ALL ABOUT CHESS AND COMPUTERS

Chess and Computers
and
More Chess and Computers
Second Edition

COMPUTER CHESS SERIES

ALL ABOUT CHESS AND COMPUTERS

DAVID LEVY and MONROE NEWBORN

Containing the Complete Works:

Chess and Computers by David Levy

and

More Chess and Computers
Second Edition

The Microcomputer Revolution
The Challenge Match
BELLE the World Champion

by David Levy and Monroe Newborn

COMPUTER SCIENCE PRESS

Computer Science Press, Inc.
11 Taft Court
Rockville, MD 20850 U.S.A.

1 2 3 4 5 6   87 86 85 84 83 82

Library of Congress Cataloging in Publication Data
Main entry under title:

All about chess and computers.

    Includes bibliographies.
    1. Chess—Data processing. 2. Chess—
Tournaments. I. Levy, David N. L. Chess and
computers. 1982. II. Levy, David N. L. More
chess and computers. 2nd ed. 1982.
GV1318.A38   1982   794.1'7   82-12497
ISBN 0-914894-75-7

Chess and Computers

David Levy

First published 1976
Copyright © David Levy 1976

Printed in the United States of America

Computer Science Press, Inc.
9125 Fall River Lane
Potomac, Maryland 20854

ISBN — 0-914894-02-1   Paper

Table of Contents

Preface

For some time now, I have felt that the time is right to write a book about Computer Chess. Ever since the first attempts at chess programming were made, some twenty five years ago, interest in the subject has grown from year to year. During the late 1950s the subject was first brought to the attention of the public by an article in *Scientific American*, and less than a decade later a chess program was competing in a tournament with humans. More recently, there have been tournaments in which the only participants were computer programs, and when the first World Computer Championship was held in Stockholm in 1974 the event was an outstanding success.

Laymen often doubt the value of investing in a subject so esoteric as computer chess, but there is definitely considerable benefit to be gained from a study of the automisation of chess and other intellectual games. If it proves possible to play such games well by computer, then the techniques employed to analyse and assess future positions in these games will also be useful in other problems in long-range planning.

I have tried to make this book both interesting and instructive. Those who understand anything at all about chess but who have no knowledge of computers, will be able to follow my description of how computers play chess. Those with a knowledge of both areas will still find much to interest them.

I have included several examples of computer play. These are intended to be entertaining, as well as illustrative of the way that programs play. I have taken particular pains to include a thorough coverage of Soviet programming efforts because these efforts have, until now, been largely ignored by the literature in the West.

I should like to thank John Littlewood who translated Vigneron's article *Les automats* from the original French. Katya Young who translated most of the material that was originally published in Russian, and my wife, Jacqueline, who helped to read the proofs. I should also like to thank David Bronstein, Mikhail Donskoy and David Slate for their help, and Ben Mittman and Monty Newborn for their efforts in promoting computer chess. Lastly, I must thank Dennis Gilles, without whom this book would probably not have been written.

David Levy
London, October 1975

Introduction

'Chess is the Art of Human Reason'.

Augustus, Duke of Brunswick, 1616

Chess is a fascinating game. Over the centuries it has come to be regarded as the intellectual game par excellence, so complex is its nature and so varied are the positions that can arise even within a very few moves. Yet chess is simple enough to be learned within a few minutes and it is a game that can be enjoyed at all levels of play from beginner to grandmaster. It has become such a popular game in the 20th Century that the number of registered players in the Soviet Union can be measured in millions, and it has been so profusely written about that there are more books available on chess than those devoted to all other sports and pastimes put together. But chess is still only a game. What then would be the value to society if someone managed to create a machine that could play perfect, or at least grandmaster level chess? This question has often been asked and before describing *how* man has tried to program computers to play chess I shall endeavour to explain *why* he thinks it is a worthwhile task.

Chess is a game of planning. To play the game well it is necessary to be able to create in one's mind a plan that conforms to the necessities and potentialities of a given position. It is true that in many positions the correct move can be found by pure calculation but it is not these positions that really distinguish the master from the amateur. A two move combination will be found by the club player nearly as often as by a master, but the correct long-term plan will be discovered much more frequently by the master than by the club player. If we could write a computer program that could play good chess we could (presumably) use similar programming techniques to solve other problems in long-range planning. Is it any more difficult to win the World Chess Championship than it is to plan the year's budget for a nation or to solve a difficult diplomatic crisis with the flair of a Kissinger? I doubt it. Probably it is easier.

I have always found it most difficult to convince non-scientists of the value of computer chess. But then fifty years ago I expect that I would have had at least as much difficulty convincing society of the value of building a machine that could smoke cigarettes. From the fact that smoking machines have since been built and that as a direct result of the research performed with these machines startling advances have been achieved in medical knowledge, I think that any non-scientist must agree that 'What use will it have?' is not a very good argument to be employed against an esoteric looking research project. A frequently heard argument of a different type, is 'If man succeeds in building a machine that can win the World Chess Championship, what fun will there be left in the game?' In reply I would say 'Boats have been sailing the seas for centuries but I still like to swim'.

In this book I explain, in rather simple terms, how computers play chess. I trace the history of computer chess in order to show how much (or little) advance has been made during the past thirty years. I describe the 'thought processes' of chess programs and discuss their limitations and their achievements. I discuss some of the stronger chess programs that have been written in recent years and I show how some of the problems of computer chess have been solved while on others there has been little or no progress.

I have written this book in such a way that it can be understood by any chess player (i.e. anyone who knows the moves and the rules of the game) even though he might never even have heard of an electronic computer, let alone know how one works. If you are interested in science but cannot play chess then your complaint is easily and painlessly remedied. I hope that my readers will find the subject of computer chess interesting and some of my examples of computer play entertaining.

1 Chess Machines

'In the opening a master should play like a book, in the middle game like a magician, in the ending like a machine'

Spielmann

Chess Automata

Although Computer Chess is the principal topic of this book, I think it worthwhile to acquaint the reader with two, pre-computer attempts to mechanize the game of chess. The more notorious of the two was the Automaton Chessplayer built by Baron von Kempelen and first exhibited by him at the Royal Palace in Vienna in 1770.

Von Kempelen was Aulic Councellor on Mechanics to the Royal Chamber and he was famed for his mechanical genius and inventiveness. The Baron's new invention was wheeled into Court by an attendant and what the amused spectators saw was a life-sized figure dressed as a Turk, seated behind a chest that was about four feet long, two feet wide and three feet high. On top of the chest was screwed a chessboard. Baron von Kempelen proudly announced that his Automaton, without any help whatsoever from himself, would play and probably defeat any member of the audience.

Naturally the audience was sceptical—after all, a small man or a boy could easily hide inside the box. But when he was questioned about the contents of the chest von Kempelen opened the front to reveal a mass of cogs and levers. He then went round to the rear of the Automaton, opened a second door and shone a candle from behind the chest so that the audience could see right through the machinery. Then he closed the rear door, went round to the front and opened a drawer at the bottom of the cabinet to show that it contained only a set of chess men. The Baron continued to perform like a conjuror, opening this door and that to the audience and showing them that the figure of the Turk contained nothing more than another set of cogs, wheels and levers.

Two members of the Automaton's first audience later wrote about their inspection of this amazing machine. One eyewitness wrote: 'I searched into its darkest corners, but found no possibility of its concealing any object of even the size of my hat'. Another said: 'It was suspected that a child was hidden in the machine. I examined with attention all parts of the table and figure and assured myself that this imputation did not have the least foundation.'

When the inspection was over, von Kempelen had the Automaton wheeled into an eclosure behind a balustrade. He removed some things from the drawer and the cabinet, adjusted some of the mechanical parts inside the 'Turk', then he closed all the doors and covered the Turk with his robe. He then set up the red and white ivory pieces on the board, took a large key from his pocket and wound up the machine whereupon the audience heard the familiar clicking sounds of a clockwork ratchet-wheel.

With the Automaton apparently ready for play, von Kempelen held up a casket that he had removed from the cabinet. This casket, he declared, held the secret of the Automaton's power. While the mechanical power that propelled the Turk's left arm to move the pieces was provided by clockwork, the secret of how the Turk was able to place the pieces on the correct squares was contained in the casket. Regrettably, Baron von Kempelen explained, he was unable to reveal the secret of the casket nor to explain it to the audience. He placed the casket carefully on a small table near the Automaton and asked for the first volunteer to come foreward and play against the Turk.

Each time the Turk came to move, its head would move from side to side and after a few moments thought it would pick up a pawn or piece in its left hand and slowly move it to a new square, all the time to the accompaniment of the whirring of clockwork. The entire audience was astonished. One old lady got up from her chair, crossed herself and retired hurriedly to a curtained window recess, wanting to have nothing to do with such sorcery. It soon became apparent that without any sort of communication from the Baron, the Turk was playing strong chess! Every ten or twelve moves the Baron would go to his machine to wind it up again, the rest of the time he had his back to the machine and remained at a distance.

The Turk was a very polite opponent. When it attacked its opponent's queen it bowed its head twice. When it gave check it bowed three times. When its opponent made an illegal move it shook its head, replaced the illegally moved piece on its original square, and extracted the penalty that was in force in those days of moving a piece of his own.

At the end of the game von Kempelen again opened the doors of the cabinet and uncovered the figure of the Turk, thereby demonstrating that no-one had climbed inside the machine since the first inspection.

Within a few years the Automaton had toured the courts of Europe and had been seen by Empress Maria Theresa and Emperor Joseph 2nd of the Austro-Hungarian Empire, and by Grand Duke Paul of

Russia. In 1783 it visited Paris where it lost occasional games against the experts at the Café de la Regence. Although most sceptics quite rightly believed there to be a human being hidden inside the machine, it was not until the Automaton reached London in 1784 that definite statements were expressed accusing the Baron of trickery. A pamphlet by Philip Thicknesse, published in London in 1784, was entitled *The Automaton Chessplayer, Exposed and Detected*. Thicknesse believed that a child was hidden inside the cabinet, and he pointed out that the Automaton was exhibited for only one hour per day because 'the invisible player could not bear a longer confinement; for if he could, it cannot be supposed that they would refuse to recieve crowns for admittance from 12 o'clock to 4, instead of only from 1 to 2.'

From London the Baron took his machine to Berlin where it so excited Frederick the Great that he bought the Automaton and its secret from von Kempelen, but once Frederick had learned the simplicity of the machine's 'secret' he was disappointed with his purchase and discarded it into a lumber room where it remained for twenty years.

In 1789 a book was published in Dresden by Joseph Friderich von Racknitz in which he described a robot of his own invention that was extremely similar to von Kempelen's Turk. Both machines used the same mechanism to reveal to the operator the moves that were being made on the board above him. Both machines were constructed so that the operator could move the head, arm and fingers of the figure. The only real difference was that von Racknitz had a far less ingenious method of concealing the player inside the machine: His player lay full length behind the drawer, and this restricted his choice of player to those under four feet in height.

Had von Racknitz' book been widely read the Automaton would probably never have seen the light of day after its confinement to Frederick's lumber room. But the book was never translated into English and presumably those interested in the machine in England and America were unable to read German or they were not aware of the existence of the book. Even those who did read the book were not entirely conversant with the workings of the machine. Poe, for example, mentioned the book in such a way that makes it clear that even after reading it he still did not understand Racknitz' idea.

Baron von Kempelen died in 1804. After his death the Automaton was brought out of retirement by Leonard Maelzel of Regensburg and when Napoleon occupied Berlin in 1806 he decided to test the

Automaton's cleverness by trying a few impossible moves against it. The first time, the figure shook its head and replaced the piece. The second time, the Automaton removed the offending piece from the board and made its own move. The third time the Automaton was so disgusted that it swept all the pieces onto the floor.

In 1809 at Schönbrunn, Napoleon decided to take the Automaton more seriously.

White: Napoleon
Black: Automaton (Allgaier)

1	P-K4	P-K4	13	P-N3	N-B6+
2	B-B4	N-QB3	14	K-N2	N×Q+
3	Q-B3	N-B3	15	R×N	Q-N5
4	N-K2	B-B4	16	P-Q3	B×BP
5	P-QR3	P-Q3	17	R-R1	Q×NP+
6	O-O	B-KN5	18	K-B1	B-Q5
7	Q-Q3	N-KR4	19	K-K2	Q-N7+
8	P-R3	B×N	20	K-Q1	Q×R+
9	Q×B	N-B5	21	K-Q2	Q-N7+
10	Q-K1	N-Q5	22	K-K1	N-N8
11	B-N3	N×RP+	23	N-B3	B×N+
12	K-R2	Q-R5	24	P×B	Q-K7mate

After Napoleon's defeat the Automaton was bought by another wealthy patron, Price Eugène de Beauharnais, who was Napoleon's stepson. The Prince paid 30,000 francs for the machine but did nothing with it for seven years and then resold it to Maelzel for the same sum plus a fifty per cent share in whatever profits might be made in the future. Maelzel continued to exhibit the machine but he was a sharp businessman and in 1825 he fled to America in order to escape from his creditors.

In 1821 an article appeared in the Edinburgh Philosophical journal, written by Robert Willis of the University of Cambridge. Willis had discovered part of the Automaton's secret—he had surmised how the human might be hidden in the machine but his explanation of how the operator viewed the chessboard and moved the pieces was completely wrong.

Fig. 1. Fig. 2.

'The drawings in figures 1 and 2 represent the general appearance of the machine. It runs on castors, and is either seen on the floor when the doors of the apartment are thrown open, or is wheeled into the room at the commencement of the exhibition.

'The exhibitor, in order to show the mechanism, as he informs the spectators, unlocks the door (A, fig. 1) of the chest, which exposes to view a small cupboard, lined with black or dark coloured cloth, and containing different pieces of machinery which seem to occupy the whole space. He next opens the door (B, fig. 2) at the back of the same cupboard, and holding a lighted candle at the opening, still further exposes the machinery within. The candle being withdrawn, the door (B) is then locked. The drawer (G G, fig. 1) in the front of the chest is then opened, and a set of chess men, a small box of counters, and a cushion for the support of the Automaton's arm, are taken out of it. The exhibitor now opens the two front doors (C C, fig. 1) of the large cupboard, and the back door (D, fig. 2) of the same, and applies a candle, as in the former case. This cupboard is lined with cloth like the other, but it contains only a few pieces of machinery. The chest is now wheeled round, the garments of the figure lifted up, and the door (E, fig. 2) in the trunk, and another (F) in the thigh, are opened. But it must be observed, that the doors (B and D) are closed.

'The chest is now restored to its former position on the floor; the doors in front, and the drawer, are closed and locked; and the exhibitor, after he has occupied some time at the back of the chest, in apparently adjusting the machinery, removes the pipe from the hand of the figure, winds up the works, and the Automaton begins to move.'

Fig. 9.   Fig. 10.

Fig. 11.

Willis pointed out the extreme difficulty of executing the movements of the chess player by machinery alone, and the extreme probability of a deception, from the eagerness of the exhibitor to display a part of the mechanism at one time, and his concealment of it at another. He then pointed out a method by which a skilled player of ordinary stature might secretly animate the automaton and imitate the movements of the chess player:

'The drawer (GG, fig. 10) when closed, does not reach to the back of the chest; it leaves a space (O) behind it, about 1 foot 2 inches broad, 8 inches high, and 3 feet 11 inches long. This space is never exposed to view.

'The small cupboard is divided into two parts by the door or screen (I, fig. 6) which is movable on a hinge, and is so contrived that when B is closed, this screen may be closed also. The machinery (H) occupies the whole of the front division as far as I: the hinder division is nearly empty, and communicates with the space behind the drawer, the floor of this division being removed.

'The back of the great cupboard is double, and the part (PQ) to which the quadrants, &c. are attached, moves on a joint (Q), at the upper part, and forms, when raised, an opening (S) between the two cupboards, by carrying with it part of the partition (R), which is composed of cloth stretched tight. Fig. 10 shows the false back closed. Fig. 11 shows the same raised, forming the opening (S) between the chambers.

'When the trunk of the figure is exposed by lifting up the dress, it will be seen that a great part of it is occupied by an inner trunk (N), which passes off towards the back in the form of an arch, (fig. 2) and conceals a portion of the interior from the view of the spectators. This inner trunk opens to the chest by an aperture (T, fig. 9) about 1 foot 3 inches high, by 1 foot broad.

'When the false back is raised, the two chambers, the trunk, and the space behind the drawer, are all connected together.

'The player may be introduced into the chest through the sliding panel (U, fig. 6), at the end. He will then elevate the false back of the large cupboard, and assume the position represented by the dotted lines in figs. 3 and 4. Everything being thus prepared, "the charm's wound up," and the exhibitor may begin his operations by opening the door (A). From the crowded and very ingenious disposition of the machinery in this cupboard, the eye is unable to penetrate far beyond the opening, and the spectator is led to conclude that the whole space is occupied with a similar apparatus. This illusion is strengthened and confirmed by observing the glimmering light which plays among the intricacies of the machinery, and occasionally meets the eye, when the lighted candle is held at the door (B). A fact too, is ascertained, which is equally satisfactory, though for opposite reasons, to the spectator and the exhibitor, viz. that no opake body of any magnitude is interposed between the light and the spectator's eye. The door (B) must now be locked, and the screeen (I) closed, which being done at the moment the light is withdrawn, will wholly escape observation.

'It has been already mentioned, that the door (B), from its construction, closes by its own weight; but as the player's head will presently be very near it, the secret would be endangered, if, in turning round the chest, this door were, by any accident, to fly open; it becomes necessary, therefore, "to make assurance double sure," and turn the key. If the circumstance should be observed, it will probably be considered as accidental, the keys being immediately wanted for the other locks.

'The opening (B) being once secured, and the screen (I) closed, the success of the experiment may be deemed complete. The secret is no longer exposed to hazard; and the exhibitor is at liberty to shape his conduct in any way he may think most likely to secure the confidence of the spectators, and lead them insensibly from the main object of pursuit. The door (A) may safely be left open; this will tend to confirm the opinion, which the spectators probably formed on viewing the candle through this cupboard, that no person was concealed within it: it will further assure them that nothing can pass in the interior without their knowledge, so long as this door continues open.

'The drawer stands next in the order of succession: it is opened, *apparently*, for the purpose of taking out the chess men, cushion, &c. but *really* to allow time for the player to change his position, (see fig. 5) and to replace the false back and partition, preparatory to the opening of the great cupboard.

'The machinery is so thinly scattered over this cupboard, that the eye surveys the whole space at one glance, and it might seem unnecessary to open a door at the back, and to hold a lighted candle there, as in the former instance; but the artifice is dictated by sound policy, which teaches that the exhibitor cannot be too assiduous in affording facilities to explore every corner and recess, which, he well knows, contains nothing that he is desirous of concealing.

'The chest may now be wheeled round for the purpose of showing the trunk of the figure; leaving, however, the front doors of the great chamber open. The bunch of keys, too, should be suffered to remain in the door (D); for the apparent carelessness of such a proceeding will serve to allay any suspicion which the circumstance of locking the door (B) might have excited, more especially as the two doors resemble one another in point of construction.

'When the drapery has been lifted up, and the doors in the trunk and thigh opened, the chest may be returned to its former situation, and the doors be closed. In the mean time the player should withdraw his legs from behind the drawer, as he will not so easily effect this movement after the drawer has been pushed in.

'Here let us pause a while, and compare the real state of the chest at this time, with the impression which, at a similar period of an exhibition of the Chess-Player has generally been left on the minds of the spectators; the bulk of whom have concluded that each part of the chest had been successively exposed; and that the whole was at that time open to inspection: whereas, on the contrary, it is evident that some parts had been entirely withheld from view, others but obscurely shown, and that nearly half of the chest was then excluded from their sight. Hence we learn how easily, in matters of this sort, the judgment may be led astray by an artful combination of circumstances, each assisting the other towards the attainment of one object.

'When the doors in front have been closed, the exhibitor may occupy as much time as he finds necessary, in apparently adjusting the machinery at the back, whilst the player is taking the position described in figs. 7 and 8. In this position he will find no difficulty in executing every movement required of the automaton: his head being above the table, he will see the chess-board through the waistcoat as easily as through a veil; and his left hand extending beyond the elbow of the figure, he will be enabled to guide its hand to any part of the board, and to take up and let go a chess man with no other "delicate mechanism" than a string communicating with the finger. His right hand being within the chest, may serve to keep in motion the contrivance for producing the noise, which is heard during the moves, and to perform the other tricks of moving the head, tapping on the chest, &c.

'In order to facilitate the introduction of the player's left arm into the arm of the figure, the latter is obliged to be drawn backwards; and to account for, and conceal this strained attitude, a pipe is ingeniously placed in the automaton's hand. This pipe must not be removed till the other arrangements are completed.

'When all is ready, and the pipe removed, the exhibitor may turn round the winder, to give the impression to the spectators of winding up a spring, or weight, and to serve as a signal to the player to set the head of the automaton in motion.

'The above process is simple, feasible, and effective, showing indisputably that the phenomena may be produced without the aid of machinery, and thereby rendering it probable that the Chess Player derives its merit solely from the very ingenious mode by which the concealment of a living agent is effected.'

A few years after Maelzel fled to America, the Automaton's secret was revealed for the first time, in an article written by Mouret, 'Director' of the Automaton from about 1819 to 1824. In 1857 *The Chess Monthly*, a New York publication, gave a fairly accurate account of the Automaton's construction and secret by Dr John Mitchell who had been co-owner of the Automaton in 1840. During the period of the Automaton's reign and that of its successor 'Ajeeb' (built in London in 1868) several accounts, accurate and otherwise, were published of its workings. However, none of these accounts was entirely complete though it has been possible, by studying all of them, to put together an accurate picture of how the 'Director' could hide inside the machine,

Fig. 12

even though to all intents and purposes the public had been shown that there was no concealed person.

The Automaton's secret lay in the drawer, which had sides of the same depth as the cabinet and went all the way to the rear. But the back of the drawer was on wheels and it stopped half way when the drawer was pushed in. The back part of the drawer, with the exception of the sides, telescoped into the front part (see figure 12). When pulled out the drawer gave the appearance of being as deep as the cabinet. When closed there was an unoccupied space behind the drawer. This space extended the full width of the cabinet (4 feet) and about half its depth (i.e. 1 foot). On the floor of this trough behind the drawer was fixed a pair of iron rails about three feet long. A stool with iron runners was placed on the rails and the operator could sit on this stool and slide backwards and forwards on the greased runners. The illusion was completed by a series of hinged sections that concealed the operator when the audience was being invited to inspect the machine, but which moved out of his way when he was working the controls.

In 1837, when Maelzel died, the Automaton was taken to a Philadelphia museum where it was destroyed by fire in 1854. Ajeeb also went to America where it too eventually perished in a fire (at Coney Island in 1929). When Ajeeb left England for the New World in 1878, yet another robot was built, this one being called the 'Mephisto'. The hidden director of the Mephisto was Gunsberg who played some of the finest games of the first era of chess automata.

White: Mephisto (Gunsberg)
Black: A. N. Other
London, c. 1883

1	P-K4	P-K4	15	N-N5	
2	N-KB3	N-QB3	16	B-K3	B-B4+
3	P-Q4	P×P	17	N.N5×BP	B-K3
4	N×P	Q-R5	18	R×B	B×B+
5	N-KB3	Q×KP+	19	N×B	B×N
6	B-K2	P-Q4	20	P-B4	Q-B2
7	O-O	B-K3	21	R-QR3	KR-K1
8	N-B3	Q-B4	22	R-N1	K-N1
9	B-QN5	KN-K2	23	P-QN4	Q-B1
10	N-Q4	Q-N3	24	Q-Q4	N×P
11	P-B4	P-B4	25	R×NP+	N-B3
12	R-K1	B-Q2	26	R×P+	K×R
13	N×QP	O-O-O	27	Q-N6+	N×R
14	B×N	N×B	28	N-B7mate	K-R1

Torres y Quevedo

The first genuine attempt to design a chess playing machine was made in 1890 by the Spanish scientist Torres y Quevedo, who built a machine that played the ending of king and rook against king. The machine always played the side with the extra rook and it would always force mate (though not necessarily in the minimum number of moves). Since it is possible to give an explicit set of rules for making satisfactory moves in this particular ending, the problem is relatively simple, but the ideas incorporated in Torres' machine were quite advanced for those days.

The machine was created as a scientific toy in order to attract attention to the feasibility of Torres' theory on automation. He described his invention in a brief interview given to the Spanish journalist Jose Maria Carretero:

'It is an apparatus that plays chess with the king and the rook as if it were a person, knowing with absolute precision all moves that occur and always mating its opponent. Besides this, it warns its opponent, in a courteous manner, of any mistakes (i.e. illegal moves-DNLL) made by its opponent by means of a light, and after its opponent has made three mistakes it ceases playing, considering that its opponent is no match for it, ... This apparatus has no practical purpose; but supports the basis of my thesis: that it is always possible to produce an automaton the actions of which always depend on certain circumstances and which obey certain rules that can be programmed when the automaton is being produced. Evidently these rules will be such as to be self-sufficient to determine the performance of the automaton without any uncertainty and at any given moment.'

Soon after it was built, Torres' machine was put on exhibition in Bilbao and Seville and it was also demonstrated at the conference of the Spanish Association for the Progress of Science in Villadolid. In 1914 the machine crossed the border into France, taking its inventor with it. It was exhibited in the laboratory of the Department of Physical and Experimental Medecine at the Sorbonne and an excellent account of its workings was given by the French scientist Henri Vigneron in *La Nature*. I am reproducing Vigneron's article here in full, because not only does it explain Torres' inventive machine, but also it gives a good account of the most interesting automata that had been built up to that time.

Robots
H. Vigneron

Mr. Torres y Quevedo, the renowned Spanish engineer, has been invited by the Franco-Spanish Research Centre to show his work in Paris. For this purpose he has brought with him some of the apparatus and machines which he has constructed and which are on display in the new laboratory of Physical and Experimental Mechanics at the Sorbonne, boulevard Raspail, whose director, Mr. Konigs, gave a warm welcome to the Spanish scientist and his machines.

Mr. Torres runs the Laboratorio de Automatica in Madrid, set up in 1907 by the Spanish government. This allows him to carry on his research into calculating machines whilst at the same time constructing machines for teaching and for the scientific research of various laboratories which depend on the State. In this way Mr. Torres is freed from financial problems and can show total impartiality in his dealings with the scientists who turn to him for help.

Mr. Torres, who has created among other things a most ingenious model of an airship, has been kind enough to provide us with highly interesting comments about himself, his work and his machines. The latter can be divided into two groups: robots and algebraic machines.

The term 'robot' is often applied to a machine which imitates the appearance and movements of a man or animal. So we are usually dealing with a machine containing its own source of energy which drives it (a spring, for example), and capable of performing certain actions, always the same, without any external influence. The most famous of these robots are the work of Vaucanson, such as the flute player which he described in a paper in 1728. In 1741 he exhibited a duck which could perform all the animal's functions, including feeding and digestion. Unfortunately his collection has not come down to us in its entirety, being scattered in many German museums. He had donated it to Queen Marie Antoinette for the Academic des Sciences, but as the king was dabbling in such matters against her wishes, she placed little value on Vaucanson's collection which was thus dispersed before reaching its destination.

There is another kind of robot which is much more interesting. Rather than imitate man's gestures, it imitates his actions and can occasionally replace him. The self-guiding torpedo, the scales which can weigh and differentiate coins automatically, and thousands of other well-known mechanisms represent examples of this type of robot. Many other examples which are much more interesting can be found in factories.

The major part of industrial progress is brought about by producing machines which can tackle work hitherto done by man. Gradually we are managing to automate most operations which were originally carried out by workmen, and we talk about complete automation when production can be achieved by the sole use of machines. Mr Torres divides this latter type of robot into two groups according to whether the circumstances which regulate their action are of a continuous or an intermittent nature.

Let us consider the self-guiding torpedo as an example of the first group. The horizontal rudder mechanism, whose task is to maintain the torpedo at a more or less fixed depth, is controlled by a chamber of compressed air which reacts to the water-pressure, and by a pendulum. Variations in depth result in the movement of a metal strip which separates the chamber of compressed air from the surrounding water; variations in tilt result in movement, relative to the torpedo, of the pendulum which remains vertical. The horizontal rudder is linked to the pendulum and the metal strip in such a way that each of these new movements compel it to return the torpedo to the required depth. We thus see that the problem here is to establish fixed mechanical linkages between three variables: pendulum, metal strip, rudder. This is the same type of problem as all those which are studied in the theory of kinematics as applied to the construction of machines, and is of no special interest to us here.

In the robots of the second group fixed linkages play no part. On the contrary, the aim is to change these links suddenly when circumstances demand. The principle is to stop or start a pulley, open or close a valve etc., usually with a very rapid movement. In other words the automation is effected by a sudden intervention at a given moment, thus controlling each different action of the machine.

In descriptions of machines we can find countless examples of these sudden interventions, but it is clear that this kind of automation does not form part of the theory of kinematics and has never been systematically studied. Mr Torres proposes to devote to it a special chapter of the theory of machines entitled 'automation' in which he would consider methods of constructing robots with much more complex programming (command) systems.

These robots will have SENSES such as thermometers, gyroscopes, dynamometers, pressure guages etc. Data received by the latter will be transmitted in the form of a movement: for example, a needle traversing a graduated scale.

These robots will have LIMBS i.e. mechanisms capable of carrying out given "orders" to perform certain operations. Such "orders" can be given by very simple means, even if complex operations are involved. This can be seen in the case of certain famous clocks like the ones at Rouen, Basle and Strasbourg, where a mechanism similar to the one used in an alarm-clock triggers off the movement of mechanical dolls which perform various actions.

Finally, these robots will have the necessary POWER in the form of batteries, water, compressed air etc., in order to keep the machines running and enable them to execute the essential operations.

Furthermore, and for Mr. Torrès this is the main problem of automation, the robots must be able to CHOOSE intelligently i.e. carry out the required operation after taking into account the data they are receiving from their "senses" or even the data already acquired. In other words, they should be able to imitate human beings by adapting their behaviour to the existing conditions.

In theory there is no difficulty in constructing apparatus for supplying the sense data, or in providing machines which will perform the operations designated by the robot. However, when it comes to constructing a robot which will determine its actions according to its ASSESSMENT of relevant data, the general opinion is that this can be done only in a few very simple cases. For example, it is thought that automation is possible for certain purely mechanical manual operations of a workman, whereas it will never be possible for those operations which demand the intervention of the mental faculties.

Mr. Torrès disagrees; for him it is self-evident that we can construct a robot all of whose actions depend on certain circumstances, numerous or otherwise, so long as we have a body of "rules" which we can impose arbitrarily at the design stage. This "program" will clearly have to be efficient enough to determine in all circumstances, without any doubt, the actions of the robot.

Not only does Mr. Torrès consider that the problem is not insoluble, but on the contrary he has provided us with a very elegant solution in the shape of a chess-playing machine. We shall describe this marvel of ingenuity later, once we have explained the guiding principles behind Mr. Torrès' method of constructing robots.

These principles basically depend on the use of an extremely simple electro-mechanical method. We said earlier that as a general rule any variation in the circumstances influencing the action of the robot will be indicated by a movement. Let us assume that it is a switch which is moved; instead of a needle moving along a graduated scale we will have an arm sweeping through a series of points, contacting each in turn.

If there are n switches and if we call the number of points linked with each of them P_1, P_2, P_3...P_n, then the total number of possible positions to be considered will be the product $P_1 \times P_2 \times P_3 \ldots \times P_n$. To each of these positions a certain operation will be linked and triggered off by a very simple mechanism such as the attraction of the armature of an electro-magnet. Thus, each position will have its own electro-magnet and in order to carry out a specific operation the electrical connections will have to be arranged in such a way that each electro-magnet will be activated when the corresponding switch is in line. In the simplest case, when only one element is involved, the solution is the one presented in figure 13. The variations of this single element are reflected in the movements of switch M which contacts in turn each of the points A, B, C, D. In the diagram the connection is being made with electro-magnet E, so the operation linked with this will be carried out as soon as the electric circuit is completed at K.

Fig. 13

*Diagram showing the connections which allow four
different operations to be carried out at choice.*

Fig. 14

Diagram showing how 24 different operations can be "selected".

In figure 14, there are three main switches M, N and P. The second involves in its movement another switch N^I, and the third brings in the Five switches P^I, P^{II}, P^{III}, P^{IV}, P^V.

M can take up positions A, B. N can take up positions E, F, G. P can take up positions R, S, T, U.

This system, then, allows 24 operations which can be carried out as soon as the corresponding electro-magnet is activated by completion of the circuit.

Of course, we can increase at will the number of switches and the number of points connected with each of them. In other words, we can increase indefinitely the number of particular cases that the robot will have to 'consider' when controlling its operations. There is no theoretical problem here, as there is no essential difference between the simplest machine and the most complex robot. Both can be reduced to a material system dependent upon the physical rules applied in their construction. The sole difference is that when these rules are complex, involving a certain amount of reasoning to deduce the corresponding manoeuvres, the machine which carries out the manoeuvres appears to possess in itself this ability to choose intelligently.

Indeed, this is the impression created by Mr. Torres' chess-playing machine. The object is to mate with rook and king against king, with a human chess player conducting the defence. As we have already stated, certain rules have to be established (programming) which the machine must always follow and which determine its response to any defence adopted by its opponent who has the black pieces.

Here are the rules applied by Mr. Torres in constructing the robot:

If the opponent plays an illegal move, a light comes on and the robot refuses to make a move. Once three such illegal moves have been made, the robot ceases to play altogether.

If, on the contrary, the defence plays correctly, the robot will carry out one of six operations, depending upon the position of the black king. In order to achieve this, Mr. Torres uses two zones on the chessboard: the one on the left consisting of the QR, QN and QB files, and the corresponding one on the right consisting of the KR, KN and KB files. We then have the six operations as shown in figure 15.

How are these operations carried out? Before we turn to the full picture given in figure 18, let us consider figures 16 and 17 which use the same graphical notation.

The black King					
is in the same zone as the rook	is not in the same zone as the rook and the vertical distance between the black king and the rook is				
	more than a square	one square, with the vertical distance between the two kings being			
		more than two squares	two squares, with the number of square representing their horizontal distance apart being		
			odd	even	zero
The rook moves away horizontally	The rook moves down one square	The king moves down one square	The rook moves one square horizontally	The white king moves one square towards the black king	The rook moves down one square
1	2	3	4	5	6

Fig. 15

The six possible operations of Torres' machine.

Fig. 16   Fig. 17

Rectangle C in figure 16 represents a slide which can move vertically. It has an arm B fixed to it at P and whose end Q can contact points P or P^1 thus connecting either circuit. The wavy line F represents an extensible electrical conductor (e.g. spring) which connects moving point β to fixed point α without hindering the movement of the slide.

In figure 17, the disc D is dragged round by friction from the central moving spindle O unless prevented by the catch A. Each time that the electro-magnet E attracts its armature A, then disc D will make one complete rotation compelling the robot to carry out a specific manoeuvre.

Now let us examine the brain of the robot:

Fig. 18
*Diagram showing how the chess player performs the various
operations according to the positions of the pieces.*

Corridor R indicates the horizontal position of the white king.
Corridor R' indicates the same for the black king.
Corridor T indicates the horizontal position of the white rook.
Corridor R_1 indicates the vertical position of the white king.
Corridor R'_1 indicates the same for the black king.
Corridor T_1 indicates the vertical position of the white rook.

There are eight discs in the diagram, 1, 1', 2, 3, 4, 4', 5, 5' which
execute the following specific manoeuvres:
1 The rook moves to the QR-file.
1' The rook moves to the KR-file.

2 The rook moves one square down.
3 The king moves one square down.
4 The king moves one square to the right.
4′ The king moves one square to the left.
5 The rook moves one square to the right.
5′ The rook moves one square to the left.

At the same time that the robot moves the piece, it also moves the corresponding slide to indicate the new position.

When the defender moves, the robot begins by comparing the new position of the black king with the one it occupied previously. If the move is illegal, a light comes on. Otherwise the circuit is completed at K and the robot carries out one of the six operations according to its programmed rules (see figure 15):

No. 1 Let us suppose that the black king is in the same zone as the white rook, for example on QB2. The current passes along arms *a* and *b* then on to *b′* connecting with electro-magnet 1′ in the present case since the rook is in the left-hand zone. If the rook were in the right-hand zone, electro-magnet 1 would be the one activated.

No. 2 The black king is not in the same zone as the rook and the vertical distance between them is more than one square. The current passes either through *a′* (the black king is in neither zone) or through *a* and *b* (the black king is not in the same zone as the rook). From there it goes to *c* and on to electro-magnet 2.

No. 3 In the third hypothesis, the vertical distance between the black king and the rook in different zones is one square, but the vertical distance between the two kings is more than two squares. The current passes from *c* to *d*, then to electro-magnet 3.

No. 4 If, in the preceding conditions, the vertical distance between the kings is two squares and the horizontal distance between them is an odd number of squares, the current passes from *d* through *e* and *f*. It then goes to electro-magnet 4 if the rook is on the QR or KN file and to electro-magnet 4′ if the rook is on the QN or KR file.

No. 5 With the same conditions as the preceding case but an even number of squares being the horizontal distance between the kings, the current passes from *d* through *e* and *f'*. It then goes to electro-magnet 5 if the black king is to the right of the white king, or to electro-magnet 5' if the opposite is the case.

No.6 Finally, if both kings are on the same file (i.e. the horizontal distance between them is zero), the current activates electro-magnet 2 via *d* and *e*.

Such are the principles behind Mr. Torres' chess-playing machine. However, what we have been unable to describe is the ingenuity required to create such a robot. It is only when one sees it at work, checking the opponent's moves then carrying out the correct manoeuvre in reply that you can understand the truth of Mr. Torres' words: 'It is not difficult to conceive the theoretical possibility of a robot determining its action at a given moment by weighing up all the circumstances it must take into consideration to carry out its assigned task. Equally one can visualize a robot carrying out a series of actions in order to achieve a certain "result".'

In Mr. Konigs' laboratory Mr. Torres also displayed other machines which were just as original. The telekine, a machine which carries out orders sent by wireless, interpreting them correctly whilst taking into account various external factors. Algebraic machines representing continuous functions by means of movements which are continuous too. A machine for solving algebraic equations, and other machines, all of which are clear evidence of the knowledge and ingenuity of this eminent engineer.

Torres machine is still in good working order and can be seen in the museum at the Polytechnic in Madrid.

2 How Computers Play Chess

'It is hopeless to try to make a machine play perfect chess'

Norbert Wiener

An electronic computer is a high speed calculating device capable of storing vast amounts of numerical information and performing elementary arithmetic operations (addition, multiplication, etc) on the various numbers contained in its storage locations. A computer program is a set of instructions, written in some language that can be 'understood' by a computer, that determines how the computer is to operate on the information (i.e. the numbers) fed to it. A simple program written in an elementary computer language might look like this:

$$READ\ X;$$
$$Y = X + 10;$$
$$PRINT\ Y;$$
$$END\ OF\ PROGRAM;$$

This program would read in the first number that it was given (probably on a punched card or paper tape) and assign this number to a storage location named X. It would then add 10 to the number stored in location X and put the result in another location named Y. The third instruction would 'tell' the computer to print out the number stored in location Y and the final instruction terminates the program.

Of course it is a far cry from a program as trivial as the one above to one that can perform complex tasks such as playing chess, but the

BLACK

18	28	38	48	58	68	78	88
17	27	37	47	57	67	77	87
16	26	36	46	56	66	76	86
15	25	35	45	55	65	75	85
14	24	34	44	54	64	74	84
13	23	33	43	53	63	73	83
12	22	32	42	52	62	72	82
11	21	31	41	51	61	71	81

WHITE

DIAGRAM 1

basic elements of a chess program are not so very much more complicated. A storage location is assigned to each square on the chess board, as in diagram 1. White's QR1 is called 11, White's K4 is called 54, and so on.

Next, a number is assigned to each piece so that if a program investigates the contents of one of these locations the number stored in that location will identify the piece. A simple coding system might be

$$pawn = 1$$
$$knight = 2$$
$$bishop = 3$$
$$rook = 4$$
$$queen = 5$$
$$king = 6$$

and a black piece might be identified by giving the negative value for that piece, so that -2 represented a black knight and -6 the black king. If a square on the chess board was empty then its storage location would contain a zero.

The reader can already see that the problem of representing a chess position inside a computer is not a difficult one. The position shown in diagram 2 is recognizable to a human with no more difficulty than that experienced by a computer in recognising its counterpart in diagram 3.

DIAGRAM 2   DIAGRAM 3

Once a computer can store a chess position, the next step is to program it to be able to generate a list of all the legal moves that can be made in a given position. Since each square on the board has its unique numerical 'name' and since the moves in chess are clearly defined, it is not difficult to see that the list of legal moves may be generated by performing simple addition and subtraction operations on the names of the storage locations for the various pieces.

As a simple example, consider the square 64 in diagram 1. If there was a king located on that square and if the king's movements were not restricted in any way then the king would be able to move to square 53, 54, 55, 63, 65, 73, 74 or 75. In more general terms, if a king is on square number n and if its movement is not restricted, it would then move to square n-11, n-10, n-9, n-1, n+1, n+9 n+10 or n+11. In order to make sure that the king can, in fact, move to any of these squares, it is necessary, for each of the squares, to ask the following questions:

1) *Is the square on the board?* This can be determined by making sure that each digit of the square's 'name' is not less than 1 nor more than 8. Thus, a king located on square 85, would not be able to move to squares 94, 95 or 96 because in each case the first digit of the square's name is greater than 8.

2) *Is the square occupied by one of the king's own men?* This can be answered by looking at the contents of the square—if it is occupied and if its occupant is identified by a number of the same sign as the king (i.e. if both are negative to indicate black or positive to indicate white) then the move is not legal.

3) *Is the square attacked by one of the opponent's men?* (For the sake of legality this question must be asked in relation to all king moves though not in relation to the moves of any other piece.) The answer to this question can be obtained by looking through the list of legal moves that can be made by each of the opponent's men.

Now that we can represent a chess position inside a computer and program the computer to generate legal moves, we must devise a means whereby the program can distinguish between good positions and bad ones. And this is where the story really begins.

A human chess master usually knows at once whether a given position is good for White or for Black or whether it is level. The bigger the advantage possessed by one side, the easier it is for the human to be sure of his assessment. In chess books we find countless occurrences of phrases such as 'White has a clear advantage', 'Black has a slight advantage' and 'The chances are equal'. Being able to make frequent, accurate assessments of this kind, is one of the stock tools of every chess master. How do they do it and how can their techniques for positional evaluation be simulated in a chess program?

The key to evaluation is knowing what to look for. A chef knows that when his rib of beef is bright red it is too rare for most tastes and when it is almost black it is overdone. Between the red state and the black the beef will go through various gradations of brown, and the experienced chef will be able to judge exactly when is the right moment to turn off the oven. He uses time as a rough guide because he knows roughly for how long he should cook the meat, but his final decision is based on its appearance. So it is with chess. A master can often get a very good idea as to which side stands better in a chess position, simply by counting the pieces. But while the number and values of the pieces on each side is often a sufficient measure, more likely than not the true assessment of a position can only be made by looking at its 'colour'—seeing how the pieces are arranged in relation to each other, and looking for features that are less obvious than material.

A chess program arrives at its assessment of a position through the use of a device called an evaluation function (sometimes known as a scoring function). This device considers various features of the position, determines how much of each feature is present in the position and calculates an evaluation (or score) by giving each of the features a numerical weighting. Before proceding into the complexities of evaluation in chess let us first consider the problem of Hamish McHaggis who has to drive from Glasgow to Edinburgh by the quickest possible route in order to arrive in time for the first round of the Scottish Championship. He has a choice of two roads, the High road and the Low road. The High road is 45 miles long of which 30 miles is motorway while the remaining 15 miles is an old road under repair. The Low road is 55 miles long but it is all motorway. Hamish knows that he can drive at an average of roughly 60 miles per hour along the motorway but that when the road is under repair he can normally expect to average only 30 miles per hour. Which road should he take? Hamish evaluates the two choices as follows:

High Road: 30 miles at 60 m.p.h. + 15 miles at 30 m.p.h.

$$= 30 \quad \times \quad \tfrac{1}{60} \quad + 15 \quad \times \quad \tfrac{1}{30} \quad = 1 \text{hour}$$

Low Road: 55 miles at 60 m.p.h.

$$= 55 \quad \times \quad \tfrac{1}{60} \quad\quad\quad\quad = 55 \text{ minutes}$$

Unfortunately, the problem of evaluating a chess position is not quite so simple. Nevertheless, computer programs set about this problem in the same sort of way as Hamish used to compare routes. In Hamish's situation there were only two features, the motorway and the road under repair, and the weightings that he gave to each ($\frac{1}{60}$ and $\frac{1}{30}$) were based on his past experience of driving along each type of road. In chess there are far more features and their weightings are extremely difficult to find, especially so as the weighting of one feature might depend on the quantity present of another. In chess two or more features are often linked together in some way, for example the value of having four of your own pieces attacking your opponent's king will vary according to how well his king is defended. But in Hamish's situation the speed at which he could drive along the motorway was in no way affected by the fact that some of the route might later be under repair.

Let us consider the simplest possible evaluation of a chess position—that based on material. If we assign the traditional values of 1 to a pawn, 3 to a knight or bishop, 5 to a rook, 9 to a queen and (say) 1,000,000 to a king, then, all other things being equal (which they rarely are), by adding the total value of the material on each side we can determine who has the advantage. If one side is a pawn up then his score on the material scale is +1. If one side sacrifices his queen and both rooks to force mate, then although he has given up 19 points on the material scale he has done so to gain 1,000,000 and so he has won the game (we can set the threshold for a win at 999,961 using the above scale). While it is quite true that if a program could look ahead along every variation right up to the end of the game it could decide what move to make entirely on the basis of material, the number of possible variations is so enormous that such a technique is not feasible (see page 38). Nevertheless, one of the strongest American programs of the early 1970s, TECH, employed only one feature in its evaluation mechanism—material.

After material, the second most important feature in chess is mobility. By mobility we mean the number of legal moves that can be made in a given position. Material and mobility are obviously linked since, in general, the more pieces we have the more moves we can make. But mobility is a very useful addition as a measure, since there are many chess positions in which the real value of a piece lies in the moves it can make rather than in its simple material measure. Possibly the best example of this is the difference in value between bishop and knight. Although many beginners' books assess these two pieces as being of equal or nearly equal value, it is well known that the value of each depends on the type of position in which it finds itself. A bishop, in a closed position with an obstructive pawn chain, is often worth far less than a knight which might be able to roam in and out of the pawn structure or to transfer quickly from one area of the board to another. On an open board, however, the bishop is nearly always superior and the reason is easy to understand—from any square on an empty board a bishop can make many more moves than a knight; the ratio varies from 13:8 in the centre of the board to 7:2 on a corner square.

Mobility also explains why three minor pieces (two bishops and a knight or two knights and a bishop) are usually better than a queen. The combined mobility of the three pieces is greater than that of the queen and the pieces therefore attack more squares.

As a further example of the use of mobility as a simple measure, consider the following well-known position.

It is White's turn to move and he has twenty legal moves. Let us consider each of the twenty in turn and count, after each one, the number of moves that White would be able to make if it were still his move:

Move	Mobility
P-K4	30
P-K3	30
P-Q4	28
P-Q3	27
P-QB4	22
N-KB3	22
N-QB3	22
P-KR4	21

P-KN3	21
P-KN4	21
P-QB3	21
P-QN3	21
P-QN4	21
P-QR4	21
P-KB4	20
N-KR3	20
N-QR3	20
P-KB3	19
P-KR3	19
P-QR3	19

These figures are not being given with the intention of proving anything conclusive, but it is interesting that the two most popular opening moves in master chess (1 P-K4 and 1 P-Q4) appear at the top end of the list. 1 P-K3 and 1 P-Q3 are hardly ever seen in strong competitions because although they increase White's mobility substantially they do not attack any squares in the opponent's half of the board. There is also the point that a position with pawns at Q3 and K4 (or Q4 and K3) offers less mobility than one with pawns at Q4 and K4. Nevertheless, in reply to 1 P-K4, the moves 1...P-K3 and 1...P-Q3 *are* frequently seen in competitive chess.

Some experiments reported in 1950 by E. T. O. Slater led him to argue that 'it does seem possible that a chess computer which was programmed, beyond immediate tactical tasks, to maximize the mobility difference between itself and its opponent over a series of moves, might play a strategically tolerable game of chess'. Slater's remarks are of value in that they were based in part on an examination of master games. What he did was to compare the mobilities of the two players in 78 arbitarily selected master games which ended with a decisive result on or before the 40th move. The average of these mobilities can be seen in the following table:

After Move	Winner's Mobility (average)	Loser's Mobility (average)	Difference
0	20.0	20.0	0
5	34.2	33.9	0.3
10	37.5	36.0	1.5
15	39.7	35.2	4.5
20	38.9	36.4	2.5

25	39.6	31.9	7.7
30	35.6	27.7	7.9
35	31.7	23.2	8.5

˒ These figures show an increase in mobility as pieces are developed, a descrease in mobility as pieces are exchanged and, in general, an increase in the difference between the winner's mobility and that of his opponent.

Slater also pointed out that many standard chess features might be regarded as merely an extension of mobility. Control of space is highly correlated with mobility; development is largely tantamount to the acquisition of increased mobility; even putting a rook on an open file may be considered as little more than increasing the rook's mobility.

If a computer program is to employ an evaluation function with the two features material and mobility, it is important to find a numerical weighting that expresses the importance of one feature relative to the other. These weightings (or coefficients as they are sometimes called) correspond to the $\frac{1}{30}$ and $\frac{1}{60}$ in Hamish's calculations. Most programmers seem to arrive at their coefficients by making a guess and then modifying it in the light of the play of their program. If their program sacrifices its pawns (and sometimes pieces) in the opening in order to achieve maximum mobility, then unless its middle game play is also Morphy-like, its mobility coefficient will be reduced relative to material. One practical way to arrive at a working value for a coefficient is to arrange for the program to play a slightly different version of itself. In one version the mobility coefficient could be set to (say) 0.01, i.e. one extra unit of material (a pawn) is worth one hundred extra units of mobility (moves). In the other version of the program the mobility coefficient could be set to (say) 0.5. The two versions of the program would then play a series of games against each other and, depending on the results, the coefficient of the loser would be changed to bring it some way towards that of the winner. Such a procedure might justifiably be called 'computer learning', since the programs would be learning to adjust their own coefficients in the light of their performance.

In his assessment of a chess position a master considers many more features than material and mobility and it is a reasonable assumption that a strong chess program should also 'consider' a number of aspects of the position. Part of the difficulty in establishing a series of numerical criteria from which a program can arrive at an accurate assessment of a position, lies in the presumption that such criteria do exist. After all, a chess master does not work in this way. His assessments are usually made, not by counting pawns and pieces, but from his 'feel' of the position. One might argue that unless this feel can be implemented in a computer program there will never be a program that can play master chess. This argument is not necessarily correct however, since it might be possible to write a strong chess program without directly simulating human behaviour (although personally I doubt it).

Having considered the relatively simple features of material and mobility, let us look at the problem if finding satisfactory numerical criteria to describe, to a program, features that are more subtle in nature. A logical addition to our list of features would be one based on the fact that the control of certain squares is of greater value than the control of certain others. It is well known, for example, that control of the centre is of vital importance in chess. If a player's pieces and pawns control the centre then some of his pieces will eventually be able to occupy strong central posts and from the centre a piece exercises more mobility than it does from (say) the edge of the board. It is therefore a good idea to find some way of weighting the squares on the board in such a way as to make central squares more attractive to a program than edge or corner squares.

We could weight each of the squares of the board according to how many moves could be made from that square when various pieces are placed there. These pieces can be taken as one queen, two rooks, two knights, one bishop (the other can never get to the same square) and however many pawns can conceiveably reach that square (e.g. from the initial position only the QP, KP and KBP can possibly reach the K3 square). This method of weighting gives us some idea of the relative values of the squares at the beginning of the game, but once pieces begin to be exchanged we must readjust the weightings to take into account the different material combination arising on the board. Then we should consider the fact that some pieces are badly placed to reach certain squares, and that the weightings for these squares should be adjusted accordingly—but how? The difficulties are just beginning!

The problem of finding some satisfactory way to measure the various features increases in difficulty as the features become less concrete in nature. Material and mobility can be measured easily, centre control with considerably more difficulty, and just how does one weight a passed pawn on the seventh rank in relation to one on the sixth, or doubled pawns on QB2 and QB3 in relation to pawns on KB2 and KB3? How to measure such features is one of the most serious problems in computer chess today.

Trees and Tree-Searching

Given the ability to generate all the legal moves from any chess position and the facility to perform some sort of evaluation on the resulting position, a computer program can play chess in better than random fashion. In fact, if it were possible to achieve, using an evaluation function, assessments that were 100% accurate, then it would be possible to write a computer program to play perfect chess without the need for any look-ahead. But just as it is not feasible to consider all possible variations with the most primitive of evaluation functions, so it is highly unlikely that anyone will ever develop an evaluation function so sophisticated that look-ahead is completely unnecessary.

When a chess master looks ahead his whole analytical search rarely encompasses many more than 100 positions. His expertise is such that he can discard from his considerations almost all the legal moves at any depth of search. This is because his 'evaluation function' enables him to reject these moves as being highly implausible and to concentrate his efforts along paths that look more fruitful. So far (1975), chess programmers have made no real pro gress in this direction. Instead, chess programs typically look at tens or hundreds of thousands of positions at each move, some examine as many as one and a half million.

The device used by a chess program to look ahead from a chess position is called a tree. Trees are not peculiar to chess programs but are used in a variety of programs that solve decision making problems. Like the arborial variety computer trees have roots and branches but traditionally they grow downwards, rather than up towards the sky.

Each chess position is represented on the tree by a 'node'. The position in which the program is considering its move is the root of the tree. Each branch of the tree represents one legal move and the node at the lower end of the branch represents the position that arises when the move represented by that branch is made from the position represented by the node at the upper end of the branch. A simple tree is shown on the next page.

The position (P_0) in diagram 5 is the one from which the program must select a move. If it follows the branch that represents R-R6 then it will reach the position in diagram 6, represented by node P_1. If it chooses the branch representing R-R7 then it will reach P_2 which represents the position of diagram 7. Similarly for R-R8 and R×P. These five nodes and four branches make up a small tree, and

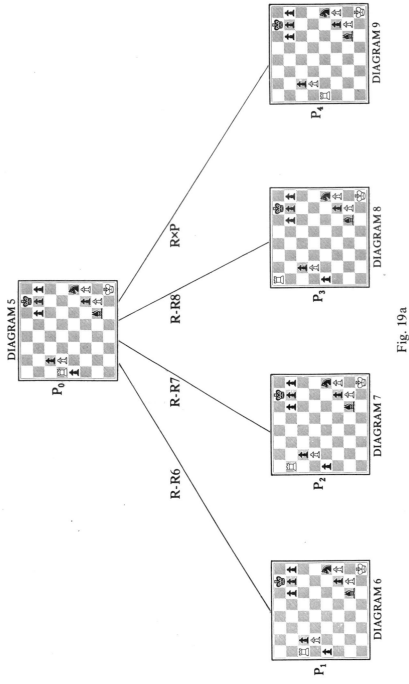

Fig. 19a

White has a choice of four moves.

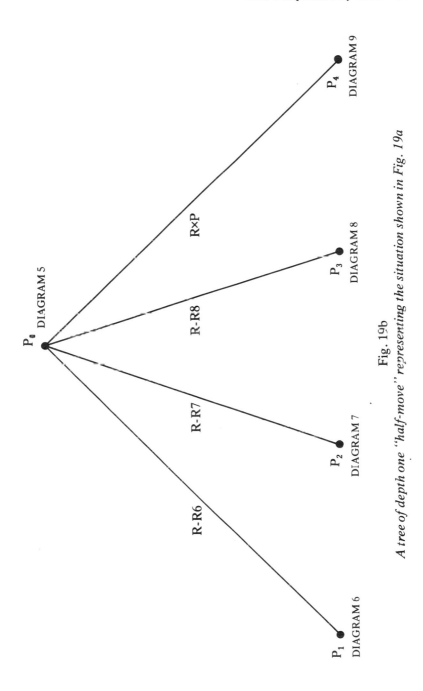

Fig. 19b

A tree of depth one "half-move" representing the situation shown in Fig. 19a by evaluating all the nodes at the lower extremities of the tree (called the terminal nodes) the program can decide which move to make. In this example the decision is simple. R-R8 leaves Black with a mobility of zero, i.e. Black has been mated. This is not true in any of the other three cases and so R-R8 is the move that would be chosen.

Now let us grow a slightly larger tree in order to see how a computer program looks ahead.

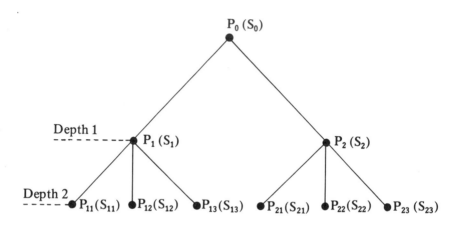

Fig. 20
A tree of depth two "half-moves".

This tree has been grown to a depth of two half-moves (or two-ply). The program is required to move from the position represented by the node P_0. It can move to the position represented by P_1, when its opponent will have a choice of moving to P_{11}, P_{12} or P_{13}; or to P_2, when its opponent will be able to choose between P_{21}, P_{22} and P_{23}. Associated with each of these positions at depth two there is a score, obtained from the evaluation function, that measures how good or bad that position is. Usually programmers adopt the convention that a high (positive) score is good for their program and that a low (or negative) score is good for their opponent.

If the program's opponent had to move from position P_1 and if it chose its best move, it would move to whichever of the three possible successor positions carried with it the best score from its own point of view. This would be the position P_{1i} for which the score S_{1i} was the minimum of S_{11}, S_{12} and S_{13}. This score, S_{1i}, would then be the score S_1 associated with the node P_1 because it would be the *best* score that could be reached from position P_1 in one half-move by the program's opponent. Similarly, the score S_2 associated with node P_2 is the minimum of S_{21}, S_{22} and S_{23}.

Clearly, the move that should be made by the program from node P_0 should be the one that maximizes its score, and the program should therefore choose whichever of P_1 and P_2 has the higher score. This score, the greater of S_1 and S_2, is the score associated with the root of the tree (P_0) and it represents the value of that position to the program assuming best play by both sides. This process of taking the maximum of the minimums of the maximums of the minimums is called, not surprisingly, the minimax method of tree searching.

Having discussed some of the many difficulties involved in finding a satisfactory evaluation mechanism for chess programs, and having thereby discarded the possibility of playing master chess using a program that searched to a depth of only one-ply, we should consider briefly the problem of searching an enormous tree using a primitive evaluation function (e.g. one employing only the single feature material). Just how big would the tree need to be for our problem to be able to play perfect chess?

Various attempts have been made to estimate the theoretical maximum of the number of possible chess games and chess positions, and Jack Good has even tried to estimate the number of 'good games' and 'good variations'. If we take into consideration the 50 move rule, then no game may last for more than 3150 moves by each side (49 piece moves, 1 pawn move or capture, 49 more piece moves, 1 pawn move or capture, ... there are fifteen units to be captured on each side and eight pawns, each of which has six moves during its life. Hence the total of $[50 \times 15] + [50 \times 8 \times 6] = 3150$). In any position, the maximum number of moves that can be made by a pawn is 4, by a knight 8, by a bishop 13, by a rook 14, by a king 7 and by a queen 27. So even if all pawns have been promoted to queens the maximum number of possible moves in any position is theoretically $8 + 8 + 13 + 13 + 14 + 14 + 7 + [9 \times 27] = 320$. (The error introduced by omitting the possibility of castling is insignificant.) Also, in any position the player on the move has the right to resign, though this naturally curtails part of the tree of possible games.

Without being in the slightest bit inaccurate, we can therefore state that the theoretical maximum of the number of possible chess games is 321^{6300} which is roughly 10^{15790}.

Some of Good's calculations produced interesting results. He considers the number of opening lines that are recorded in the 10th edition of *Modern Chess Openings* (about 10,000) given on average to a depth of twelve moves by each side. The average number of moves considered in each position is $10000^{\frac{1}{24}} = 1.48$, almost of all of which are lines that have been played or analysed by good players. The Dutch psychologist Adrian de Groot, whose work we shall discuss later, concluded that for the whole game the figure is not much higher than 1.48. Good makes the reasonable assumption that the average number of moves considered in each position by a chess master lies between 1.6 and 1.9. This may seem rather low when one looks at a master's annotation of one of his own games and sees that often he considered three or more moves. But when the number of positions in which a move is obvious or forced (e.g. a simple recapture) is taken into consideration, Good's assumption seems quite justified.

Good uses his statistic to show that the number of 'good' games of not more than 40 moves on each side lies between 10^{15} and $10^{20.5}$ and that the number of good variations up to Black's 40th move lies between 10^{17} and $10^{22.5}$. He also makes the amusing observation that if 1.75 is the correct average during the opening, then *Modern Chess Openings* ought to run to fifty volumes, i.e. only one fiftieth of good opening lines are at present recorded. Perhaps this is not without a tinge of truth. Up to the 1960s most players would have only one book on the openings, a book that contained something about everything. Nowadays the tendency is towards having a library of openings books. The Batsford series of monographs already contains 17 volumes, with more coming each season.

The number of possible chess positions, assuming that no pawn has yet been promoted, is of the order of

$$\frac{64!}{32! \times [8!]^2 \times [2!]^6}$$

or roughly 10^{43}. (N! means $1 \times 2 \times 3 \times \dots \times N$). The reader who wishes to verify this figure should remember that there are a maximum of 32 pieces to be arranged on the chessboard, with 64 squares to choose from, and that each of the eight white pawns is the same as every other white pawn, each white rook, white knight, and white bishop the same as the other, etc. Allowing for promotions the number is less than 2×10^{50}.

These figures are truly astronomic. But even if one considers a reasonable statistic, such as all games that last 40 moves, then assuming an average choice of 30 moves per position, the number of games is 10^{120} which is far more than the number of atoms in the universe. This fact leads us rapidly to the conclusion that if each atom in the universe were a computer and if all these computers worked together then they would still not be able to play the first move in the perfect game of chess in anything less than millions of years, by which time all the computers would have died of old age.

By now the reader will understand some of the more obvious problems facing the chess programmer. It is not feasible to write a program that plays perfect chess by examining every possible variation. It seems impossible, for the moment at least, to design an evaluation function sufficiently sophisticated to enable a program to play good chess by examining only a small tree. The answer lies somewhere between these two extremes. Clearly there must be some sort of look-ahead but equally obviously it must be directed in some way so that only trees of manageable size are examined.

3   The Early History of Computer Chess

'Many have become chess masters — no one has become the master of chess.'
    Tarrasch

Shannon

On March 9th 1949 Claude E. Shannon, a research worker at Bell Telephone Laboratories, Murray Hill, New Jersey, presented a paper at a New York convention. His paper was called *Programming a Computer for Playing Chess* and its enormous significance lies not in the fact that it was the first paper to be published on the subject but that many of Shannon's original ideas can still be seen in today's programs. Shannon did not claim that computer chess itself was of any practical importance but he did realize that a satisfactory solution to the problem might result in progress being made in other areas of automatic problem solving. In particular, he listed the possibility of building machines (i.e. writing programs) that could design electronic circuits, handle complex telephone switching problems, translate from one language to another, make strategic decisions in simplified military operations, orchestrate a melody or handle problems of logical deduction.

   Shannon proposed several features which might be included in the evaluation function:

1) *Material Advantage*
2) *Pawn formation:*
   (a) Backward, isolated and doubled pawns.
   (b) Relative control of the centre (pawns at K4, Q4, KB4, QB4).
   (c) Weakness of pawns near the king (e.g. an advanced KNP).
   (d) Pawns on opposite coloured squares from bishops (i.e. if you have only one bishop you should put your pawns on squares of the other colour).
   (e) Passed pawns.
3) *Positions of pieces:*
   (a) Advanced knight (at K5, Q5, KB5, QB5, K6, Q6, KB6, QB6) especially if protected by a pawn and free from attack by enemy pawns.
   (b) A rook on an open or semi-open file.

(c) A rook on the seventh rank.

(d) Doubled rooks.

4) *Commitments, attacks and options:*

(a) Pieces which are required to guard other pieces and, there-fore, committed and with limited mobility.

(b) Attacks on pieces which give one player the option of exchanging.

(c) Attacks on squares adjacent to the enemy king.

(d) Pins, where the pinned piece is of value not greater than the pinning piece, e.g. a knight pinned by a bishop.

5) *Mobility.*

Shannon described two different types of strategy for growing chess trees. The most primitive strategy, which Shannon referred to as a type-A strategy, is to grow the tree to a fixed depth along every branch and then to search for the best move by using the minimax method. This strategy would require the use of only a limited amount of storage in the computer's 'memory' provided that the tree was grown and searched in the most efficient manner.

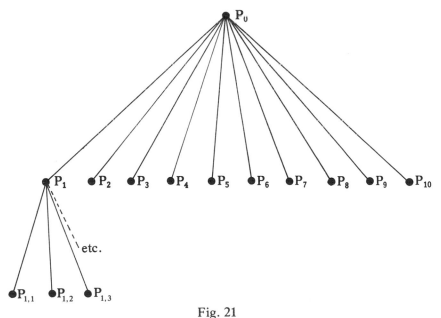

Fig. 21
A tree of depth two half-moves.

The above tree has a root P_0 and then branches from the root. From each of the nodes P_1, P_2, P_3, ... etc., there are also ten branches. If the whole tree were grown before minimax was applied it would be necessary to store 111 nodes in the computer's memory, and associated with each node would be quite a lot of information such as a list of all the squares attacked by each piece, a list of all pieces defended by their own men, etc.

Since storage is always at a premium when solving complex problems on a computer, it is worthwhile devoting some thought to the question of how best to search this tree. Let us first generate the move represented by the branch leading to position P_1. We are interested in discovering which is the best move for the program's opponent from position P_1, and so we wish to compare the scores of positions $P_{1,1}$, $P_{1,2}$, $P_{1,3}$ ... $P_{1,10}$. We generate position $P_{1,1}$ and remember its score and the move leading to that position. We next generate node $P_{1,2}$. We compare the score of $P_{1,2}$ with that of $P_{1,1}$ and if this score is better, for the program's opponent, than the score of $P_{1,1}$, then we discard all the information about $P_{1,1}$ and replace it with the corresponding information about $P_{1,2}$. Then we proceed to generate $P_{1,3}$, compare it with the best node (descended from P_1) so far discovered, and retain all information about whichever of them is the best. In this way we can proceed to generate and examine all the descendants of P_1 without using more storage space than we would require to deal with only two of the descendants.

When we have finished examining all the descendants of P_1 we can assign to P_1 the score corresponding to the best of $P_{1,1}$, $P_{1,2}$ ... etc. We can then discard all the information concerning P_1 except for the move leading to that position from P_0 and the score associated with P_1. We can then examine all the descendants of P_2, one at a time, in the same way, and compare the best result (which will be the score associated with P_2) with the score associated with P_1. Whichever of P_1 and P_2 is the worst for the program has all its information discarded.

By searching the tree in this way, it is never necessary to store information about more than five nodes:

1) The root of the tree (P_0). Also, the positions arising from:
2) The best move from the root found so far (this is at depth 1)
3) The move from the root that is currently under consideration (also at depth 1)
4) The best successor found so far from the move currently under consideration at depth 1 (this will be at depth 2)

5) The depth 2 move currently under consideration.

So by using this method we can search a tree of 111 nodes without ever storing more than 5 of them. It is easy to see that for a tree of depth n-ply (or half-moves) it is necessary only to store information about 2n+1 of the nodes — a dramatic saving for a large tree. There are three major disadvantages of Shannon's type-A strategy, all of which were pointed out by Shannon himself. In a typical middle game position there are more than 30 moves to choose from. After just one move by each side there are roughly 1,000 terminal nodes to be evaluated. After three moves by each side there are 10^9 terminal nodes and even at the rate of one evaluation every micro-second (which is very optimistic) it would take about 16 minutes to make each move. And even with an exhaustive tree search to a depth of six half-moves it would not be possible to play chess at a high standard because of the number of important variations that were more than six-ply long. A human master examines some variations to a depth of only one-ply and others to a depth of twenty or more. It is vital that a chess program be given the facility to examine some variations in depth while rejecting others. The inability to examine deep variations is the second disadvantage of the type-A strategy.

The third disadvantage can be shown by the following simple example.

If a program with a fixed depth search of 2-ply were to analyze this position, part of its analysis would include the variation 1 R-B8ch R×R. Here the program would terminate its look-ahead and assess the position. Seeing that it is a rook down it would proceed to analyse the other variations at its disposal and would eventually choose one of them. It would certainly not play 1 R-B8ch because as far as it could 'see' this variation loses a rook for nothing. Yet 1 R-B8ch is a move that would be made by any human player with very little thought, because the human would see the merit in analysing just a little further. It is obvious to the human player that it is not sensible to evaluate a position that arises in the middle of a sequence of captures, checks or direct threats — we only evaluate positions that are 'quiescent'.

Shannon introduced the notion of quiescence (he called it 'stability') into his second type of strategy. This 'type-B' strategy had two distinct advantages over its predecessor:

1) It examined forcing variations as far as possible and evaluated only quasi-stable positions;

2) It selected the variations to be analysed by some process that prevented the machine from wasting its time in totally pointless evaluation.

These two criteria could equally be applied to a strong human player.

Shannon's admittedly crude interpretation of the concept of quiescence was somewhat inadequate for the purposes of writing a strong chess program, but it is interesting to note that many of today's chess programs are just as deficient in the same area. Shannon's proposal was to call a position approximately stable if no pieces were *en prise*. This, if taken to include all checks (i.e. position in which a king is *en prise*), is not sufficient to ensure good, or even satisfactory tactical play, since there are other, equally serious threats that one might be under even though one's pieces were all safely protected and free from attack.

Turing and Hand Simulations

In 1951 Alan Turing wrote about the results of his work on computer chess at the University of Manchester. Turing was one of the outstanding workers during the early years of computer science and he was convinced that games constituted an ideal model system in which studies of machine intelligence could first be developed. This view is widely held today by those who work in the field of artificial intelligence but in Turing's day his opinion was greeted with some scepticsm.

Turing's earliest thoughts on the subject of computer chess date from 1944, when he discussed some of his ideas with various friends and colleagues. Around 1947-48 he and D. G. Champernowne devised a one move analyser called the TUROCHAMP and at the same time Donald Michie and S. Wylie designed a rival analyser named MACHIAVELLI. These analysers were sufficient to enable their creators to simulate the play of a computer that was searching to a depth of one-ply. They simply calculated, by hand, the scores associated with all the positions at a depth of one and then made the move leading to the position with the highest score. A match between the two was arranged but never completed. Thirteen years later, in 1961, MACHIAVELLI did play a game with another analyser (SOMA) designed by Maynard Smith.

SOMA used an evaluation function in which three features were of paramount importance — material, mobility and 'swap-off values'. For material calculations each pawn was worth 10 points, knights and bishops 30, rooks 50 and the queens were worth 90 if they were not on the back two ranks and the player had not castled, otherwise they were worth 100. This deterred moving the queen from the back two ranks before castling.

The mobility score was not a simple count of the number of moves that could be made by all pieces, but a weighted measure that placed a greater value on attacking certain squares than on attacking certain others. For every square attacked 1 point was scored. For every square attacked that was adjacent to the enemy king an extra 2 points were scored. For each attack on one of the four central squares an extra 1 point was scored. These 'attacks' took into account pinned pieces by assuming that if a piece was pinned it did not actually attack any squares, and the feature also allowed for transparent attacks, whereby, for example, if two rooks are on the same file they can both be considered to be attacking an enemy piece on that file because the attack by one of the rooks is being supported from behind by the other one. The squares attacked by each piece are ennumerated separately and added, so that if a square were attacked by four white pieces this added four times the usual square attack value to White's score.

The most interesting feature of SOMA was the swap-off values. These values determined, in a very simple way, whether or not a particular exchanging sequence was likely to be profitable, without the necessity of performing any look-ahead whatsoever. I am amazed that no real chess program has ever used swap-off values as they would considerably improve the accuracy of the evaluation of terminal positions. Swap-off values are calculated in the following way. Assume that a white piece of value v_0 is attacked by n white pieces of value v_1, v_2, ... v_n in ascending order of value, and by N black pieces of values

$u_1, u_2, \ldots u_N$ in ascending order of value. Calculate:

$w_1 = v_0$
$w_2 = v_0 - u_1 + v_1$
$w_3 = v_0 - u_1 + v_1 - u_2 + v_2$
$w_4 = v_0 - u_1 + v_1 - u_2 + v_2 - u_3 + v_3$ etc.

and

$b_1 = v_0 - u_1$
$b_2 = v_0 - u_1 + v_1 - u_2$
$b_3 = v_0 - u_1 + v_1 - u_2 + v_2 - u_3$
$b_4 = v_0 - u_1 + v_1 - u_2 + v_2 - u_3 + v_3 - u_4$ etc.

These two series are calculated until one side or the other runs out of pieces with which to capture on the square occupied by v_0.

If the number of white pieces n, is greater than or equal to the number of black pieces N, then the series ends at b_N and the swap-off value S = the largest value of b, or, if smaller, the smallest value of w preceding this. If n is less than N then the series ends at w_{n+1} and S = the smallest value of w, or, if larger, the largest value of b preceding this.

In calculating swap-off values it is important to remember that if piece X only attacks the square under consideration by virtue of the transparency of another piece Y (e.g. white queen at Q1, white rook at Q2 — the white queen attacks Q3 by virtue of the transparency of the rook) then even if the value of Y is greater than that of X, v cannot precede v_y in the series because there is no possibility of capturing with X before Y has captured.

Lets us examine a concrete example.

It is Black's move and we wish to determine whether or not he should capture on Q4.

$v_0 = 1$

$v_1 = 3$ (knight) $\qquad u_1 = 3$ (bishop)
$v_2 = 3$ (bishop) $\qquad u_2 = 5$ (rook)
$v_3 = 5$ (rook) $\qquad u_3 = 9$ (queen)

$w_1 = v_0 = 1$
$w_2 = v_0 - u_1 + v_1 = 1 - 3 + 3 = 1$
$w_3 = v_0 - u_1 + v_1 - u_2 + v_2 = 1 - 3 + 3 - 5 + 3 = -1$

and

$b_1 = v_0 - u_1 = 1 - 3 = -2$
$b_2 = v_0 - u_1 + v_1 - u_2 = 1 - 3 + 3 - 5 = -4$
$b_3 = v_0 - u_1 + v_1 - u_2 + v_2 - u_3 = 1 - 3 + 3 - 5 + 3 - 9 = -10$

To summarize our results so far:

$$w_1 = 1 \qquad b_1 = 2$$
$$w_2 = 1 \qquad b_2 = -4$$
$$w_3 = -1 \qquad b_3 = -10$$

Since n (i.e. 3) is equal to N (also 3) the series ends at b_3. The swap-off value S is the largest value of b (i.e. -2) or, if smaller, the smallest value of w preceding this (i.e. -1). Since -1 is not less than -2, the swap-off value is -2. We can verify this by examining the position. If Black captures White's QP he loses at least 2 points on the usual material scale, since the lowest valued piece with which he can make the capture will immediately be lost and he will therefore have given up 3 points in order to win 1. The capture can be seen to be disadvantageous from the fact that the swap-off value is negative.

By using swap-off values when evaluating terminal positions in which captures are feasible, it is quite possible to determine that a certain position offers an advantageous exchanging sequence without actually searching that part of the game tree in which the exchanges occur.

The three principal features of SOMA's evaluation mechanism were weighted in the following way:

SCORE = [SQUARE ATTACK × 10] + MATERIAL + SWAP-OFF + r

where r represents the small residual score that took into account castling and the other minor features mentioned in the previous paragraph. It took a human operator about five minutes to make the calculations for a single move. MACHIAVELLI worked along similar lines but it had more instructions concerning chess strategy and rather less tactical insight.

White: SOMA
Black: MACHIAVELLI

1 P-K3

This move increases the score for White's position by 8 points: 4 new squares attacked by the bishop, 3 by the queen and 1 because the pawn now attacks a centre square and an ordinary square whereas before it moved it attacked two ordinary squares.

Three other moves also increase SOMA's score by 8 points: 1 P-K4. 1 N-KB3 and 1 N-QB3. In such cases, where there is a tie, the move is chosen at random from those with the maximum score.

1 ...	P-K4
2 P-Q4	N-QB3
3 N-QB3	P-Q4
4 N-B3	P-K5
5 N-K5	B-QN5
6 N×N	P×N
7 B-Q2	N-B3
8 P-QR4	B-Q3
9 P-KR4	

White's last two moves have increased the mobility of his rooks!

| 9 ... | B-KN5 |
| 10 B-K2 | Q-Q2 |

11 O-O	O-O-O
12 P-B3	B-KB4
13 P×P	B×P
14 B-R6+	K-N1
15 N×B	N×N
16 Q-K2	

SOMA is only a one move analyser and so it does not see ...N-N6 coming.

16 ...   Q-K3

MACHIAVELLI's designers ascribe this tactical oversight to the fact that their 'program' prefers development to material gain.

| 17 B-R5 | N-N6 |
| 18 Q-B3 | |

Obviously (to a human) White should play 18 Q-Q3.

18 ...	N×R
19 R×N	P-B3
20 R-Q1	Q-K5
21 Q×Q	

SOMA doesn't know that a material advantage of 20 to 18 is much better than one of 29 to 27.

21 ...	P×Q
22 P-Q5	P×P
23 R×P	B-K4?

Black can win another exchange by 23...B-R7ch 24 K×B R×R. SOMA would have found this combination because after

23...B-R7ch there would be two white pieces en prise: the king with a value of 100 and the rook with a value of 5. The only black piece en prise would be the bishop (worth 3) and so the swap-off value of the move would be +2.

24 R-N5+   K-R1

25	B-N7+	K-N1
26	B×KP+	K-B1
27	B-B5+	R-Q2
28	B×R+	K×B

Here the game was agreed drawn because neither program had been taught anything about the endgame.

During the course of his research on computer chess, Turing tried to program both the TUROCHAMP and the MACHIAVELLI on the Ferranti Mark 1 computer at Manchester, but he never completed the programming and so was unable to play them against each other automatically.

The significance of Turing's work lay largely in the fact that he was the first person to design a program that could play chess. Admittedly the one game 'played' by his 'program' was really a tedious hand simulation, but if we make the reasonable assumption that Turing's arithmetic was correct then we have every reason to regard this game in the same vein as those played by real live computers.

Turing used a simple evaluation function in which material was the dominating factor. He grew his game tree to a depth of two ply along all branches and then examined all 'considerable' moves at deeper plies, stopping a variation when a 'dead' position was reached (i.e. a position from which there are no 'considerable' moves). He defined 'considerable' moves as those that:

a) Capture an undefended piece;
b) Recapture a piece;
c) Capture a defended piece with one of lower value;
d) Give mate.

To play a game by hand using such a scheme must have taken a great deal of time and patience. Before making a move Turing would have to consider in the region of 1,000 terminal positions and perform evaluations for many of them. If the material evaluations were equal for two or more positions at depth one, then positional factors were used to break the tie. This positional value did not take into account all the pieces on the board, but only all those of the side on the move as well as his opponent's king. The features employed in Turing's positional evaluation were:

1) *Mobility:*

For the queen, rooks, bishops and knights, add the square roots of the number of moves that the piece can make, counting a capture as two moves. (For the sake of simplicity Turing approximated the square roots to one place of decimals.)

2) *Piece safety:*

For the rooks, bishops and knights add 1 point if the piece is defended once, and 1.5 if it is defended at least twice.

3) *King mobility:*

For the king use the same method of scoring as for the pieces, but do not count castling.

4) *King safety:*

Deduct points for the king's vulnerability, defined as the number of moves that a queen could make were it on the square occupied by the king.

5) *Castling:*

Add 1 point if castling is still legally possible at a later stage of the game (i.e. if neither the king nor the rook has yet moved), add another point if castling is immediately possible or if the castling move has just been made.

6) *Pawn credit:*

Score 0.2 points for each rank advanced and 0.3 points for each pawn defended by one or more non-pawns.

7) *Checks and mate threats:*

Score 1 point for the threat of mate and 0.5 points for a check.

The material values assigned to each of the pieces was:

Pawn=1, knight=3, bishop=3.5, rook=5, queen=10.

The game played between Turing's hand simulation and a weak human opponent is given below.

White: 'Program'
Black : Human

Manchester 1951

1	P-K4	P-K4	
2	N-QB3	N-KB3	
3	P-Q4	B-N5	
4	N-B3	P-Q3	
5	B-Q2	N-B3	
6	P-Q5	N-Q5	
7	P-KR4		

Strangely enough, even though such moves would be almost unthinkable in a game between reasonable human players, they are not uncommon in computer games. The reason is not hard to find. The program's positional 'judgement', is governed by its evaluation function which, in turn is designed to incorporate various chess rules-of-thumb (called heuristics in computer jargon). Two of the heuristics embodied in Turing's evaluation function, as well as in the evaluation functions of many more recent programs, are (1) Advance your pawns (exemplified by the bonus of 0.3 for each rank advanced); and (2) Increase your mobility (score the square root of the number of moves that a piece can make). The move 7 P-KR4 scores a bonus of 0.6 for advancing the pawn two ranks, and it increases to mobility of White's KR from 2 (for which it scores 1.4) to 4 (for which it scores 2).

7 ...	B-N5
8 P-R4	

Thematic!

8 ...	N×N+
9 P×N	B-KR4
10 B-QN5+	P-B3

Obviously 10...N-Q2 would be better.

11 P×P	O-O
12 P×P	R-N1
13 B-QR6	Q-R4
14 Q-K2	N-Q2

Black can win back one pawn by 14...B×P! 15 Q×B Q×B.

15 R-KN1	N-B4
16 R-N5	

Turing and others have commented that this move was made using the 'Heads in the sand' approach. The program is faced with the loss of its advanced QNP and it staves off this material loss as far as possible. By playing 16 R-N5 the program appears to be avoiding reality — it simply pushes reality (in this case the loss of the QN7 pawn) over its horizon. Now, after Black moves his attacked bishop and White retreats his own bishop, the capture of the QN7 pawn has not been averted, but its capture will occur at a depth too great for the program to see at this point. This move is the earliest example of what is known today as the 'horizon effect'.

The amusing thing is that 16 R-N5 is White's best move, but Turing and many later writers have overlooked the reason.

16 ...	B-N3

17 B-N5?

An aimless move. 17 B-QB4 was obviously the best choice since if Black were then to capture the QNP White could play 18 P-R5 trapping the bishop

(18...P-KR3 19 R×B). If Black meets 17 B-QB4 with 17...K-R1, avoiding the pin along the KN1-QR7 diagonal, White wins by 18 P-R5. e.g. 18...P-B3 19 R×B P×R 20 P×P, and it is impossible for Black to prevent White from mating him by Q-B1-R1 or P-B4 and Q-R5. 17...K-R1 18 P-R5 P-R3 is also no good because of 19 P×B P×R 20 Q-B1 etc. It seems that Black must reply to 17 B-QB4 with 17...N-K3 18 B×N P×B, when White has an excellent position.

17 P-R5 at once is not good becuase of 17...N-K3.

So it would appear that in the diagrammed position Turing's program had a clear advantage.

| 17 ... | N×NP |
| 18 O-O-O? | |

18 B-QB4. threatening 19 P-R5, probably gives White a won game. 18 P-R5 P-KR3 19 P×B P×R 20 B-QB4 is also very difficult to meet.

The program, however, is more attracted by the bonus attached to castling.

| 18... | N-B4 |

Now it is too late for P-R5 which can be met by ...N-K3, and 19 B-QB4 N×RP is also good for Black.

| 19 B-B6 | KR-B1? |

19...N-K3 was essential for obvious reasons.

20 B-Q5	B×N
21 B×B	Q×P
22 K-Q2?	

22 P-R5 wins for White.

| 22 ... | N-K3 |

At last, but it should be too late.

| 23 R-N4? | |

23 B×N was correct. Now Black's knight becomes a nuisance.

| 23 ... | N-Q5? |

23...N-B5 followed by 24...N×B would have put an end to White's K-side play.

24 Q-Q3	N-N4
25 B-N3	Q-R3
26 B-B4	

26 R.Q1-KN1 gives White a winning attack.

| 26 ... | B-R4 |
| 27 R-N3 | |

Why not go back to N5?

27 ...	Q-R5
28 B×N	Q×B
29 Q×P??	

After 29 Q×Q R×Q 30 R.Q1-KN1 P-N3 31 K-K3, White could unravel his rooks and keep a big advantage because of the superiority of his own bishop over that of his opponent.

| 29 ... | R-Q1 |

White had overlooked the strength of this 'deep' move. The program only looked to a depth of two half moves and so when it considered 29 Q×P it was unable to see to the position in which its queen was captured (which was at depth four).

30 Resigns

Turing summed up the weakness of his 'program' by describing it as a caricature of his own play. 'It was in fact based on an introspective analysis of my thought processes when playing, with considerable simplifications. It makes oversights which are very similar to those which I make myself, and which may in both cases be ascribed to the considerable moves being inappropriately chosen. This fact might be regarded as supporting the glib view which is often expressed, to the effect that "one cannot program a machine to play a better game than one plays oneself".'

Another interesting parallel that may be drawn between the play of this program (and others) and weak human players is that members of both groups often, through no fault of their own, find themselves in positions in which a win can be forced through some relatively simple tactical idea, but without realising that such a tactical opportunity might be present they fail to search for it and hence they fail to find it. Most club players, when faced with the position at move 17 (and the similar ones that followed) would have realized that White's KB belongs on the QR2-KN8 diagonal and that P-R5 was likely to be very strong if it were played at the correct moment. The concept of trapping and winning an immobile piece (Black's QB in this case) and the idea of the attack on Black's weak KB2 and KR2 squares, are both simple and common enough for them to occur to any reasonably experienced chess player. It should merely be a question of working out in which order the moves should be played and in calculating one or two variations. Since computers are flawless in calculation the only problem would seem to be in thinking of this plan, but planning is one area of problem-solving in which computer programs, even today, are still in their infancy.

In November 1951 one of Turing's colleagues at Manchester University, Dr. Prinz, wrote a program to solve simple mate-in-two problems. Since such problems can be solved quite easily by conducting a three-ply search, Prinz's program was little more than an intellectual exercise. It contributed nothing to the more general problems of computer chess.

The Los Alamos Program

The next well documented account of experiments in chess programming appeared in 1956, following the work of five scientists (Kister, Stein, Ulam, Walden and Wells) at the Los Alamos Scientific Laboratory in New Mexico. The Los Alamos group mentioned a slightly earlier program, reported in an article in *Pravda* that had been written for a BESM computer in Moscow, but the *Pravda* article did not give a detailed account of the method by which their program had been written nor the results of its play beyond the statement that a fair chess player was able to beat the machine.

The game played by the Los Alamos program was not really chess but a miniature version of it, played on a 6×6 board omitting the bishops. For its first move each pawn could advance only one square and castling was not permitted. They found that although the game was much simpler than chess it nevertheless retained much of the flavour of the real game. The program ran on a MANIAC computer whose speed was 11,000 operations per second, and it was able to perform an exhaustive search to a depth of four-ply in about 12 minutes on average. Since, in real chess, the number of legal moves at each stage would be almost twice as great, the time taken to make a move in the real game would have been in the region of three hours for an exhaustive four-ply search.

The program employed an evaluation function using only two features, material and mobility. The first game played by MANIAC matched the program against itself. The programmers reported that '...like any game between beginners it contained weak moves, but in general we were very pleased with the quality of the play.' Several changes in the program were then made to correct the most obvious of the remedial weaknesses. For example, the program seemed to have a mortal fear of checks, since its mobility after a check was almost nil, and it tended to sacrifice material to avoid being checked.

An improved version of the program was then matched against a strong player from Princeton, Dr. Martin Kruskal, who gave MANIAC odds of a queen. The game took many hours to play and attracted wide local interest. After about fifteen moves Kruskal had not recouped any material and had even started calling his opponent 'he' instead of 'it'. As the game progressed it appeared that Dr. Kruskal might lose, but around move nineteen the program chose a weak continuation and Kruskal was able to win its queen by threatening mate. After the program had been forced to give up its queen for a pawn it had no chance.

The program was then matched against a young lady member of the laboratory who had been taught to play chess one week earlier with the express intention of playing against MANIAC. She had been coached during the week in the principles of the game and in elementary combinations, and she had played several games against players of average strength. This is the way the game proceeded:

White: MANIAC
Black: Human

1 P-K3   P-QN3
2 N-KR3
A good idea in 6×6 games —

the knight is quite aggressively placed, attacking K4 and KB5.

2 ...   P-K3
3 P-QN3   P-N3
4 N-N1   P-QR3
5 P×RP?

A dreadful strategic error, giving Black's QN its undeserved freedom and leaving White with an isolated QRP. Better would have been 5 N-K2 intending 6 N-Q4+ N×N 7 NP×N with a good game.

5 ...   N×P

6 K-K2?	N-Q4
7 N×N	NP×N+
8 K-K1	P-R3
9 P-QR3	R-N1
10 P-R4	

The program made these last two moves because they increase the mobility of its QR — the rule 'advance your pawns' had not been programmed. This is a good example of a program playing the right moves for the wrong reason.

| 10 ... | R-R1 |
| 11 P-R5 | |

11 ...	K-K2
12 Q-R3	Q-N2
13 Q-R2+	K-N2
14 R-N1?	R×P
15 R×Q	R×Q
16 R-N1	

To prevent the back rank mate!

| 16 ... | R-QR2 |

Passive — Nimzowitsch would never have removed his rook from the fifth rank.

17 P-R3	R-R3
18 RP×P	P-Q3
19 N-R3+	K-K1
20 P-N5+	K-K2
21 P×R=Q	N-Q2
22 Q×KP+	K-Q1
23 N-N5 mate	

The Bernstein Program

'Chess is not only one of the most engaging but also one of the most sophisticated of human activities. The game is so old that we cannot say when or where it was invented; millions of games have been played and thousands of books have been written about it; yet the play is still fresh and forever new.' Thus began an article by Alex Bernstein and Michael de V. Roberts in the June 1958 issue of *Scientific American,* in which the authors described to the public a program that they had developed together with Timothy Arbuckle and M. A. Belsky. It is true that Shannon had expressed his ideas in the pages of *Scientific American* (inter alia) eight years earlier, but Shannon's paper was purely theoretical in nature whereas the Bernstein/Roberts article described a program that could play a reasonable game on a real live computer (in their case an IBM 704, which could perform as many as one billion calculations per day).

The Bernstein/Roberts article had more than a touch of the 2001s about it. 'You sit at the console of the machine with a chessboard in front of you and press the start button. Within four seconds a panel light labelled "Program Stop" lights up on the console and now you make your choice of black or white: to choose black you flip a switch on the console; if you want white, you simply leave the switch as it is. Suppose you have picked black. To begin the game you press the start button again. The machine now "thinks" about its first move... Some lights flash on the console but the computer is working so swiftly that it is impossible to say just what these flashes mean. After about eight minutes the computer prints out its move on a sheet of paper.' If the human opponent made an illegal move the computer would print out "PLEASE CHECK LAST MOVE". At the end of the game it printed the game score and the words "THANK YOU FOR AN IN-TERESTING GAME".

Their program had an evaluation function that used four features:
1) *Mobility:*
  The number of available moves for each side;
2) *Area control:*
  The number of squares completely controlled by each side;
3) *King defence:*
  The number of controlled squares around each king;
4) *Material:*
  The ratio of the program's material score to that of its opponent.

By using a ratio as their material measure instead of the difference between White's material and Black's, the programmers introduced the well known heuristic 'swap off when you are ahead in material'.

The program searched to a depth of four-ply. In order to ensure that its moves could be made within a reasonable space of time, instead of considering every move in a given position it chose the best seven moves as selected by a number of 'decision routines'. These decision routines examined a position to determine whether a certain state existed — if it did then certain moves were generated and added to a 'plausible move table'. The questions asked by the decision routines were:

1) *Is the king in check?:*
  If the answer was yes then the program looked to see if it was in check from more than one piece, in which case it would generate only king moves. If the king was only in check from a single piece then the

program generated interposing moves and moves that captured the checking piece. If the answer to question (1) was no, the program went to the next question.

2) (a) *Can material be gained?*
    (b) *Can material be lost?*
    (c) *Can material be exchanged?*

If the answer to question 2(a) was yes, the program listed those moves which gained material in the plausible move table; if 2(b) was yes, the program found which moves would put the attacked pieces in safety and entered them in the table; and if 2(c) was yes it entered the exchanging moves in the table.

At the end of question 2, if the storage locations in the plausible move table were not yet full, the program went on to the following questions:

3) *Is castling possible?*
4) *Can a minor piece be developed?*
5) *Can any pieces occupy the critical squares created by pawn chains?*
    (These are the squares that are normally referred to in chess books as 'weak' squares.)
6) *Can open files be occupied?*
7) *Can any pawn be moved?*
8) *Can any piece be moved?*

This decision routine procedure was stopped either if the plausible move table was filled, or if the answer to question 3 was yes. The logic behind this second criterion is that castling is such an important element in bringing the king to safety that none of the less important routines should be questioned.

The ordering of these routines was very important. At the beginning of the game questions 1, 2 and 3 do not apply and questions 4 and 7 were the only ones that generated moves. In the middle game, questions 2, 5 and 6 generate the most moves. In the endgame it was questions 5, 6, 7 and 8 that were the most often used.

This decision routine process resulted (hopefully) in the seven most plausible moves being stored in the table. The program performed a depth-four search, considering, at each stage, the seven most plausible moves. It therefore examined 7 positions at a depth of 1-ply, 49 at depth 2. 343 at depth 3 and 2401 at depth 4: a total of 2800 position — quite manageable for a computer. The program played a passable amateur game at the rate of one move in about eight minutes.

Here is a game that the program lost against a skillful opponent. The program's first four moves are not unreasonable but by the middle game it had betrayed its chief weakness: namely, a heavy bias towards moving attacked pieces rather then defending them. Since the program only searches to a depth of four-ply it is obvious that a five-ply (or in human terms, three move) combination will escape its notice. Since it is heavily materially biased it would always accept a sacrifice, but then so did Capablanca, Bernstein and other outstanding players.

White: IBM 704
Black: Human

1	P-K4	P-K4
2	B-B4	P-QN3
3	P-Q3	N-KB3
4	B-KN5	B-N2
5	B×N	Q×B
6	N-KB3	P-B3
7	O O	P-Q4
8	P×P	P×P
9	B-N5+	N-B3
10	P-B4?	

White could win a pawn by 10 N×P (Q×N 11 R-K1), but after Black's 11th move the material assessment of the (then current) situation would reveal that Black was a piece up for a pawn. That Black was going to lose his queen on the next move is something that was one ply too deep to be 'seen' by the program.

10	...	P×P
11	B×N+	Q×B
12	P×P	

Better is 12 R-K1.

| 12 | ... | P-K5 |
| 13 | N-N5 | Q-N3 |

14	N-KR3	P-K6
15	P-B3	B-B4
16	R-K1	O-O
17	N-B3??	

This move shows up a deficiency in the decision routines — there is no routine that asks the question "Can I give check?" nor one that asks "Can I attack an enemy piece?" and so Black's next move would not be in the top seven.

17	...	P-K7+
18	N-B2	B×P
19	P-KN3	P×Q=Q
20	N.B3×Q	Q-B7
21	P-N3	QR-Q1
22	P-KR4	

Another deficiency in the system. The answers to questions 1-6 were all 'no'. Question 7 generated all six legal pawn moves and question 8 generated piece moves at random but unfortunately for the program the plausible move list was full after the first piece move was discovered. The program then went on to depth 2 where questions 2(a) generated the move 22...R×N. All replies to ...R×N fail to save further material loss by White but the program has no mechanism for searching for alternative moves at depth zero. The program is then in the unfortunate situation of knowing that it is about to make a move that will lose material and that it is not allowed to add new moves to the plausible move list.

22   ...   R×N
23   Resigns

Early Soviet Programs

Although it was not very widely publicized, there was almost as much research in computer chess in the USSR during the mid-late 1950s as there was in the USA. As early as 1956 V. M. Kurochkin wrote a program to solve chess problems. His program ran on the Strela computer and it could find a two move mate quicker than most human solvers (two to four minutes) but three and four move mates required ten to twelve minutes or even longer. Kurochkin pointed out that problem solving programs must conduct an exhaustive search and because of this they consider many moves which would normally be considered bad by human players. In this respect problem solving programs do not contribute anything to the more general task of writing a chess playing program.

A year or two later, V. D. Kukushkin wrote a program to play the ending of king and two bishops against king, but the first attempt at writing a program that could play a complete game was made by G. Sehlibs, whose program performed an exhaustive three-ply search. No games played by Sehlibs' program were published and no mention was made of how strong or weak was its play.

The first well publicized chess program written in the Soviet Union made its debut in 1961. It was written at the Styeklov Mathematical Institute of the USSR Academy of Sciences by a team including Professor M. Shura-Bara, I. Zadykhailo, E. Lyubinsky and V. Smilga (a Soviet Candidate-Master). A description of their work was published in the 8th bulletin of the 1961 Tal-Botvinnik World championship Match and from an interview with Professor Shura-Bara that formed part of that description I should like to quote two sentences: 'Working with these aims in mind we have not repeated the experiments of Western Scientists who have tried to load their computers with a huge mass of variations. We want to teach a computer to assess a chess position just like a human player assesses it.' I find it rather interesting that the Professor claimed that the Americans had 'tried to load their computers with a huge mass of variations' — Was this statement propaganda or was the good professor unaware of what had been done in the USA?

This program employed seven features in its evaluation mechanism:

1) *Material:*

   pawn = 1; knight = bishop = $3\frac{1}{2}$; rook = 5; queen = $9\frac{1}{2}$; king=10^9

2) *Mobility:*

   A special bonus is assigned to king mobility since 'the more squares available to him, the less likely he is to be mated'. Had the program used a deep look-ahead, this special bonus would probably have resulted in the king becoming too exposed!

3) *Defence of Pieces:*

   Attacks on enemy pieces were considered less important than the loss of the program's own men, even though the attacked piece might be much more valuable than the piece lost. This heuristic, to some extent, preserved the program from gross blunders.

4) *Pawn Structure:*

   Advanced pawns were given a bonus while backward and isolated ones were assigned a penalty.

5) *Centre Control:*

   The program was encouraged to occupy the centre with pawns and to support the centre with pieces.

6) *Pins:*

   Special consideration was given to pieces pinned against the king.

7) *King Protection:*

   The pawns nearest the king were discouraged from moving, with the exception of the QP and KP.

Let me again quote from the Russian description of the program. 'Despite the restricted nature of the program from the point of view of an experienced player, the machine has already had definite successes in practical play. It is perfectly possible that as the elements of positional judgement are refined, the machine will make huge leaps forward on the road to strengthing its play.'
[Qualitative leaps forward is a Marxist term — the transformation of quality into quantity and vice versa is one of the rules of dialectical materialism. — Translator]

The program performed no look ahead and so its play was rather limited. It took between 30 and 58 seconds to make each move.

In the following game the program played against a girl from the Styeklov Institute who had only recently learned to play.

White: Program
Black: Beginner

1 P-K4!
It is advantageous to occupy the centre with pawns.

1 ...   P-K4
2 Q-R5
Attacking a large number of squares, including some in the centre, and attacking the KP.

2 ...   P-KN3
3 Q×KP+   N-K2
4 Q×R   P-Q4
5 N-QB3
The program found this developing move more appealing than the capture of the KRP.

5 ...   P-KR4
6 N×P   N×N
7 P×N   Q-K2+
8 K-Q1
The program tries to avoid having pieces pinned against its king.

8 ...   B-N5+
9 N-B3   K-Q2
10 B-N5+   P-QB3
11 P×P+   P×P
12 B-K2   N-R3
13 B×N   R-N1
14 Q-Q4+   K-B2

15 Q×P+   K-Q3
16 Q×R+   Q-B2
17 Q×B+   Q-K2
18 Q×Q+
'At this point (according to eye witnesses) the girl was so put out by the onslaught of the machine that she preferred not to play any further.'

The next game was played against a more experienced opponent.

White: Program
Black: Amateur
1 P-K4   P-K4
2 P-Q4

Why did the program not play 2 Q-R5 as in the previous game? The answer is that 2 Q-R5 did not please the programmers and so they made a slight adjustment to the mobility feature of their evaluation function.

2 ...   P×P
3 Q×P   N-QB3
4 Q-Q5

The theoretical move, 4 Q-K3, blocks the line of the QB, while the move played gives White's queen more squares to attack.

4 ...	N-B3
5 Q-KB5	N-Q5
6 Q-K5+	N-K3
7 B-K3	N-N5
8 Q-KR5	N×B
9 P×N	B-B4
10 K-Q2	

This move satisfies two criteria. It guards the KP and gives the king more free squares (thereby 'reducing' the chance of mate). It should also be mentioned that the program had not been taught to castle, and therefore it finds nothing wrong in moving its king.

10 ...	Q-B3
11 N-QB3	

Guarding against the threats 11...Q×NP and 11...Q×B, but overlooking a third threat

through its lack of look-ahead.

11 ...	Q-B7+
12 Q-K2	B×P+
13 K-Q3	

Again looking for freedom — on Q1 the king would have no moves.

13 ...	N-B5+
14 K-B4	N×Q
15 N.N1×N	P-Q3
16 N-Q1!	

Not even the programmers had expected such a "lively" move from the machine.

16 ...	Q-B3

16...Q-K8 keeps the bishop.

17 N×B	Q×P
18 R-Q1	Q×RP+

and the program soon resigned.

Newell, Shaw and Simon

Alan Newell, John Shaw and Herbert Simon began their work on computer chess in 1955 when they were working together at Carnegie Institute of Technology (now Carnegie Mellon University) in Pittsburgh. During the following two or three years however, their major interest lay in developing programs that discovered proofs for theorems in symbolic logic and so progress on chess was slow. That area of Artificial Intelligence is not, in fact, far removed from computer chess, since proving theorems and playing chess involve the same problem: reasoning with heuristics that select fruitful paths of exploration in a fast growing tree of possibilities.

The NSS program was constructed from a basic set of modules, each module being associated with a particular goal in chess. Typical goals are king safety, material balance, centre control, development, attack against the king and pawn promotion. Each goal has associated with it a collection of processes: a move generator, a static evaluation function and an analysis generator.

The move generator associated with each goal proposes various moves relevant to that goal. They carry the burden for finding positive reasons for doing things. Thus, only the centre-control generator will propose P-K4 as a good move in the opening and only the material balance generator will propose moving out of danger a piece that is *en prise*.

Each move proposed by a move generator is assigned a value by an analysis procedure whose job it is to decide on the acceptability of a move once it has been generated. The value assigned to a move is obtained from a series of evaluations, one for each goal, so that each goal takes the place of the features referred to in our earlier discussions. (In fact we may consider goals and features to be conceptually equivalent.) The score associated with a given position is made up of a number of components, each component corresponding to one goal (or feature). Each component expresses the acceptability or otherwise of a position from the viewpoint of the goal corresponding to that component.

The NSS program was careful to evaluate only positions that were "static" (i.e. quiescent) with respect to every one of the goals. As a simple example of how their program analysed, let us consider the situation shown in figure 22.

P_0 is the initial position from which the program must make a move. The move M_1 has been proposed by one of the move generators and in order to decide on its acceptability the analysis procedure must obtain a value for the resulting position P_1. Considering each of the three goals on the program's goal list in turn, an attempt is made to produce a static evaluation. For P_1 this attempt is successful for the first and second goals, yielding values of 5 and 3 respectively. However, the third goal does not find the position P_1 dead and generates two moves, M_2 and M_3. Move M_2 produces a position P_2 for which all three goals are able to make a static evaluation. M_3 produces a position P_3 for which the first goal does not find the position static but instead generates the move M_4 to resolve the instability of position P_3 with respect to this goal, and the second goal also fails to find the position P_3 static and generates the move M_5. The third goal does find P_3 static and so it generates no further positions. The moves M_4 and M_5 lead to positions P_4 and P_5 respectively, both of which are found to be static with respect to each of the three goals. Now that it is unnecessary to generate any more positions it is safe to perform a minimax search in order to determine the score that should be associated with P_1.

An example of the goals used is centre control. This goal always

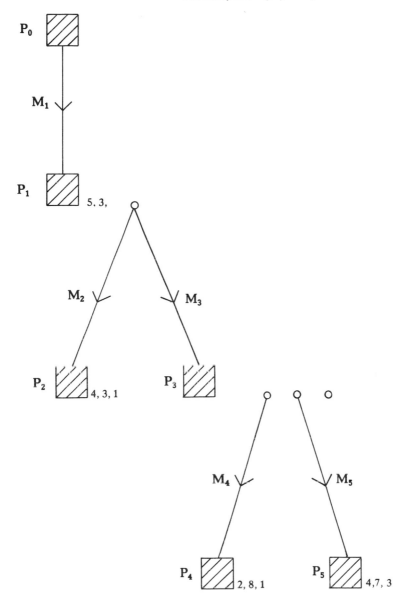

Fig. 22
An analysis tree with sample scores for each of three goals.

operates unless there are no more centre pawns to be moved to the fourth rank. The move generator for centre control attempts to make moves as follows:

1) Move P-K4, P-Q4 (these are called primary moves).
2) Prevent your opponent from making his primary moves.
3) Prepare your own primary moves by:
   (a) Adding a defender to your K4 or Q4 square;
   (b) Eliminating a block to moving the KP or QP.

The static evaluation for centre control simply counts the number of blocks that prevent making the primary moves.

The move generator for centre control is concerned only with the two primary moves P-K4 and P-Q4. It will propose these moves if they are legal and it is the responsibility of the analysis procedures for all the goals to reject the moves if there is anything wrong with them, e.g. if one of the moves puts a pawn *en prise*. Thus, after 1 P-Q4 P-Q4, the centre control move generator will propose 2 P-K4 but the evaluation routine of the material balance goal will reject this move because of the loss of material that would result from 2...P×P.

If the primary moves cannot be made the centre control generator has two choices: to prepare them or to prevent the opponent from making his own primary moves. If the program is written so that it prefers prevention to preparation then it will generally play more aggressively in the opening.

The move generator approaches the subgoal of preventing the opponent's primary moves (whenever this subgoal is evoked) in the following way. It first determines whether the opponent can make one of these moves by trying the move and then obtaining an evaluation of it from the opponent's viewpoint. If one or both of the primary moves are not rejected, then prevention will serve some useful purpose. Under these circumstances the centre-control move generator will generate preventative moves by finding moves that bring another attacker to bear on the opponent's K4 and Q4 squares or that pin a defender of one of these squares. Among the moves that this generator will normally propose are N-KB3, N-QB3, P-KB4 and P-QB4.

The move generator prepares its own primary moves by first determining why the moves cannot be made without preparation — i.e. whether the pawn is blocked by one of its own pieces, or whether the fourth rank square is unsafe for the pawn. In the first case the move generator proposes moves for the blockading piece, in the second case it finds moves that will add support to the fourth rank square, drive away or pin attackers, and so on.

The task of the evaluation routine for centre control is essentially that of the devil's advocate — to ensure that moves proposed by some other goal will not be made if they jeopardize control of the centre. When the program begins to 'think' about making its move, a preliminary analysis is carried out to establish that some particular chess situation (a 'state') exists. This state evokes a set of goals appropriate to it and the goals are put onto a list with the most crucial ones first. This goal list then controls the remainder of the move making procedure. What kind of game the program will play clearly depends on what goals are available to it and chosen by it for any particular move. One purpose of this modular construction is to provide flexibility over the course of the game in the kinds of consideration the program spends its efforts on. For example, the goal of denying stalemate to the opponent would only be invoked in certain endgame situations where the opponent is on the defensive and his king is in a constrained position.

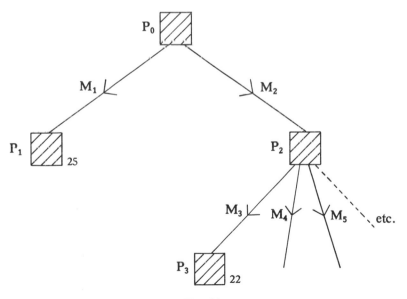

Fig. 23

An analysis tree with sample scores,
illustrating the alpha-beta algorithm.

The importance of considering the most crucial goals first lies in a sophisticated form of the minimax method whose first use in game playing programs was in the NSS chess program. This method of tree searching guarantees to find the minimax solution to a tree search (i.e. it will always make the move that would be chosen by a minimax search) but it does so very much faster, by eliminating from its consideration whole sections of the tree. How this method works can be illustrated by the tree on the preceding page.

Let us assume that the program has to move from position P_0 and that it has determined that to make move M_1, to position P_1, would give it a score of 25 (the program is trying to maximize its own score and minimize its opponent's). Now it comes to consider the move M_2, to position P_2, and in order to evaluate P_2 it must first consider M_3, M_4, M_5, ... etc. and evaluate positions P_3, P_4, P_5, ... etc. Or must it? If the program makes the move M_2 and its opponent replies with M_3, leading to position P_3 whose score is 22, then we can say at once that the program is already worse off than if it had moved M_1 for a score of 25. It is true that the program's opponent might have an even better move in M_4, M_5, or one of the other 10,000 moves at its disposal, but it is not necessary to look at all these thousands of moves to realize that M_2 is inferior to M_1.

This method of tree searching is called the alpha-beta algorithm. An algorithm is a method that guarantees finding the solution to a problem if a solution exists, and it is important to distinguish it from a heuristic which aims to reduce the effort in finding a solution but which does not give any guarantee as to results. This algorithm derives its name from the fact that it is only necessary to keep track of two values, alpha and beta, in order to operate the algorithm. At any point in the tree search, alpha is the best (backed-up) score that can be achieved by the program in the light of the branches examined so far. If analysis of another of the program's alternative moves reveals that its opponent could, if that move were made, reduce alpha, then the program knows that it is not necessary to look at the offending branch any more — it is inferior. The program cuts off that part of the tree in which the inferior move lies (in the above diagram it would cut off the part of the tree beginning with position P_2.) Such cutoffs are called alpha-cutoffs. A similar situation occurs if the program discovers that its opponent would be ill advised to make a particular move because that move would increase the value of beta. This situation would cause what is called a beta-cutoff. Alpha-cutoffs occur only at odd depths (when it is the opponent's move) and beta-cutoffs at even depths (when it is the program's move). The savings that can be made by using the alpha-beta algorithm under its optimal conditions, are enormous. If a tree has N terminal nodes that would need to be generated and evaluated using the minimax method, only $2\times\sqrt{N}$ terminal nodes need to be generated and evaluated if the alpha-beta algorithm is used under optimal conditions. Thus, for an exhaustive search to a depth of 4-ply, which would typically involve in the region of 1,000,000 terminal nodes, only 2,000 terminal nodes would need to be generated and evaluated using optimal alpha-beta searching. For optimal conditions it is simply necessary to examine the best move first, then the second best move, and so on. In this way it is possible to maximize the number of cutoffs. Now the reader can understand why Newell, Shaw and Simon placed so much importance on having the most important goals at the top of the goal list. For minimax searching the order would be unimportant but for efficient alpha-beta searching it is critical.

The following game was played by Herbert Simon against the NSS program CP-1 which was running on the RAND JOHNNIAC computer at Carnegie Institute of Technology. This computer operated at about half the speed of the IBM 704 used by Bernstein and his colleagues and the program's moves took from 2-50 minutes. The program had three goals: material balance, centre control and development.

White: CP-1
Black: H. Simon

1	P-Q4	N-KB3
2	N-QB3	P-Q4
3	Q-Q3?	

Chess programs can often be seen to move their queens at a very early stage of the game. The usual reason is that the development feature (or in this case the development goal) does not give more credit for developing minor pieces than it does for developing major ones. In this instance the

move might also have been promoted by the centre control goal, since White's move adds a protector to the K4 square.

3	...	P-QN3
4	P-K4	B-N2
5	P×P	N×P
6	N-B3	P-K3
7	B-K2	B-K2
8	B-K3	O-O
9	O-O	N-Q2
10	KR-K1	P-QB4
11	QR-Q1	Q-B2
12	N×N	B×N

13 P-QR4?

Obviously 13 P-B4 is best, at least it is obvious to a human. The move generator for the material balance goal would have generated the moves 13 P-B4, 13 P-QR3 and 13 P-QR4. Moves such as R-R1 are not generated because the rook has another function — adding support to White's control of the centre. There is nothing in the programmer's description of their move gnerators to explain why the program preferred the weakest of the three moves but it is clear that their centre control mechanism should have been designed to give a bonus for attacking Black's Q4 square even though there is no black pawn on Q2 or Q3.

13 ...	QR-B1
14 Q-B3	B-KB3
15 B-QN5	

Black was threatening 15...PxP 16 QxQ RxQ 17 NxP BxN 18 BxB RxP, so by attacking the knight White saves his pawn.

But did White make this move for the right reason? It seems more likely to me that the program feared 15...BxN 16 BxB P-K4 (this is one of the primary moves) and that its 15 B-QN5 was aimed at attacking a piece that adds support to one of the primary moves. Once its centre control move generator had proposed the move B-QN5, the program would have examined the exchanging sequences beginning with 15...PxP and found that they did not win material for Black.

Other 15th moves proposed by the program's move generators would be seen to lose a pawn and so 15 B-QN5 would be the only acceptable move. But what a strange way to find it!

15 ...	BxN
16 PxB	KR-Q1
17 BxN?	

Aimless. White could have held the pawn by moving his queen — after 17...PxP 18 BxP BxB 19 RxB, Black cannot capture the QBP because his knight would be lost.

| 17 ... | QxB |

Attacking the QRP as well.

18 P-N3	PxP
19 Q-Q2	Q-B3
20 B-B4	QxQBP
21 QxQ	RxQ
22 R-QB1	R.Q1-QB1
23 R.B1-Q1	R.1-B6
24 P-N4	R.B6xP
25 B-N3	P-Q6

26 R-QB1

The program does not know about forks.

26 ... B-N4

Nor does its opponent: 26...P-Q7 27 R×R P×R=Q+ 28 K-N2 Q-

Q8 wins at once.

27 R×R   P×R
28 B-K5   P-B8=Q
29 R×Q   B×R

At this point the programmers resigned for their program.

The Anderson/Cody Program

In 1959 a Canadian program was demonstrated at the University of Toronto. It was written by Frank Anderson, an International Master, and Bob Cody, and it ran on an IBM 605 computer. The program did not play a complete game but dealt only with simple pawn endings (the most complex was king and two pawns v king and pawn). The programmers devised a unique strategy that enabled their program to play these endings perfectly. Their first version could cope with more than 180,000 different positions, a figure that was increased in subsequent versions of the program. When the program was demonstrated at the Canadian Conference of Scientists it played against more than 50 different opponents, each of whom was allowed to choose his own starting position, given the small number of pawns. In each case the program played perfectly.

Unfortunately, the strategy that enabled these endings to be programmed successfully was never documented and the programmers no longer have any written record of it, nor are they able to remember it. In fact Frank Anderson confessed to me recently that even at the time he couldn't explain why some of their strategies worked.

The Kotok Program

In 1961 Alan Kotok wrote a chess program for his bachelor's thesis at Massachusets Institute of Technology. His program was written under the guidance of John McCarthy, one of the leading figures in the world of Artificial Intelligence, who was then a professor at M.I.T.

Kotok's program performed a variable depth search. It looked ahead until a stable position had been reached or until its depth of search reached an arbitary maximum. In order to avoid growing enormous trees the program examined fewer and fewer successor positions as the depth of search increased. Moves were proposed by a plausible move generator whose job it was to find moves that fulfilled various goals. In this respect Kotok's work was similar to that of Newell, Shaw and Simon. The plausible move generator supplied 4 moves at the root of the tree, 3 at the next level, then 2, 2, 1, 1, 1, 1, 0, 0, ... etc. In addition to the plausible moves considered at each level the program examined captures and checks.

Kotok's evaluation function used four features: Material, Pawn Structure, Centre Control and Development. Looking at the board from the side of the player about to move, Kotok weighted the sixteen centre squares in the following way.

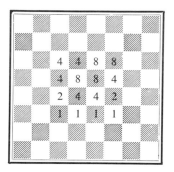

Presumably these weightings were designed to give more credit for attacking squares in the opponent's half of the board, and for attacking squares near his king (the weights 4, 4, 8, 8, for the squares on the sixth rank were adjusted to 8, 8, 4, 4, if the opponent had castled on the left hand side of the board).

Each centre square point was worth one-sixtieth of a pawn at the beginning of the game. After 20 moves centre control became less important and after move 30 the feature was discarded.

The program assigned points for each developed piece: 1 for a pawn, rising to 3 or 4 for the other pieces. Each development point was worth one-fifteenth of a pawn at the start of the game but this value too was diminished as the game progressed.

Pawn structure points were each worth one-twentieth of a pawn: For each pawn on an open file the program scored 8 pawn structure points, for each isolated pawn −1, for a backward pawn −5, for a doubled pawn −3 and for a passed pawn 10.

Kotok's work began in the Spring of 1961. By the time that he presented his thesis in 1962 his program had played four long game fragments, calculating for between five and twenty minutes per move. It played rather poor chess (even for a program) and in one of the four game fragments it made an illegal move, advancing a pawn two squares when the intervening square was occupied. After graduating from M.I.T. Kotok's interest in computer chess died but his program remained alive. When McCarthy left M.I.T. to take charge of the Artificial Intelligence Laboratory at Stanford University he took Kotok's program with him and improved its tree searching mechanism.

At the end of 1966 a four game match began between the Kotok/McCarthy program, running on Stanford University's IBM 7090 computer, and a program developed at the Institute of Theoretical and Experimental Physics in Moscow which used a Soviet M-20 computer. The Soviet program was written by Arlazarov, Adelson-Velsky, Bitman (a Soviet Master), Uskov and Zhivtovsky.

In two of the games both progams used a basic three-ply search, in the other two they searched to a depth of five-ply. The result of the match was an outstanding success for the Soviet program, even though it had been written along the lines of Shannon's primitive type-A strategy and run on a slower machine. The American program, as we have already shown, used Shannon's type-B strategy.

The Soviet program won two games and the other two were agreed drawn when one of them reached move 40. (This agreement, made before the start of the match, was prompted by the abysmal endgame play of both programs.) In the two unfinished games the Soviet program had advantages which would certainly have proved decisive in human master play.

The following article by Arlazarov and Bitman describes the basic elements of their program and analyses the four games of the match. It first appeared in *Shakhmaty v SSSR,* number 2 1968.

Will Machines Ever Outplay Man?   (USSR v USA)

Even now a lot of chess players are of the opinion that the outcome of a game which has reached a certain position depends not only on the position itself but also on the creative personalities of the players. And this is really so if the chess players are not able to calculate the variations to a sufficient number of moves ahead. In reality, though, the total number of positions which can occur is finite, and in consequence in any given position, including the starting position, the result is uniquely determined.

We have to stress that what we have said above is not just a question of chess or philosophical credo, but it is a fact which can be proved mathematically. Thus, the starting position is drawn or won for White or even won for Black, although we do not yet know which of the three possibilities is the case. If we were able to create a computer which could analyse all possible variations an arbitrary number of moves ahead, then, naturally, we should be able to resolve this question. Unfortunately (or luckily) there is no such machine; moreover, there never can be one. This fact, however, does not exclude the possibility of creating a computer, which with its 'iron fist' would be able to defeat any man. People have learned to play chess quite well, and in doing so a human being comes far short of calculating all possible continuations in every position, but rather chooses a small number of them for further analysis. It is only because of this that it is possible to consider main variations quite deeply. This is the strength of a human being, but also his weakness.

A computer can work out the moves and estimate the advantages of the resulting positions much faster than human beings. So, if we can teach a machine to consider only the sensible continuations, then its advantage over a human being will become unquestionable. By the way, a computer plays even more creatively than a man. It does not have stereotypes and it more often finds unexpected and therefore beautiful solutions. The question now is, precisely what does our expression 'sensible' mean? The strength of the computer's play depends to a large extent on the answer to this question.

The principles underlying the choice of sensible moves in the American and Soviet programs differ considerably. The completed games allow us to point out the strong and weak sides of these two approaches. The procedure of the American program was closer to that of a human being. On the first move it chose seven continuations by some criteria and for each of these it considered seven possible replies by the opponent. On its second move the program selected only five possibilities for each side. At each succeeding level the number of continuations chosen was reduced and from a certain point only a single-stranded variation was considered.

We, on the other hand, considered all possible continuations for both sides up to a certain level and thereafter only forcing ones:

captures and checks. The merit of the first method is that the computer can look quite deeply into the position after the chosen moves; however, the possibility of a bad blunder at the beginning of the variation is not excluded.

Thanks to the fact that the Soviet program does not throw out anything during the first few moves it simply cannot fall into such transparent traps. On the other hand, in choosing among the variations analysed our computer can err in not considering quiet moves deeply enough, even though forced variations can drag on as far as the fifteenth half-move. We define the depth of the calculations in our programs as the number of half-moves up to the beginning of the forced variations. For example, when we claim that the program plays the game with a depth of calculation of two half-moves it means that the computer considers its own move (really half a move) and the opponent's reply and then examines the consequences of forced variations following on the previous moves.

A forced variation can lead not only to the gain of material, but also to the acquisition of various positional advantages as a result of exchanges. These calculations are done by the chess estimating function [The scoring function — DNLL]. This takes into account such factors as the mobility of pieces, control of the centre and open lines and the safety of the king, and in respect of the pawn structure considers such factors as the phalanxes, support points, passed pawns, doubled pawns, isolated pawns, isolated pawns on an open file and so on. This estimating function is mainly intended for the opening and middle game, as, indeed, is the whole program.

In the endgame, however, it is more important to devise a plan for a few moves ahead, because the opponent has less opportunity to hinder its realization. Besides, there are considerably fewer plans for the endgame than in the middle game. So, by the end of the game, one can see the final position of very long variations and one can often be sure that a chain of simple moves will lead there.

A program for the endgame will have to be constructed in quite a different way from middle game programs, and the ideas underlying such a program have yet to be worked out properly. The American mathematicians had not yet studied the problem of the endgame either, so it was agreed only to continue the match games up to the fortieth move.

Game 1
White: USSR (Three half-moves)
Black: USA

1 P-K4   P-K4
2 N-QB3   N-QB3
3 N-B3   B-B4
4 B-B4

In   this   position,   which
occurred in the third game as
well, the program found the
stronger line 4 N×P when playing
five half-moves.

4 ...   N-B3
5 O-O   O-O
6 P-Q3   P-Q3
7 B-K3   B-KN5
8 P-KR3   B-R4
9 B-Q5

The developing moves have
finished and the program does
not know what to do. Here a
human being might have played 9
N-QR4   followed   by   P-B3,
livening the pawns up in the
centre. It seems though that three
half-moves are just not sufficient
for seeing the advantages of the
resulting position.

9 ...   B-Q5

It appears that the American
program suffers from the same
difficulties.

10 P-KN4

In this the program had a
'human' idea. It reckons that this
move forces an advantageous
exchange.

10 ...   B×N
11 QNP×B   B-N3

12 B-N5   R-K1
13 R-N1   R-N1
14 Q-K2

In the variation 14 R×P R×R 15
B×N.QB6 the three half-moves
have run out and White is still
short of material. A computer
playing four [five-DNLL] half-
moves would have played 14 R×P.

14 ...   K-R1
15 P-Q4   K-N1

It might appear that in playing
14...K-R1 Black was preparing to
reply 15...P×P against 15 P-Q4,
to be followed by 16 P×P B×P 17
B×B P-Q4, winning a pawn, since
White cannot play B×RP+. In
fact, however, neither of the
machines saw this line.

16 Q-B4

It is curious that White
'thought' five times as long over
this bad move as over most other
moves.

16 ...   N-QR4

17 B×N

Feeling that something is
wrong the program makes an

intermediate exchange. After 17
B×N Q×B 18 Q-Q3 its counting
has finished and it thinks all is
well.

17 ...	Q×B
18 Q-Q3	P-B3
19 P×P	P×P

Our program considered the
move 19...Q-B5 to be best for
Black, thinking that after 20
B-N3 P×P Black wins back the
pawn. And if 20...B×P, then it
had a pretty variation in reserve:
21 B×KBP+ K×B 22 Q×B Q×Q
23 N-N5+ and 24 N×Q.

This is an example of the
complex combinations the
computer can carry out without
even noticing the simple
intermediate exchange 20...N×B,
because after 21 RP×N B×P it
thought it was all right.

20 B-N3	R.N1-Q1
21 Q-K3	P-N3
22 R.B1-Q1	R-Q3
23 P-N5	Q-K2
24 R-Q3	R×R
25 P×R	R-Q1
26 R-R1	

White thinks that Black should
play 26...N×B and therefore
occupies the open file in advance.

26 ...	Q-Q3
27 P-Q4	P×P
28 P×P	N×B
29 P×N	P-QR4
30 R-R4	Q-K3
31 N-K5	Q-K1
32 P-B4	R-Q3
33 P-B5	

Our program did not see that
this move won a pawn, but made
the move out of positional
considerations.

33 ...	B-R4
34 N-B4	

Now it can see.

34 ...	R-Q1
35 N×NP	R-N1
36 N-B4	B-Q8
37 R-R3	B-B7

Because game two had reached
the fortieth move it was decided
to call a halt to the match and
agree a draw in this game since
neither of the opponents had an
overwhelming advantage.

Game 2
White: USA
Black: USSR (Three half-moves)

1 P-K4	N-KB3
2 P-K5	N-Q4
3 N-KB3	P-K3
4 B-N5	P-QR3
5 B-R4	P-QN4
6 B-N3	B-N5

This is a typical case of a
positional mistake due to an
insufficient depth of calculation.
Black develops a piece and prevents 7 P-Q4, not noticing that
after 6...B-N5 7 P-B3 B-B4 (three
half-moves have come to an end!)
White nevertheless plays 8 P-Q4.

7 N-B3	N-B5
8 O-O	B-N2
9 P-Q4	B.N5×N

10 P×B	N-Q4
11 B×N	B×B
12 B-R3	P-Q3
13 P×P	

Our program considered the move 13 P×P to be very weak. Its assessment of the position changed sharply in its own favour.

13 ...	P×P
14 R-K1	N-B3
15 R-K3	O-O
16 Q-K2	B-B5
17 Q-K1	Q-B2
18 B-N4	P-QR4
19 B-R3	K-R1

However strange it may seem this is not just for 'something to do'. Black is intending to play 20...P-B4, which it cannot do immediately because of the answer R×P.

20 N-N5	P-R3
21 N-K4	R.B1-Q1
22 N×P	R×N
23 B×R	Q×B
24 P-QR3	N-K2
25 R-K5	N-B3

Now if 26 R-K3 then the game would be drawn by repetition.

26 R-QB5	P-K4
27 Q-K4	R-R3

It is only now that the computer can see that 27...R-QB1 can be followed by 28 P-QR4. According to assessments printed out by our computer, its position is worsening very fast. Here we have an example of a position in which the strategy of a deep analysis of a small number of moves does better than a short but comprehensive analysis. White's moves R-QB5, Q-K4 and P-QR4 are essential to any reasonable line of play, while Black cannot interfere with his opponent's plan even by means of the most exotic variations.

28 R-Q1	P-N3
29 R-Q2	P-N4

Defending against the threat of Q-K3, winning a pawn.

30 R-Q1

White can no longer find any move to improve his position.

30 ...	P-R5
31 R-Q2	P-B3

To strengthen such a position is difficult even for a human being. In any case it would need a subtle plan lasting quite a number of moves. This, of course, is beyond the computer's capacity while it has such a shallow depth of calculation. Having no plan Black makes a very weak move. It saw, of course, the reply 32 Q-N6 but considered that after 32...Q-B1 it was quite safe. A chess player would never have ended the analysis of a variation in such a position, except perhaps to conclude that it was acceptable.

32 Q-K3	P×P
33 P×P	N-K2
34 Q-KN3	Q×Q
35 RP×Q	

Against 35 BP×Q the program was going to play 35...R-K3 and the best variation for both sides (following this move) went like this: 36 P-N4 P-B4 37 P×P N×P, getting rid of the weak pawn, since 38 R×N is not possible because of 38...R-K8+ 39 K-B2 R-KB8+ and 40...R×R.

35 ...	N-Q4
36 R-B8+	K-R2
37 R-KB8	P-QN5
38 P×P	N×P
39 P-QB3	N-Q4
40 R-QB8	Drawn

From a chess player's point of view, of course, this position is easily won for Black, but both computers showed such a total lack of comprehension of the game that there was no point in examining it further.

Game 3

White: USSR (Five half-moves)
Black: USA

1 P-K4	P-K4
2 N-KB3	N-QB3
3 N-B3	B-B4
4 N×P!	

This move was quite a surprise for us, since the computer attaches a high value to the right to castle. Nevertheless, the positional advantages secured seem to have pushed the scale in favour of 4 N×P (as against 4 B-B4). Our program gave as the best variation for both sides: 4...B×P+ 5 K×B N×N 6 P-Q4.

4 ...	N×N
5 P-Q4	B-Q3
6 P×N	B×P
7 P-B4	

With this move White 'issued' the following optimal sequence: 7...B×N+ 8 P×B N-B3 9 Q-Q4.

7 ...	B×N+
8 P×B	N-B3
9 P-K5	

As in games between human beings plans can change during the play: in its preliminary calculations our program intended to play 9 Q-Q4, but now it can see new possibilities. It is interesting that the line 9 B-B4 was rejected by the program because of 9...N×P 10 B×P+ K-B1!? and Black wins a pawn because of the threat on ...QB6 and a queen check on ...KR5.

9 ...	N-K5
10 Q-Q3	

The variation given by the program was this: 10...P-Q4 11 P×Pep N×QP 12 B-R3. Note however, that in calculating six half-moves ahead the program did not find the strongest move in the position: 10 Q-Q5!

Why did that happen? Evidently because in the line 10...N×P 11 Q-B4 Q-R5ch 12 P-N3 black is obliged to make a sixth half-move, after which White enters a forcing variation

which wins a knight. Thinking
only five half-moves ahead, in the
position after 12 P-N3 it appears
that Black wins a pawn and so the
move 10 Q-Q5 is rejected.

10 ...	N-B4
11 Q-Q5	N-K3
12 P-B5	N-N4

In making its twelfth move
our program expected 12...P-
QB3 13 Q-Q3 N-B4 14 Q-Q6.

| 13 P-KR4 | P-KB3 |
| 14 P×N | P×P |

15 R×P!
This simple tactical coup
would have been found even with
a calculation for one half-move.

15 ...	R-B1
16 R×P	P-B3
17 Q-Q6	

After the program made this
move it 'announced' that Black's
only salvation from mate was the
variation beginning with the moves
17...Q-B3 18 P×Q K-Q1.

| 17 ... | R×P |

Black prefers a faster finish.

| 18 R-N8+ | R-B1 |

If 19...K-B2 then 20 B-QB4
mate.

19 Q×Rmate

Game 4
White: USA
Black: USSR (Five half-moves)

1 P-K4	N-KB3
2 P-K5	N-Q4
3 N-KB3	N-N5

This looks senseless. The
program is really trying to play
4...P-Q4 and the interpolation of
4 P-B3 N.N5-B3, will not, in the
program's opinion, improve
White's position.

4 B-N5	P-QB3
5 B-R4	P-Q3
6 P-Q4	Q-R4
7 P-B4	

A bad blunder which our
program did not expect when it
played 6...Q-R4.

7 ...	N-B7++
8 K-B1	N×R
9 N-B3	Q-N5

The program can see that in
quiet continuations White wins
the knight on R1. Now it
manages to keep the extra rook
(at least for the present).

10 Q-K2	P×P
11 P×P	B-K3
12 Q-Q1	B×P+
13 N-K2	P-QN4
14 B-B2	N×B

15 Q×N	B×P
16 N.K2-Q4	Q-B5+
17 K-N1	P-QB4
18 Q-Q2	P×N
19 N×P	P-K3
20 N-B3	N-B3
21 Q-N5	R-Q1
22 B-Q2	Q-B8+

The computer is not looking for 'beauty': it is simply winning a pawn.

23 B-K1	Q×P
24 Q-B4	B-Q4

25 Q-N3	Q-K7
26 B-B3	P-N5
27 B-K1	B×N
28 P×B	Q×B+
29 K-N2	Q×KP
30 Q-R4	P-QR4
31 R-QB1	N-Q5
32 R-B1	N×P!

The program did not find this move in its earlier analysis. If now 33 K×N, then 33...R-Q5! wins the queen.

33 Q-R3	R-Q6
34 Q-N3	N-K8+
35 R×N	R×Q+
36 K-B1	Q-QN4+

The program was intending to play here 36...R-N8+ but then found a more lucrative continuation.

37 R-K2	R-QR6
38 K-K1	R-R8+
39 K-Q2	

After this the program can see that it is mating.

39 ...	Q-Q4+
40 K-K3	R-R6+
41 K-B4	Q-KB4 mate

The problem of creating a chess computer belongs to a young branch of cybernetics — heuristic programming. There is one task facing this discipline the solution of which would have practical applications: to work out methods of orienting in a continuously changing situation depending on a large number of factors which cannot be subjected to a complete mechanical analysis. Chess is an excellent model of such a situation.

In the course of work on chess programs some very valuable heuristic methods have been found which shorten the analysis many times over. Remembering the best moves in deep analyses, the use of forced variations and certain *a priori* evaluations of moves and positions are among these techniques. The heuristic methods discovered in the course of creating chess programs have already found application in the study of networks, finding the minimum of functions of several variables and also in working out the results of some physical experiments.

And as far as the eternal question (which excites all chess players) is concerned of whether the computer will defeat man, the authors of this article are bold enough to claim that it will happen in the next ten to fifteen years.

The Moscow program used an evaluation function with four features:

1) *Pawn Structure*
   Four aspects of pawn-structure were considered:
   (a) Central Pawns: For each side the central squares are K4, Q4, K5, Q5, K6 and Q6. For each pawn on one of the central squares a bonus of 10 points was given.
   (b) The Pawn Phalanx: Two pawns on the same rank and on neighbouring files are called a phalanx. N pawns on the same rank and on neighbouring files are counted as N-1 phalanxes. For each phalanx a bonus of 4 points was scored.
   (c) Isolated and Doubled Pawns: Doubled pawns are only penalised if they are also isolated, and isolated pawns that are not doubled are only penalised if they are on a semi-open file. For each such pawn a penalty of 12 points is deducted.
   (d) Passed pawns: For each passed pawn score a bonus of 32 — 4×S where S is the number of ranks separating the pawn from the queening square.

2) *Mobility*
   For each square attacked by a piece, a bonus is scored according to the piece that is doing the attacking. For the king this bonus is 0, for the queen 1, for a rook 2, for a knight or bishop 5 and for a pawn 0.
   This method of scoring encourages minor pieces to be developed before major ones.

3) *Castling*
   When a player castles he scores a bonus of 11 points, but if he

forfeits the right to castle he suffers a penalty of 11.

4) *Material*
    The ratios of the values of the pieces are:
        pawn = 1
        bishop = knight = $3\frac{1}{2}$
        rook = 5
        queen = 10

The Stanford-Moscow match did much for the development of computer chess by creating the stimulus for further work in the USA. Even as the match was taking place, a new program was being developed at M.I.T., and the next eight years saw an explosion of interest in the subject. Computer competitions became more and more frequent and some scientists believed that a master standard chess program was not far away.

4 The Modern Era of Computer Chess

'I think that the problem can be solved only by chess specialists using their creative experience'.

Botvinnik

The Greenblatt Program

Beginning in mid-November 1966, a chess program was developed on a PDP-6 computer at the Artificial Intelligence Laboratory at M.I.T. The program was written primarily by Richard Greenblatt, then an undergraduate student, with the assistance of Donald E. Eastlake III. The program was written quickly—by February 1967 it was ready to play in a local tournament where it lost four games and drew one to achieve a rating of 1243 on the United States Chess Federation scale. In March 1967 it played in another tournament, winning one game and losing four. Its performance rating for that event was 1360 and its overall rating went up to 1330. One month later it scored two wins and two losses for a performance rating of 1640. The program was named Mac Hack VI and it was made an honorary member of both the U.S.C.F. and the Massachusets Chess Association.

Greenblatt's program contained several powerful interaction aids for locating errors in the program and for improving its performance. These aids included facilities to look, on a cathode ray screen, at the evaluation of any selected node on the game tree, to examine all the factors that caused a move to be considered plausible, to look at the main variation of the program's analysis from each depth-one position analysed, and to examine statistics on how long the computation took and how many plausible moves were generated at any point. By the use of these facilities and by playing hundreds of games against the program within a few months, Greenblatt was able to produce a program that was efficient, fast and relatively free of 'bugs' (programming errors).

Greenblatt's plausible move generator had three basic functions. It selected the moves that it considered plausible, put them into their order of merit so as to optimize the advantage of using the alpha-beta algorithm, and calculated certain positional and 'developmental' values that would decide the program's move if several moves led to the same static value. The major reason for the quality of the program's play was that considerable chess knowledge was programmed in. In fact there were about fifty chess heuristics used in computing the plausibility of moves, though many of the fifty were only applicable in special cases or at certain stages of the game.

Each square was assigned a value during each plausible move computation, corresponding roughly to the estimated worth of having another piece bearing on the square or the cost of moving away a piece presently attacking the square. The principal criteria used for assigning these values included the closeness of the square to the centre of the board, its proximity to the opponent's king, and its occupation by one of the program's own pieces which is *en prise*. Small values were given for occupation of the square by one of the program's pieces and for its closeness to the opponent's side of the board.

The current developmental value of a piece is the sum of the values for the squares it attacks, plus values accumulated for actual attacks on enemy pieces. When a move is being considered for plausibility the new development value of the piece is calculated assuming the piece to be on its new proposed location. The difference between the new and old developmental values is used as a factor in assessing plausibility, encouraging developing moves and discouraging antipositional ones. Gains or losses in development resulting from blocking or unblocking the opponent's or the program's pieces were also considered in the developmental value. Other factors were added to encourage attacking the opponent's pieces, his weak pawns, his pinned pieces and pieces defending other pieces etc.

Greenblatt noticed that sometimes his program would give a high plausibility value to an antipositional move because it attacked an enemy piece. If the attack led to material gain, all was well and good; but if the opponent could simply move the attacked piece away then the move was a pointless waste of time. So moves were scored separately on their positional merit and if this proved bad then the move would be rejected if there was a more positional move leading to the same terminal score.

The evaluation function used five features: Material balance, piece ratio, pawn structure, king safety and centre control. The piece ratio term was aimed at promoting exchanges when the program was ahead in material and avoiding them when behind. Greenblatt's pawn structure feature was slightly more reliable than those used in earlier programs because it made allowances for backward pawns as well as for doubled and isolated ones.

The program's tree search was conducted along the lines of

Shannon's type-B strategy, with variable widths of search at different levels of the tree. At the root of the tree the fifteen most plausible moves were chosen and ordered. For each of these the fifteen most plausible reply moves were chosen and ordered. Then the nine most plausible replies to these, then nine replies to them and seven moves at depth five. These are the basic settings that were used when the program played tournament games. The only way that the program could fail to consider the indicated number of moves is either that the requisite number of moves simply did not exist or that the alpha-beta algorithm produced a cutoff before all these moves at any node had been examined. Just as efficient tree searching was sometimes responsible for the basic settings not being reached, so it was often the case that the basic width had to be increased in order to allow for safe checks to be considered, as well as captures (at the first and second level) and at least some of the moves of a reasonable number of pieces. The logic behind this last heuristic is quite sound. If all the moves of a single piece are highly plausible (e.g. those of a queen because it is *en prise*) then the rest of the board might not be looked at because the number of plausible moves might have reached the basic setting. But by examining the moves of a few other pieces it might be possible to find a clever tactical blow that succeeds even though the queen is left *en prise*.

The program kept a record of each position considered during its search for a move, together with information concerning the value of that position. If the position arose again during the search, either on part of the same tree (by transposition) or as part of a different tree (e.g. when the program was considering a later move) then the position could be looked up in the table and its value retrieved. This often avoided the necessity of evaluating the same position twice, and it also detected draws by threefold repetition.

If two moves were found by the search to lead to the same static evaluation, the move with the higher plausibility value was preferred. However, in some situations this move was not the most desirable one to make. In order to take such cases into account, two types of modification were made to the values found at the lower levels of the tree. The first modification subtracted a few points if the current move being investigated was marked as being developmentally poor by the plausible move generator. The second modification subtracted small amounts for moving pieces that had already moved higher up in the tree. This had the effect of avoiding moving pieces twice in the opening, avoiding making moves that result in the moved piece being attacked and forced to retreat, and avoiding making a two move manoeuvre when the manoeuvre was possible in one move. The program's performance was improved by introducing a secondary search whenever the normal tree search resulted in a new candidate for the best move at the top level. What was done was to move down the principal variation for that move as far as the variation was computed by the plausible move generator, and then to conduct an additional search, usually limited to two plies although captures and checks could increase this number. The value obtained by the secondary search is then used in place of the value found for the principle variation if it is worse for the side to move. Here is a simple example to illustrate the concept of the secondary search.

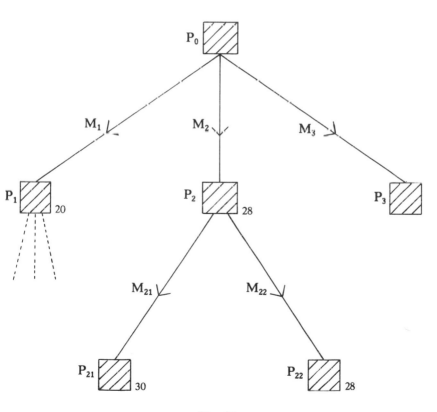

Fig. 24
*An analysis tree with sample scores illustrating
the concept of a secondary search.*

The program has to move from position P_0. It generates its plausible moves and orders them according to their apparent merit with the best one first. It then examines the apparently best move, M_1 and the resulting position P_1, by looking at the tree below P_1 and backing up the scores in the susal way. Let us say that P_1 is found to have a backed up score of 20.

The program now looks at M_2 and the resulting position P_2. After examining the tree below P_2 (i.e. P_{21} and P_{22}) the program comes to the conclusion that the score for P_2 is 28 and that the principal variation consists of the moves M_2, M_{22}.

This decision would put M_2 at the top of the list of candidate moves, but before doing so the program checks its analysis by conducting a secondary search from position P_{22}. If this secondary search comes up with a score of less than 28 then this new score is the one assigned to P_2. Otherwise P_2 is assigned a score of 28 and the move M_2 goes to the top of the list of candidates. The search then continues with M_3.

Another feature that was new to chess programs was the use of a small library of opening variations. This 'book' was compiled by two M.I.T. students, Larry Kaufmann, who represented the USA in Student Chess Olympiads, and Alan Baisley, an Expert on the U.S.C.F. scale.

The following game was played by Mac Hack VI when it was only two months old. It is the first tournament game played by a computer, and its opponent was rated 2190 on the U.S.C.F. scale, i.e. almost a Master.

White: Human
Black: Mac Hack VI

	White	Black		White	Black
1	P-KN3	P-K4			
2	N-KB3	P-K5	11	B-N2	O-O
3	N-Q4	B-B4	12	O-O	B-N5
4	N-N3	B-N3	13	Q-B2	R-K1
5	B-N2	N-KB3	14	P-Q4	P-B4
6	P-QB4	P-Q3	15	B-K3	P×P
7	N-B3	B-K3	16	N×P	N-K4
8	P-Q3	P×P	17	P-KR3	B-Q2
9	B×P	QN-Q2	18	P-N3	B-QB4
10	P×P	R-QN1	19	QR-Q1	Q-B1
			20	K-R2	N-N3
			21	B-N5	R-K4
			22	B×N	P×B
			23	N-K4	P-B4

24	N-KB6+	K-N2	40	Q×B	Q-K2
25	N×B	Q×N	41	Q-R4+	K-N3
26	N-B6	R.1-K1	42	B-B5+	K-N2
27	N×R	R×N	43	Q×RP+	K-B1
28	Q-B3	P-B3	44	Q-R8+	K-B2
29	R-Q3	R-K7	45	Q-QR8	Q-B2
30	R-Q2	R×R	46	Q-Q5+	K-N2
31	Q×R	N-K4	47	K-N2	Q-K2
32	R-Q1	Q-QB2	48	P-KR4	K-R3
33	B-Q5	K-N3	49	P-N4	K-N2
34	P-QN4	B-N3	50	P-R5	Q-K7
35	Q-B2	N-B3	51	P-R6+	K-B1
36	B-K6	N-Q5	52	P-R7	Q×KBP+
37	R×N	B×R	53	K×Q	K-K2
38	Q×P+	K-N2	54	P-R8=Q	P-R3
39	Q-N4+	K-R3	55	Q-K6 mate	

The next game is the first ever won by a computer program in tournament play. It was played in the second round of the Massachusets State Championship, March 1967.

White: MacHack VI
Black: Human (1510)

1	P-K4	P-QB4
2	P-Q4	P×P
3	Q×P	N-QB3
4	Q-Q3	N-B3
5	N-QB3	P-KN3
6	N-B3	P-Q3
7	B-B4	P-K4
8	B-N3	P-QR3
9	O-O-O	P-QN4
10	P-QR4	B-R3+
11	K-N1	P-N5
12	Q×QP!	B-Q2

If 12...Q×Q 13 R×Q P×N 14 R×N.KB6 B-Q2 (say) 15 N×P and

White is two pawns up. Presumably Human missed the fork of the two knights by White's rook.

13	B-R4	B-N2
14	N-Q5	N×P
15	N-B7+	Q×N
16	Q×Q	N-B4
17	Q-Q6	B-KB1
18	Q-Q5	R-B1
19	N×P	B-K3
20	Q×N.B6+	R×Q
21	R-Q8 mate	

By the time that MacHack VI had played in one or two tournaments it had attracted considerable public attention. This became even more the case when it discovered a nice, 9-ply combination that was reputedly missed by some of the U.S. Masters who were shown the same position.

Here MacHack found:

1 ...   R×P+!
2 K-N1

If 2 R×R N-R7+ 3 K-K2 (or 3 K-N1 Q×R+ 4 K×N Q×R and Black is a rook ahead) 3...Q-N7+ 4 K-Q1 Q-N8+ 5 K-K2 R-N7 mate.

2 ...   R×R
3 Q-R8+   K-B2
4 Q-B6   R×R+
5 Resigns

MacHack VI started a resurgence of interest in computer chess. It was on show in Edinburgh during August 1968 at the triennial congress of the International Federation for Information Processing (IFIP) where it took on all comers and scored about 50% — not a bad result when one realizes that many computer scientists are also stronger than average chess players.

The 'Levy Bet'

Immediately after the IFIP '68 congress, the Department of Machine Intelligence and Perception at Edinburgh University held one of its annual 'Machine Intelligence Workshops'. These meetings brought together many of the most prominent workers in the field of artificial intelligence and the proceedings of the workshops have been published as a well-known series of books by Edinburgh University Press *(Machine Intelligence 1, ... etc)*.

The Machine Intelligence Workshops were hosted by Donald Michie, Professor of the Edinburgh University department, and during the workshop it was traditional for him to arrange a number of cocktail parties and other social events. It was during one of these parties that my now famous bet was born. I was talking to John

McCarthy, Professor of Artificial Intelligence at Stanford University and one of the world's leading authorities on the subject, and he expressed the opinion that it would only be a matter of time before computer programs could play chess as well as a Grandmaster. I replied that I did not think there would a program that could beat me within ten years and both he and Michie said that they were sure I was wrong. Intrigued by this challenging opinion I offered to bet each of them £250 that I was right, i.e. that no program would be able to beat me in a match by the end of August 1978. They both accepted the bet with confidence, and my only regret is that I did not make it for a much larger sum, but in those days I was earning less than £1,000 per annum and £500 sounded like a lot of money.

The following year I was asked to present a paper at the Machine Intelligence Workshop and during the course of my presentation I was heckled by Professor Seymour Papert of the Artificial Intelligence Laboratory at M.I.T. Papert was so sceptical at some of my assertions that I asked him whether he would like to come in on my bet and increase it by £250. He said that he was quite sure that within five years, not ten, I would be beaten by a computer program, but I felt that it would have been unfair of me to bet with him on such a short time span. So we agreed that he would become a third member of the consortium. At the time of writing it is already two years since Papert's proposed time limit expired. I do not think that his optimism requires any further comment.

In 1970 the Association for Computing Machinery (ACM) held the first chess tournament in which all of the participants were computer programs. The tournament was held in New York as part of the ACM's annual convention and it attracted six entries and widespread publicity. The winner of the tournament was a program called CHESS 3.0 which was written at Northwestern University, Evanston, Illinois. The program will be described in some detail later in this chapter.

The ACM tournament in 1970 was such a success that it was decided to repeat it the following year, and since then it has become a regular event and it usually proves to be the most popular attraction at the ACM convention. I was invited to be the tournament director at the 1971 competition in Chicago where the number of contestants was increased from six to eight. As well as being concerned with the rules of the competition and ensuring fair play, my job was to give a running commentary to the audience so that spectators could understand what was happening in the games. Since 1971 I have performed these duties each year and I must say that I find them far more entertaining than watching most Grandmaster tournaments.

During the 1971 competition I was talking to some of the programmers about my bet. Professor Ed. Kozdrowicki, then of the Bell Telephone Laboratories at Murray Hill, New Jersey, felt sure that I was going to lose and he even offered to increase the bet by $1,000 (about £400). I was still an unprosperous programming assistant and I was afraid to take on such a 'big' committment so I said that I would take £250 of his action and Professor Ben Mittman, one of the tournament organizers and the head of the Evanston installation that had produced the champion program Chess 3.5 (the son of Chess 3.0) took the remainder of the bet. A few hours after Kozdrowicki came in on the bet his program reached the following position in its game against GENIE, programmed by Herbert Raymond at the Fleet Computer Centre in San Diego.

In this position it would appear that White had some advantage. He has at his disposal two different mates in one (38 B-B4 and 38 Q-N2) as well as various mates in two, three, four or indeed almost any number of moves. But because of a defect that occurs in many chess programs, it was this plethora of mating continuations that led to COKO's tragedy. Had there been only one forced mate COKO would have played it, but because

there was more than one mate, and because COKO was unable to distinguish between the value of a mate in one and the value of a mate in two, three or four, it chose between these mating continuations at random.

38 K-B1

This is just as good, from the program's point of view, as giving mate on the move, since mate still cannot be prevented.

| 38 ... | P-KB4 |

39 K-B2

And this just as good as giving mate on the move . . .

39 ...	P-B5
40 K-B1	P-N5
41 K-B2	P-B6
42 K-B1	P×P
43 K-B2	P×R=Q

Now White has one last chance to end the game with a single blow.

44 K-B1???		52 Q×Q+	K×Q
But this is inexplicable.		53 P-K4	K×P
44 ...	Q×B+	54 P-K5	P-N7
45 K-Q2	Q×P+		
46 K-B1	Q-N8+		
47 K-B2	Q×RP+		
48 K-B1	Q-R8+		
49 K-B2	Q-QN8+		
50 K-Q2	P-N6		
51 Q-B4+	Q-N6		

By now COKO's programmers had seen enough and they resigned on behalf of their program. Ed Kozdrowicki was heard to be muttering something about a bad bet as he left the playing hall.

So by August 1971 my bet had grown to £1,000. By this time I had become an International Master but the standard of the best chess programs had improved little, if at all, since I made the first bet three years earlier. As time went on I became more and more confident and I was therefore delighted in the Autumn of 1974 when Donald Michie offered to up the stakes. He wanted to increase his stake in the original bet to £500, thereby increasing the total wager to £1,250 (roughly $2,900), and to add a rider that if I did lose this bet then the program that beat me would have been written either by him or under his direction. Since, at that time, the world's strongest chess programs was KAISSA, written in Moscow, and since I knew that KAISSA's success in the first World Computer Championships in Stockholm (August 1974) would mean more financial support and programming effort for the Moscow group, I felt confident that in the unlikely event that anything did turn sour on me it would be from the East the my victor would come, and not from the West. I therefore accepted both parts of Michie's new wager but I turned down his 'offer' to extend the period of the bet from August to December 1978. After all, by August 1978 the value of my winnings will have already been substantially eroded by inflation.

So much for my bet. Let us now look at some of the more recent efforts at producing an electronic Grandmaster.

Soviet Research

Between the time of the Moscow-Stanford match in 1967 and the birth of the KAISSA program in 1971 (see page 108) only one Soviet chess program was heard of. It played very weakly and was annihalated in a game played against the readers of the newspaper 'The Ural Worker'

(Uralsky Rabochy). Each week the program's move would be published in the newspaper and the readers were invited to send in their suggestion for reply moves. The move that received the most votes was played. The game was published in *Shakhmanty v USSR,* number 8 1968, with notes by Polugayevsky. No details were revealed either concerning the computer or its programmers, perhaps because of the poor play of the program. Here is the game with Polugayevsky's annotations — presumably this is the first mass contest against a computer in history.

White: Readers
Black: Program

1 P-K4   N-QB3

A move suggested by Nimzowitsch. It is not very popular and has almost disappeared from tournaments, but the computer has its own 'theoretical taste', which does not coincide with the conclusions of contemporary chess theory.

2 P-Q4   P-Q4
3 N-QB3   P×P

The computer prefers to take the pawn. 3...P-K3 is more cautious.

4 P-Q5   N-K4
5 B-KB4

White is quite right in not hurrying to recapture the pawn. By chasing the knight White tries to make the development of Black's king's side more difficult.

5 ...   N-N3
6 B-N3   P-KB4?

It seems that a computer also has human weaknesses — it can be just as greedy as a human being. The computer does not want to part with the extra pawn, and moreover it threatens 7...P-B5.

However, the move ...P-KB4 is obviously antipositional. It weakens the king and opens the KN1-QR7 diagonal. Furthermore, the computer appears to have forgotten one of the most important principles in chess — the principle of development. 6...P-QR3 would have been a better solution and if 7 N×P, then 7...N-KB3 8 N×N (8 Q-Q4 P-K4! 9 B×KP N×N 10 Q×N Q-K2) 8...KP×N. White's position is better but Black will succeed in completing his devlopment. Instead of 7 N×P, 7 Q-Q4 is stronger. After 7...N-K3 8 O-O-O, White still has pressure.

7 B-N5+   B-Q2
8 N-R3!

The readers have correctly determined the weak points in their opponent's camp. The white knight is aiming at K6.

8 ...   P-QB3!

A natural move, but since it was made by the computer it

deserves an exclamation mark. This move bears witness to the great possibilities of the electronic chess player. Evidently the computer is able to assess the position correctly. Black's Achilles' Heel is the square K3 and the computer correctly decides not to allow the exchange of his white-squared bishop, which is the only piece defending that square.

9 B-QB4   Q-N3

White's main threat of 10 N-KN5 followed by 11 P×P and 12 B-B7 mate is noticed by the computer, which prepares to castle queen's side in order to remove the king from the danger zone. However, it does not manage to realize this plan.

Black's position was compromised by his sixth move, but he should have tried as an emergency measure to neutralize his main enemy — the bishop on QB4. The computer should have 'paid attention' to 9...P-N4. For example: 10 P×P P×B 11 P×B+ Q×P or 10 B-N3 P-B4 11 P-R4 P-QB5 12 B-R2 P-QR3. And in spite of the strong move 13 P-B3 for White, Black can still put up a fight.

10 Q-Q2   Q-B4

The computer is alert. It avoids the trap prepared by the humans: 10...O-O-O 11 N-R4 and the queen has nowhere to go.

The computer also refuses the 'Greek gift' — the pawn on QN7:

10...Q×NP 11 R-QN1 Q-R6 12 R×P with an overwhelming advantage for White. Who could say after this move that the computer thinks in a primitive way?

11 P×P

In order to profit from his advantage in development White has to open the game up.

11 ...   B×P

As will transpire later 11...P×P 12 O-O-O N-B3 is correct.

12 B-K6!

Well played! Now Black's king's side is frozen and White can calmly prepare for the decisive attack.

12 ...   N-R3

What would a chess player have played in this position? He would have chosen the lesser evil: 12...R-Q1 13 B-KB7+ K×B 14 Q×R P-KR3, but the computer cannot part with the exchange. We should note however that the computer's combinative ability is not too bad: it saw the piquant variation: 12...P-KR3 13 O-O-O N-B3 14 B-QB7 and then 15 Q-Q8+.

13 O-O-O   N-K4

How else can he defend against 14 B-QB7? If 13...Q-R4 then 14 N-KN5 R-Q1 15 Q×R+ Q×Q 16 R×Q+ K×R 17 R-Q1+ K-K1 18 B-QB7 wins.

14 N-KN5   N.R3-N5

Otherwise 15 B×N follows.

15 P-KB3   P-KN3

It has to give up the knight. The fight is over, but the computer (like some chess players) does not like resigning in time.

16 P×N   B-N2
17 B×N   Q×B

This leads to an attractive finish. the computer 'did not like' 17...B×B 18 B-B7+ followed by 19 N-K6+ and Black loses his queen.

Could the computer have seen the final combination? Perhaps, but even a computer is entitled to count on his opponent's mistakes...

18 Q-Q8+!   R×Q
19 B-B7+

and the computer resigned.

The electronic chess player will undoubtedly try to take revenge on the readers in a fresh match. The future will show whether he can succeed.

Throughout his notes Polugayevsky makes the common mistake of referring to the computer when he really means to say the program. He also calls the computer 'he' instead of 'it' in his final note, as do many humans when they are playing against a computer program. — DNLL

The Northwestern Program

The Program written at Northwestern University won the first four ACM tournaments (1970, '71, '72 and '73). It finished second, behind KAISSA, at the first World Computer Championship in Stockholm (1974) and it was second, behind RIBBIT, at the fifth ACM tournament (San Diego 1974). It regained its ACM title at Minneapolis in 1975. The program was written by Larry Atkin, Keith Gorlen and David Slate while they were students at Northwestern university, and it was improved a little each year, even after its programmers graduated. At the time of writing, Atkin and Slate are working as systems programmers in the same laboratory at Evanston, and Gorlen is with the U.S. Public Health Service at Bethesda, Maryland.

The version of the Northwestern program that first appeared in the ACM tournaments was called CHESS 3.0. As the program has grown in age and strength so its name has been amended and it is currently (1975) called CHESS 4.4. Here is a brief description of how the program decides on its moves.

The program performs a depth-first tree search using the alpha-beta algorithm. The way in which the program grows the tree is interesting — there is a special routine (segment of the program) whose job it is to choose the next move to be searched or to decide not to search any more moves from some particular node. To choose a move this routine invokes one of fifteen selector modules, each of which is a different move selection algorithm. A module may select a move and /or it may determine which module is to be used the next time the selection routine is called into operation for the same node. Here is a list of the modules and their functions:

START:
   This module initializes a node. It calls *GENMOV* to generate and evaluate the legal moves.

LIBRARY:
   The program has a library of positions that have been 'learnt' and this library is searched for a move applicable to the current position. When a position is added to the library a suggested move is also added, this move being either the book move, in the case of a stored opening variation, or the move actually played in that position, in the case of a position already encountered.

ENDPOINT:
   is evoked to terminate the search of a branch by returning a final evaluation for that branch.

CHPRUNE:
   tries to find a checking move whose score suggests that it is worth looking at for reasons other than the check.

LMBLAS:
   looks at the best variation of the previous move tree to see the program's expected reponse, at that time, if the opponent makes the move predicted by that tree. A human analyses in much the same way — if his opponent makes an expected move a human master will first consider the move that he had planned to make when making his previous move.

ISTBST:
   chooses the move having the best score from the evaluation function, i.e. the apparently best move.

BSTLAS:

chooses the move which turned out best at the last node examined at the same ply level. This is another human approach — if a particular move is strong in reply to one of our opponent's moves, then maybe the same move will be strong in reply to another of his moves.

MORBST:

selects up to L best valued moves, where L is a pre-set limit. The limits were usually different for different levels in the tree, though at any one level the limit was the same. It is this limit parameter that determines the width of search and hence, to a great extent, the time taken to make a move.

COMBO:

selects a number of the most promising moves as determined by a 'combination potential' score.

FLEX:

selects moves in almost the same way as *MORBST* but with the difference that it only tries to find moves that defend against a threat not met by previously searched moves.

BANANA SUPER BEYOND:

selects moves at ply 1 whose scores are not high enough to justify a full depth search by previous modules. *SUPER BEYOND* moves are searched to a depth of 3-ply and, if their score looks good, to full depth by the *EXPAND* module. The purpose of *SUPER BEYOND* is to solve such problems as the difficulty of transferring a piece from one square to a better one by passing through a worse one. e.g. a human player would not normally put his knight on, say, KR3 unless he intended to move it to a good square such as KB4. But since such an operation takes 3-ply it is a good idea to examine a number of moves to that depth.

BEYOND:

selects all moves that are not chosen by *SUPER BEYOND* and examines them to a depth of 2-ply. This module is inexpensive in terms of time, but it catches certain kinds of moves that would otherwise not be examined.

EXPAND:

re-searches moves that pass the tests set by *BEYOND* and *SUPER BEYOND*. This expansion takes the search to full depth.

QUIESCE:

varies the depth of search according to the degree of quiescence of the position.

DONE:
terminates the selection of moves from the node currently under consideration.

The program's library of positions can be augmented in two different ways. If the program is in *LEARN* mode then any position added to its library will have a move associated with it. If the program ever reaches this position during the course of a game it will automatically make that move, by-passing the usual tree search. If the program is set in *ANALYSIS* mode it continually monitors its progress throughout the game. When the evaluation of a current position is significantly different from what was expected during an earlier look-ahead analysis the program assigns credit or blame to its previous four moves and puts these assigned scores into the library. If the same position is encountered in the future, the program uses the credit or blame score to supplement the information gleaned during the normal look-ahead search.

The current version of the Northwestern program, CHESS 4.4, employs an evaluation function with 53 features, and when playing at tournament rates (40 moves in 2 hours) it examines an average of 250,000 positions each time it calculates its move. Of the three members of the programming team only one is a strongish player — David Slate has a USCF Expert's rating. The continued success of their program owes more to the excellence of their programming and to their foresight in building in a number of useful interactive facilities that help them improve their program's play and diagnose its faults.

The following game was played in the third round of the 3rd ACM tournament, Boston 1972. At the time of this tournament there was a little thing going on in Iceland between Fischer and Spassky. Possibly prompted by some of the publicity surrounding that match, some of the programs complained during the tournament about spectators in the front row chewing gum and others who were talking too loudly.

White: CHESS 3.6
Black: TECH

1	P-K4	P-K4	
2	N-KB3	N-QB3	
3	B-N5	N-B3	
4	O-O	B-B4	
5	N-B3	P-Q3	
6	B×N+		

CHESS 3.6 likes to double its opponents' pawns.

6	...	P×B	
7	P-Q4	P×P	
8	N×P	O-O	

9 B-N5

Obviously CHESS 3.6 could find nothing clear after 9 N×P Q-K1 10 N-Q5 Q×P 11 N×N+ P×N.

9 ...   B-KN5
10 Q-Q3

It took CHESS 3.6 over 6½ minutes to decide on this move. 10 B×N Q×B 11 Q×B B×N leads nowhere for White.

10 ...   B×N
11 Q×B   R-N1
12 B×N

Never missing an opportunity to double its opponent's pawns.

12 ...   Q×B
13 Q×Q   P×Q
14 P-QN3   R-N5
15 P-KR3   B-K3
16 P-N4!

Excellent. Fixing Black's KBPs.

16 ...   R-Q5

16...P-Q4 looks more logical, but after 17 P-B3 P×P 18 N×P P-KB4 19 N-B6+ K-N2 20 N-R5+ White still has the edge.

17 QR-Q1   R×R
18 N×R

The knight is better placed on K3 than on QB3.

18 ...   K-N2
19 N-K3   K-N3
20 P-KB4   K-N2
21 K-N2   R-QN1
22 K-B3   R-N4
23 P-B4   R-QR4
24 P-KB5   B-Q2
25 R-B2   R-K4
26 R-Q2   P-QR3

Black can do nothing.

27 P-KR4   P-B4

A serious positional error, creating a hole for White's knight. Reshevsky annotated this game in the *New York Times* and claimed that after 27...P-R3 the position would be even. I. J. Good tried to refute Reshevsky's assessment with the continuation 28 N-N2, threatening 29 N-B4, 30 N-R5+ and 31 N×P, but both Reshevsky and Robert Byrne pointed out that 29 N-B4 could be met by 29...K-B1 and 30 N-R5 by 30...K-K2, defending the KB3 pawn. There is also the point that 28 N-N2 can be met by 28...P-KR4 29 P-N5 P×P 30 P×P P-Q4 equalizing.

The only thing that this analysis proves is that after 27...P-R3 White cannot achieve anything with 28 N-N2. However, White's position must surely be superior. He can continue with 28 K-B4 (to prevent the freeing manoeuvre ...P-KR4; P-N5 P×P; P×P P-Q4, since now the rook would be *en prise)* and then play P-N4 preparing for an eventual P-B5.

28 N-Q5   B-B3
29 N×QBP   B×P+
30 K-B4   P-KR4
31 P×P   P-R4
32 R×P   B×P
33 P-R6+!

'A stroke of genius' — Reshevsky.

a matter of technique.

35	...	R-K7
36	K×B	R-KB7+
37	K-K5	R-R7
38	N-Q5	K-N4
39	N-B3	R-R5
40	R×P	K×P
42	N-K4	R-R4+
42	K-Q6	K-N3
43	R-QR7	P-R5
44	R×P	K-B2
45	R-R7+	K-N3
46	P-R4	R-B4
47	P-R5	R-B6
48	R-QN7	K-B4
49	N×P	R-B6
50	P-R6	R-R6
51	P-R7	Black lost

33	...	K-N3
34	P-R5+!	K×P.R4
35	R×P	

White wins a piece. The rest is on time

The Northwestern program has an impressive record against other chess programs. In the first three ACM tournaments it played 10 games and won them all. In the fourth tournament it scored 3½ out of 4 and it was not until the first World Championship tournament in 1974 that CHESS 4.0 (as it was then called) lost a 'serious' game to another program (see page 120). Later in the same year CHESS 4.0 lost another game to a computer program, this time to RIBBIT from the University of Waterloo. RIBBIT became the first program to stop CHESS 4.0 from winning the ACM tournament.

CHESS 4.0 has not only been successful against other programs. It competed in a tournament with 50 humans at Northwestern University during the winter of 1973/4 and finished in a tie for third place with a score of 4½ out of 6. The average rating of its opponents was 1537 and its performance rating for the tournament was 1736 which places it in the middle of class B on the USCF scale.

TECH

The Technology chess program was written by James Gillogly at Carnegie-Mellon University. Its name, TECH, is derived from the basic philosophy that underlines Gillogly's work — he wanted to produce a program that relied almost entirely on technology (i.e. fast computers) and hardly at all on chess heuristics. The aim was to write a program that would simply generate all legal moves to a fixed depth, then evaluate the terminal positions only with respect to material. We have already explained that such an approach can never lead to a program that plays perfect chess, but Gillogly's idea was not to create a Grandmaster program, rather to produce a standard of play against which other programs could be measured. In order to justify the effort of developing a more complex program it would be necessary that the more complex program could defeat TECH. Since TECH's performance would improve with an increase in computer speeds it could always be used as a 'bench-mark' program.

Gillogly's first experiments showed that this ultra-primitive approach did not result in a useful program, since the standard of play was low for any reasonable depth of search. The program often reached a position that was strategically hopeless before it was able to achieve anything by tactics, and it even made tactical blunders through evaluating non-quiescent positions. Gillogly therefore decided to devote a small percentage of the program's computation time to chess heuristics.

His move generator mechanism consists of two main parts: positional and tactical analysis. The positional analysis routine sorts the moves at the top level of the tree so that the moves with the best superficial positional scores are examined first. This helps to get the most out of the alpha-beta algorithm. No tactical considerations are included in the positional analysis. The tactical analyzer is a 'brute-force' tree search which investigates all moves to a fixed depth and evaluates terminal positions provided that they conform to a simple quiescence criteria. The alpha-beta algorithm will select the move at ply-1 that is seen to be materially the best. If there are two or more moves of equal material merit then the first of these is chosen since that is the one whose superficial positional score is the highest. One feature of the Technology program that is (in 1975) unique among chess programs is that it uses its opponent's thinking time for its own analysis. While its opponent is thinking it predicts its opponent's move and then begins to compute its reply. If the opponent makes the predicted move then TECH's clock time will be small. In many cases TECH can reply immediately because it predicted its opponent's move long before its opponent had decided on it.

The most important part of the program (in terms of playing ability) is the tactical analysis component (i.e. the brute force search). All moves are searched to a fixed depth, usually 5-ply, and then all captures are examined and all captures in reply to these captures, and so on until there are no more captures. Even though the alpha-beta algorithm was employed, this search strategy results in as many as 500,000 terminal positions being examined when the program is choosing its move in a tournament game. This is only made possible by the simplicity of the evaluation function (material being the only feature used) and the efficiency of the move generator. Captures are recognized and sorted during move generation with the highest valued captures being put first on the list. This helps speed up the tree search since the refutation of a weak move is often a capture.

The positional pre-sorting routine discriminates between moves of equal material value. When used in conjunction with the tactical search routine it can often achieve a satisfactory position from the opening, even though it knows no opening theory. The program distinguishes between five phases of the game and for each phase it employs different heuristics for the positional pre-sort at the top of the tree. Among heuristics that are used throughout the game are one to encourage exchanges when TECH is ahead in material and one to adjust the basic maximum depth for the tactical analysis on the basis of how much time, on average, TECH has for each move before the next time control. If the program has significantly more time available per move than it used (on average) on its previous nine moves, then its depth of search is increased. If it used more time on its previous moves then the depth is decreased.

TECH considers the opening to be the first eight moves. The most important heuristic in the opening evaluation is occupation of the centre. Each square on the board is weighted with a desirability value ranging from 0 points for the corners to 8 points for the centre. Each move represents a gain or loss of centre control, e.g. the move 1 N-KB3 would yield a gain of 5 points for centre control. This is multiplied by a priority factor for the piece that moves: pawn=1, queen=1, rook=2, bishop=3, knight=4, and king=−1. These weightings encourage the development of knights before bishops, of minor pieces before major pieces (i.e. bringing out the queen is discouraged during the opening) and it encourages castling by giving the king a negative priority value so that it scores the greatest number of centre control points when it is in a corner.

Each move in the opening is given a final positional score of the centre control term plus the value of whichever of the following heuristics apply to the move:

Pawn from K2 to K4: 30 points
Pawn from K3 to K4: 2 points
Pawn from Q2 to Q4: 20 points
Pawn from Q3 to Q4: 2 points
K-side castling: 30
Q-side castling: 10
N-R3: −15
Putting a piece on K3 or Q3 where it blocks a pawn: −50
Moving a K-side piece: 2
Playing the Petroff Defence: −50
Pawn captures towards the centre: 5
Pawn catures away from the centre: −5
Pawn captures leading to doubled isolated pawns: −10
Advancing a rook's pawn: −10
Capturing an undefended centre pawn: 50
Capturing a defended centre pawn: −15

The best way to show the effectiveness of these heuristics is to give some examples of TECH's opening play. Remember that TECH is playing purely from first principles — it has no 'book' knowledge whatsoever.

1) TECH-DAVID, 2nd ACM Tournament, Chicago 1971. 1 P-K4 P-K3 2 P-Q4 Q-R5 3 N-QB3 N-QB3 4 N-B3 Q-R4 5 B-Q3 Q-N5 6 O-O P-B3 7 B-K3 P-QR3 8 Q-K2 P-KN4.

2) TECH-CHESS 3.5, 2nd ACM Tournament, Chicago 1971. 1 P-K4 P-QB4 2 N-KB3 N-QB3 3 P-Q4 P×P 4 N×P N-B3 5 N-Q3 P-Q3 6 B-QB4. Fischer's favourite move! Not bad for a program that knows no theory. 6...P-K3 7 O-O P-QR3 8 B-K3 N-K4.

3) COKO III-TECH, 2nd ACM Tournament, Chicago 1971. 1 P-K4 P-K4 2 N-KB3 N-QB3 3 B-B4 N-B3 4 P-Q3 P-Q4 5 B×P N×B 6 P×N Q×P 7 N-B3 B-QN5 8 O-O B×N.

4) SCHACH-TECH, 3rd ACM Tournament, Boston 1972. 1 P-Q4 P-Q4 2 P-QB4 P×P 3 N-KB3 N-QB3 4 P-K4 P-QN4 5 P-Q5 N-N5 6 B-N5 N-KB3 7 B×N KP×B 8 B-K2 B-QB4.

5) TECH-USC, 3rd ACM Tournament, Boston 1972. 1 P-K4 P-QB4 2 N-KB3 N-QB3 3 P-Q4 P×P 4 N×P N-B3 5 N-QB3 P-Q3 6 B-QB4 P-K4 7 N-B5 B-K3 8 Q-Q3 N-QN5.

6) CHESS 3.6-TECH, 3rd ACM Tournament, Boston 1972. 1 P-K4 P-K4 2 N-KB3 N-QB3 3 B-N5 N-B3 4 O-O B-B4 5 N-B3 P-Q3 6 B×N+ P×B 7 P-Q4 P×P 8 N×P O-O. For the continuation of this game see page 100.

7) OSTRICH-TECH, Play-off for second place, ACM tournament 1972. 1 P-QB4 P-K4 2 N-QB3 N-KB3 3 P-K4 N-B3 4 P-Q3 B-B4 5 B-N5 O-O 6 N-B3 P-Q3 7 B-K2 B-K3 8 O-O N-Q5.

8) TECH-COKO III, Play-off for second place, ACM tournament 1972. 1 P-K4 P-K4 2 N-KB3 N-KB3 3 P-Q4 B-N5+ 4 B-Q2 B×B+ 5 QN×B P×P 6 N×P O-O 7 B-B4 N×P 8 N×N P-Q4.

These examples should be sufficient to convince the reader that it is quite possible to get reasonable positions in the opening without having any book knowledge.

TECH considers the middle game to begin with move nine and it continues until one side has less than 1950 points worth of material (in the initial position each side has 4420 on TECH's scale). The centre control heuristic is still used in the middle game but the priority factors are slightly altered: pawn=3, knight=4, bishop=3, rook=2, queen=1 and king=1. Since the pieces have usually found good squares by the middle-game, this factor has less influence than in the opening. Each move is credited with a mobility term which is, as usual, the number of potentially legal moves available after the move is made. Movement of a piece into at the area near the opponent's king is rewarded in the same way as the centre control heuristic, and the net gain is again multiplied by the priority value for that piece. The pawn heuristics are the same as in the opening except that advances of wing pawns score −5 instead of −10. If TECH is ahead in material, piece captures score a 10 point bonus. Moving a piece which blocks a KBP or QBP scores 5.

The third, fourth and fifth phases are devoted to three different types of endgame, endgame with pawns, general endgames and endgames with only pieces. The most important goals in pawn endgames are advancing one's own passed pawns and blocking those of one's opponent. Each move is credited with the net gain in the realm of passed pawns and this allows TECH to escort its own pawns towards promotion and to block the advance of its opponent's pawns.

Pawn moves are weighted by the rank of their destination and by whether they are opposed.

Rank	Opposed	Unopposed
3	2	3
4	1	5
5	3	10
6	4	13
7	-	23
8	-	80

If TECH has more than one pawn on a file only the first is given this bonus; the other pawns on the same file lose 10 points.

As in the pawn endgame, TECH's main goal in the general endgame is to promote. The pawns are given the same weights for advancing as in the previous paragraph. The material value of a pawn is raised by 20% but if TECH has 2 pawns or less then their material value is increased by 90%. This would mean, for example, that if TECH had a knight and two pawns against a bishop and one pawn it would not allow its opponent to sacrifice the bishop in return for the two pawns. A move which places a rook behind a passed pawn of either colour is rewarded with 15 points. The centre control term uses priorities of pawn=0, knight=4, bishop=3, rook=1, queen=1 and king=4. This encourages centralisation of the king.

Unlike the other forms of endgame, TECH's goal in the endgame with pieces is to drive its opponent's king to the edge in order to deliver mate. This is achieved by doing a small (2-ply) tree search and using a special evaluation function that was largely invented by the Northwestern University programming team.

TECH has always been one of the stronger programs of the present generation. At the second ACM tournament, Chicago 1971, it finished in a tie for second place from a field of eight programs. It subsequently won the play-off. At the third tournament in Boston, the following year, TECH again tied for second place but this time it was defeated in the play-off by OSTRICH. In 1974, when there were twelve competing programs in the fourth ACM tournament at Atlanta, TECH tied for fifth place. The program that finished second in Atlanta was TECH II, written at M.I.T. by Alan Baisley, Stan Kugell and James Cooper. (Baisley was instrumental in adding the opening library to Greenblatt's program in 1967). One of the refinements of TECH is its storage of all positions evaluated during the tree search. If a position occurs again later in the same search (by transposition) or during the search for the next move, it is retrieved from storage and the score associated with it is used instead of being computed for a second time. Since 1973 Gillogly appears to have moved on to other pastures, leaving TECH II to participate in the American and International arenas.

While TECH was active it competed in a number of human tournaments as well as three of the annual ACM events. Between May 1971 and March 1972 it participated in seven human tournaments scoring 12 points from 31 games. Its current (July 1975) USCF rating is 1243 which makes a mockery of some programmers' claims that their programs deserve ratings of 1600-1800.

Let us close this biography of TECH with one of the best games of its career.

White: COKO III
Black: TECH
2nd ACM Tournament
Chicago 1971

1	P-K4	P-K4
2	N-KB3	N-QB3
3	B-QB4	N-B3
4	P-Q3	P-Q4
5	B×P	N×B
6	P×N	Q×P
7	N-B3	B-QN5
8	O-O	B×N
9	P×B	O-O

Black has achieved a perfectly satisfactory game from the opening.

10	N-N5	B-B4
11	R-N1	P-KB3
12	P-QB4	

A normal computer move, attacking the opponent's queen, but Black soon takes advantage of the weakness at White's Q4.

12	...	Q-B4
13	N-R3?	B×N
14	B K3	N-Q5
15	P×B	Q-B3
16	P-QB3?	N-B6+
17	K-R1	N-Q7+
18	P-B3	N×R.B8
19	Q×N	P-B4
20	R-N5	P-B5

20...P-K5 would open up White's king.

| 21 | R-B5 | Q-K3 |
| 22 | B-B1 | P-B3 |

Threatening 23...P-QN3.

| 23 | P-Q4 | QR-K1? |

This move was due to a bug in the program. 23...P×P is obvious and correct. Now Black loses a pawn.

24	R×KP	Q-N3
25	R×R	Q×R
26	Q B2	Q-K3
27	Q-B1	R-B4

28 P-KR4	P-B4!
29 P-Q5	Q-Q3
30 Q-R3	Q-K4
31 Q-B1	Q×BP
32 P-Q6	Q-Q5
33 Q-K2	Q×QP
34 Q-K8+	R-B1
35 Q-R4	R-B4
36 Q-K8+	R-B1
37 Q-R4	Q-K3

TECH knows that it is ahead and so avoids threefold repetition of position.

38 Q-N3	Q-K7!
39 P-KR3	R-Q1

Forcing the win of the queen.

40 B×P	R-Q8+

And here COKO's programmers resigned.

KAISSA

Following the success of the Moscow program in the match against Stanford in 1967, little was heard from the Soviet Union about computer chess except for some of Botvinnik's theoretical results (see chapter 5). But this did not mean that Soviet scientists had lost interest in the subject. In 1971 a group of programmers at the Institute of Control Science began to rewrite the program that had been used in 1967, and by the following year it was ready, in its new form, to play a match against the readers of the newspaper *Komsomolskaya Pravda*. The two game match was conducted in the same way as the game played against *The Ural Worker* (see page 94). On most Sundays throughout 1972 the newspaper published KAISSA's moves in each of the two games and the readers sent in their suggested replies. In every case the move suggested by the majority of the readers was chosen and KAISSA's reply was published the following week. KAISSA drew one game and lost the other. The previous year Spassky had played two games against the readers of the same newspaper and scored one win and one draw. Obviously the combined force of the readership of *Komsomolskaya Pravda* produces rather strong chess and so it is reasonable to assume that KAISSA is also no rabbit.

KAISSA's basic look-ahead was set at 7 ply, with further analysis along variations that involve captures and other forcing moves.

Game 1
White: KAISSA
Black: Readers

| 1 P-K4 | P-QB4 |
| 2 N-QB3 | |

After 40 minutes thought and an examination of over half a million positions.

2 ...	N-QB3
3 N-B3	P-Q3
4 B-N5	B-Q2
5 O-O	P-KN3
6 P-Q4	P×P
7 B×N	P×N
8 B×P	R-N1
9 B-Q5	B-N2

If 9...P×P 10 B×NP R×B 11 Q-Q4, forking the two rooks.

| 10 P-QN3 | N-B3 |
| 11 B-K3 | |

Before making this move KAISSA examined more than 1,500,000 positions.

11 ...	Q-B2
12 Q-Q4	P-QR4
13 B-QB4	O-O
14 QR-K1	B-B3
15 P-K5	B×N
16 P×P	P×P
17 P×B	N-R4
18 Q-Q3	B-K4
19 B-Q4	K-N2
20 R-K3	

KAISSA predicted that the continuation would be 20...P-B3 21 B×P B×P+ 22 K×B P-Q4+ 23 B-K5.

| 20 .. | P-B3 |
| 21 R.1-K1 | |

But now KAISSA changed its mind.

21 ...	N-B5
22 Q×BP	R.N1-B1
23 P-QR4	Q-Q2
24 B×B	BP×B
25 K-R1	Q-R6
26 R-KN1	N-Q4
27 Q×RP	R-QB4
28 Q-R7+	R-QB2
29 Q-R5	R-QB4
30 Q-R7+	R-KB2

Avoiding the draw

31 Q×R.B5	P×Q
32 B×N	R-B5
33 R×P	R×BP
34 B×R	Q×B+
35 R-N2	

Declared drawn, since the readers cannot afford to refuse the repetition of moves by 35...Q-Q8+ 36 R-N1 Q-B6+.

Game 2
White: Readers
Black: KAISSA

1 P-QN3

This move was chosen by the newspaper before the readers had been invited to send in their suggestions.

1 ...	P-K4
2 B-N2	N-QB3
3 P-QB4	P-B3
4 N-QB3	B-N5
5 N-Q5	KN-K2
6 P-QR3	B-Q3
7 P-N3	O-O

8 B-N2	N-N3	23 B×KP	N-K2
9 P-K3	P-B4	24 B×QNP	R-N1
10 N-K2	R-K1	25 B-K4	N-B4
11 Q-B2	P-K5	26 N-Q5	P-R4
12 P-Q3	P×P	27 P-KN4	N-K2
13 Q×P	R-B1	28 N×N+	R×N
14 P-B4	B-K2	29 P-N5	P×P
15 P-KR4	P-KR3	30 P-KB5	N-B2
16 P-R5	N-R1		
17 P-K4	P-Q3		

After examining 2,877,000 positions

18 O-O-O	R-B2
19 N×B+	Q×N
20 N-B3	B-K3
21 N-Q5	Q-Q2
22 N-K3	P×P

KAISSA correctly thought that 30...B-B2 31 P-R6 P×P 32 Q-QB3 R-K4 33 Q×R would have been even worse.

31 P×B	Q×P
32 B-Q5	Q-K6+
33 Q×Q	R×Q
34 QR-B1	Resigns

Thus KAISSA made its public debut. When the newspaper games ended the programming team continued to work on the program. Altogether about ten people were involved, including G. Adelson Velsky, Dr. V. Arlazarov, Dr. M. Donskoy and A. Bitman, a Soviet Master who works at the Institute of Control Science.

KAISSA uses a complex evaluation function involving many features. In fact it is so complex that when I asked Mikhail Donskoy about it he replied '...I don't even remember what is in it'.

The program uses the now familiar method of searching all moves to a specified depth and then considering only captures, checks, other forcing moves and moves that are replies to checks. An upper bound of 30-ply has been put on the depth of these forcing variations but this depth is reached very seldom during the tree search.

KAISSA uses the alpha-beta algorithm with the slight modification that before the search for a move begins the values of alpha and beta are not set to −infinity and +infinity (as is usually the case) but to rather narrower limits between which the value of the current position is known to lie. In this way the search is reduced still further.

An improvement in the performance of the alpha-beta search is obtained by using what the programmers call the 'best move service'. They point out that in chess the number of possible moves (less than 10,000) is far smaller than the number of possible positions and that a classification of moves is therefore much easier than a classification of positions. The underlying principle of the best move service is that a move that was the best in many similar positions would most likely be plausible in the current position. For each level ten moves are stored. These are the moves that were most frequently the best ones in other position at this level. When ordering the moves from a particular position these 'best moves' are put at the head of the list and hence they are considered earlier. The application of the best move service produced a ten-fold reduction in the time taken to search trees whose basic depth was 5-ply.

Another innovation was the idea of introducing a dummy move at certain points in the game tree. If it is White's turn to move and Black makes a 'blank' move then it is White's turn to move once again. If White can now gain a material advantage then the previous White move must have carried this threat. Under some circumstances a threat can be used to create a cut-off in the search process and this technique can therefore lead to a further reduction in the search time. Another use of the discovery of threats is that they can be included in the list of moves that need to be examined.

KAISSA is able to reduce its search still further by being able to recognize positions that are analogous to positions already examined. If a move is absurd in a particular position then it is likely to be absurd in similar positions and it can therefore be excluded from the search until such time as circumstances appear that change the variation arising after the absurd move. A simple example of this strategy can be shown by considering the following position.

Under normal circumstance a chess program would always consider the moves Q-Q4 and Q-N5 when making a move from this position, and KAISSA's use of the blank move would normally result in these two moves being considered because they are threats. But in the present position both moves are absurd because they put the white queen *en prise*. Let us assume that White plays 1 P-QR3 and that Black replies 1...P-QR4. Now most programs would once again consider Q-Q4 and Q-N5 even though both moves are still absurd *for the same reasons*, but KAISSA has a list of all the squares attacked by each of Black's pieces and it would not consider Q-N5 until Black's KRP had advanced, nor would it examine Q-Q4 until the black knight had moved. This is how a human plays chess and KAISSA's programmers point out that the standard of a human's play increases with the accuracy with which he determines when a move rejected earlier as absurd should be re-examined. KAISSA defines absurd moves as those that lead to the immediate loss of material. The only problem in implementing this 'method of analogies' is in deciding when the position has changed sufficiently to warrent re-examining a move that was rejected earlier. KAISSA's programmers have made some progress in solving this problem but their research is beyond the scope of this book.

The KAISSA program runs on a British built ICL 4/70 computer. A version of the program exists that could run on an IBM computer which would be faster and which would therefore allow a greater depth of search and hence stronger play by the program. So far the programmers have been unable to try the IBM version of their program (there are no IBM machines in the Soviet Union) but it is hoped that one will be made available for KAISSA's use at the 1977 World Computer Championship which is due to take place in Toronto. Dr. Arlazarov is of the opinion that if his program can have the use of the biggest and fastest IBM computer then it would be able to play with the strength of a Soviet Candidate-Master. If that proves to be true I might have to work hard to make sure of winning my bet!

KAISSA's first appearance outside the Soviet Union came in August 1974 when it participated in the first World Computer Championships in Stockholm. It won two of its games very convincingly, it was temporarily in trouble in a third and totally lost for much of the game in the vital last round. But in the end KAISSA won all four games and with them the title of World Champion.

5   Computer Chess Tournaments

'In tournaments it is not enough to be a connoisseur of chess. One must also play well.'

Siegbert Tarrasch

During the course of the preceding pages I have often referred to events in which the only participants were computer programs. At the time of writing seven such events have been held: Five ACM tournaments, one tournament in Canada in 1974 and one World Championship tournament (also in 1974). The ACM tournaments show every sign of increasing in popularity, with more and more programming groups expressing an interest every year. Although the number of programs that compete at these tournaments is usually limited to twelve, there are often as many as twenty that apply to take part. When selection is necessary programs are chosen or rejected largely on the basis of sample games that are sent in by the programmers.

Holding events of this type brings many benefits. Firstly, they act as a testing ground for those who have been working on chess programs. The programmers can compare their progress with that of their colleagues and they can exchange ideas, either informally or at one of the panel discussions that are now becoming a regular feature of the ACM tournaments. Manufacturers of computing equipment are usually only too happy to co-operate with tournament organizers in loaning teletypes or other items that are necessary to link the playing hall with the various computers via telephone lines. In return the manufacturers get some inexpensive publicity. The tournaments attract widespread interest (the 1972 ACM event was reported on the front page of the *New York Times*) and contribute to the aim of making the man in the street feel less uneasy about the increasing proliferation of computers. Lastly, computer tournaments are great fun for the participating programmers and the spectators. During one of the games at Atlanta in 1973 there were more than 200 people standing at midnight (at least as many were occupying all the seats).

When computer programs play each other in tournaments it is very rare for their computers to be present in the tournament hall. Most computers are much too large, too sensitive and too valuable to be transported hundreds or thousands of miles. The best known exception is the OSTRICH program, written by Monty Newborn and George Arnold at Columbia University, which runs on a Data General

Supernova computer that is small enough to be transported a few hundred miles without difficulty (it was the only computer present at the ACM tournament in Boston). More recently, the TELL program, written in Zürich by Johann Joss, has appeared on the international scene. It plays on a Hewlitt Packard computer that is small enough to be taken almost anywhere.

The usual way of communicating between the playing hall and the computer installation is by telephone. A normal telephone headset is clipped into a device called a modem which transforms the sounds that come through the telephone into impulses that can be decoded by a teletype or some other device. When the computer wants to communicate its move to the programmer, it sends a signal along the telephone line (via another modem situated in the computer room) and this signal appears as a move typed out in the tournament hall. Occasionally there is too much interference on the telephone line and the programmers are reduced to speech communication — they receive the moves from an operator in the computer room and give back the reply moves to the operator who types them in on the computer's console.

People often ask me how it is possible to be certain that it is the computer who makes all the moves? After all, a Grandmaster might be present in the computer room to make the occasional move for the program. Perhaps you have heard the story about Lasker playing a strong, blind player from whom he kept his identity secret. After Lasker had made a few tremendously powerful moves the blind man lifted his head, smiled and said, 'Ah, Dr. Lasker I presume.' Just as a Grandmaster's style can be recognized by a strong player, so a program's style can, to some extent, be recognized. In particular, if one knows that a program can only search to a depth of, say, 9-ply, and it unleashes an 11-ply combination, then something is probably wrong. But just to make sure that fair play was observed, one of the rules of the first World Championship tournament required that an impartial observer be present at every computer site. If I had any cause for suspicion (I was the tournament director) I could always communicate with the impartial observer by 'phone.

A few special rules are necessary for computer tournaments. The time limit is usually 40 moves in 2 hours and 10 moves in every subsequent half hour, which is not uncommon in human events, but each program is allowed up to three 20-minute breaks during a game so that if there is technical trouble of some sort at the computer installation the program will not be penalized.

Perhaps the most important special rule is that there must be no manual adjustment of program parameters during a game. Once the width and depth of search have been set by the programmers they are not allowed to change them, even though their program may be getting into bad time trouble. However, if the program asks a questions such as 'how much time do I have left before the next time control?' then the programmers may answer it. By instructing a program to ask this question at frequent intervals it is possible to avoid time trouble, nevertheless programs do still lose on time even in overwhelming positions.

Two amusing examples of a defective time-control mechanism were seen in the fifth ACM tournament, San Diego 1974.

White: KCHES6
Black : TECH II

1 P-K4	P-K4
2 N-KB3	N-QB3
3 B-B4	N-B3
4 N-N5	P-Q4
5 P×P	N×P
6 P-Q4	

Up to now TECH II had consumed a total of 10 minutes and 50 seconds. Now it thought for 86 minutes, leaving it with only 23 minutes for its remaining 34 moves.

6 ...   P×P

This move is in all the books! It isn't really worth 86 minutes.

From here the numbers in brackets indicate the length of time, in seconds, which TECH II spent on each of its remaining moves.

7 Q-B3	B-K3 (75)
8 N×B	P×N (28)
9 Q-K4	B-N5+ (19)
10 P-QB3	P×P (9)
11 P×P	N×P (6)
12 Q-N4	N×N+ (97)
13 K-K2	N-Q5+ (19)
14 K-K3	N-B7+ (60)
15 K-K2	N-B6+ (11)
16 K-B3	N×R (49)
17 B-KN5	O-O+ (19)
18 K-N3	N-K5+ (27)
19 Q×N	Q×B+ (14)
20 K-R3	Q-R4+ (16)
21 K-N3	B-Q3+ (27)
22 P-B4	Q-N4+ (27)
23 K-R3	Q-R3+ (19)

24 K-N4   R×P+ (12)

KCHES6's   programmers
resigned for their program while
TECH II still had more than 14
minutes remaining on its clock.

TECH's programmers could at
least be thankful that their
program knew it was short of
time after its lengthy deliberation
at move 6.

What happened to TECH II in the following round was somewhat
more tragic.

TECH II — RIBBIT

This position was reached after RIBBIT's 22nd move. TECH II had
45 minutes at its disposal for the next 18 moves and it has a number of
forced mates to choose from, one beginning with Q-KN6+ and the
others, slightly longer, beginning with R-B7. Possibly confused by the
multiplicity of wins available, TECH II thought and thought and
thought and ... finally it lost on time without making another move.

By winning this game RIBBIT reached a score of 3 out of 3. In the
fourth and final round it faced Chess 4.0, the defending champion,
and RIBBIT made amends for its poor play against TECH II.

White: RIBBIT
Black: CHESS 4.0

1 P-K4	P-QB4
2 P-QB3	P-Q4
3 P×P	Q×P
4 P-Q4	P×P

Up to this point RIBBIT was
following its opening book but

now it had to think for itself.
CHESS 4.0 knew the theory of
this line two moves further.

5 P×P	N-QB3
6 N-KB3	B-N5
7 N-B3	Q-Q3?

As Tarrasch once commented,
'Up to this point Black has been
following well-known analysis,

but now he makes a fatal error — he begins to use his own head.'
Correct is 7...Q-QR4 or 7...B×N when White has only a slight advantage.
The move chosen by CHESS 4.0 presents White with a winning initiative.

8 P-Q5	N-N5
9 B-QN5+	B-Q2
10 B×B+	K×B

If 10...Q×B 11 N-K5 Q-B4 12 Q-R4+ K-Q1 13 N×P+ Q×N 14 Q×N and White has an extra pawn and an overwhelming position.

11 B-K3	Q-QR3?
12 N-K5+	K-K1
13 P-QR3	Q-Q3
14 Q-R4+	N-QB3
15 P×N	P×P
16 N×QBP	P-K4
17 N×RP+	Q-Q2
18 Q×Q+	K×Q

and White eventually won.

In my opinion CHESS 4.0 was rather unlucky to lose its ACM title by just one mistake. Computer games are usually so riddled with errors that against some programs CHESS 4.0 could have survived after its weak seventh move. But the winning ideas were easy for RIBBIT to spot because they all involved checks and direct threats to Black's queen and knight. Full credit must be given to RIBBIT for the manner in which it won material and exchanged into an easily won ending, but I feel that it was rather given the game on a platter. This, coupled with RIBBIT's lucky win against TECH II two rounds earlier, leads me to conclude that as of November 1974 it was still CHESS 4.0 that was the strongest program in the Western World.

World Computer Championship, Stockholm 1974

The ACM tournaments have all proved so popular that it seemed natural to organize a World Championship tournament. The idea was born on the last night of ACM 73 in Atlanta. Ben Mittman, Monty Newborn and I approached the organizers of the 1974 IFIP Congress in Stockholm and they were very enthusiastic and extremely helpful. Thirteen programs from eight countries were admitted to the tournament and there were others who had to be refused places because of insufficient space in the tournament hall. Having an odd number of competitors in a Swiss System tournament presents no real problem since the programs are seeded on the basis of the two games submitted with their entry and the program seeded last is given the bye in the first round. In this way none of the strongest programs get the bye, and if a program that has had the bye wins in the next round it can then be given a tough opponent to make up for the bye.

At the Stockholm tournament there was one program from the Soviet Union (KAISSA), four from the USA, one from Canada, three from Britain and one from each of Norway, Switzerland, Austria and Hungary. From its previous games the Hungarian program PAPA looked to be the strongest entry but some last minute changes made to the program seemed to have an adverse effect on its play.

The first round produced few surprises. KAISSA defeated the Austrian entry and the four American programs also won, but PAPA lost to the weakest of the British Programs.

White: KAISSA
Black: FRANTZ

1 P-K4	P-K4
2 N-KB3	N-QB3
3 B-N5	P-Q3
4 P-Q4	P×P
5 Q×P	KN-K2

Normal in this position is 5...B-Q2 but FRANTZ's opening knowledge extended only as far as its previous move. Although the text move is inferior, it was once played by a Soviet Grandmaster.

6 O-O	P-B3
7 B-KB4	B-K3
8 N-B3	Q-B1

More natural is 8...P-QR3.

| 9 QR-Q1 | B-B2 |

With the 'idea' of 10...Q-N5

10 Q-N4?

Strong is 10 Q-Q3, followed possibly by 11 B-B4 in order to take advantage of Black's weakness along his KN1-QR7 diagonal. The text move inexplicably puts the white queen on a diagonal that will soon be opened in his opponent's favour.

10 ...   P-QR3!

| 11 B×N+ | N×B |
| 12 Q-R4 | |

White should play 12 Q-R3 and if 12...P-Q4 13 Q-R4. e.g. 13...P-QN4 14 N×NP P×N 15 Q×P Q-R3 16 Q×Q R×Q 17 P×P with adequate compensation for the piece. But this continuation was 11-ply deep and not all the moves were forced, so KAISSA could not have seen it.

12 ...   P-QN4

| 13 Q-R3 | P-Q4 |

13...P-N5? 14 Q-R4 P×N 15 Q×N+ solves all of White's problems.

14 P-QN4

Forced

14 ...	B×P
15 Q-N2	P×P
16 KR-K1!	

Stronger than 16 N×KP O-O when White has nothing for the pawn.

16 ... P-B4?

All computer programs are materialists and FRANTZ is no exception. Black should be satisfied with just one pawn and look to the safety of his king. After 16...O-O 17 R×P B-B4, Black has an extra pawn and a good game. After the text move Black keeps two pawns instead of one but his king is immediately in trouble.

17 N-K5

Missing a nice combination: 17 N×KP! P×N (if 17...B×R 18 Q×KNP R-B1 19 N-B6+ etc.) 18 Q×P R-KN1 (or 18...B×R 19 Q×R+ K-K2 20 B-N5+ K-K3 21 Q-B6 mate) 19 R×P+ N-K2 (or 19...B-K2 20 Q-B6) 20 Q-K5 B-R6 21 B-N5 with a decisive attack.

The text, however, is also strong.

17 ... N×N

The best chance. If, for example, 17...B×N 18 Q×B N-Q1 then 19 B-N5 N-K3 (if 19...Q-K3 20 Q×P) 20 Q-B6+ K-B1 21 N×B K×N 22 R-Q7+ K-N3 23 Q×N+ K×B 24 R×NP+ and mate in a few moves.

18 B×N

Now White's pressure on the long diagonal gives him more than enough pressure for the pawns.

18 ... B×N

19 B×B?

It is moves like this that confirm that it is a computer making the moves at the other end of the telephone line and not a human. If White recaptures with his queen Black is immediately lost, since 19...O-O 20 B×NP R-K1 21 B-R6 leads to mate, while most other moves are refuted by 20 Q-B6+ K-B1 21 B×BP with an overwhelming position.

19 ... R-KN1
20 P-B3! Q-N2
21 B×P

Or 21 P×P P×P 22 B×P Q-N3+ 23 K-R1 Q-N3 24 Q-K5+ B-K3 25 Q×KP when Black exchanges queens into a roughly equal ending.

21 ... Q-N3+
22 B-Q4

Not 22 K-R1 Q-N3 23 P×P P-B5 24 Q-K5+ B-K3 and Black wins.

22 ... Q-N3

23	P-N3	O-O-O
24	P×P	P×P
25	B-B6	R-Q4!
26	R×R	B×R
27	Q-K5	Q-B2
28	R-Q1	B×P
29	Q×KP	K-N1
30	B-K5	R-K1

Correct was 30...Q-K3 when White is hard pressed to find compensation for his lost pawn.

31	Q-B6!	Q-N3

If 31...R×B it is mate in two. Black can hold out longer with 31...R-KB1, though after 32 Q-QN6+ K-R1 33 Q×RP+ K-N1 34 Q×P+ K-B1 35 Q-R6+ K-N1 36 Q-QN6+ K-B1 (or 36... K-R1 37 B×P) 37 Q-R7 B-Q4 38 R-N1 he can resign.

32	Q×BP+	K-R1
33	R-Q7	Q-B4
34	Q-B6 mate	

The second round provided the biggest upset of the tournament. CHESS 4.0, which was hitherto undefeated in competition against other computer programs, succumbed to a devastating positional piece sacrifice against its compatriot CHAOS.

White: CHAOS
Black: CHESS 4.0

1	P-Q4	P-Q4
2	P-QB4	P×P
3	N-KB3	N-KB3
4	P-K3	P-K3
5	B×P	P-B4
6	Q-K2	P-QR3
7	O-O	P-QN4
8	B-N3	B-N2
9	R-Q1	QN-Q2
10	N-B3	B-Q3
11	P-K4	P×P
12	N×QP	Q-N1
13	P-N3	

The game Friedman-CHESS 4.0, Northwestern University tournament 1973/4 went 13 N-B3 P-N5 14 N-QR4 B×KP 15 P-KR3 O-O 16 B-K3 Q-N4 17 Q×Q P×Q 18 N-N6 N×N 19 B×N B-Q4 20 B-B2 KR-B1 21 R-Q2 B-KB5 22 B-K3 B×B 23 P×B B×P 24 QR-Q1 N-Q4 25 K-B2 R×B? 26 R×R B-

B5 (CHESS 4.0 had intended 26...B-N6 but now realized that this move would have lost to 27 R-R1) 27 R.Q1-QB1 P-B4 28 N-K5 P-N6 29 N×B? P×R 30 N-R3 P-N5 31 N×P R-QB1 32 P-QN3 N-B6 33 K-B3? (Better is 33 K-K1) 33...N-R7 34 R-Q1 R×N 35 R-Q6 K-B2 36 P-N3 N-B8 37 R-Q4 N×P 38 R×P N-Q7+ 39 K-B4 K-B3 40 R-N6? P-N4 mate.

The text is recommended by theory but now, for the first time in the game, CHESS 4.0 is out of its openings book and must think for itself.

13 ...	P-N5

Now CHAOS is also out of its book.

14	N-R4	B×KP

14...O-O has also been played, but CHESS 4.0 is as materialistic as the next program.

15	P-B3	B-N3?

The 'book' continuation is 15...P-K4 16 N-K6 P×N 17 P×B B-B4+ 18 N×B N×N 19 Q-B4 Q-N4 when Black has repelled the attack and remains ahead in material.

16 N×P!

This sacrifice was obviously based on purely positional considerations since CHAOS could not possibly have analysed as far as move 24. To the best of my knowledge this was the first example of a positional sacrifice being made by a computer program.

16 ...   P×N
17 Q×KP+   B-K2
18 R-K1   Q-Q1
19 B-KB4

Threatening 20 B-B7 Q×B 21 Q×B mate

19 ...   K-B1
20 QR-Q1   R-R2
21 R-QB1

21 B-Q6 N-KN1 22 N-B5 wins at once, e.g. 22...N×N 23 B×B+ Q×B 24 Q-B8+ etc. But the text move, which threatens 22 R-B8!, can hardly be bad.

21 ...   N-KN1
22 R.B1-Q1   P-QR4

Black is completely lost. There is no good move.

23 B-Q6   B×B
24 Q×B.Q6+   N-K2
25 N-B5   B-B4
26 P-N4   Q-K1
27 B-R4   P-N6
28 P×B   P×P
29 B×N   P-R8=Q
30 R×Q   R-R3
31 N×R   Q-Q1
32 K-B2

Inexplicable!

32 ...   K-B2
33 Q-K6+   K-B1
34 Q×N+   Q×Q
35 R×Q   K×R
36 N-B5   R-QN1
37 R×P   R×P+
38 K-N3

and White eventually won.

When the third round began there were three programs with 2 out of 2: CHAOS, KAISSA and OSTRICH. OSTRICH was given black against CHESS 4.0 and by move eleven OSTRICH had thrown away the game. The encounter between KAISSA and CHAOS almost led to an internaticnal incident, before it finally resolved in favour of the Soviet program.

White: KAISSA
Black: CHAOS

1 P-K4	P-QB4
2 N-KB3	N-QB3
3 P-B3	P-Q4
4 P×P	Q×P
5 P-Q4	B-N5
6 B-K2	P-K3
7 O-O	N-B3
8 B-K3	

Black has played rather passively and White has the initiative from the opening.

8 ...	P×P
9 B×P	

9 P×P is more natural, followed by N-B3 with a very active game.

9 ...	P-K4!?
10 P-KR3	P×B
11 P×B	B-Q3!?

Preparing a dangerous looking attack. The alternative was 11...P×P forcing the exchange of queens.

12 P×P	N×NP
13 N-B3	Q-KR4

Threatening 14...B-R7+ 15 K-R1 B-N6+ with a draw by perpetual check.

14 P-KN3	K-Q2?

After 14...O-O-O, or even 14...O-O, the position would be rather unclear. But now White has a completely won game.

The explanation for CHAOS'

blunder is that it scores highly for surrounding its king with its own pieces and the text move puts its king next to two of its own men, with the possibility of adding further reinforcements by ...QR-Q1 and ...KR-K1. This is an excellent example of how a simple heuristic can lead to disaster.

15 N-KR4
15 P-Q5 would have been devastating, since 15...N.B3-K4 loses to 16 N×N+ and 17 B×N+.

15	...	P-B4
16	P-Q5	

But now this gives Black tremendous counterplay by driving the QB3 knight to the K-side where it can join in the attack on White's king. Both 16 Q-R4 and 16 Q-N3 were strong continuations.

16	...	N.B3-K4
17	Q-B2	KR-KB1
18	B-Q3	N×B?

Black should play 18...P-KN4

19 B×P+ K-K2 when White seems to be quite lost.

19	Q×N	QR-K1

Now 19...P-KN4 can be met by 20 N-B3 or first 20 Q-N5+.

20	N-N5	P-B5
21	N×B	K×N
22	Q-R3+	K-B2
23	Q×P	Q-B2

23...P×P 24 QR-B1+ is no better for Black.

24 KR-B1+
It is more accurate to check with the other rook.

24	...	K-Q3
25	Q-B5+	K-K4
26	P-Q6+	K-K3

27 R-K1+
Instead of typing in this move, one of the CHAOS programmers input 27 R-B1 by mistake. For a while no-one noticed the error and the game continued (27 R-B1) 27... K-Q2 28 Q-B7 mate. Of course this move is not mate when White's rook is on KB1 but

everyone in the tournament hall thought that the rook was on K1. Mikhail Donskoy, confident that the game was over, said goodbye to his colleage in Moscow (they were using speech communication because the telephone line was too unreliable for modems) and replaced the telephone receiver. A few seconds later CHAOS printed out the move 28...K-K3.!

When a move has been input incorrectly the usual procedure is to return to the position where the accident happened and resume the game with the correct move. Donskoy tried to reopen the telephone line to Moscow but on enquiring at the Stockholm exchange he was told that it would take at least a few hours. Obviously it was very important to finish this game in the proper manner before the last round began but Donskoy was not at all certain that he would be able to get the use of his computer before 7.30 p.m. the following evening when the final round was due to begin.

In case it proved impossible to play the game out, I made the following decision. The game would be adjudicated a win for White and in order to get an estimate of the number of moves needed to win*, Donskoy and I would play, in consultation, against the CHAOS program. We tried to predict the moves that

KAISSA would make, deliberately avoiding the best moves in some positions. Our game ended: (27 R-K1+) 27...N-K6 28 P×P Q-Q2 29 R×N+ K-B3 30 R.R1-K1 Q-N5+ 31 N-N2 R-QR1 32 Q-K5+ K-N3 33 R-KN3 P-R4 34 R×Q+ P×R 35 Q-KN5+ K-R2 36 R-K7 R-B2 37 R×R K-R1 38 Q×P .N7 mate.

The following morning however, Donskoy was able to telephone to Moscow and the resumption of the game was fixed for 5.00 p.m.

27	...	N-K6
28	P×P	Q-Q2
29	P-B5+!	K-B3
30	R×N	R-Q1
31	R-K7	Q-R5
32	Q-K5+	K-N4
33	N-B3+	K-N5
34	R×KNP+	K-R4
35	Q-R2+	Q-R5
36	Q×Q mate	

* In the event of a tie for one of the top places, a tie-breaking system was to be used to determine which two programs would play off for whatever prize was at stake. The tie breaking system involved adding the number of moves in games won to half the number of moves in games drawn and subtracting the number of moves in games lost. The program with the lower total was declared to have the better tie-break score.

Everyone wanted to see CHESS 4.0 playing KAISSA in the last round but the pairing system would not permit it. KAISSA was given black against OSTRICH and for much of the game the Soviet program was faced with a forced loss.

White: OSTRICH
Black: KAISSA

1 N-KB3	P-K3
2 P-Q4	N-KB3
3 B-N5	P-Q4
4 P-K3	B-K2
5 N-B3	B-N5

Kaissa believes more in the power of the pin than in the old rule 'you shouldn't move the same piece twice in the opening'.

6 B×N	B×N+
7 P×B	Q×B
8 B-Q3	P-B4
9 O-O	O-O
10 Q-Q2	N-B3
11 P×P?!	Q-K2

Better was 11...R-Q1 but KAISSA wants to restore material equality as quickly as possible.

12 P-B4!

Otherwise White can never undouble his pawns.

12 ...	P×P
13 B×BP	Q×P
14 Q-Q3	R-Q1
15 Q-K4	P-QN4?

Black can maintain a slight advantage with 15...N-Q5! 16 N×N Q×B, when White's isolated QBP might cause him some problems in the ending.

16 B-Q3	P-B4

16...P-N3 is less weakening.

17 Q-KR4   P-K4

Black should have played the developing move 17...B-Q2 but the text looks more active.

18 P-K4

Stronger is 18 P-QR4!, e.g. 18...P×P 19 B-B4+ K-R1 20 N-N5; or 18...P-K5 19 B×NP P×N 20 B×N.

18 ...	P-B5
19 KR-K1	B-N2??

I cannot understand how KAISSA, with a basic look-ahead of 5-ply, could overlook White's manoeuvre. 19...P-KR3 would be found by most chess programs.

20 N-N5	P-KR3
21 N-K6	Q-N3
22 N×R	R×N
23 P-R4	P-N5
24 B-B4+	K-R1
25 QR-Q1	N-Q5
26 R-QB1?	

White can win more material by 26 Q-K7, threatening both the KP and the crushing move P-K5. If 26...R-QB1 27 B-N3 and both 27...N×P and 27...N×B can be met by 28 R-Q7.

26 ...	B-B3!
27 P-QB3!	

White cannot defend the QRP. If 27 B-N3 P-B6!

27 ...	P×P
28 R×P	B×RP
29 Q-K7	N-B3

30 Q-KB7   Q-B4
31 R-Q3

A good alternative is 31 R.K1-QB1.

31 ...   N-Q5
32 B-Q5   B-N4?

Black can force a draw by 32...N-K7+! 33 K-B1 (33 K-R1 is much worse for White than the game continuation because his rook is not on the KR-file) 33...B-N4 34 R-Q2 (if 34 K×N Q-B7+ or 34 R-KR3 N-B6+ 35 K-N1 N×B) 34...N-N6+ 35 K-N1 N-K7+ etc.

33 R-KR3   N-K7+
34 K-R1   Q×P

35 R-Q1?

Missing a forced win by 35 R×P+!! P×R 36 Q-B6+ K-R2 37 Q-K7+ K-N3 38 Q-KB7+ K-N4 39 Q-KN7+ K-R4 40 B-B7+ K-R5 41 Q×RP+ K-N5 42 B-K6 mate. But this was too deep for OSTRICH.

35 ...   Q-N3
36 R-QN1   R-QB1
37 B-K6!   R-Q1?

After 37...B-Q2! White has no more than a draw by 38 R×P+

P×R 39 Q-B6+ K-R2 40 Q-B7+.

38 Q-N6   Q-N2
39 Q-B5?

White can still win with the rook sacrifice on KR6: 39 R×P+ P×R 40 Q×P+ Q-R2 41 Q-B6+ Q-KN2 42 Q×R+ K-R2 43 B-B5+ K-R3 44 Q-R4 mate. After Monty Newborn had returned home he tried OSTRICH out on this position but gave it an extra ply of look-ahead — OSTRICH found the win!

It is perhaps worth mentioning that 39 B-B5 K-N1 40 R×P would also be decisive.

39 ...   Q-QB2
40 R-R4?

The rook sacrifice still wins.

40 ...   N-Q5
41 Q-R3?

Missing the winning opportunity for the last time.

41 ...   N×B
42 Q×N   B-Q6

Now Black is probably winning.

43 R-N1   B-B5?

Why not take the pawn?

44 Q-B5   B-K7

To prevent 45 R-R5.

45 R-R1   P-QR4
46 Q-N6   P-R5

46...P-B6! would also have been strong.

47 R-K1   B-B5
48 R-R1   P-R6
49 R-QN1   Q-Q3!
50 Q×Q   R×Q
51 R-R3   P-R7
52 R-QB1   R-Q5

More convincing would have been 52...B-Q6 followed by 53...B×P and 54...B-N8.

53	R.R3-QB3	R×P
54	R-R1	R-Q5

Threatening to advance the KP.

55	R×B	R×R
56	P-N3	P-B6

The back rank mate threat still prevents the capture of Black's QRP.

57	P-R3	R-B7
58	R-Q1	R-Q7
59	R-QB1	P-K5
60	P-N4	P-K6
61	K-N1	P-K7
62	K-B2	R-Q8
63	R-B8+	K-R2
64	K×P	P-K8=Q
65	R-B2	R-Q6+
66	K-B4	P-N4+
67	K-B5	R-KB6mate.

A game full of human interest.

With this victory KAISSA took first place in the tournament and with it the title of World Champion. Mikhail Donskoy was presented with a gold medal that had been specially commisioned for the event by the British publisher Mr Robert Maxwell. Mr. Maxwell was present during the last round of the tournament and he was able to make the presentation in person. Richard Nixon was so disappointed with OSTRICH's numerous missed wins that he resigned the US Presidency a few minutes after this last game ended and his resignation speech was relayed to the spectators.

In order to satisfy the bloodthirsty spectators and as a friendly gesture between the Soviet programming team and the group from Northwestern University, an exhibition game was arranged the next day between CHESS 4.0 and KAISSA. CHESS 4.0 won the toss and chose White. Here is the score of that encounter — the Fischer-Spassky match of the computer world.

White: CHESS 4.0
Black: KAISSA

1	P-K4	P-Q4
2	P×P	N-KB3
3	P-Q4	N×P
4	N-KB3	P-KN3
5	B-K2	B-N2
6	O-O	O-O

7	R-K1	B-B4
8	N-R4	P-K4?

I cannot understand this move. Black is saddled with doubled, isolated pawns, his king position is weakened and White gets the advantage of the two bishops.

9	N×B	P×N
10	P×P	N-N5

11 Q×Q	R×Q
12 B-KN5	R-Q2
13 N-R3	B×P
14 P-QB3	N.N5-B3
15 N-B4	P-QR4
16 B-B3	P-B3
17 B-R6	P-R5
18 QR-Q1	R×R
19 R×R	K-R1?

Wasting time. The king should be moving towards the centre, ready for the endgame.

20 B×N

Peculiar. White helps his opponent to complete his development and simultaneously gives up the bishop pair. This game shows that the positional judgement of even the best chess programs still leaves much to be desired.

20 ...	N×B
21 P-B4	P-N4

Or 21...B-Q3 22 N×B P×N 23 R×P followed by 24 R×P and White is two pawns ahead.

22 P×B	P×N
23 P×P	R-Q1
24 R-KB1	K-N1
25 R×P	R-Q8+
26 K-B2	N-Q1
27 B-B4	P-B3
28 K-B3	

Hereabouts White begins to play without a plan. This is typical of computer programs and one of the fundamental problems of computer chess. Of course the endgame should be an easy win and there are probably dozens of winning plans but...

28 ...	R-KB8+
29 K-K4	R-QR8
30 P-QR3	R-K8+
31 B-K3	

If 31 K-Q4 N-K3+ 32 K×P R-K5+ and it is Black who wins. The correct plan for White is to bring his king back to KB2 and then either advance his K-side pawns or go after Black's Q-side pawns. But CHESS 4.0 wants to keep its king centralized and because of this Black's counterplay can develop quite successfully.

31 ...	R-K7
32 R-B2	R-K8
33 R-Q2	N-K3
34 R-Q6	N-B4+
35 K-B3	N-Q6
36 B-Q4	P-B4
37 B-K3	K-B2
38 R-Q7+	K-N3
39 R-KN7+	K×P
40 R×P	N-K4+
41 K-B4	N-Q6+
42 K-K4	N×P

43 P-N4??

A terrible oversight. After 43 K-B3 N-Q6 44 R-R5 N-K4+ 45 R×N K×R 46 B×P, White's two connected pawns guarantee him a win.

43 ...   N-Q8

Why CHESS 4.0 overlooked this simple threat I do not know.

44 P-N5+   K-N3
45 R-R6+   K-N2
46 K-Q5   R×B
47 K×P.B4   R×P+
48 K-N5   R×P
49 P-R4   R-R6

If 49...R QN6+ 50 K×RP P-B5 51 P-R5 R-N7 52 R-QB6 P-B6 53 R-B7+ and Black has no hope of winning.

50 K×BP   N-N7
51 P-R5   P-R6
52 R-KN6+   K-B2
53 R KB6+   K-N1

54 R-KN6+   K-B2
55 R-KB6+   K-K2

KAISSA is ahead on material and so it avoids the draw by repetition.

56 P-R6   N-R5+
57 K-N4   P-R7
58 R-B1   N-B6
59 K-N3   P-R8=Q

KAISSA sees an opportunity to win a pawn!

60 R×Q   N-K5+
61 K-B4   N×P
62 R-R6   N-B2
63 R-R7+   K-K3
64 R-R6+   K-B4
65 K-Q4   N×P

And indeed KAISSA has won a pawn, but there is no hope of it being able to win the game. At this point I adjudicated the game a draw.

6 Current Research and Future Prospects

'But probably computers, in the future, can help chess players. If you have an adjourned game and you have a good program,... as to me I am a little bit lazy and so I need a good computer.'

Boris Spassky

The games played at the first World Computer Championship serve as an accurate guide as to the current state of the art. In my opinion, the standard of play exhibited in Stockholm was not outstandingly better than that of Bernstein's program (1957) or even of Turing's hand simulation. It is true that the programs of today do not make gross tactical blunders so often as those of twenty years ago, but in terms of strategical concepts the advances that have been made during the past two decades are negligible.

There is a logical reason for this. Programmers realize that the defects that are most obvious are those due to tactical weakness. Even a very poor chess player can criticize a program for leaving its queen *en prise* or overlooking a mate. But the subtle inadequacies of chess programs, the lack of planning and the lack of a good grasp of strategic concepts, these are not noticed by inexperienced players. It is therefore not surprising that most of the effort that has gone into chess programming since Shannon's day has been directed towards the problems of tree searching (i.e. tactics) — how best to grow the tree and how to search it in the most efficient manner.

The Dutch psychologist Adrian de Groot has conducted a number of experiments among Grandmasters and Masters in an attempt to analyse their thought processes. He asked various players to look at a number of chess positions and for each position they were requested to speak their thoughts so that de Groot could note down their analysis trees. Among the more important of his results, from the point of view of chess programming at least, was the fact that it is not the depth of their calculation that distinguishes Grandmasters from Masters. Many chess programmers seem to think that if they could run their program on a much faster computer it would play very much better. While I would agree that increased computing speeds, and hence deeper tree searches, will improve programs' tactical play, I doubt whether a master standard program will exist even when computers are 1,000 or 10,000 times faster than they are today. Increased computing speeds will be felt most in the area of tactical play, and since chess is essentially a game of strategy there must be a limit on how far one can go with tactics. I have often asked chess programmers the question: 'If I gave you a routine that played perfect tactical chess, that saw every trick and every combination, that never lost material through a trap and never overlooked a possibility to win material by force, how would you set about writing a master strength chess program?' So far, no-one has yet been able to offer me any kind of an answer.

Another part of de Groot's research was devoted to examining the number of positions that a strong player considers during the course of his analysis. The result will probably amaze inexperienced players — it is usually less than 50. Why then is it necessary for chess programs to examine hundreds of thousands of positions before making a move? Something must be wrong. I think that there is enormous scope for future research into the problem of static evaluation. If a chess master analyses by using a lot of information about each of a small number of positions, why are so many programmers trying to do the converse? In my opinion a really strong chess program will be written only when someone produces an extremely sophisticated evaluation mechanism.

Automatic learning is another area of computer chess that has been almost uncharted. It is interesting that there has been a program written that can play draughts (checkers) at championship level and one of the most important features of that program is that it learns from experience. So far there have been very few attempts to implement any kind of learning in chess programs and it is usually possible to win the same game countless times against the same program.

Recently there has been an attempt to teach a chess program attacking patterns. A program written at the University of Southern California can take 'snapshots' of particular combinations of pieces and code these snapshots together with some numerical value. Every time the program considers a position it looks in its snapshot library to see if it recognizes any features of that position. For example, a human player knows that if his opponent has a knight on KB3, a queen on Q1 and if the KP is not on K2, then the move B-KN5 will pin the knight. The snapshot: bishop on KN5, opponent's knight on KB3, opponent's queen on Q1, no pawn on opponent's K2, is stored in the human player's mind because it is a frequently occuring theme in chess. He recognizes at once a situation in which B-KN5 is a plausible looking move.

How successful have the U.S.C. programmers been? Anyone reading their article in the June 1973 issue of *Scientific American* might have been misled into assuming that they had made great progress. Suffice it to say that when the program competed at the ACM tournament in Atlanta (August 1973) it finished in a tie for 10th-11th places (out of 12).

The endgame also offers great scope for original research. It is fairly well known that the endgame is the phase that sorts out the masters from the club players. Anyone who has watched a chess master giving a simultaneous exhibition will have noticed that the master often tried to reach the endgame as quickly as possible. This is because he knew that in the endgame his superior strength would be emphasized and that he would almost inevitably be able to outplay his opponent, even if he had no objective advantage.

In 1967 Barbara Huberman wrote a Ph.D thesis called 'A Program that plays Chess Endgames'. The object of her research was not to write a general endgame playing program but to investigate the problem of translating heuristics from chess books to computer programs. She discovered that the problem is not an easy one, nevertheless, she managed to write a program that could mate with king and rook against king, king and two bishops against king, or king bishop and knight against king. It is interesting to note that eight years later, to the best of my knowledge, no competitive program can perform all three of these standard mates.

The difficulty of writing a good endgame program is frequently underestimated by chess programmers. In August 1973, at the ACM tournament in Atlanta, I offered to bet any or all of the programming teams that by the time of the following year's tournament they could not write a routine to play the ending of king, rook and pawn against king and rook, correctly for both sides. In order to defeat my challenge the routine would have to demonstrate that it could win a number of 'won' positions and that it could draw, from the defending side, a number of 'drawn' ones. The CHAOS programmers took my bet for $100 and in November 1974 they paid up without even submitting their efforts to a formal test. At that time I offered the same bet for another one year term but no-one would take me on. In the book *Rook Endings* by Levenfish and Smyslov there are 47 pages devoted to that one endgame.

In December 1974, when my wife and I were visiting Moscow, I made the same bet with Dr. Arlazarov. I did not wish to corrupt him with the offer of a cash bet and so I suggested a wager of twelve bottles of vodka (if I won) against twelve bottles of Scotch. The period of the bet was to expire at the end of 1975, and the arbiter was to be Grandmaster Yuri Averbakh, President of the Soviet Chess Federation and one of the world's leading endgame experts. I suggested to Averbakh that he give the program the task of winning two or three theoretically won positions, with him playing the defence, and that he tried to win against the program from two or three different theoretically drawn positions. Just after the beginning of 1976 I received a telegram from Moscow saying: "KAISSA successfully examined by Averbakh on December 27th".

Winning a case of Scotch is not KAISSA's most notable achievement however. A routine written a little earlier enables it to play the endgame of queen and knight's pawn against queen perfectly. When the program reaches a won position it prints out something like "I will win in 34 moves", and if its opponent makes a mistake then it prints "That was a mistake — now I will win in 17 moves". This feat is all the more remarkable when one realises that this particular ending has been argued about in the chess literature for decades, and even such authorities as Botvinnik have been unsure as to exactly which positions were won and which ones were drawn.

In the USSR Zonal tournament at Vilnius in August 1975, Bronstein reached a position with queen and knight's pawn against queen in his game with Tseshkovsky. At the second adjournment, Bronstein telephoned the KAISSA programmers and asked them to look in their program's library to see what winning procedure it would adopt in his particular position. "And they gave me a plan that was so beautiful I would never have found it by myself". Bronstein sat down to resume his game, Tseshkovsky soon went wrong and the game was won. It was only later that it was discovered that at the end of the critical variation the program had made a mistake, overlooking a stalemate possibility, and that this particular variation should end in a draw. "But probably there is still a win" Bronstein said a few months later.

It has often been stated that since psychology is an important element in master play, no computer program will ever win the World Chess Championship because programs cannot employ any psychological devices. Until recently I agreed with this argument but I changed my opinion when I read a short paper written by Donald Michie.

Michie's work was prompted by the fact that although perfect play is assumed when searching an analysis tree (either by a human or a computer program), in the real-life game both sides are susceptible to error. The way in which Michie's research relies on this susceptibility can best be shown by considering a small analysis tree.

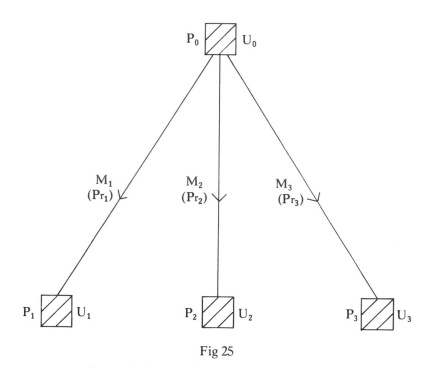

Fig 25

An analysis tree with utilities instead of scores.

Associated with each position is not a score in the normal sense but a 'utility' which, for a terminal node, is the same as the usual score, but for a non-terminal node it has a completely different significance. In figure 25 the position P_0 has a utility U_0 associated with it and the positions P_1, P_2 and P_3 (reached by making the moves M_1, M_2 and M_3 respectively from P_0) have associated with them the utilities (in this case the scores) U_1, U_2 and U_2 respectively. In the case of a normal analysis it would be assumed that the player to move from position P_0 would automatically make the move leading to the best utility and that this utility would be the one associated with the position P_0. Michie, however, assumes that instead of there being a probability of 1 that the move made is the one leading to the best utility (and there being a probability of 0 of any other move being made), there is a finite probability Pr_N that move N will be made from position P_0 (Pr is always greater than 0, and less than 1 unless there is only one legal move). This argument is quite reasonable. If move M_1 wins a pawn (say) and moves M_2 and M_3 achieve lesser aims, then in a normal tree search it would be assumed that $Pr_1=1$ and that $Pr_2=Pr_3=0$ (i.e. that M1 would definitely be the move made). By assigning small values to Pr_2 and Pr_3 Michie takes into account the possibility that one of the moves M_2 or M_3 *might* be the move played. He then calculates the utility U_0 from the formula

$$U_0=Pr_1 \times U_1+Pr_2 \times U_2+Pr_3 \times U_3$$

In the case of the usual type of tree search, U_0 would be equal to U_1 because $Pr_1=1$ and $Pr_2=Pr_3=0$. But with Michie's method the actual value of U_0 bears some relation to the fact that the player to move from position P_0 might not necessarily choose move M_1, even though it wins a pawn.

Calculating the utilities is easy enough once the probabilities are known. In order to determine the probabilities Michie introduces the notion of discernability, which measures the degree to which a particular player can discern which move is best in a given position. Discernability is directly related to the strength of the player and inversely related to the number of moves separating the position under consideration from the end game tree: next-move mates and stalemates and fully discernible even to a beginner, but next-move utilities are not so easy to estimate.

Michie argued that since a player's discernibility from a particular position is related to his strength and to the number of moves that the utility associated with that position has been backed-up, it is possible to calculate a value of discernibility (d) for every position. As a measure of the strength of the player concerned we could use, for example, his rating on the Elo scale. Michie further suggests a relationship between the relative probabilities of making the various moves from a given position, the discernibility applicable in that position and the utility associated with each move. From these relationships he calculates the utilities.

Michie's paper gives an example to show that from a given position different moves might be 'best' against players of different strengths. But in my opinion the most interesting application of his work is one that he himself had not considered when he wrote his paper. If, in calculating the discernability for a given position, the numerical measure of the player's strength is adjusted according to his stylistic preferences, it would be possible in many situations to steer the game into positions that one's opponent did not like to play. For example if a program were particularly good at tactical play, and if its opponent was known to dislike being under attack on the K-side, then in sharp situations where the program was attacking on the K-side its own playing strength would be considered to be greater than usual while its opponent's strength would be considered to be a little weaker. Such situations could be spotted a few moves ahead in the game tree and they might well result in the program steering the the game in a direction that was more suitable for it from a psychological viewpoint even though on a purely numerical assessment a different continuation might have been followed. In order to put this strategy into practice it would only be necessary for a program to 'know' its own weaknesses and strengths and for it to be told something about its opponent (his playing strength and the types of position that he did or did not like to play). Thus, the computer Grandmasters of the future might well play positionally against Tal and tactically against Petrosian.

Now that computer chess is becoming so popular there are a number of strong players who have interested themselves in the subject. If Botvinnik is right in thinking that the problem can only be solved with the help of strong players, the next few years should see much more rapid progress that the last twenty. Botvinnik's own line of research involves an 'algorithm' that is based on a knowledge of how many moves it would take each of the pieces to reach each of the squares on the board. His ideas are explained in his book 'An Algorithm for Chess' which has been translated into English and retitled *Computers, Chess and Long-Range Planning*. Botvinnik claims that his algorithm is so powerful that it could find the 23-ply deep combination that he discovered in his famous game with Capablanca at the A.V.R.O. tournament in 1938. Botvinnik's programming team is now working hard in an attempt to produce a strong program in time for the 1977 World Computer Championship. When I first told him about my bet, in March 1970, he said to me: 'I feel very sorry for your money'. When my wife and I visited him at his home in Moscow in December 1974 he was not quite so sorry for me!

There is a growing number of strong chess players in the West who are taking an active interest in computer chess. Hans Berliner, a former World Correspondence Champion, wrote his Ph.D thesis on the development of a tactical analyser. He has written a chess program but it is not yet strong enough to make it worth entering the ACM tournaments. Charles Kalme a U.S. Senior Master who was once invited to represent the U.S.A. in an Interzonal (he declined and gave up chess for mathematics) has been associated with the program written at the University of Southern California. He has not been discouraged by the program's lack of success and he is currently working on some more abstract aspects of the problem at the psychology department of the University of Indiana.

Michael Clarke, a former British Correspondence Chess Champion, has devised a special purpose programming language for writing chess programs. This, in my opinion, is a real step forwards, since it makes it much easier for chess experts with no programming knowledge to help programmers write good chess programs.

Perhaps the most esoteric line of research currently being pursued is Ron Atkin's work at the University of Essex. He has shown that there exists a relationship between the chess pieces, the squares on the board and the moves that can be made by the pieces, which possesses a geometrical representation in 53 dimensional space. He argues that it is possible to interpret the course of a game of chess as the expansion and contraction of two geometrical structures (one for White and one for Black) in this 53 dimensional space, and that positional theories can be expressed in a way that are particularly well suited to expression in a computer language. William Hartston, an International Master, is collaborating with Atkin.

Conclusions

Since 1948, when Shannon wrote his classic paper, there has been very little conceptual progress in computer chess. I think that there is no doubt that I shall win my bet in 1978, but with so many different programming efforts under way I think that I will ask for odds when I offer the bet for another ten year period. But for the moment at least, man is still master over the computer.

7 Stop Press

Since the typescript of this book was handed to the publishers, some startling news appeared on the subject of computer chess. This news will not only have grave implications so far as my bet is concerned, it will also change the game of chess completely. I was shocked when I read this report in the April 1975 issue of *Scientific American* and I tried to contact Richard Pinkleaf at once to make him an offer for his program. Unfortunately he was not available to take my call — he had gone to Moscow for a vacation.

I shall leave my readers with this news item, reproduced here by kind permission of *Scientific American*.

There were rumours late in 1974 that π would soon be calculated to six million decimal places. This may seem impressive to laymen, but it is a mere computer hiccup compared with the achievement of a special-purpose chess-playing computer built in 1973 by the Artificial Intelligence Laboratory at the Massachusetts Institute of Technology. Richard Pinkleaf, who designed the computer with the help of ex-world-chess-champion Mikhail Botvinnik of the USSR calls his machine MacHic because it so often plays as if it were intoxicated.

Unlike most chess-playing programs, MacHic is a learning machine that profits from mistakes, keeping a record of all games in its memory and thus steadily improving. Early in 1974 Pinkleaf started MacHic playing against itself, taking both sides and completing a game on an average of every 1.5 seconds. The machine ran steadily for about seven months. At the end of the run MacHic announced an extraordinary result. It had established, with a high degree of probability, that pawn to king's rook 4 is a win for White. This was quite unexpected because such an opening move has traditionally been regarded as poor. MacHic could not, of course, make an exhaustive analysis of all possible replies. In constructing a 'game tree' for the opening, however, MacHic extended every branch of the tree to a position that any chess master would unhesitatingly judge to be so hopeless for Black that Black should at once resign.

Pinkleaf has been under enormous pressure from world chess leaders to destroy MacHic and suppress all records of its analysis. The Russians are particularly concerned. I am told by one reliable source that a meeting between Kissinger and Brezhnev will take place in June, at which the impact on world chess of MacHic's discovery will be discussed.

Bobby Fischer reportedly said that he had developed an impregnable defense against P-KR4 at the age of 11. He has offered to play it against MacHic provided that arrangements can be made for the computer to play silently and provided that he (Fischer) is guaranteed a win-or-lose payment of $25 million.

The reaction of chess grandmasters to MacHic's discovery was mild compared with the shock waves generated among leading physicists by last year's discovery that the special theory of relativity contains a logical flaw.

Bibliography

This is a virtually complete list of English and Russian language books, articles and papers on computer chess published up to July 1975.

Part One — English

ACM (1971): *Computer Chess Programs*. Proceedings of the 1971 Annual Conference, Association for Computing Machinery, pp. 97-113.

Adelson-Velsky, G. M., Arlazarov, V. L., Bitman A. R., Zhivotovsky, A. A. and Uskov A. G. (1970): *Programming a Computer for Playing Chess*. Russian Mathematical Surveys, volume 25, number 2, pp. 221-262.

Adelson-Velsky, G. M., Arlazarov V. L., and Donskoy M. V. (1975): *On Some Methods of Chess Play Programming*. Artificial Intelligence.

Adelson-Velsky G. M., Arlazarov V. L., and Uskov A. V. (1966): *Program Playing Chess*. A report on the Symposium on 'Theory and Computing Methods in the Upper Mantle Problem'. Original in Russian, English translation privately circulated.

Arbuckle T., Belsky M. A., Bernstein A. and Roberts M. de V. (1958): *A Chess Playing Program for the IBM 704 Computer*. Proceedings of the Western Joint Computer Conference, pp. 157-159. (Panel discussion pp. 171-172).

Arnold G. and Newborn M. M. (1972): *A Chess Playing Program: THE OSTRICH*. Privately circulated.

Atkin L. (1975): *CHESS 3.6: A Chess Playing Computer Program*. M.Sc. dissertation, Computer Science Department, Northwestern University.

Atkin L., Gorlen K. and Slate D. (1972): *Chess 3.5*. Privately circulated.

Atkin R. H. (1972): *Multidimensional Structure in the game of Chess*. International Journal of Man-Machine Studies, volume 4, pp. 341-362.

Atkin R. H. and Witten I. H. (1973): *Mathematical Relations in Chess*. In 'Computer Chess' — Proceedings of a One Day Meeting on Chess Playing by Computer, Ed. Bell A. G., Chilton: Atlas Computer Laboratory pp. 37-79.

Baylor G. W. and Simon H. A. (1966): *A Chess Mating Combinations Program.* Proceedings of the Spring Joint Computer Conference, pp. 431-447.

Bell A. G. (1970): *How to Program a Computer to Play Legal Chess.* Computing Journal, volume 13, pp. 208-219.

Bell A. G. (1972): In 'Games Playing with Computers', Bell A. G., London: Allen & Unwin.

Berliner H. J. (1970): *Experiences Gained in Constructing and Testing a Chess Program.* Proceedings of the International Electrical and Electronic Engineering Symposium on Systems Science and Cybernetics.

Berliner H. J. (1973): *Some Necessary Conditions for a Master Chess Program.* Proceedings of the 3rd International Joint Conference on Artificial Intelligence, pp. 77-85.

Berliner H. J. (1974): *Chess as Problem Solving: The Development of a Tactics Analyzer.* Ph.D. dissertation, Computer Science Department, Carnegie-Mellon University.

Berman V., Ruben I., Swartz F., Toikka W. and Winograd J. (1973): *CHAOS.* Privately circulated.

Bernstein A. and Roberts M. de V. (1958): *Computer vs Chess Player.* Scientific American, volume 198, pp. 96-105.

Boos G. (1972): *The Viking.* Privately circulated.

Botvinnik M. M. (1970): *Computers, Chess and Long-Range Planning.* London: Longman.

Carlson F. R. and Zobrist A. L. (1972): *The USC Chess Program.* Privately circulated.

Carlson F. R. and Zobrist A. L. (1973): *An Advice-taking Chess Computer.* Scientific American, volume 228, number 6, pp. 93-105.

Ceruti F. and Smith R. (1972): *SCHACH.* Privately circulated.

Chase W. G. and Simon H. A. (1973): *Skill in Chess.* American Scientist, volume 61, number 4, pp. 394-403.

Clarke M. R. B. (1973): *Some Ideas for a Chess Compiler.* In Artificial and Human Thinking, edited by Elithorn A. and Jones D., pp. 189-198. Amsterdam: Elsevier.

Crocker S. D., Eastlake D. E. III and Greenblatt R. D. (1967): *The Greenblatt Chess Program.* Proceedings of the Fall Joint Computer Conference, pp. 801-810.

Cooper D. W. and Kozdrowicki E. W. (1973): *COKO III: The Cooper-Koz Chess Program.* Commications of the ACM, volume 16, pp. 411-427.

Gillogly J. J. (1972): *The Technology Chess Program.* Artificial Intelligence, volume 3, pp. 145-164.

Good I. J. (1968): *A Five year Plan for Automatic Chess.* In 'Machine Intelligence 2', Eds. Dale E. and Michie D., pp. 89-118. Edinburgh: Oliver and Boyd.

Good I. J. (1969): *Analysis of the Machine Chess Game J. Scott (White), ICL-1900 versus R. D. Greenblatt, PDP 10.* In 'Machine Intelligence 4', Eds. Meltzer B. and Michie D., pp. 267-269. Edinburgh: Edinburgh University Press.

Huberman B. J. (1968): *A Program to Play Chess End Games.* Stanford Technical Report CS 106.

Kalme C. I. (1974): *The Basic Search Routine for Selecting a Move in Chess.* Indiana Mathematical Psychology Program report.

Kalme C. I. (1974): *Incorporating Chess Knowledge Within the Framework of Computer Chess.* Indiana Mathematical Psychology Program report.

Kalme C. I. (1974): *Teaching Chess at the Human and Machine Levels.* Indiana Mathematical Psychology Program report.

Kister, J., Stein P., Ulam S., Walden W. and Wells M. (1957): *Experiments in Chess.* Journal of the Association for Computing Machinery, volume 4, pp. 174-177.

Kitov A. I. and Krinitsky N. A. (1962): *The Solution of Chess Problems* followed by *Programme-controlled computers playing chess.* In 'Electronic Computers', pp. 106-108. Oxford: Pergamon. (This is a translation of *Elektronnye Tsifrovye Mashinii i Programmirovannye* published in Moscow in 1959.)

Kotok A. (1962): *A Chess Playing Program for the IBM 7090.* B.Sc. Thesis. Massachusets Institute of Technology, Artificial Intelligence Project Memo 41.

Kent P. (1973): *A Simple Working Model.* In 'Computer Chess' — Proceedings of a One Day Meeting on Chess Playing by Computer, Ed. Bell A. G., pp. 15-27. Chilton: Atlas Computer Laboratory.

Levy D. N. L. (1971): *Computer Chess — A Case Study on the CDC 6600.* In 'Machine Intelligence 6', Ed. Meltzer B. and Michie D., pp. 151-163. Edinburgh: Edinburgh University Press.

Levy D. N. L. (1971): *Computer Chess — Past, Present and Future.* Chess Life and Review, volume 28, number 12, pp. 723-726.

Marsland T. A. and Rushton P. G. (1973): *A Study of Techniques for Game Playing Programs.* Proceedings of the World Organization of General Systems and Cybernetics, Ed. London: Gordon & Breach.

Marsland T. A. and Rushton P. G. (1973): *Mechanisms for Comparing Chess Programs*. Privately circulated.

Maynard Smith J. and Michie D. (1961): *Machines that Play Games*. New Scientist, volume 12, pp. 367-369.

Michie D. (1966): *Game-Playing and Game-Learning Automata*. In 'Advances in Programming and Non-Numerical Computation', Ed. Fox L., pp. 183-200 (incorporating an appendix by Maynard Smith J., *Rules of Somac*. pp. 196-200). Oxford: Pergamon.

Michie D. (1974): *A Theory of Evaluative Comments in Chess*. University of Edinburgh Machine Intelligence Project Memorandum MIP-R-105.

Mittman B. (1973): *Can a Computer Beat Bobby Fischer?* Datamation, June 1973, pp. 84-87.

Newborn M. M. (1975): *Computer Chess*. New York: Academic Press.

Newell A. (1955): *The Chess Machine*. Proceedings of the Western Joint Computer Conference, pp. 101-110.

Newell A., Shaw J. C. and Simon H. A. (1959): *Chess Playing Programs and the Problem of Complexity*. IBM Journal of Research and Development, volume 2, pp. 320-335. Reproduced in 'Computers and Thought', Ed. Feigenbaum E. A. and Feldman J. A., pp. 39-70.

Newell A. and Simon H. A. (1965): *An Example of Human Chess Play in the Light of Chess Playing Programs*. In 'Progress in Biocybernetics, volume 2' Ed. Schade J. P. and Weiner N., pp. 19-75. Amsterdam: Elsevier.

Pitrat J. (1968): *Realization of a General Game-Playing Program*. In 'Information Processing 68' pp. 1570-1574. Amsterdam: North Holland Publishing Co.

Pitrat J. (1971): *A General Game-Playing Program*. In 'Artificial Intelligence and Heuristic Programming', Eds. Findler N. V. and Meltzer B., pp. 125-155. Edinburgh: Edinburgh University Press.

Scott J. J. (1969): *A Chess-Playing Program*. In 'Machine Intelligence 4', Eds. Meltzer B. and Michie D., pp. 255-266. Edinburgh: Edinburgh University press.

Shannon (1950): *A Chess-Playing Machine*. Scientific American, volume 182, pp. 48-51.

Shannon (1950): *Programming a Computer for Playing Chess*. Philosophical Magazine, volume 41 (7th series), pp. 256-275.

Slater E. (1950): *Statistics for the Chess Computer and the Factor of Mobility*. Symposium on Information Theory, pp. 150-152. London: Ministry of Supply.

144   *Bibliography*

Tan S. (1972): *Representation of Knowledge for Very Simple Pawn Endings in Chess*. Ph.D. thesis, Edinburgh University Department of Machine Intelligence and Perception.

Tan S. (1973): *A Knowledge Based Program to Play Chess End-Games*. In 'Computer Chess' — Proceedings of a One Day Meeting on Chess Playing by Computer, Ed. Bell A. G., pp. 81-88. Chilton: Atlas Computer Laboratory.

Turing A. M. (1953): *Digital Computers Applied to Games*. In 'Faster than Thought', Ed. Bowden B. V., pp. 286-295. London: Pitman.

Two journals that publish news of computer chess research are:
i) SIGART (originally SICART) — The Journal of the ACM Special Interest Group on Artificial Intelligence.
ii) FIRBUSH — The Journal of the Machine Intelligence Research Group, University of Edinburgh.

Part Two — Russian
(This list does not include references to works for which an English translation exists and is mentioned above.)

Adelson-Velsky-G.M. and Arlazarov V. L. (1974): *Metodii Usilenya Shakhmatny Program*. In 'Problemii Kybernetiky, volume 29', Ed. Jablonskogo S. V., pp. 167-168.

Arlazarov V. L. and Bitman A. R. (1968): *Obigrayetlii Mashina Cheloveka?* Shakhmatny v SSSR, number 2 1968 pp. 9-11.

Belensky V. (1964): *Yeshe ob Elektronnikh Shakhmatistakh*. Shakhmaty (Sahs), number 16 1964, pp. 21-26.

Botvinnik M. M. (1961): *Lyudi i Mashini za Shakhmatnoy Doskoy*. Shakhmaty v SSSR, number 3 1961, pp. 78-80.

Botvinnik M. M. *Lyudi i Mashini za Shakhmatnoy Doskoy*. Shakhmaty v SSSR, number 3 1961, pp. 78-80.

Donskoy M. V. (1974): *O Programmye, Igrayushei v Shakhmaty*. In 'Problemii Kybernetiky, volume 29', Ed. Jablonskogo S. V., pp. 169-200.

Gik E. and Murakhveri V. (1968): *Na Dvukh Lektsyakh M. Botvinnika*. Shakhmaty v SSSR, number 8 1968, pp. 18-19.

Gulyayev A. (1970), *Kak Igrat c Mashinoy?* Shakhmaty v SSSR, number 10 1970, pp. 14-15.

Korobinskogo N. and Pekelisa V. (1956): *Mashina Delayet Vibor*. Nauka i Zhisn, number 6.

Korobinskogo N. and Pekelisa V. (1958): *Bestrasstnii Partner*. Tekhnika — Molodezhi, number 3.

Leonidov K. (1961): *Match: Chelovek-Mashina.* Leningradskaya Pravda, December 1st 1961.

Polugayevsky L. (1968): *Poebinok c Uralskim Robotom.* Shakhmaty v SSSR, number 8 1968, pp. 18-19.

Smilga V. (1956): *Vosmozhen li Shakhmatnii Avtomat?* Shakhmaty v SSSR, number 6 1956, pp. 176-177.

Tumanov V. (1961): *'Luchshii Khod'* — *Za 58 Sekund.* Bulletins of the World Championship Match Botvinnik-Tal, 1961, number 8, pp. 4-5.

Zagoriansky E. (1959): *Mashina i Shakhmaty.* Shakhmaty v SSSR, number 3 1959, pp. 68-69.

More Chess and Computers

Second Edition

The Microcomputer Revolution
The Challenge Match
BELLE The World Champion

David Levy
Monroe Newborn

Computer Science Press, Inc.
11 Taft Court
Rockville, MD 20850 U.S.A.

2 3 4 5 6   87 86 85 84 83 82

Contents

Preface

This is my fourth work for Computer Science Press, Inc., who have done much to help the advancement of computer chess by publishing regularly on the subject. The present volume was written in cooperation with Monty Newborn. Chapter 5 is his exclusive contribution. In addition, he assisted in coordinating material. This book is intended to be a sequel to *Chess and Computers*, and to bring the reader of that work up to date on developments that have taken place in the field during the past three years. However, it is by no means essential for those interested in the subject to have read the earlier work before they can follow the present one - simply consider *More Chess and Computers* as a state of the art survey.

Perhaps I should devote a few words to the future of this series of books on computer chess. I will not be writing any more tournament books but will condense the results and games of the most important computer chess tournaments into a succession of books which will appear at three yearly intervals, following the triennial IFIP Congress at which the World Computer Championship is held. The next volume in this series may therefore be expected after the 1980 IFIP Congress which is due to take place in Melbourne.

Computer Chess is a discipline which is attracting widespread interest from scientists and from the chess playing public. At the present time there is considerably less literature being published on the subject than on human chess. Within a decade or so I expect this situation to change dramatically - as computer programs begin to become regular winners of Grandmaster tournaments there is no reason why they cannot be used to annotate games in chess periodicals and to 'write' articles on new ideas in the openings. It would not surprise me at all if, within a decade, there were at least half a dozen monthly magazines devoted largely or exclusively to the latest games and exploits of computer programs. Ten years ago I would not have believed possible the progress that has since been made. Now nothing would really surprise me (very much).

David Levy
London, June 1979

This edition contains a postscript describing four major computer chess tournaments that were held after our original manuscript was submitted to the publishers. The hero of this material is BELLE, a program written by Ken Thompson and Joe Condon of Bell Telephone Laboratories. BELLE is performing very near Master level as the games show. Twenty-four games are presented and we believe the reader will be impressed by their quality. The next few years should be most exciting.

Monty Newborn
Montreal, November 1980

Acknowledgement

This edition contains a postscript describing four major computer chess tournaments that were held after our original manuscript was submitted to the publishers. The hero of this material is BELLE, a program written by Ken Thompson and Joe Condon of Bell Telephone Laboratories. BELLE is performing very near Master level as the games show. Twenty-four games are presented and we believe the reader will be impressed by their quality. The next few years should be most exciting.

Monty Newborn
Montreal, November 1980

To Lily and Floyd and the memory of Pumpernickel.

"A fool sees not the same tree that a wise man sees."

William Blake

1 The Levy Bet - End of an Era

In August 1968—I attended a conference on Artificial Intelligence at Edinburgh University's Department of Machine Intelligence and Perception. At a cocktail party one evening during the conference, I happened to be playing a friendly game of chess with John McCarthy, a professor of Artificial Intelligence at Stanford University and one of the world's leading authorities in his field. I won the game, and he remarked that although he was not strong enough for me, he thought that within ten years there would be a computer program that could beat me. You can imagine my reaction. I was the reigning Scottish Chess Champion at the time, and here was this inexpert player telling me that in only a few years I would succumb to a computer program! I said something roughly equivalent to (but more polite than) "put your money where your mouth is," and I offered to bet Professor McCarthy £500 (then worth $1,250) that he was wrong. Our host for the evening, Professor Donald Michie, who was sitting on the floor only a couple of feet away, joined in our debate and agreed to take half of the bet, McCarthy taking the other half.

A year later I returned to Edinburgh to deliver a paper at the Machine Intelligence Workshop. In the audience was Professor Seymour Papert of the Massachusettes Institute of Technology. He was so sure I was wrong that he wanted to take the bet for a five-year period, but I wouldn't let him. He therefore joined the original duet, adding £250 to the bet.

In 1971, a fourth member of the consortium was added: Professor Ed Kozdrowicki of the University of California at Davis wanted to bet me $1,000 that I was wrong, and at that time the bet had only seven years to run. A thousand dollars seemed like an awful lot of money to me at that time—I was suffering the usual impecuniousness of the chess master—so I took only £250 of the action ($650), and my friend Ben Mittman, who runs the computer center at Northwestern University, took the rest of Professor Kozdrowicki's bet. (Later that same day Kozdrowicki's program, COKO III, failed to play a mate in one, then failed again, and again—and finally lost! Ed rushed out of the room mumbling something about a bad bet . . .)

That is how things stood for four years. Then, in the winter of 1975, Donald Michie made me an offer I couldn't refuse. He wanted to increase his original £250 bet to £500 and to add a further £500 bet that if I did lose it would be a program developed by him or under his guidance. I accepted both bets without hesitation, feeling that the second bet gave me a kind of insurance policy: if I was going to lose the original bet it would almost certainly be to the Northwestern program or to Russia's KAISSA.

My original bet was now up to £1,250 (now worth only $2,500) because of the sinking value of the pound Sterling), and that is where it finished.

The Challenges

Until 1977 there seemed to be no point in my playing a formal challenge match against any chess program simply because none of them were good enough. But when CHESS 4.5, written by David Slate and Larry Atkin, began to do well in human events (winning the 1977 Minnesota Open, for a rather remarkable example), it was time for me to face up to my responsibilities and to defend the human race against the coming invasion.

My first match was arranged by Donald Michie, who was then a visitor at Carnegie-Mellon University in Pittsburgh. The conditions of the match were that I would play two games, but that if I won the first game the match would be over since it would then be impossible for the program to score the 1½ points required to beat me. The game was played on April 1st under really excellent playing conditions. I was seated in a closed room with a T.V. camera, a video display unit, and one or both of CHESS 4.5's programmers. The camera was linked to a television set in an auditorium where perhaps 400 people watched the game at one time or another. Hans Berliner commented on the game throughout, and when it was over I went into the auditorium to say a few words about how I felt while I was playing the game. I must say that those responsible for organising the match in Pittsburgh did a wonderful job and I have never participated in an event where the players were more comfortable. The organisors even arranged for the moves of the game to be transmitted over the ARPA satellite network so that hundreds of people were able to follow the course of the game (including McCarthy at Standford and Papert at M.I.T.).

I won the toss and chose Black in the first game. This choice of colour was decided by the fact that in the eight blitz games that I had played against the program a few days earlier, I had repeatedly got very good positions from the opening with my favourite Dragon variation as Black, but had only been able to get slight advantages with White. The night before I played the game I went along to inspect the playing conditions but was asked to leave the playing room because Berliner was modifying the program's opening book. I happened to wander into the auditorium where I noticed the printer that was to be used to keep the audience up to date with the progress in my game, and as I glanced down I saw that the printing head was moving. So there I stood, watching the printer, as Berliner did his best to bolster up the program's knowledge of the Dragon Variation!

White: CHESS 4.5
Black: Levy

Pittsburgh, April 1st 1977
Sicilian Defence

1 P-K4	P-QB4
2 N-KB3	P-Q3
3 P-Q4	P×P
4 N×P	N-KB3
5 N-QB3	P-KN3
6 P-B3	B-N2
7 B-K3	O-O
8 Q-Q2	N-B3
9 B-QB4	

In a couple of blitz games the program had played 9 O-O-O against me and I had replied 9...P-QR3 to take the program out of its book. It then played 10 NxN?! and after 10...P×N I won both games with a direct assault down the QN-file. Berliner's changes were designed to improve the program's play from move 9 onwards but instead of playing 9...B-Q2, the move which he had prepared the previous evening, I thought that once again I would try to trick the program.

9 ... P-QR3
Against a human player I would give this move a question mark because it is too slow. Against this program it deserves an exclamation point because when the program does not know what to do against the Sicilian it captures on QB6.

10 N×N?!
There are two reasons why the program' made this move. Firstly, my QB3 knight attacks two central squares and so in a sense it appears to be more valuable than White's

Q4 knight. Also, all programs know that isolated pawns are weak and my QRP now becomes isolated. Since the text strengthens my pawn centre I was quite happy.

10 ... P×N

11 O-O N-Q2
Against a human I would never transfer this knight from the king side, where it is needed for defence, to the queen side, but I knew that CHESS 4.5 does not know how to mount a K-side attack.

12 P-B4	N-N3
13 B-K2	B-K3

Intending ...N-B5.

14 P-QN3?
The move I expected and a mistake, 14 B-Q4 is correct, but programs are quite prone to making weakening pawn moves because they have little understanding of strong and weak squares.

14 ... N-B1
Continuing my policy of doing nothing, or very little, apart from encouraging the program to weaken its position.

15 P-QR3

Intending to meet ...Q-R4 with P-QN4, but 15 B-Q4 was still correct.

15 ...   Q-R4

Encouraging another pawn advance.

16 P-QN4

Thank you!

16 ...   Q-B2

17 P-B5

Now White's K5 square is weak and his KP is in some danger of becoming isolated.

17 ...   B-Q2

18 B-R6

The right idea but the wrong way to set about it. The correct plan begins with 18 K-R1, followed by R-B3, B-R6 and R-R3. It is easy for a human to find such a plan but not for a computer program. CHESS 4.5 was looking roughly six half-moves deep along every single variation and then examining checks and captures at deeper levels. While this process enables it to see 25 half-moves or more along tactical paths, it does not allow it to examine the

seven half-move continuation beginning with 18 K-R1 simply because White's moves are all "quiet" moves, i.e. not captures or checks.

Now the reader will understand why I was not afraid to move my knight at move eleven. I was absolutely confident that the program would not have the conceptual ability to mount such an attack. In the auditorium however, Hans Berliner was telling the audience that the program had the advantage at this stage (before B-R6) - a statement which may have been true in a human v human game but which was certainly not true in a computer program v human encounter.

18 ...   Q-N3ch

19 K-R1   Q-Q5!

It is this manoeuvre which refutes White's 18th move. The exchange of queens leads to an ending in which the weaknesses in the program's pawn structure must ultimately prove fatal.

20 Q×Q   B×Q

21 R-B3

If 21 B×R B×N 22 B-R6 B×R 23 R×B P×P 24 P×P B×P, winning a pawn. CHESS 4.5 would certainly have seen this variation and rejected it.

21 ...   B-N2

22 B×B   K×B

23 R-QN1   N-N3

24 R(3)-B1

Aimless play. In this type of position it is essential to have some sort of plan.

24 ...   KR-QN1

25 QR-Q1   P-B3

Possibly not necessary, but I wanted to avoid any tactical possibilities at a later stage which might involve P-K5 or P-B6ch by White.

28	...	R-QB1
29	R-Q3	R-B4
30	R-N3	R(1)-QB1
31	R(1)-B3	P-R5
32	P-R4	

26 P-QR4?

This move was based on the analysis of 419,165 positions and a look-ahead which extended to 22 half-moves. The program thought at this point that it had an advantage equivalent to roughly half a pawn, but in fact the text makes the win very easy for Black. Were it not for this move, or some other equally weak response from the program, it would have taken many moves to exploit White's weaknesses.

26	...	P-QR4
27	P-N5	BP×P
28	RP×P	

28 B×P B×B P×B R-QB1 would not be very much different from the game continuation. Now White thought that it was seven-eighths of a pawn ahead!

CHESS 4.5 still thought that it was ahead (by half a pawn).

32	....	P-R6
33	P×P	

But now it realized that the truth was somewhat different and it printed out an evaluation of three-quarters of a pawn in Black's favour.

33	...	P×P
34	R-K3	B-K3
35	P-R5	P-N4
36	N-Q5	P-R7
37	R-QR3	B×N
38	P×B	R×BP
39	B-Q1	R-Q7
40	K-R2	R-B8
41	B-N3	P-R8=Q
42	R×Q	R×R
43	R-K3	

At this point the programmers decided to resign for their program.

After this game David Slate and Larry Atkin said that they thought it unlikely that they would challenge me again until August 1978 because they realized that their program needed a substantial improvement before it would have a chance of victory. But CHESS 4.5 is not the only strong program in the world. Since KAISSA had finished first at the 1974 World Computer Championships, Donald Michie, who had taken the role of leader of the consortium who had bet against me, thought that a match between myself and KAISSA would be worthwhile, particularly in view of the fact that at the second World Championship in Toronto, KAISSA would be running on an IBM machine, rather than the slower ICL computer used in 1974, and there was the additional possibility that an Amdahl computer might be available. A match was set up for Toronto, a few days after the end of the World Championship, but it proved impossible to get the program working on an Amdahl computer in time for the match. A postponement of a few days was agreed, and I set up a board and clock in my motel room in Columbus, Ohio, from where I was communicating with Toronto by telephone and Donald Michie waited anxiously for something to happen on the Amdahl 470 V/6 in Sunnyvale, California. Again nothing happened. Finally, after a 29 hour journey that involved a sandstorm and a broken aircraft engine, I arrived in Montreal one cold afternoon in December 1977 to play against KAISSA from a room at McGill University. The match had been set up by Monty Newborn and this time all systems at Sunnyvale were 'go'. As at Pittsburgh, this was scheduled as a two game match, and once again I won the toss. This time I chose white. It should be mentioned on behalf of KAISSA's programmers, Mikhail Donskoy and Vladimir Arlazarov, that the group at Sunnyvale were very green at managing KAISSA. Newborn feels they didn't know how to take full advantage of the Amdahl and consequently KAISSA was probably below top form.

White: Levy
Black: KAISSA

Montreal, December 17th 1977
English Opening (by transposition)

1   P-Q3

This move was designed to take KAISSA out of its openings book and to avoid an early clash of forces. I was following my dictum of doing nothing but doing it well, and waiting for the program to dig its own grave.

1	...	N-QB3
2	P-QB4	P-K4
3	P-KN3	B-B4

Already an inaccurate move. The bishop has no real future on the QR2-KN8 diagonal since White can blunt its attack by P-K3.

4	B-N2	N-B3
5	N-QB3	O-O
6	P-K3	Q-K2

A pointless move that puts the queen on a bad square.

7	KN-K2	B-N3
8	O-O	P-Q3
9	P-QR3	B-N5

9 ...P-QR4 was necessary, to prevent White's next move.

| 10 | P-QN4 | Q-K3 |
| 11 | N-Q5 | B × N |

I was pleased when KAISSA made this move but could not understand why it should do so. Black's bishop is undoubtedly a better piece than my knight.

12 Q×B   N-N5

13 B-Q2

I also considered 13 B-R3 P-B4 14 P-K4, but rejected it as being unnecessarily sharp.

13 ...   QR-N1

I was threatening 14 P-B5! P×P 15 P×P B-R4 (or 15 ...B×P 16 N×P) 16 B×B N×B 17 N×P, forking Black's queen and rook.

14 P-QR4   P-QR3

Relatively best was 14 ...P-QR4 15 P-N5 N-Q1 16 N×B P×N, though White can then win a pawn by 17 B-R3 P-B4 18 P-K4 N-R3 19 B×N Q×B 20 B×BP.

15 P-R5   B-R2
16 P-N5   P×P
17 P×P   P-K5!

The best swindling try. If now 18 P×N Q×N 19 B×P, Black replies 19...Q-R4, saving the piece. Best was 18 P×P N(B3)-K4 19 P-N6, but who makes the best moves after a 29

hour journey? In any case, the move that I chose was quite sufficient.

18 P×N   Q×N
19 Q×N   Q×QP
20 KR-Q1   P-B4
21 Q-N5   P×P
22 B-KB1   Q-N6
23 R(Q1)-B1   P-R3
24 Q-N6

24 ...   Q-N2

Forced. Black must guard against 25 R×P and 25 B-B4ch forking king and queen. If 24...R-B3 25 Q×R! P×Q 26 B-B4ch Q×B 27 R×Q.

25 P-R6   Q-B1

On 25...Q-R1 I had planned 26 B-B4ch, and if 26...P-Q4 27 B×Pch! P×B 28 R×P and mate on KN7.

26 R×P   R-B3
27 Q-R5   Q-Q2
28 R(R1)-B1   B-B4
29 R(B1)×B!   P×R
30 R×R   P×R

Black's 28th move was designed to win material, but in doing so Black left its king fatally exposed. Programs still seem to be unable to judge when material is not the most important feature in a position.

31	Q-N6ch	Q-N2
32	Q × P(B5)	

At this point the game was adjudicated by Camille Coudari, a Canadian Intentional Master. White has a material advantage and numerous threats, as a result of which Black is totally lost. e.g.: (a) 33 P-R7 R-R1 34 Q-Q5ch, winning the rook; (b) 33 B-B4ch K-R1 34 B-B3 R-KB1 35 P-R7 and then 36 P-R8 = Q R × Q 37 B × P winning the queen; (c) 33 Q × KP, threatening 34 P-R7 etc. Coudari therefore adjudicated the game a *win for White*.

With the bet having only several months to run, Slate began devoting half of his working time to a new program, a complete rewrite that would be named CHESS 5.0. I had decided some time ago that I wanted to play my final match in a blaze of publicity (the deadline was the end of August 1978), and I had tried to persuade the Canadian National Exhibition to sponsor it. After various difficulties the match was finally scheduled at CNE.

About three weeks before leaving England for Toronto, I received a most unexpected challenge from Richard Greenblatt of M.I.T. Greenblatt, it will be recalled, was the author of the program MACHACK VI, which achieved fame around 1957 by finding a pretty Rook sacrifice that had been overlooked by a number of U.S. masters. Although very little news of chess had been emanating from M.I.T.'s Artificial Intelligence labs during the past decade, scientists there were known to be working on a piece of hardware designed to do nothing but analyze, generate, and evaluate chess positions at the rate of 150,000 per second!! This machine, called CHEOPS, would be used by an improved version of the Greenblatt program in the following way: whenever the main program reached a position it considered strategically satisfactory, CHEOPS would take a look at the further tactical possibilities. This enabled the program to avoid numerous traps.

I agreed to a two-game match against the Greenblatt MACHACK-CHEOPS program. Since I had wagered that I would not lose a match, I needed to score only one point in the two games. The rate of play for all my challenge matches had been agreed at forty moves in two hours followed by twenty moves per hour. Under these conditions the following game was played in Cambridge, Massachusetts, on August 23, 1978.

White: MACHACK-CHEOPS
Black: Levy

Sicilian Defence

1	P-K4	P-QB4

Since I knew nothing about this program's style or openings repertoire, I thought it best to play something with which I was reasonably familiar rather than try to confuse the program from the outset.

2	N-KB3	P-Q3
3	P-Q4	P × P

4 N×P N-KB3
5 N-QB3 P-KN3
6 P-B4

I began to smell a rat. I knew that U.S. international masters Ken Rogoff and Norman Weinstein had visited M.I.T. a few days earlier, and I was worried that one of them might have busted a line in my book on the Dragon Sicilian. But now it was too late to turn back.

6 ... B-N2!

This move, which used to be considered a grave error, is probably Black's best reply.

7 P-K5 N-R4
8 B-N5 ch

Not 8 P-KN4?? N×P 9 B×N P×P winning a pawn.

8 ... B-Q2
9 P-K6 P×P
10 N×P B×N ch
11 P×B

Thus far both sides have been following a well-known path which used to be thought very good for White.

11 ... Q-B1!

A relatively new idea, maintaining threats against QB6, QN4, and K3, which I think rehabilitates 6 ...B-N2. During the game, however, I could not help worrying that the program was about to unleash a crushing innovation, courtesy of Rogoff or Weinstein. All of my opponent's moves thus far had been played without hesitation. But now it "thought" for a couple of minutes, so I knew that my earlier fears were unfounded. I learned later that the opening book had been prepared by Ken Church, one of Greenblatt's research students, and he had not even used my book!

12 Q-Q4 N-KB3
13 Q-B4 N-B3
14 N-Q4 N×N

Exchanging into a slightly favourable end-game.

15 P×N

If 15 B×B ch Q×B 16 P×N (or 16 Q×N Q-K3 ch and White's King is the more exposed) 16 ...R-QB1 with a good game for Black.

15 ... Q×Q
16 B×Q B-B4!

More accurate than 16 ...R-QB1 17 B-Q3 when it is not clear that Black has any advantage.

17 B-N5 ch

To stop me from castling; not that I would want to.

17 ... K-B2
18 B-B4 ch P-Q4
19 B-Q3!

Excellent judgement. After 19 B-N3 the bishop would be badly placed and Black would pile up on the QB-pawn without worrying about counterplay along the QN-file. Black can capture on Q3 at once, saddling White with doubled, isolated pawns, but in fact this would leave Black's knight without a really good square.

19	...	KR-QB1
20	O-O	

I was told after the game that the strategic part of the program wanted to trade bishops on KB5, but CHE-OPS realized that this would leave the QB-pawn indefensible. When the program castled, the audience, who had been following this thought process, let out a cheer. I was happy because the text move shows that the program did not understand what was going to happen. The King is needed in the middle to protect the QB2/Q3 structure.

20	...	R-B2
21	R-N1	QR-QB1
22	B-K3?!	N-K5
23	R-B3	

White's rather aimless play here-abouts is reminiscent of the way CHESS 4.6 played against me in Pittsburgh.

23	...	N-Q3
24	R-N2	P-N3

25	P-QR4	B×B

Now that my pieces are on their best square and the QN-pawn is protected it is time to cash in on the weaknesses of White's pawn structure.

26	P×B	R-B6
27	R-R3	P-KR4
28	B-Q2	R-B7
29	R×R	R×R
30	B-K1	N-B4
31	P-R5	P×P
32	B×P	N×P
33	R-K3	R-R7
34	B-B7	P-R4

Outside passed pawns seem aw-fully strong against chess programs (CHESS 4.6 v. Levy, *Chess Life and Review*, June 1977).

35	R-K1	P-QR5
36	B-K5	N-B3
37	B-R8	P-R6
38	R-Q1	R-QB7
39	B-R1	P-R7
40	P-R3	N-R4
41	P-Q4	N-N6
42	P-B5	R-B8
43	R×R	

Greenblatt resigned for his program because of 43 ...N×R, 44 ...N-N6, etc.

Greenblatt asked me to play the second game at 30-30 speed, and I agreed. It was a dull game, in which I outplayed the program in a Rook ending only to reach a position in which my extra pawn might not have been enough to win against best play, but MACHACK, after very cleverly seeing a number of tricks, went completely wrong and lost.

The Main Event
The final match to decide the bet began on August 26 at the Canadian National Exhibition in Toronto. CHESS 5.0 was not ready in time, so I·played its predecessor, CHESS 4.7. I was seated in an almost soundproof booth, wearing a tuxedo. The program was represented by David Slate (his

partner was vacationing in England), David Cahlander, and John Douglas, the latter two of Control Data Corporation. Cahlander had built a special chessboard with a switch beneath each square to enable the program to detect its opponents' moves. The switches are activated by magnets in the bases of the chess pieces. This board also indicates the program's moves automatically, by lighting up the departure and arrival squares as well as the other squares along the moving piece's path. Soon a robot will move the pieces for the program and punch the clock button.

The Toronto match was scheduled for six games. I therefore needed three points to collect my wager; my opponent needed three and a half to make me famous.

The notes to the five games of the Toronto match are by CHESS 4.7 and myself. The first line of each note contains four items of information: (1) The program's assessment of its position, expressed in pawns (thus, after 3...N-KB3 in game 1, CHESS 4.7 considered itself to be 0.13 of a pawn behind); (2) In parentheses, the number of positions evaluated when considering this move; the number of seconds taken by the program over its move; and the number of iterations performed by the program's search process (this is the depth, in ply, of the exhaustive part of the search).

The second line of annotation is the program's predicted continuation, i.e., its opinion of the best line of play for both sides.

In some positions I have added a note of my own, and this always follows the program's comments.

GAME 1
White: Levy
Black: CHESS 4.7
                    Reversed Pirc
1 **P-KN3**   **P-Q4 (book)**
2 **B-N2**   **P-K4 (book)**
3 **P-Q3**   **N-KB3**
-0.13 (230,531; 76; 6)
4 N-QB3 B-QB4 5 N-R4 N-R3 6
B-Q2
4 **N-KB3**   **N-B3**
-0.15 (208,660; 69; 6)
5 P-Q4 P×P 6 N×P B-N5 7
N×N P×N
5 **O-O**   **B-Q2**
-0.13 (339,183; 118; 6)
6 B-Q2 B-QB4
6 **P-N3**   **B-QB4**

-0.20 (281,184; 96; 6)
7 N-B3 P-Q5 8 N-QR4 B-QN5 9
N-N5
7 **B-N2**   **Q-K2**
-0.26 (384,803; 129; 6)
8 N-B3 O-O 9 N-QN5
8 **P-QR3**   **P-K5**
-0.43 (346,157; 116; 6)
9 P×P P×P 10 KN-Q2 O-O 11
N×P N×N 12 B×N Q×B 13
Q×B Q×BP
9 **N-K1**   **O-O**
-0.54 (557,445; 195; 6)
10 P×P P×P 11 P-QN4 B-N3 12
N-Q2
10 **P-Q4**   **B-Q3**
-0.56 (207,493; 67; 6)
11 N-QB3 P-QR3 12 P-B4 K-R1

11 P-K3

Before you all rush off letters complaining about my opening play, permit me to point out that when faced with a strong computer program I try to play the opponent, not the position. It was my plan to create a situation in which nothing was happening and then to expand gradually on the Queenside. Unfortunately, the program had read my article in the June 1977 *Chess Life and Review* and found out how to attack on the Kingside.

11 ...   N-KN5!
-0.55 (677,730; 264; 6)
12 P-R3 N-B3 13 N-QB3 P-QR3 14 P-B4

12 P-R3??

12 P-QB4 must be played but even then 12 ...Q-N4 is strong. I completely overlooked Black's 13th move.

12 ...   N × KP!!
-0.62 (1,508,192; 509; 8)
13 P × N Q-N4 14 Q-K2 Q × P 15 N-QB3 Q-R7ch 16 K-B2

The program replied instantly, indicating that it had expected 12 P-R3 and had already worked out its reply while I was thinking!

13 P × N   Q-N4
-0.62 (189,389; 66; 6)
14 Q-K2 Q × P 15 N-QB3 Q-R7 ch 16 K-B2

14 P-KN4

Realizing that I was completely busted, I thought my only hope was to sacrifice the Exchange to get the queens off.

14 ...   Q × P ch
-1.43 (196,923; 67; 6)

15 K-R1 Q-N6 16 K-N1 Q-R7 ch 17 K-B2

15 R-B2   B-N6
-2.31 (264,087; 78; 6)
16 Q-Q2 B × Rch 17 Q × R Q × Q ch 18 K × Q

16 Q-K2   Q × R ch
-2.47 (328,495; 89, 7)
17 Q × Q B × Qch 18 K × Q P-B4 19 P × P B × P

Of course it would be crushing to take with the bishop and keep the queens on so that my king would die of exposure, but the program knows that it should trade down when materially ahead.

17 Q × Q   B × Q ch
-2.47 (325,505; 85; 8)
18 K × Q P-B4 19 P × P

18 K × B   P-B4!
-2.45 (275,094; 80; 7)
19 P × P B × P 20 K-K3 B-Q2 21 N-Q2 QR-K1

19 P × P   N-K2
-2.46 (419,456; 125; 7)
20 K-N1 N × P 21 N-QB3 B-B3 22 R-B1 N-K6

20 P-B4   R × P ch
-2.34 (292,433; 84; 7)
21 K-N1 P-B3 22 B-QB1 QR-KB1 23 B-K3 R/4-B3

21 K-N1   P-B3
-2.23 (504,277; 153; 7)
22 P-QR4 N-N3 23 N-QB3 N-R5 24 B-R3 R-K1

22 N-QB3   R-R4
-2.24 (1,024,267; 315; 7)
23 N-K2 N-N3 24 K-R2 N-R5 25 N-N3 R-N4

23 K-R2   R-KB1
-2.20 (586,076; 177; 7)
24 B-QB1 N-B4 25 P × P P × P 26

N × QP N × P
24 N-Q1   **N-N3**
-2.67 (560,787; 167; 7)
25 R-B1 N-B5 26 R-B3 P × P 27
B × P P × P 28 R × P R × P ch 29
R × R B × R
25 R-B1   **B × P!**

-3.11 (574,126; 166; 7)
26 B × B R-B8 27 N-K3 R-B7 ch
28 N-N2 R × N ch
I had seen this coming but was
powerless to prevent it.
26 B × B   **R-B8**
-2.53 (1,091,773; 279; 8)
27 N-K3 R-B7ch 28 K-N1 R × B
29 B-K6ch K-R1 30 P × P R × NP 31
P × P R × N 32 P × P
27 N-N2   **R-B6**
-3.33 (956,766; 239; 8)
28 K-N1 R/4 × B 29 P × P P × P 30
R-B5 N-K2 31 R-B7
28 P × P   **R/4 × B ch**
-3.22 (1,030,153; 245; 8)
29 K-N1 P × P 30 R-B5 N-K2 31
R-B7 N-B3 32 N-B2
29 K-N1   **P × P**
-3.20 (338,469; 94; 8)
30 R-B8 ch R-B1 31 R × R ch

K × R 32 N/1-K3 N-K2 33 K-B2
30 R-B8 ch   **N-B1?**
-3.06 (1,293,137; 366; 9)
31 N-B3 R-Q6 32 N-B4 R/Q-N6
ch 33 N-N2 R-N4 34 R-B7 R/6-N6
31 B-B3   **R-Q6**
-4.71 (578,439; 145; 8)
32 N/1-K3 R/R × N 33 N × R
R × N 34 K-B2 R-B6 ch 35 K-K2
32 N/1-K3   **R/R × N**
-4.74 (462,088; 121; 9)
33 N × R R × N 34 B-N4 R-N6 ch
35 K-B2
33 N × R   **R × N**
-3.55 (516,744; 135; 9)
34 B-N4 R-KB6 35 R-Q8
34 B-N4
My first threat of the game, but I
was not too happy about being three
pawns down.
34 ...   **R-KB6**
-3.47 (487,332; 137; 8)
35 R-Q8 P-KR3 36 B × N R × B 37
R × P P-KN4 38 R-Q7
35 R-Q8   **P-KR3**
-3.47 (708,097; 195; 8)
36 B × N R × B 37 R × P P-KN4 38
R-K5 R-B5 39 R-K7
The program no doubt saw that
35 ... R-B4 36 B × N R × B 37
R × P would be followed by the win
of the K-pawn or the QN-pawn and
probably did not analyse past that
point.
36 R × P   **R × P**
-4.30 (758,637; 202; 8)
37 R-QR5 P-R3 38 R-K5 P-K6 39
R-K7 R-Q6 40 K-N2 R × QP 41
R × KP
37 R-Q8   **R-KB6**
-3.12 (1,682,751; 473; 9)
38 R-K8 R-B5 39 K-N2 P-KN4 40

P-Q5 P-KR4 41 B×N R×B 42
R×P
38 R-R8   P-KN4
-3.32 (732,704; 204; 8)
39 R-K8 P-K6 40 P-Q5 P-KR4 41
B×N R×B 42 R×P
39 P-Q5   P-KR4
-3.25 (571,760; 159; 8)
40 R×P R-B4 41 R-R8 K-N2 42
R-K8 N-R2 43 R×P R×P
40 P-Q6   K-N2
-3.31 (501,877; 138; 8)
41 R×P R-B2 42 B-B3 ch K-N3
41 R×P   R-B2
-2.47 (677,184; 182; 9)
42 R-R5 K-N3 43 R-K5 R-B5 44
R-N5 P-N3 45 R×P N-Q2
42 R-R5
Suddenly the position is no longer
totally hopeless - it is merely
hopeless.
42 ...   K-B3
-2.24 (1,312,720; 363; 9)
43 K-B2 P-N3 44 R-N5 K-K3 45
K-K3 R-B4 46 R×P N-Q2
43 B-B3 ch   K-N3
-2.53 (667,411; 183; 9)
44 R-K5 R-B5 45 R-N5 R-B6
44 R-K5   R-B6
-2.47 (1,568,177; 429; 9)
45 B-N4 R-B5
45 B-N4   R-B5
-1.55 (672,852; 184; 8)
46 R-K7 R-N5 ch 47 K-B2 N-R2
48 R×NP N-B3 49 B-B3
46 R-K7   R-B2
-1.20 (781,421; 217; 8)
47 R×KP N-Q2 48 R-K7 P-R5 49
K-N2 P-N5 50 B-B3
47 R×KP   R-Q2
-1.23 (579,012; 157; 8)
48 K-N2 P-R5

48 R-K7   P-R5
-1.33 (754,845; 201; 9)
49 K-N2 P-N5 50 B-B5 K-B4 51
B-N4 P-N3 52 P-R4 K-N4
49 K-N2   P-N5
-1.34 (357,150; 99; 8)
50 K-R2 P-N3 51 P-R4 K-B4 52
B-B3 P-N6 ch 53 K-R3 R×P 54
K×P
50 K-R2?!
50 B-B5 would have prevented ... P-N3.
50 ...   P-N3
-1.31 (468,777; 129; 8)
51 K-N2 R-Q1 52 B-K1 P-R6 53
K-N3 R×P 54 K×P
51 K-N2   R-Q1
-1.31 (536,589; 148; 8)
52 K-R2 K-N4 53 B-Q2 ch K-B4
54 B-B3 N-Q2 55 K-N2
Help! Black is beginning to untan-
gle his pieces.
52 P-R4   N-Q2
-1.45 (875,466; 246; 8)
53 B-B3 N-B4 54 R-N7 ch K-B4
55 R-B7 ch K-K3 56 R-B4
53 P-R5   N-B3
-1.63 (929,565; 244; 9)
54 P×P N-Q4 55 B-K1 N×R 56
P×N P-R6 ch 57 K-N3 R-K1
I was expecting 53 ...P×P 54
B×P R-QR1 and hoping that 55 B-
B3 might hold.
54 P×P
Material equality at last. Now I
thought I had a draw: if my opponent made one more mistake, then
maybe ...
54 ...   N-Q4
-1.61 (900,747; 234; 9)
55 B-K1 N×R 56 P×N P-R6 ch
57 K-N3 R-K1 58 P-N7 K-B4

55 P-N7!

At this point in the proceedings the computer got sick and the doctors were called. Twenty-five minutes later, with the program still having plenty of time on its clock, it played

55 ...   N×R

-1.54 (491,772; 125; 8)

56 P×N R-K1 57 B-Q6 K-B2 58 P-N8 = R R×R 59 B×R K×P

A brilliant decision. 55 ... N×B does nothing for Black, if only because of something like 56 R-K4 N-B3 57 R×P ch K-R4 58 R-QB4. Also 55 ... N-B5 ch 56 K-R1 looks good for White. CHESS 4.7 had probably found the only way for Black to draw!

56 P×N   R-KR1!

+0.03 (242,230; 58; 8)

57 B B3 P-R6 ch 58 K-N3 R-K1 59 B-R5 K-B4

On 56 ... R-K1 57 B-R5 wins.

57 B-Q6   K-B3

-1.30 (294,755; 71; 9)

58 K-R2 K-K3 59 P-N8 = Q R×Q

58 P-N8 = Q   R×Q

-0.75 (397,940; 89; 11)

59 B×R K×P 60 B-B7 K-B2 61 B-Q8 P-R6 ch 62 K-N3 K-N6 63 K×P P-R7

59 B×R   K×P

-0.53 (383,817; 77; 12)

60 B-B7 K-B2 61 B-Q8 P-R6 ch 62 K-N3 K-N3 63 B-B7 K-N4

60 B-B4   K-B3

-0.57 (378,895; 76; 12)

61 B-Q6 K-B4 62 B-K7 P-R6 ch 63 K-N3 K-N3 64 B-Q6 K-N4

61 B-Q2   K-N3

-0.55 (549,063; 110; 12)

62 B N4 K-N4 63 B-K7 ch K-R4 64 B-B6 P-R6 ch 65 K-N3

62 B-K1   K-N4

-0.53 (531,415; 106; 12)

63 K-R2 K-R4 64 B-N4 K-N3 65 B-K7 P-R6 ch

63 B-B2   K-R4

-0.47 (551,712; 111; 13)

64 K-R2 P-R6 65 B-N3 K-N3 66 B-B7 K-B4 67 K-N3 K-N4 68 B-N8 P-R7

64 B-K1

And David Slate offered me a draw on behalf of his program.

A remarkable game, and the first time a computer program has ever drawn with an international master under tournament conditions. Before the match David Slate had had some doubts as to whether his program was ready for me, but this game removed them.

The next day saw game two of the match, in which the program was faced with more difficult problems from an early stage.

GAME 2
White: CHESS 4.7
Black: Levy

Sicilian Defence

1 N-QB3(book)   P-QB4
2 P-K4(book)   N-QB3

3 P-B4(book)   P-QR3 +

To take the program out of the book. I have played this system as White several times and would not feel comfortable on the other side.

4 N-B3

David Cahlander and David Levy relaxing before a game.

+0.27 (534,448; 176; 7)

4   ...   P-Q3 5 B-B4 N-R4 6 B-K2 B-Q2 7 O-O

4 ...   P-KN3

5 P-Q4

+0.40 (536,940; 177; 7)

5   ...   P×P 6 N×P B-N2 7 B-K3 P-Q3 8 B-K2

5 ...   P×P

6 N×P

+0.42 (285,587; 92; 7)

6   ...   B-N2 7 B-K3 N-R3 8 B-K2 O-O 9 O-O

6 ...   B-N2

7 B-K3

+0.36 (454,059; 146; 7)

7   ...   P-K4 8 N×N NP×N 9 B-B4 P×P 10 B×BP

7 ...   P-Q3

8 N×N?

+0.31 (222,023; 69; 6)

8   ...   P×N 9 B-K2 R-N1 10 B-Q4 P-K4

After making this strategic error against my Sicilian last year, the program was altered in an attempt to prevent it from exchanging in similar situations. Some of the factors causing this exchange were eradicated, but apparently not enough of them.

8 ...   P×N

9 B-K2

+0.10 (360,727; 115; 6)

9   ...   R-N1 10 Q-B1 N-B3 11 B-Q4 P-B4

9 ...   R-N1

10 Q-B1

+0.04 (1,185,859; 395; 7)

10   ...   B×N ch 11 P×B Q-R4 12 B-Q2 N-B3 13 P-B4

10 ...   Q-R4

11   B-Q2
+0.14 (239,111; 82; 6)
11   ...   Q-N5   12   R-QN1   N-B3
13   P-K5   P × P   14   P × P
11   ...   Q-N3
12   N-R4
+0.14 (267,191; 89; 6)
12   ...   Q-N2   13   R-QN1   N-B3
14   B-B3   O-O
12   ...   Q-R2
13   N-B3
+0.01 (271,911; 89; 6)
13   ...   B-Q5   14   N-Q1   N-B3
15   P-B3   B-B4
13   ...   B Q5
14   N-Q1
-0.10 (732,542; 246; 7)
14   ...   N-B3   15   P-B3   B-N3   16
Q-B2   B-N5   17   B × B   N × B
14   ...   N-B3
15   P-B3
-0.10 (524,256; 168; 7)
15   ...   B-N3   16   Q-B2   B-Q2   17
P-B5   P × P   18   P × P
15   ...   B-N3
16   Q-B2
-0.20 (1,444,961; 497; 7)
16   ...   B-N5   17   B × B   N × B   18
P-KR3   N-B7   19   N × N   B × N   ch   20
K-K2
16   ...   N-N5
17   Q-R4
0.00 (262,998; 90; 6)
17   ...   Q-N2   18   P-QR3   N-B3   19
P-K5   P × P   20   P × P
17   ...   O-O
18   B × N
+0.03 (1,082,139; 357; 7)
18   ...   B × N   19   Q × BP   B-N8
20   P-N4   QR-B1   21   Q-Q5
If   18   Q × BP   N-B7 exchanging
knights   and   then   bishops,   and

White's exposed king must cost him
the game.
18   ...   B × B
19   Q × BP
-0.23 (617,331; 202; 7)
19   ...   B-N8   20   P-N4   B-R7   21
N-B2   B-Q2   22   Q-Q5
19   ...   B × N
20   K × B
+0.37 (286,488; 85; 7)
20   ...   B-K6   21   P-QN4   KR-B1
22   Q-Q5   R-N4   23   Q-N3
20   R × B   B-K6 is equally horrible
for White.
20   ...   B K6
21   P-QN3
+0.33 (520,425; 157; 7)
21   ...   B × B   22   K × B   KR-B1
23   Q-R4   Q-B7 ch   24   K-Q3
21   ...   B × B
22   K × B
-0.43 (949,692; 253; 8)
22   ...   KR-B1   23   Q-R4   Q-B7 ch
24   K-Q3   Q × NP   25   QR-KB1   R-R1
22   ...   QR-B1
23   Q-R4
-0.60 (849,366; 233; 8)
23   ...   Q-B7   ch   24   K-Q3
Q × NP   25   P-B4   Q-B6 ch   26   K-Q4   P-
B4
23   ...   Q-B7 ch
24   K-Q3
-1.16 (783,833; 227; 8)
24   ...   Q × NP   25   Q-Q4   Q-B6
ch   26   K-B2   Q × P   27   QR-KB1   Q-N4
24   ...   Q × NP
25   Q-Q4
-1.17 (360,866; 111; 7)
25   ...   Q-B6 ch   26   K-B2   Q-K7
ch   27   K-N1   Q-N7   28   R-N1   Q × P
25   ...   Q-B6 ch
26   K-B2

-1.27 (1,952;740; 571; 9)

26 ... Q-K7 ch 27 K-B1 P-B4
28 P×P R×BP 29 Q-Q2 Q×Q ch
30 K×Q R×KBP

26 ...   Q-K7 ch
27 K-B1

-1.27 (422,483; 130; 7)

27 ... P-B4 28 P×P R×P 29
Q-Q2 Q×Q ch 30 K×Q R×KBP

27 ...   P-K4
28 P×P

-0.46 (448,407; 128; 8)

28 ... P×P 29 Q×P KR-K1 30
Q-QR5 R×P 31 P-B4 Q-N7

28 ...   P×P
29 Q×P

-1.02 (882,932; 263; 8)

29 ... KR-Q1 30 Q-B4 R-Q6
31 Q-K5 KR-Q1 32 Q-QR5 Q×KP

29 ...   KR-K1
30 Q-N3

-0.57 (371,857; 104; 7)

30 ... R×P 31 Q-R3 P-B4 32
P-B4 QR-K1 33 K-N1

30 ...   R×P
31 Q-R3

-2.21 (306,863; 89; 7)

31 ... P-B4 32 K-N1 R-K6 33
Q-R4 R/K×P 34 R-K1

31 ...   R-Q1
32 Q-B1

-7.25 (518,359; 135; 8)

32 ... Q-K6 ch 33 K-N1 R-Q7
34 R-N1 Q×P 35 R×P ch RP×R
36 Q×P R×KRP

32 ...   Q-Q7 ch
33 K-N1

-0.72 (142; 0; 2)

33 ... P-B4

33 ...   R-K7
34 Q×R

-20.21 (477,123; 127; 8)

34 ... Q×Q 35 R-K1 Q×R ch
36 K-N2 R-Q7 ch 37 K-R3 Q×R

34 ...   Q×Q
35 R-K1!

-21.71 (658,057; 146; 9)

35 ... Q×R ch 36 K-N2 R-Q7
ch 37 K-R3 Q×R 38 K-N4 R×KRP
39 P-R3

Otherwise it is mate in four.

35 ...   Q×R ch
36 K-N2

-23.54 (624,008; 133; 9)

36 ... R-Q7 ch 37 K-R3 Q-K4
38 P-N4 Q×P ch 39 K-R4 Q×R 40
P-R3 R×P

36 ...   R-Q7 ch
37 K-R3

-20.21 (80; 0; 2)

37 ... Q×R

37 ...   Q×R

The remaining seventeen moves
are of no interest. In all fairness to
the program, I should say that it
occasionally saw ways I could have
forced mate which I myself did not
see.

38 K-N4

mate in 7 (934,994; 239; 8)

38 ... Q-K8 39 K-R4 Q-K1 40

K-R3 Q-K4 41 P-N4

38 ...   **P-R4 ch**
39 K-B4
mate in 6 (1,341,883; 344; 8)
39 ... Q-K8 40 P-N4 Q-K7 ch
'39 ...   Q-B8 ch
40 K-B5
-21.66 (52; 0; 2)
40 ... R×KRP
40 ...   **Q-B4 ch**
41 K-B6

mate in 5 (91,249; 24; 6)
41 ... Q-K3 ch 42 K-N5 Q-K4
ch 43 K-R6 R-Q3 ch 44 K-R7 Q-K2
ch 45 K-R8 R-Q8 mate
41 ...   **Q-B1 ch**
42 K-N6
mate in 4 (5,205; 1; 4)
42 ... R-Q3 ch 43 K-N5 Q-B3
ch 44 K×P Q-B4 ch 45 K-R4 R-R3
mate

42 ...   **R-Q3 ch**
43 K-N5
mate in 3 (7,168; 2; 4)
43 ... Q-B3 ch 44 K×P Q-B4
ch 45 K-R4 R-R3 mate
43 ...   **Q-N2 ch**
44 K-R4
mate in 4 (743,709; 190; 8)
44 ... Q-B3 ch 45 K-R3 Q×P
46 P-R3 R-Q7 47 P-R4 Q-N5 mate

44 ...   **R-Q7**
45 P-N4
mate in 4 (1,033,390; 268; 8)
45 ... R×P ch 46 K-N3 Q-Q4
ch 47 P-B4 Q-Q7 48 P×P
45 ...   **R×P ch**
46 K-N3
mate in 3 (23; 0; 2)
46 ... R×P

46 ...   **Q-Q4 ch**
47 P-B4
mate in 2 (144; 0; 2)
47 ... Q-Q7 48 P×P Q×QRP
47 ...   **P-R5 ch**
48 K×R
mate in 3 (9,983; 2; 6)
48 ... Q-Q7 ch 49 K-R1 P-R6
50 P-R3 Q-N7 mate
48 ...   **Q×P ch**
49 K-N2
mate in 5 (502,918; 107; 9)
49 ... Q-Q6 50 K-B1 P-R6 51
P-N5 Q-K7 52 P-R3 P-R7 53 P-N6
P-R8=Q mate
49 ...   **Q-N6 ch**
50 K-B1
mate in 5 (418,175; 90; 9)
50 ... Q-R7 51 K-Q1 Q×P 52
K-B1 P-R6 53 K-Q1 P-R7 54 K-B1
P-R8-Q mate
50 ...   **P-R6**
51 K-Q2
mate in 4 (285,700; 65; 8)
51 ... P-R7 52 K-K2 P-R8=Q
53 P-R3 Q-KN8 54 K-Q2 Q/8-Q8
mate
51 ...   **P-R7**
52 K-K2
mate in 3 (62,883; 15; 6)
52 ... P-R8=Q 53 P-R3 Q-
KN8 54 K-Q2 Q/8-Q8 mate
52 ...   **P-R8=Q**
53 K-B2
mate in 2 (31,274; 8; 4)
53 ... Q/8-Q8 54 P-R4
53 ...   **Q/8-R7 ch**
54 K-K1
mate in 1 (266; 0; 2)
54 ... Q/6-N8 mate
54 ...   **Q/6-N8 mate**

After the second game there was a five-day break before hostilities resumed. In game three my do-nothing-but-do-it-well strategy scored another convincing victory.

GAME 3
White: Levy
Black: CHESS 4.7
English Opening

1   P-QB4   N-KB3
                  (book)
2   P-QR3
Out of the book again.
2   ...   N-B3
-0.22 (331,999; 112; 7)
3 N-KB3 P-Q4 4 P×P N×P 5 P-K4 N-B5
3   N-QB3   P-Q4
-0.24 (380,122; 126; 7)
4 P×P N×P 5 N-B3 B-B4 6 P-Q4 P-K3
4   P×P   N×P
-0.22 (184,293; 58; 7)
5 P-Q4 P-K4 6 P×P N×N 7 Q×Q ch K×Q 8 P×N N×P
5   P-Q3
To encourage
5   ...   N×N
-0.35 (330,662; 96; 7)
6 P×N P-K4 7 N-B3 B-K2 8 R-QN1 0-0
... as in game two.
6   P×N   P-K4
-0.26 (217,302; 71; 7)
7 N-B3 B-K2 8 P-K4 B-KN5 9 B-K3 0-0
7   P-N3   B-K2
-0.30 (305,903; 102; 6)
8 B-N2 B-KN5 9 R-N1 Q-B1 10 B×N ch P×B
8   B-N2   Q-Q3
-0.20 (405,822; 137; 6)

9 Q-N3 O-O 10 B-K3 K-R1 11 B-K4
9   N-B3   B-K3
-0.21 (630,434; 215; 6)
10 N-N5 O-O 11 O-O
10 O-O   O-O
-0.16 (432,068; 147; 6)
11 B-Q2 P-B4 12 Q-N1 QR-N1 13 N-N5 B×N 14 B×B
11 Q-R4
Intending to put pressure on the QNP with KR-N1
11 ...   Q-B4
-0.23 (418,702; 145; 6)
12 B-Q2 P-QN4 13 Q-B2 P-B3 14 B-K3
12 B-Q2   P-QN4?
-0.15 (808, 838; 275; 6)
13 Q-B2 P-B3 14 P-K4 N-Q4 15 N×N P×N
A typical program failing; it weakens its pawn structure without sufficient provocation.

13 Q-B2   P-B3
-0.04 (753,664; 249; 7)

14 B-K3 Q-Q3 15 P-QR4 P-N5 16
N-Q2 P-QR4 17 P×P N×P
14 KR-N1   QR-Q1
-0.24 (572,717; 198; 6)
15 R-KB1 P-QR4 16 K-R1 Q-N3
17 P-B4
15 Q-N2
Not 15 B-K3 N-Q5! 16 Q-N2
Q×BP!
15 ...   R-N1
-0.23 (252,760; 79; 6)
16 B-K3 Q-Q3 17 N-Q2 P-QR3
18 N-K4
16 B-K3   Q-Q3
-0.24 (522,533; 175; 7)
17 Q-B2 P-QR4 18 R-KB1 P-B4
19 N-N5 P-B5 20 N×B Q×N
17 N-Q2
Intending N-N3 or N-K4, followed by N-B5 or B-B5.
17 ...   B-Q4
-0.23 (204,311; 62; 6)
18 N-K4 Q-Q1 19 N-B5 P-B4 20
N-K6 B×N 21 B×N
18 B×B ch   Q×B
-0.14 (568,218; 175; 8)
19 Q-B2 P-QR3 20 P-QR4 P-B4
21 P-QB4 P×BP 22 Q×P
19 Q-N3
The program can analyse far more
deeply in the ending than in the
middlegame because there are fewer
pieces on the board and also fewer
possible moves. For this reason I
usually try to avoid the endgame
until the program has compromised
its position - which it has done here.
I felt that Black's poor pawn structure would soon prove fatal.
19 ...   Q×Q
-0.26 (246,373; 73; 8)
20 N×Q P-B4 21 R-KB1 P-QR4

22 P-B3 P-R5 23 N-Q2
20 N×Q   P-B4
-0.21 (254,511; 76; 7)
21 P-QR4 P-QR5 22 P×P R×P
23 N-Q2 R×R ch 24 R×R
21 B-B5   B-Q3!
-0.21 (336,741; 99; 7)
22 K-R1 P-QR4 23 B×B P×B 24
N-Q2 P-Q4
The exchange on B4 would permit
White's knight to enter the game
with great effect.
22 R-N2   K-R1
-0.26 (760,764; 232; 7)
23 QR-N1 P-QR3 24 P-K4 P×P
25 P×P B×B 26 N×B
When it does not know what else
to do the program puts its king "into
safety". CHESS 4.7 is aware that
the king should be nearer the corner
in the middlegame and centralised
in the endgames. I suppose the
threshold between middle- and endgame is not sufficiently defined - the
program thinks it is still in the
middlegame.
23 QR-N1   P-QR3
-0.27 (424,892; 126; 7)
24 P-B3 P-B5 25 K-R1 N-K2 26 P-
N4 B×B 27 N×B
24 B×B   P×B
-0.33 (228,547; 67; 7)
25 N-Q2 P-B5 26 P-B4 N-Q5 27 P-
K4 P×NP 28 RP×P
25 N-Q2   P-B5
-0.26 (332,840; 100; 7)
26 P-K4 P×P e.p. 27 P×P P-Q4
28 R-KB1 N-K2 29 R×R ch R×R
26 K-N2   P×P
-0.27 (706,961; 211; 7)
27 RP×P QR-Q1 28 P-QB4 P×P
29 N×P P-Q4 30 R-N6 R-B1

27   RP × P   QR-Q1
-0.13 (697,027; 202; 7)
28 P-QB4 P × P 29 N × P P-Q4 30 R-N6 R-B1
28   P-R4!   N-R2!
-0.04 (302,424; 83; 7)
29 R-QR1 P × P 30 R × P N-N4 31 N-K4 R-R1
Perceiving that 28 ... P × P 29 R-N6 would be extremely unpleas-ant for Black.
29   N-K4   P × P
-0.02 (701,727; 188; 8)
30 R-N6 P-Q4 31 N-B5 N-N4 32 N × P/4 R-R1 33 R-N7
30   R-N6   P-Q4
+0.17 (583,538; 152; 8)
31 N-B5 N-N4 32 N × P/4 R-R1 33 P-QB4 N-R6 34 R/1-N3
31   N-B5   N-N4
+0.23 (942,370; 258; 8)
32 N × P/4 R-QR1 33 R-K6 KR-K1 34 R × R ch R × R 35 P-QB4
32   N × P/4   R-QR1
+0.16 (496,625; 144; 7)
33 R-N2 P-K5 34 P × P P × P 35 P-QB4 N-Q4
33   P-QB4
Remember what I said about passed pawns!
33   ...   P × P
+0.42 (635,379; 163; 8)
34 P × P N-R6 35 R-QB1 QR-B1 36 P-B5 P-QR4 37 R-B3
34   P × P   N-Q5
+0.53 (970,480; 264; 8)
35 P-K3 N-B6 36 P-B5 N-Q7 37 R-Q1 N-B5 38 R-N7
35   P-K3   N-B6
+0.60 (2,637,333; 730; 9)
36 P-B5 N-N4 37 R-N7 N-K5 38 P-B4 P × P 39 KP × P QR-Q1

36   P-B5   N-N4
+0.60 (476,059; 135; 7)
37 R-N7 N-K5 38 P-B4 P × P 39 KP × P QR-Q1
Or 36 ... N-Q7 37 R-N4 and the Black knight has nothing to do.
37   P-B6   N-K5
+0.56 (391,981; 112; ;7)
38 P-B4 P × P 39 NP × P N-Q7 40 R-QR1 N-B5
38   P-B7   R × P ch
-0.02 (1,379,960; 397; 8)
39 K-N1 KR-KB1 40 R-N8 N × P 41 R/1-N4

With this move the program warned "Be careful!" (but I was not told of this until after the game). In fact, Black has no defence to the threat of 39 R-N8 ch in conjunction with N-N6.
39   K-N1   KR-B1
-0.63 (879,932; 252; 7)
40 R-QB6 QR-B1 41 N-N6 N-Q7 42 R/1-QB1 N-B6ch 43 K-N2
40   R-N8   P-KR4
+9.46 (460,002; 114; 8)
41 R × R R × R 42 R-N8 ch K-R2 43 P-B8 = Q R × R 44 Q × R N × P 45 Q × P
41   R × R   R × R
+11.61 (787,096; 176; 10)
42 R-N8 ch K-R2 43 R × R N-Q3 44 R-Q8 N-B1 45 R × N K-N3 46 N-B5
42   R-N8 ch   K-R2
+15.55 (794,632; 178; 10)
43 R × R N-Q3 44 R-Q8 N-K5 45 P-B8 = Q N × P 46 K-N2 P-R5 47 R-R8 ch K-N3 48 R × P

David Slate resigned for his program.

I now had a lead of 2½-½ and needed only one draw in the last three games to win my bet. I had demonstrated to everyone's satisfaction that my do-nothing strategy worked to perfection, so I considered it worthwhile to experiment in game four by attempting to beat the program at its own game, playing sharp, tactical chess and endeavoring to outanalyze CHESS 4.7. This was the result.

GAME 4

White: CHESS 4.7

Black: Levy

Latvian Gambit

1 P-K4(book)   P-K4
2 N-KB3(book)   P-KB4
3 P×P
+0.76 (455,388: 153; 7)
3 ... P-K5 4 N-K5 N-KB3 5 B-N5 Q-K2 6 N-B4

3 ...   P-K5

4 N-K5
+1.06 (647,160; 215; 7)
4 ... Q-N4 5 Q-N4 Q×Q 6 N×Q N-KB3 7 N×N ch P×N

4 ...   N-KB3

5 N-N4
+0.53 (211,585; 69; 6)
5 ... N-B3 6 N-QB3 N×N 7 Q×N P-Q4

5 ...   P-Q4

6 N×N ch
+0.76 (268,819; 88; 7)
6 ...Q×N 7 Q-R5 ch K-Q1 8 N-B3 P-Q5 9 N-N5

6 ...   Q×N

7 Q-R5 ch
+0.55 (189,803; 64; 7)
7 ... K-Q1 8 N-B3 P-B3 9 P-KN4 P-KN3 10 P×P P×P 11 N×P P×N 12 Q×P ch B-Q3 13 Q×KP R×P 14 R×R B×R

The program is a pawn up and is thus quite willing to trade queens.

7 ...   Q-B2

8 Q×Q ch   K×Q
9 N-B3   P-B3
10 P-Q3
+0.62 (300,808; 92; 7)
10 ... B×P 11 P×P B×P 12 N×B P×N 13 B-B4

10 ...   P×P

11 B×P
+1.34 (341,668; 106; 7)
11 ... N-Q2 12 B-KB4 N-B4 13 P-KN4 K-N1 14 O-O N×B 15 P×N

11 ...   N-Q2

12 B-KB4
+1.34 (642,724; 198; 7)
12 ... K-N1 13 O-O N-B4 14 P-KN4 N×B 15 P×N

12 ...   N-B4

13 P-KN4
+0.32 (287,237; 86; 7)
13 ...P-KR4 14 B-K2 P×P 15 P-N4 N-R3 16 B×N P×B

13 ...   N×B ch

14 P×N
+0.13 (318,041; 88; 8)
14 ...P-KR4 15 P-B3 P×P 16 P×P R-R5 17 R-KB1 R×NP

14 ...   B-B4

Preventing O-O-O and therefore encouraging O-O; the program likes to castle when its pieces have been developed.

15 O-O
+1.20 (592,278; 182; 7)
15 ... P-QN3 16 N-R4 B-K2 17 QR-Q1 B-R3 18 KR-K1

15	...	P-KR4
16	N-R4	

+0.26 (422,519; 125; 7)

16 ...B-Q5 17 B-K3 B×B 18 P×B P×P 19 N-B5

16	...	B-Q5
17	B-K3	

+0.16 (750,709; 200; 8)

17 ... B×B 18 P×B P×P 19 P-K4 R-R6 20 N-B5 P-QN3

17	...	B-K4
18	P-Q4	

+1.06 (497,290; 153; 7)

18 ... B-Q3 19 P-KR3 P-QN3 20 KR-B1 B-Q2 21 B-N5 P×P 22 P×P

18	...	B-Q3
19	P-KR3	

+0.77 (337,183; 106; 7)

19 ... R-K1 20 KR-K1 K-N1 21 B-Q2 B-Q7 22 N-B5 B×N 23 P×B

19	...	P-QN3
20	KR-K1	

+1.02 (770,702; 236; 7)

20 ... P×P 21 P×P B-R3 22 B-N5 K-N1 23 QR-B1

20	...	B-Q2
21	N-B3	

+0.72 (169,446; 51; 6)

21 ... P×P 22 P×P R-R5 23 P-B3 R-R7

21	...	P×P
22	P×P	

+0.60 (368,992; 108; 7)

22 ... R-R5 23 P-B3 R-R7 24 B-B2 QR-R1 25 K-B1

22	...	R-R5
23	P-B3	

+0.35 (234,136; 67; 7)

23 ... QR-R1 24 K-B1 R-R6 25 K-K2 R-R7 26 B-B2

23	...	QR-R1

24	K-B1!	

+0.32 (412,942; 120; 7)

24 ... R-R6 25 K-K2 R-R7 ch 26 B-B2 K-N1 27 K-B1

24	...	B-N6?

The immediate 24 ... B-QB1 is better, and if 25 K-K2 (even worse for White is 25 N-K2 B-R3) 25 ... R-R7 ch 26 K-Q1 (not 26 B-B2?? B-N6 27 R-KB1 R-K1 ch winning a piece) 26 ... R×P with an overwhelming position.

25	R-K2	

+0.54 (292,595; 84; 7)

25 ... R-R8 ch 26 B-N1 B-Q3 27 QR-K1 K-N1 28 P-N3

25	...	B-B1
26	K-N2	

+0.75 (356,720; 103; 7)

26 ...R-R6 27 B-N1 B-R3 28 R-K6 B-N2 29 N-K2

26	...	B-Q3
27	B-N1	

+0.54 (226,239; 67; 7)

27 ... B-Q2 28 QR-K1 K-N1 29 K-B1 R-R8 30 P-N3

27	...	R-R6
28	QR-K1	

+0.60 (744,584; 223; 7)

28 ... B-Q2 29 P-R3 K-N1 30
P-N4 R-R8 31 K-B1
28 ...   R-N6 ch
29 K-B2
+0.45 (252,687; 74; 7)
29 ... R/N-R6 30 R-Q1 B-B5
31 P-N4 B-QR3 32 R/Q-K1
29 ...   R/R-R6
30 R-K3
+1.01 (448,775; 135; 7)
30 ... B-R3 31 N-K2 B×N 32
R/1×B P-B4 33 P×P B×P
30 ...   B-R3
If 30 ... B-B5 31 R-K7 ch K-
B3 32 R/1-K3! with N-K2 to follow.
Had I noticed these defensive re-
sources earlier I would have played
24 ... B-QB1.
31 N-K2
+0.77 (238,329; 68; 7)
31 ... B×N 32 R/1×B P-B4 33
R-R3 P×P 34 R×P ch K-N1
31 ...   B×N
32 R/1×B
+0.66 (228,450; 65; 7)
32 ... P-B4 33 R-R3 P-R4 34
R-K6 B-B5 35 R×NP P×P
32 ...   P-B4

33 P-B4!
+0.14 (541,278; 158; 8)
33 ... R×R 34 R×R R×R 35
K×R P×P ch 36 K-Q3 B×P 37
B×P
I have overlooked this move.
33 ...   R×R
34 R×R
+0.24 (1,233,406; 334; 10)
34 ... R×R 35 K×R P×P ch
36 K-Q3 K-N1 37 B×P B×P 38 P-
N3 K-B2
34 ...   R-R5
34 ... R×R 35 K×R P×P ch 36
K-Q3! gives White a won bishop
ending.
35 K-N3
+1.06 (842,547; 233; 9)
35 ... R-R8 36 B-B2 P×P 37
R-Q3 R-QB8 38 B×P R-B7 39 K-
B3
35 ...   R-R8
36 B-B2
+1.17 (369,782; 105; 8)
36 ... P×P 37 R-Q3 R-KB8 38
R×P B-B4 39 R-Q2 B×B ch 40
R×B R×R 41 K×R
36 ...   R-Q8!
37 R-R3
+1.43 (847,921; 237; 9)
37 ... P×P 38 R×P ch K-B1
39 K-B3 R-Q7 40 R-Q7 B-B4 41
R×P R×P 42 B×P B×B 43 R×B
R×P
37 ...   P×P
38 R×P ch
+2.34 (503,780; 143; 9)
38 ... B-K2 39 K-B3 R-Q7 40
R-N7 P-Q6 41 B-B4 R-K7 42 B×B
R×B 43 R×P ch
38 ...   K-B1??
38 ... K-K1 39 R×P P-Q6 40

K-K3 R-QN8 would probably have been sufficient to win.

39   R-Q7

+2.53 (699,230; 188; 9)

39 ... R-Q6 ch 40 K-N2 R-B4 41 R×P R-Q7 42 P-N4 B-K2 43 R×P R-N7

39   ...   R-Q6 ch??

An idea that fails because of White's 48th move. Correct is 39 ... B-B4 40 R×P P-Q6 41 B×B ch P×B when CHESS 4.7 would almost certainly not have been able to win; it may even have lost because of the passed Q-pawn.

40   K-N2

+1.61 (1,285,544; 337; 10)

40 ... B×P 41 R×P B-K6 42 B×B R×B 43 R×P R-K7 ch 44 K-B3 R×P

40   ...   B-B4

41   R×P

+2.66 (656,375; 172; 9)

41 ... R-Q7 42 P-N4 B-K2 43 R×P P×P 44 K-B3 P-QN4 45 R-K4

41   ...   R-Q7

42   P-N4

+2.75 (474,441; 126; 9)

42 ... B-K7 43 K-B3 R×P 44 B×P B×P 45 B×P K-K2 46 R-Q4

42   ...   B×P

43   R-Q8 ch

+2.74 (800,572; 212; 9)

43 ... K-B2 44 R×P R-N7 45 R-Q7 ch B-K2 46 R-R7 R-B7 47 K-B3

43   ...   K-B2

44   R-Q7 ch

+1.54 (1,774,804; 498; 9)

44 ... B-K2 45 K-B3 K-K1 46 R×P R×P 47 R-Q5 R-R6 ch 48 K-K4

44   ...   K-B1

45   R×QP

+3.03 (290,158; 77; 8)

45 ... R-N7 46 K-B3 B-K2 47 R-R4 B-B4 48 R-R8 ch K-B2

45   ...   R-N7

46   K-B3

+2.67 (629,351; 165; 9)

46 ... B-B4 47 R-Q8 ch K-B2 48 B×B P×B 49 R-Q7 ch K-B3 50 P-R4

46   ...   B-B4

47   R-Q8 ch

+2.66 (957,241; 234; 10)

47 ... K-B2 48 B×B P×B 49 R-Q7 ch K-B3 50 P-R4 R-QR7 51 R-R7 P-B5

47   ...   K-K2??

The final blunder. I had still not noticed White's next move and assumed that the program was going to play 48 B×B ch, when either 48 ... P×B or 48 ... K×R 49 B-Q4 R×P 50 B×KNP would produce the unbalanced type of endgame at which the program fares less well due to its inferior understanding of passed pawns.

After 47 ... K-B2 I don't think the program could have won.

48   B-R4 ch!

+3.22 (359,796; 90; 9)

48 ... K-B2 49 P-N5 P-N3 50 P×P ch K×P 51 R-QR8 K-B4 52 R-R7

The end.

48   ...   K-B2

49   P-N5

+4.13 (583,453; 156; 9)

49 ... P-N3 50 R-Q7 ch K-B1 51 P×P R×P 52 P-B5 P-N4 53 K-B4

49 ...	P-N3
50	R-Q7 ch

+4.17 (1,184,309; 294; 10)

50 ... K-N1 51 P×P R×P 52 P-B5 P-N4 53 P-B6 P-N5 54 R-Q8 ch B-B1

50 ...	K-B1
51	P×P

+4.31(520,678; 136; 9)

51 ... R×P 52 P-B5 R-R6 ch 53 K-N4 R-R5 ch 54 K-R5 P-N4 55 B-N3

51 ...	R×P
52	P-B5

+4.40 (1,055,542; 283; 9)

52 ... R-R6 ch 53 K-N4 R-R5 ch 54 K-R5 P-N4 55 P-B6 R-K5 56 B-N3

52 ...	R-R6 ch
53	K-N4

+4.50 (1,751,564; 473; 10)

53 ... R-R5 ch 54 K-R5 R-Q5 55 R-QN7 R-Q1 56 P-B6 K-N1 57 R-N7 ch K-B1

53 ...	R-R5 ch
54	K-R5

+4.67 (938,513; 247; 10)

54 ... R-Q5 55 R-KR7 R-KB5 56 P-B6 K-N1 57 P-B7 ch K-B1 58 R-R8 ch K-K2 59 R-K8 ch K-Q2

54 ...	R-Q5
55	R-B7

+7.43 (2,260,258; 579; 10)

55 ... R×B ch 56 K×R K-N1 57 P-B6 B-B7 ch 58 K-N4

55 ...	B-K2
56	P-B6

+8.43 (564,536; 130; 9)

56 ... B-Q1 57 P-N7 ch K-N1 58 K-N6 B×P 59 P×B R-N5 ch 60 B-N5

56 ...	**Black resigns.**

So the experiment failed, but computer persons all over the world will finally have something to rejoice about.

For the fifth game I returned to my no-nonsense approach.

GAME 5
White: Levy
Black: CHESS 4.7

English Opening

1	P-QB4	N-KB3(book)
2	P-QR3	P-B3(book)

Slate added this move to the program's openings library after the third game.

3	P-Q3	P-Q4(book)
4	Q-B2	

No, I am not mad: there is a perfectly valid reason for these moves. In a blitz game between CHESS 4.6 and GM Michael Stean in London 1977, the program opened 1 P-K4 P-QN3 2 P-Q4 B-N2 3 N-QB3 P-QB4 4 P×P. If the program likes to exchange centre pawns for wing pawns, who am I to stop it?

4 ... P×P
-0.23 (159,200; 53; 6)
5 P×P P-K3 6 P-K4 B-QB4 7 Q-Q3 Q×Q 8 B×Q

5 Q×P P-K4
-0.23 (262,590; 88; 6)
6 N-KB3 B-K3 7 Q-B3 P-K5 8 N-K5

So now I have a Sicilian pawn structure!

6 N-KB3   B-Q3
-0.33 (1,378,458; 463; 7)
7 QN-Q2 O-O 8 Q-KR4 P-QN4 9
N-K4 N×N 10 Q×N
7 P-KN3   B-K3
-0.35 (481,922; 166; 6)
8 Q-KR4 QN-Q2 9 B-R3 B×B 10
Q×B
8 Q-B2   QN-Q2
-0.36 (397,130; 133; 6)
9 B-N2 Q-N3 10 B-K3 B-N6 11 Q-
B3
9 B-N2   O-O
-0.34 (486,236; 164; 6)
10 O-O Q-N3
10 O-O   Q-N3
-0.23 (347,711; 116; 6)
11 B-K3 B-N6 12 Q-B3 N-Q4 13
B×Q N×Q 14 N×N P×B
11 QN-Q2   Q-B4
-0.20 (240,297; 72; 6)
12 N-B4 B×N 13 P×B P-QN4 14
P-N3
12 Q-N1
I wanted to keep the queens on
the board as long as I could to force
the program to examine as many
moves as possible at each level; its
search would therefore be shallower
than otherwise.
12 ...   P-KR3
-0.34 (319, 129; 100; 6)
13 N-K4 N×N 14 P×N P-B3 15
B-K3
13 P-QN4   Q-N4
-0.27 (248,491; 80; 6)
14 Q-B2 N-N5 15 B-N2 B-K2 16
P-R3
14 Q-B2   N-N3
-0.21 (827,004; 297; 6)
15 B-N2 P-QR4 16 QR-N1 N-N5
17 N-K4

15 B-N2   P-QR4
-0.11 (906,758; 327; 6)
16 P-Q4 P-K5 17 N×P N×N 18
Q×N P×P
16 P-QR4   Q-R3
-0.25 (242,170; 75; 6)
17 P×P Q×RP 18 B-B3 Q-B4 19
P-R5
17 P×P   Q×RP
-0.02 (2,037,120; 663; 7)
18 N-N3 B×N 19 Q×B P-K5 20
N-R4 P×P 21 Q×QP
The game is becoming sharper
than I had intended, but with
Black's queen offside I was very
happy with the situation.

18 B-B3   Q-B4
-0.16 (322,247; 103; 6)
19 N-N3 B×N 20 Q×B N×P 21
B×P B×B 22 R×N R×R 23
Q×R
19 KR-B1   QN-Q2
-0.21 (754,910; 258; 6)
20 P-K3 KR-Q1 21 Q-Q1 Q-R2 22
N-B4
The threat was simply 20 B×P.
20 P-R5   Q-R2
-0.40 (371, 312; 137; 5)
21 R-B1 Q-R3 22 K-R1 N-Q4

21 Q-N2   N-N5
-0.27 (215,498; 81; 5)
22 P-Q4 B-Q4 23 P-R3 B×N 24
N×B
22 N-K4   B-B2
-0.36 (255,626; 99; 5)
23 B-N4 P-KB4 24 N-B5 KR-K1
22 ... P-KB4 23 N×B Q×P ch
24 K-R1 leaves Black with insufficient compensation for the piece.
23 P-R3   P-KB4
-0.24 (361,794; 129; 6)
24 P×N P×N 25 P×P B×NP 26 B-
N4
24 P×N   P×N
-0.22 (197, 085; 69; 6)
25 P×P B×NP 26 R-Q1 P-B4 27
Q-N3 ch K-R2
25 P×P   B×NP
-0.23 (186,831; 71; 5)
26 R-Q1 B-K3 27 P-K3 B-N5
26 B-K1
Unnecessary overprotection. The
immediate 26 KR-N1 was stronger,
but Black cannot easily prevent
White's plan anyway.
26 ...   N-B4
27 KR-N1
At this point the computer became indisposed and required twenty-five minutes' consultation with its medical team. When it had recovered, only twenty minutes remained for the thirteen moves to the time control, but CHESS 4.7 managed to find the best defensive moves that I could see in the position.
27 ...   QR-K1
-0.40 (115,603; 40; 5)
28 Q-B2 B×N 29 P×B R-Q1
28 B-Q2
The point. White will put pressure

on the Black knight defending QN2.
28 ...   R-B2
-0.24 (246,864; 92; 5)
29 Q-B2 N-Q2 30 Q-N2 B×N 31
P×B
If 28 ... N×P 29 B-K3 Q-R3
(29 ... N-B4 30 R-QB1 B-Q3 31
Q-B2) 30 Q×NP Q×KP 31 Q×B
R-B2 32 Q×P forking rook and
knight.
29 B-K3   B-Q3
-0.15 (231,595; 84; 5)
30 Q-B2 B×N 31 P×B QR-KB1
30 Q-B2   B×N
+0.12 (454,716; 152; 6)
31 P×B R-R1 32 R-QB1 P-QN3
33 P×P Q×R 34 R×Q R×R ch 35
B-KB1
31 B×B   R-R1
+1.34 (167,734; 57; 5)
32 R-Q1 B-K2 33 QR-B1 P-QN3
34 P×P
32 R-QB1   P-QN3
+1.02 (115,827; 39; 5)
33 Q-N2 P×P 34 Q-B3 R×B 35
P×R
33 K-N2
If 33 P×P Q×R 34 R×Q B×R
ch 35 K-N2 R-R4, it is not immediately clear that White can win.
33 ...   Q-N2
+1.02 (113,042; 37; 5)
34 Q-B4 K-B1 35 B×N P×B
34 P×P   R×R
+1.54 (124,580; 37; 6)
35 R×R N-K3 36 R-R7 Q-B1 37
R×R K×R
35 R×R   N-K3
+1.61 (142,725; 49; 6)
36 R-R7 Q-B1 37 B-R5 R-B1 38
Q-Q1
36 R-R7   Q-B1

+3.10 (458,007;131; 7)
37 Q-B4 R-B3 38 P-N7 Q-K1 39
R-R6
37   Q-R2   R-B3
+2.15 (177,738; 51; 6)
38 R-R8 B-N1 39 B-N4 K-B2 40
B-QB5
38   R-R8   B-N1
+5.01 (296,439; 86; 7)
39 B-N4 K-B2 40 Q-R7 ch B×Q
41 R×Q B×P 42 B×B
39   B-N4   K-B2
+5.01 (722,578; 206; 7)
40 Q-R7 ch B×Q 41 R×Q B×P
42 B×B R-N3
40   Q-R7 ch   B×Q

+5.24 (1,010,509; 258; 10)
41 R×Q B×P 42 B×B K-K2 43
R-QR8 R-B2 44 B-KR5 R-B1 45 R-
R7 ch K-Q3
41   R×Q   B×P
+5.26 (602,264; 157; 9)
42 B×B K-K2 43 B-KR5 K-Q3 44
B-N4 K-Q2 45 R-QR8 R-N3
42   B×N ch   R×B
+5.24 (903,909; 230; 10)
43 B×B K-B3 44 R-B7 K-N3 45
B-B5 K-R2 46 R-R7 K-N3 47 K-B3
43 B×B
Once again the computer failed
and David Slate decided to resign
the game and the match.

Thus ended an era in the annals of computer chess. I had proved that my 1968 assessment had been correct, but on the other hand my opponent in this match was very, very much stronger than I had believed possible when I started the bet. When sending me his cheque for £250 Professor John McCarthy expressed a sentiment with which I concurred - he said that had I lost to a brute force program he would not have felt that the science of Artificial Intelligence was responsible for my defeat. McCarthy, Michie and Papert all paid promptly and with good sportsmanship, just as I would have done had I lost the bet. Only Edward Kozdrowicki did not. At the time of going to press (Autumn 1979) he has had more than a year to pay but has refused all attempts to persuade him to do so.

In order to stimulate further work in computer chess I have decided to offer a prize of $1,000 US to the first programming team who writes a program that beats me in a four or six game match. The magazine **Omni** has generously added $4,000 to my own offer so there is now a $5,000 prize, with no time limit, waiting for someone. In addition to this offer I am prepared to wager up to $10,000 U.S. that no-one collects the prize before January 1st 1984. Up to now I have not had any takers but one person has told me that he is considering it - Claude Shannon, the father of computer chess.

Courtesy of United States Chess Federation, Chess Life & Review, *Vol. XXXIII, No. 11.*

2 The State of the Art

In this chapter I shall illustrate the progress that has been made in computer chess during recent years by giving some of the better games played by the Northwestern University program and pinpointing some of the program's better results. I shall also comment on some specific areas where, in my opinion, little or no progress has been made. The chapter on computer chess tournaments in my earlier book *Chess and Computers* shows the state of the art five yeas ago (summer 1974). At that time CHESS 4.0 had played some interesting games but none of which a strong club player could be proud. Within a year that statement was no longer true. At the 1975 ACM tournament in Minneapolis, CHESS 4.4, the latest version of the program, won a game against CHAOS which, in my opinion, remains to this day the best game ever played between two computer programs. In my book of that event I gave this game with copious notes which I intend to repeat here (with apologies to anyone who already owns the book of the 1975 event).

White: CHAOS
Black: CHESS 4.4

Modern Benoni

David Slate and Larry Atkin kindly supplied me with a copy of CHESS 4.4's printout and so I am able to give a lot of information that is not normally included in the annotation of a computer game. This information includes:

1) The CPU time (in seconds) taken to compute each move;
2) The number of positions examined in computing the move;
3) The program's current assessment of the position—a positive score indicates that the program considers the position to be better for White, and 64 evaluation points are roughly equivalent to one pawn;
4) The sequence of moves predicted by CHESS 4.4 (i.e. the continu-

ation that the program considers to represent best play for both sides).

This information is given *in italics* in order to distinguish it from my own comments.

1	P-Q4	N-KB3
1	P-QB4	P-B4
3	P-Q5	P-K3
4	N-QB3	P×P
5	P×P	P-Q3
6	P-K4	P-KN3
7	B-K2	

This move took CHESS 4.4 out of its openings book, since the move expected by CHESS 4.4 was 7 N-B3 when 7...B-N2 is met by 8 B-K2. After CHESS 4.4's next move and CHAOS' reply, the game is back in book so far as CHESS 4.4 is concerned. From CHAOS' point of view the opening never leaves book until move fifteen.

7 ... **B-N2**

CPU time: 172 seconds
positions: 213,130
assessment: 30
predicting: 8 B-KB4 0-0 9 N-B3 B-N5 10 0-0

| 8 | N-B3 | 0-0 |
| 9 | 0-0 | R-K1 |

While CHESS 4.4 is still in book it naturally takes no time to compute its move and it does not examine the game tree, assess the current position or predict the forthcoming continuation.

10	N-Q2	N-R3
11	P-B3	N-B2
12	P-QR4	P-N3
13	N-B4	B-QR3
14	B-N5	P-R3
15	B-R4	

From here on, both programs are thinking for themselves. It would perhaps be as well to make some general comments concerning this variation of the Benoni. White's strategy revolves around his attempt to keep a firm grip on the centre and to prepare the advance P-K5. If this advance can be effected without conceding anything, White normally has a clear advantage. Black therefore keeps an eye on his K4 square to prevent White's breakthrough, and at the same time Black tries for counterplay on the Q-side, based on the advance ...P-QN4. If Black can play this advance with impunity before White makes any progress in the centre (or on the K-side), then it is Black who will get the advantage.

These are the considerations that would affect the choice of moves of a human player, but while both programs "know" this variation up to move fifteen, neither of them "understands" it. In my opinion it is at least as important to teach programs the ideas behind the openings as it is to teach them the openings themselves. One simple way in which this could be done is to store the general ideas behind a variation, as well as specific thematic moves, with each of the opening variations in the program's library. This would enable programs to give more than a cursory glance at the thematic moves and it would help them to find moves that conformed to the general requirements of the position. In this variation, for example, Black should always be considering the feasibility of playing ...P-QN4 and a general Q-side advance.

15 ... **P-KN4**

CPU time: 115 seconds
positions: 129,779
assessment: 18
predicting: 16 B-B2 N-R4 17 Q-Q2 N-B5

Ken Thompson (center) follows his program's progress in a game against the Northern University program. David Cahlander and David Slate have their backs to the camera.

The usual move here is 15...Q-Q2.

16 B-B2

Weaker is 16 B-N3, putting pressure on Black's QP, but then Black can continue with either 16...B×N 17 B×B P-R3, followed by ...Q-Q2 and an early ...P-QN4; or 16...N-R4 and now:

(i) 17 N×QP B×N (or 17...B×B 18 N×B N×B 19 N×R N×Nch 20 Q×N Q×R and Black has the advantage of bishop and knight for rook and pawn) 18 N×R (not 18 P×B B×B 19 Q×B N×B 20 P×N Q×N winning a piece) 18...N×B 19 P×N B-Q5ch 20 K-R1 B×B 21 Q×B Q×N, with a big advantage to Black; or

(ii) 17 B×P?? B(R3)×N 18 B×N B×B 19 B×Q B×Q, and Black has won a piece.

I have given these examples to illustrate the tactical complexity of the position. Since chess programs are more likely to excel at tactics than they are at strategical planning, it is obviously in their best interests to play sharp variations such as this one. After all, human players are advised to choose opening variations that suit their style, so why should the same advice not hold good for computer programs?

16 ...   N-R4

CPU time: 73 seconds
positions: 84,729
assessment: 20
predicting: 17 B-K3 Q-B3 18 Q-Q2 Q-N3

17 P-R5?

A serious strategic error, since now Black could play 17...P-N4 with a strong Q-side attack. Just as I would advocate storing a list of "good moves" and "good ideas" with each opening variation, I would also suggest storing a list of strategic errors that should be avoided unless there was some substantial tactical justification. The move P-R5 would be high on my list of "bad moves" for positions with this particular Q-side pawn-structure.

White could preserve its advantage with 17 N-K3.

17 ...   N-B5
CPU time: 60 seconds
positions: 69,748
asessment: —30
predicting: 18 P×P P×P 19 B-N3 N Bch 20 Q×N B×N(B6) 21 P×B N×P 22 R×B N×P.

For the first time in the game CHESS 4.4 (correctly) thinks that it has the advantage. Note that when the main variation involves captures the depth of look-ahead is extended—here it was 10-ply.

18 P×P   P×P
CPU time: 65 seconds
positions: 76,015
assessment: —3
predicting: 19 B-Q3 Q-B3 20 Q-B2 N×B 21 Q×N

19 B-K3

On K3 White's bishop is undefended, and this allows the ensuing combination (which, incidentally, is not Black's strongest continuation). 19 N×NP is also bad because of 19...B×N 20 N×R (or 20 B×B

R×B 21 R×R N×R, winning a piece) 20... B×B and 21...B×R winning a piece. In fact White is already lost since there is no satisfactory defence to the threat of 19...N×Bch 20 Q×N P-N4 and 21...P-QN5.

19 ...   B×N(B6)
CPU time: 71 seconds
positions: 85,486
assessment: —47
predicting: 20 P×B B×N 21 B×B R×R 22 Q×R N(2)×P

The text is the beginning of a long combination that is based on the exposed position of White's K3 bishop. Note that the key move of the combination, the capture of White's QP by a black knight, was predicted in a slightly different guise on the previous move.

Considerably stronger than the text however, was 19...N×Bch 20 Q×N P-N4, followed by ...P-QN5 with an easy win. But CHESS 4.4 was using an exhaustive 5-ply search, and for a variation to be examined at a depth greater than 5 it was necessary that the move at depth 6 be a capture (or, in some cases, a check). Since this condition is not satisfied by the continuation 19...N×Bch 20 Q×N P-N4 21 N-R5 P-QN5 22 N-B6, CHESS 4.4 would have no reason to look further and see that 22...B×Q 23 N×Q P×N wins a piece. This sort of oversight could be omitted by widening the restriction on moves considered at depths beyond the exhaustive search level. Instead of considering only captures (and some checks) programs could also consider all checks and direct threats, i.e. moves that attack undefended pieces or pieces of greater value than the attacking piece. This would naturally lead to a slowing down of the search process but in my opinion such a search strategy is an essential part of a good tactical analyser.

20 P×B   B×N
CPU time: 110 seconds
positions: 127,171
assessment: —47
predicting 21 B×B R×R 22 Q×R N(2)×P
Eliminating this knight is an essential part of Black's plan, since it guards the bishop on White's K3. Note that 20...N×Bch 21 Q×N P-N4 22 N-R5 P-QN5 no longer wins material because White can reply 23 P-QB4.

21 B×B   R×R
CPU time: 231 seconds
positions: 340,406
assessment: —38
predicting: 22 Q×R N(B5)×QP 23 B-Q2 N-B3 24 B-Q3 P-Q4
The text is essential so as to decoy

the white queen away from her defence of the Q5 square. If 21...N(B5)×QP 22 B×N R×R (or 22...N×B 23 Q×N and Black has lost a piece) 23 B×KBPch, and White has the advantage. Note that even though the depth-5 move in the predicted continuation, 23...N-B3 (remember that 21... R×R is at depth-1), is not a capture or a check, CHESS 4.4 is still searching to a depth of 7-ply. This is because the reduction of material on the board has reduced the average number of branches at each node (the "branching factor") and so a greater depth of search can be conducted within the same time span.

22 Q×R   N(B2)×P?
CPU time: 247 seconds
positions: 364,618
assessment: —25
predicting: 23 B-B1 N-B3 24 B×N P×B 25 R-Q1 Q-B2
The text is inferior to 22...N(B5)×QP (which CHESS 4.4 was originally intending to play—see the prediction at move 21). The reason that it is inferior is the very continuation predicted by 4.4 itself: 23 B-B1(or Q2) N(Q4) moves 24 B×N P×B, and White has excellent compensation for the pawn in Black's weakened K-side. So although CHESS 4.4 can predict the correct continuation, its assessment of the resulting position is obviously incorrect. This sort of example convinces me that if a chess programmer was presented, by his fairy godmother, with a routine that played perfect tactical chess, he would still be unable to

write a really strong chess program because chess is essentially a game of strategy. I would not wish to give the impression that I consider tactics to be unimportant, but I do feel that too much effort has been devoted to tactics and not enough to strategy.

23 B × N(Q5)   N × B
CPU time: 118 seconds
positions: 180,178
assessment: —42
predicting: 24 B × BP N × P 25 B-N4 N-K7ch 26 K-R1 R-K4

A really sophisticated tactical analyser would realise that it is essential to recapture on Q4, simply from the lack of threatening, capturing, and checking alternatives. The greater part of the 118 seconds search time was consumed in the exhaustive part of the search.

24 B × BP   N × P
CPU time: 171 seconds
positions: 243,234
assessment: —27
predicting: 25 B-K3 Q-B2 26 Q-N2 N-R5 27 Q-N5 R-R1

If 24...QP × B 25 R-Q1, picking up the knight.

25 B-N4   N-K7ch
CPU time: 223 seconds
positions: 303,678
assessment: 20
predicting: 26 K-B2 Q-B2 27 R-Q1 (if 27 K × N Q-B5ch and 28...Q × B—D.L.) 27...Q-B5 28 Q-N2 P-N4 29 R × P

CHESS 4.4 is showing bad judgement by predicting 26 K-B2. With queens still on and the position so open, such a move would be very dangerous.

26 K-R1   N-B5
CPU time: 125 seconds
positions: 173,776
assessment: 33
predicting: 27 Q-Q4 N-K3 (otherwise 28 B-B3) 28 Q × QP Q × Q 29 B × Q

Note that with White's queen in the middle of the board (after the predicted 27 Q-Q4) the branching factor increases and the depth of exhaustive search is reduced from 7-ply to 6.

27 R-Q1   Q-R1
CPU time: 96 seconds
positions: 131,952
assessment: 41
predicting: 28 Q-Q4 Q-R5 29 Q × QP Q-B7 30 R-Q2

28 B × P

As CHESS 4.4 had suggested, White would do better to keep the queens on, so as to take advantage of Black's vulnerable K-side.

28 ...   Q × Q
CPU time: 69 seconds
positions: 95,554
assessment: 49
predicting: 29 R × Q R-Q1 30 B × N P × B 31 R-R7

CHESS 4.4's evaluation function is once again proved wrong. The rook ending reached in the predicted line is better for Black because of the passed QNP.

29 R × Q   N-K7
CPU time: 143 seconds
positions: 211,158
assessment: 24
predicting: 30 R-R7 R-QB1 31 P-R3 N-Q5 32 R-N7 R-B3

30 R-QN1   R-QB1
CPU time: 94 seconds

positions: 141,154
assessment: 17
predicting: 31 P-R3 R-B3 32 P-K5
N-B5 33 R-N2 N-Q6

At this point CHESS 4.4 typed out "Be careful", warning its opponent against the trap 31 R × P R-B8 mate.

31 P-R3   R-B3
CPU time: 105 seconds
positions: 157,243
assessment: 21
predicting: 32 B-K7 N-B6 33 R-R1
R-B2 34 B-Q6 R-Q2

32 B-K5   K-R2
CPU time: 166 seconds
positions: 244,363
assessment: 21
predicting: 33 K-R2 P-B3 34 B-N8
N-B6 35 R-R1 P-N4

33 R-K1   R-B7
CPU time: 120 seconds
positions: 181,346
assessment: 17
predicting: 34 R-QN1 R-B4 35 B-Q6
R-B3 36 P-K5 K-N3

34 K-R2   P-N4
CPU time: 91 seconds
positions: 135,433
assessment: 16
predicting: 35 R-QN1 R-B4 36 B-Q6
R-B3 37 P-K5 N-B6

35 R-QN1   R-B4
CPU time: 211 seconds
positions: 325,677
assessment: 22
predicting: 36 B-Q6 R-B3 37 B-K5
P-B3 38 B-N8 N-B6

It is strange that although CHESS 4.4 assesses the predicted continuation as being in White's favour, it does not try repeating the position

(in its prediction) by 37...R-B4.

36 B-Q6   R-B3
CPU time: 193 seconds
positions: 301,748
assessment: 23
predicting: 37 B-N8 N-B6 38 R-N2
R-B5 39 R-Q2 P-KN5

37 B-B8   R-B7
CPU time: 120 seconds
positions: 178,803
assessment: 4
predicting: 38 B-Q6 N-Q5 39 K-N1
K-N3 40 B-K5 N-K7

38 R-QR1
Not 38 R × P N-B5 39 R-N6
R × Pch 40 K-R1 P-R4, followed by
...R-N6 and Black will win.

38 ...   N-B5
CPU time: 124 seconds
positions: 179,683
assessment: —15
predicting: 39 R-KN1 K-N3 40 B-Q6
K-B3 41 B × N P × B

39 R-KN1   K-N3
CPU time: 258 seconds
positions: 373,054
assessment: —11
predicting: 40 B-Q6 R-N7 41 B-K5
R-R7 42 B × N P × B

40 B-N4   P-B4
CPU time: 165 seconds
positions: 240,201
assessment: —18
predicting: 41 B-Q6 R-K7 42 B × N
P × B 43 R-N1 P × P

41 P × Pch   K × P
CPU time: 272 seconds
positions: 408,598
assessment: —17
predicting: 42 B-Q6 P-R4 43 B-R3
R-R7 44 B-Q6 R-K7

42 B-Q6   R-N7

CPU time: 234 seconds
positions: 349,264
assessment: —30
predicting: 43 B-R3 R-R7 44 B-N4
P-R4 45 B-Q6 R-Q7

43 K-R1   K-B3?
CPU time: 177 seconds
positions: 259,498
assessment: —23
predicting: 44 B×N P×B 45 R-R1
P-N5 46 R-R7

A human player would recognise that Black's winning chances virtually disappear with the forthcoming exchange, but such conceptual assessments are beyond the capability of programs.

44 B×N   P×B
CPU time: 109 seconds
positions: 181,647
assessment: —27
predicting: 45 R-R1 P-N5 46 R-R6ch K-N4 47 R-R5ch K-R5 48 R-R7 P-N6

45 K-R2   P-N5
CPU time: 106 seconds
positions: 169,718
assessment: —19
predicting: 46 R-Q1 P-N6 47 R-Q6ch K-N4 48 R-Q5ch K-R5 49 R-Q7

46 R-QB1   P-N6
CPU time: 200 seconds
positions: 307,809
assessment: —25
predicting: 47 R-B6ch K-N4 48 R-QN6 R-N8 49 R-N5ch K-N3 50 R-N7 P-N7

CHESS 4.4 was now searching to a depth of 9-ply.

47 R-B6ch   K-N4
CPU time: 148 seconds
positions: 232,952
assessment: 51
predicting: 48 R-B5ch K-N3 49 R-B4 R-QB7 50 R×BP P-N7 51 R-KN4ch K-B4 53 R-B6 ch

48 R-B5ch   K-N3
CPU time: 197 seconds
positions: 305,443
assessment: 64
predicting: 49 R-B4 K-B4 50 R-B5ch K-K3 51 R-B6ch K-B4 52 R×RP R-R7 53 R-R7
10 ply!

49 R-B6ch   K-R4
CPU time: 132 seconds
positions: 211,024
assessment: 61
predicting: 50 R-B5ch K-R5 51 R-B4 R-Q7 52 R×BPch K-N4 53 R-B7 P-N7

50 R-B5ch   K-N3
CPU time: 111 seconds
positions: 174,421
assessment: 64
predicting: *

51 R-B6ch   K-N4
CPU time: 101 seconds
positions: 160,033
assessment: 64
predicting: *

52 R-B5ch   K-B3
CPU time: 156
positions: 239,191
assessment: 64
predicting: **

*No prediction in these positions because of a complicated side-effect of CHESS 4.4's transposition table. For the same reason, some later positions have only shallow predictions.

53   R-QN5

CHAOS refrained from 53 R-B6ch because although it considered Black to have the advantage it did not consider this advantage to be so great as to warrant it playing for a draw. After 53 R-B6ch Black might try 53...K-N2, but after 54 R-B7ch K-B1 (or 54...K-K1 55 R-B8ch K-B2 56 R-B4) 55 R-B4, White picks up the KBP.

The CHAOS programmers might be considered to have been rather unlucky here—had CHAOS' evaluation function calculated Black's advantage to be 0.0002 more than its actual assessment, that score would have been over the threshold beyond which CHAOS *would* have played for a draw!

53   ...   K-N3
CPU time: 89 seconds
positions: 146,942
assessment: —4
predicting: 54 P-R4 R-N8 55 K-R3 P-R4 56 R-N6ch K-B2 57 R-QR6

54   K-N1   R-N8ch
CPU time: 344 seconds
positions: 538,972
assessment: 59

predicting: 55 K-R2 K-B3 56 R-KR5 K-N2 57 R-R4 P-N7 58 R-N4ch K-B3 59 R × Pch K-K4

55   K-R2   K-N2
CPU time: 138 seconds
positions: 212,473
assessment: 60
predicting: 56 R-N6 P-N7 57 P-R4 K-B2 58 R-N4 K-B3 59 R × BPch K-K4

56   R-N4   P-N7
CPU time: 235 seconds
positions: 328,543
assessment: —34
predicting: 57 R-N6 P-R4 58 P-R4 K-B2

57   R-N6   K-B2
CPU time: 116 seconds
positions: 186,533
assessments: —20
predicting: 58 P-R4 P-R4

58   P-R4?
This move is a mistake inasmuch as Black is able to win the KRP by force but although he is then a pawn up, the position should still be a draw with correct play.

58   ...   K-N2
CPU time: 141 seconds
positions: 225,755
assessment: 60
predicting: 59 R-N4 K-N3 60 R-N5 P-R4 61 R-N4 K-B3 62 R × BPch K-K4

59   P-R5   K-B2
CPU time: 136 seconds
positions: 215,660
assessment: —37
predicting: 60 R-N4 K-K3 61 R-N6ch K-K4 62 R-N5ch K-B3 63 R-N7 K-K4

60   R-N8   K-K3

CPU time: 292 seconds
positions: 454,779
assessment: —40
predicting: 61 R-N6ch K-B4 62 R-N5ch K-B3 63 R-N7 K-N4 64 R-N5ch K-R5

From CHESS 4.4's predicted continuation we can see the difficulties facing White. At the end of the predicted variation White is in zugzwang*—if his rook moves off the fifth rank he loses the KRP while if it moves off the QN-file Black wins by 65...R-KR8ch 66 K×R P-N8 = Qch etc. It is this motif of the rook sacrifice that gives Black whatever winning chances there are in this ending.

61 R-N7 K-B4
CPU time: 225 seconds
positions: 354,367
assessment: —33
predicting: 62 R-N5ch K-B3 63 R-N4 K-N4 64 R-N5ch K-R5 65 R-N4 K×P 66 R×BP

So CHESS 4.4 knows that it is winning the KRP.

62 R-N5ch K-B3
CPU time: 87 seconds
positions: 138,706
assessment: —35
predicting: 63 R-N7 K-N4 64 R-N5ch K-R5 65 P-N3 P×Pch 66 K-N2 R-QR8 67 R×P

In this predicted variation, CHESS 4.4 has seen that 66 K×P lost to 66...R-N8ch followed by 67...P-N8 = Q.

63 P-N3??
The losing move. This was probably prompted by the horizon effect: since White is forced to lose a pawn (CHAOS would have seen the fate of its KRP) it prefers to lose the KNP to the KRP since its king is then attacking Black's undefended KNP. The loss of the KRP is pushed over the horizon and CHAOS does not realise that even though the black KNP is attacked, it is never possible for White to play K×P because of the reply...R-N8ch.

Had White kept its rook on the QN-file, Black had only one winning try. This consists of a five stage plan:
(1) Win the KRP as shown above.
(2) Bring the king to QB7. If White plays K-R3 at any stage then ...R-KR8ch allows Black to promote the NP. Also, if White's rook moves off the QN-file without giving check, Black can play ...R-KR8ch.

**zugzwang — A german word used to describe a position in which the player whose turn it is to move loses *because* it is his move.

When Black's king is on QB7 Black threatens to move the rook to QB8 followed by ...K-N8, ...R-B7, ...K-B8 and P-N8 = Q. So as soon as Black plays ...K-QB7, White must give check with his rook on the QB-file to drive Black's king away from the protection of the NP. White then returns with his rook to the QN-file and Black cannot move his rook because the NP will be *en prise*.

(3) Black marches his king from QB7 to KB7.

(4) Black advances his KRP to R6, forcing White to play P × P. It is vital however, that Black plays the move ...P-R6 when White's rook is not on QN3, protecting the KBP.

(5) After White has played P × P, Black replies ...K × P, and if White then plays P-R4 he is lost after K-N5. In any case White cannot prevent the advance of the KBP.

The reason that this plan fails is that White can play R-QN3 in reply to Black's K-KB7, so that after P-R6; P × P, Black cannot pick up the white KBP. Whether CHAOS would have found this defence or whether it would have overlooked the full force of the threat ...P-R6, I do not know.

Incidentally, I asked David Slate to see what his program would have done had CHAOS not played 63 P-N3. "Surprisingly, the program found most of the winning try, winning the king rook pawn, getting its king to K7 (*not* KB7), and then playing ...P-R6! However, playing White, I refused to play P × P. Black

played immediately ...P × P, I recaptured K × P and the game was drawn,"

63 ...   P × Pch
CPU time: 95 seconds
positions: 151,156
assessment: —134
predicting: 64 K-N2 K-K3 65 R-N3 K-B4 66 R-N5ch K-B5 67 R-N7 K-N4 68 K × P K × P

An 11-ply prediction! When capturing the KNP CHESS 4.4 typed out "That was easy".

64   K-N2   K-K3
CPU time: 183 seconds
positions: 309,719
assessment: —134
predicting: 65 5-N3 K-B4 66 R-N4 K-N4 67 R-N5ch K-R5 68 R-N7 K × P 69 K × P

65   R-N3   K-B4
CPU time: 215 seconds
positions: 361,557
assessment: —134
predicting: 66 R-N5ch K-B5 67 R-N4ch K-N4 68 R-N5ch K-R5 69 R-N7 K × P 70 K × P

If CHESS 4.4 considered checks (as well as captures) beyond its exhaustive search depth, it would realise that White's last move in its predicted variation is a loser.

66   R-N6   K-N4
CPU time: 228 seconds
positions: 360,169
evaluation: —151
predicting: 67 R-N3 K × P 68 R-N6 K-N4 69 R-N5ch K-B3 70 R-N6ch K-K4 71 R × RP

67   R-N5ch   K-R5
CPU time: 136 seconds
positions: 212,588

assessment: —151
*predicting: 68 R-N7 K×P 69 R-N6
K-N4 70 R-N5ch K-B3 71 R-N6ch
K-K4 72 R×RP*

68 R-N8   **K×P**
CPU time: 90 seconds
positions: 138,265
assessment: —154
*predicting: 69 R-N5ch K-N3 70 R-
N6ch*
"That was easy."

69 R-N5ch   **K-N3**
CPU time: 94 seconds
positions: 148,694
assessment: —161
*predicting: 70 R-N6ch K-B4 71 R-
N5ch K-K3 72 R-N6ch K-Q4 73 P-
B4 R-QR8 74 R×NP*

70 R-N6ch   **K-B4**
CPU time: 97 seconds
positions: 150,410
assessment: —159
*predicting: 71 R-N5ch K-K3 72 R-
N6ch K-Q4 73 R-N5ch*

71 R-N5ch   **K-K3**
CPU time: 143 seconds
positions: 217,260
assessment: —168
*predicting: 72 R-N6ch K-Q4 73 R-
N5ch K-Q5 74 R-N7 K-K6 75 R-N4
P-R4 76 K×P*

72 R-N6ch   **K-Q4**
CPU time: 239 seconds
positions: 372,605
assessment: —275
*predicting: 73 R-N5ch K-B3 74 R-N3
P-R4 75 K×P R-N8ch 76 K-R4 P-
N8=Q 77 R×Q R×R 78 K×P*
12-ply!
"Be careful."

73 R-N5ch   **K-B3**
CPU time: 195 seconds

positions: 302,090
assessment: —275
*predicting: 74 R-N3 P-R4 75 K×P
R-N8ch 76 K-R4 P-N8=Q 77 R×Q
R×R 78 K×P.*
"Be careful."

74 R-N3   **P-R4**
CPU time: 172 seconds
positions: 288,717
assessment: —276
*predicting: 75 K×P R-N8ch 76 K-
R4 P-N8=Q 77 R×Q R×R 78
K×P K-B4*
"Be careful."

75 P-B4   **P-R5**
CPU time: 170 seconds
positions: 286,037
assessment: —282
*predicting: 76 P-B5 K-Q4 77 P-B6
K-K3 78 R-N6ch K-B2 79 R-N4
K×P 80 R×RP*

76 R-N8

76 ...   **K-Q4**
CPU time: 101 seconds
positions: 170,279
assessment: —364
*predicting: 77 R-N4 K-K3 78 R-N5
K-B3 79 R-N7 K-B4 80 K-R3*

Of course Black can win by playing 76...P-R6ch 77 K×RP R-KR8ch 78 K×P P-N8=Q, but CHESS 4.4 must have realised that with its king defending its KNP (from KN5 or KB5) it could reach a similar position with an extra pawn (the KNP). In fact with the black king on KN5 there is the threat of mate by ...P-R5.

77   R-N5ch   K-K5
CPU time: 199 seconds
positions: 351,300
assessment: —538
predicting: 78 P-B5 K-B5 79 P-B6 P-R6ch 80 K×P R-KR8ch 81 K-N2 P-N8=Q 82 R×Q R×R
"Be careful."

78   R-N6   K-B4
CPU time: 161 seconds
positions: 297,277
assessments: —541
predicting: 79 R-N5ch K-N5 80 R-N5ch K×P 81 R-N4ch K-B4 82 R-N4 K-N4

79   R-N5ch   K-N5
CPU time: 141 seconds
positions: 268,418
assessment: —538
predicting: 80 R-N5ch K×P 81 R-N4ch K-K6 82 R-N4 K-Q6 83 R-N5 K-K7 84 R-K5ch K-Q7

80   R-N5ch
"Oh, you had that."

80   ...   K×P
CPU time: 12 seconds
positions: 36
assessment: —299
predicting: 81 R-N4ch K-K6 82 R×RP

81   R-N4ch   K-K6
CPU time: 203 seconds

positions: 381,628
assessment: —531
predicting: 82 R-N4 K-Q6 83 R-N8 K-B7 84 R-QB8ch K-Q7 85 R-Q8ch K-K7 86 R-K8ch K-Q6

82   R-N4   K-Q6
CPU time: 196 seconds
positions: 357,893
assessment: —533
predicting: 83 R-N7 K-Q5 84 R-N3 K-B5 85 R-N6 K-B6 86 R-QB6ch K-Q7
"Be careful."

83   R-N5   K-B6
CPU time: 99 seconds
positions: 179,205
assessment: —529
predicting: 84 R-N8 K-B7 85 R-QB8ch K-Q7 86 R-Q8ch K-K7 87 R-K8ch K-Q8

84   R-QB5ch   K-N5
CPU time: 201 seconds
positions: 372,503
assessment: —680
predicting: 85 R-B7 R-N8ch 86 K-R3 R-KR8ch 87 K-N4 P-N8=Q 88 R-QN7ch K-B5 89 R×Q R×R 90 K×P
12-ply!!
"Be careful."

85   R-B6   R-N8ch
CPU time: 148 seconds
positions: 265,377
assessment: —1009
predicting: 86 K-R3 K-R4 87 K×P P-N8=Q 88 R-B5ch K-N5 89 R-KN5 Q-K5ch 90 K-R5

86   K-R3
"Oh, you had that."

86   ...   R-KR8ch
CPU time: 138 seconds
positions: 252,691

assessment: —987
predicting: 87 K-N4 P-N7 88 R-QN6ch K-B5 89 R × P P-N8 = Qch 90 K-B5

The text is certainly the most accurate but it is rather greedy. After 86...P-N8 = Q 87 R-QN6ch K moves 88 R × Q R × R 89 K × P, Black is "only" a rook and a pawn ahead. After the text however, Black's material advantage is greater.

87 K-N2
"Oh, you had that."

87 ... K-R4!!
CPU time: 173 seconds
positions: 307,636
assessment: —1013
predicting: 88 R-B5ch K-N3 89 R-B8 R-R7ch 90 K-B3 R-KB7ch 91 K-N4 P-N8 = Q 92 K × P

If 87...P-N8 = Q 88 R-QN6ch K moves 80 R × Q R × R and this time Black is "only" a rook and two pawns ahead. But by moving his king off the QN-file, Black ensures himself an even greater advantage: If now 88 K × R P-N8 = Qch 89 K-N2 Q-K5ch and 90...Q × R

88 R-B5ch K-R3
CPU time: 120 seconds
positions: 206,274
assessment: —1179
predicting: 89 R-B6ch K-N2 90 R-KN6 P-N8 = Q 91 R-N7ch K-B3 92 K-B3 R-KN8

89 R-B6ch K-N2
CPU time: 170 seconds
positions: 286,919
assessment: —1175
predicting: 90 R-B6 P-N8 = Q 91 R-B7ch K-N3 92 R-B6ch K-B4 93 K-B4 Q-R8
"Be careful."

90 R-K6 P-N8 = Q
"That was easy."

CHESS 4.4's greed has at last been justified—it has promoted a pawn and kept all of its material. The remainder of the game is of no interest.

91 R-K7ch K-B3
92 K-B3 Q-B4ch
93 K-K2 P-N7

And CHAOS' programmers resigned for their program.

The following year, 1976, the Northwestern program decided that the time had come to show human tournament players what it could do. It entered the class B section at the annual Paul Masson tournament in Saratoga, California, and just to ensure that the humans did not have any cause for complaint it was decided in advance that the program would not claim any prize money that it might win. The program, by now CHESS 4.5, was running on a CDC Cyber 176. The result of the tournament was a win for CHESS 4.5, which achieved a performance rating of 2184 (i.e. high U.S. Expert). The program's games were not really of the caliber of a 2184 player but showed quite clearly that its unsuccessful opponents were psyched out, playing moves that they would not have chosen against a strong human opponent. I have noticed this syndrome quite often when watching humans battling against computer programs; most people whom I have quizzed about their computer games confessed to feeling unnerved in competition with a non-human adversary. Others have simply underestimated the strength of the program. Herein lies a whole new area of psychology - the study of human reactions to intellectual encounters with computers.

The most impressive result achieved by CHESS 4.5 in Saratoga was a win in an exhibition game played against an A-player (rating 1886). This game was played at a fast time limit (30 moves in 30 minutes), a factor which helps the program for reasons explained in chapter 3 on blitz play.

White: A. Hough
Black: CHESS 4.5

Modern Benoni

1	P-Q4	N-KB3
2	P-QB4	P-B4
3	P-Q5	P-K3

This might be called the program's favourite weapon. It has won some fine games with this defence.

4	N-QB3	P × P
5	P × P	P-Q3
6	N-B3	P-KN3
7	P-KN3	B-N2
8	B-N2	O-O
9	O-O	B-N5
10	N-Q2	Q-K2
11	P-KR3	B-Q2

Now Black threatens ...P-QN4, a thematic move in the Modern Benoni.

12	P-QR4	N-R3
13	N-B4	N-K1
14	Q-N3	N-N5
15	B-B4	P-KN4

A difficult move to assess. On the one hand it weakens Black's K-side, but it does have the advantage of driving away the KB4 bishop before White can play N-K4.

16	B-Q2	P-KR3
17	K-R2	N-B2
18	P-R5	P-B4

Black should continue with 18...N-N4; the text is too loosening. But it is not yet possible for programs to consider long term positional ideas, and so a move which is overtly aggressive will often be made even though it is not sound.

19	P-B4	QR-N1

19...N-N4 is essential.

20	P-K4	BP × P
20	...	

Forced - White threatened 21 P-K5.

21	N × KP	

Black's position is hopeless.

21	...	N(5) × P

| 22 | P × P | Q-K3 |
| 23 | N(K4) × QP | |

Why not capture on KR6?

| 23 | ... | P × P |
| 24 | QR-K1 | Q-N3 |

25 N-K3

Mistakenly going into complications in time-trouble.

25	...	Q × N
26	N × N	B-K3
27	R × B	N × R
28	R-K1	R-B7

Presumably White overlooked this move. Now that the KN2 bishop is pinned White does not have the combination based on R × N followed by N-K7ch and B-Q5.

| 29 | R × N | Q × R |

White lost on time

In any case White is lost. If 30 N-K7ch or 30 N-B6ch, Black can reply 30...K-B2.

The Northwestern program's next real test came in February 1977 when it entered the Minnesota Open Championship. David Slate and Larry Atkin expected their 'baby' to score 2-4 and thought that 3-3 would be a real success. CHESS 4.5 surprised everyone by scoring 5-1 and taking the title on tie-break. Once again I felt that some of the 'blame' for its victory must be attributed to the fallible psyche of its opponents, as seen from the following game.

White: CHESS 4.5
Black: Fenner (2016)

Sicilian Defence

1	P-K4	P-QB4
2	N-KB3	P-K3
3	P-Q4	P × P
4	N × P	P-QR3
5	P-QB4	N-KB3
6	B-Q3	Q-B2
7	O-O	B-B4
8	N-N3	B-R2
9	N-B3	N-B3
10	B-N5!	

Taking advantage of the vulnerability of Black's K-side caused by manoeuvering his bishop over to QR2.

| 10 | ... | N-K4 |
| 11 | B × N | P × B |

Now Black cannot very well castle K-side.

| 12 | Q-K2 | P-Q3 |

13   K-R1

Preparing P-B4.

13 ...	**B-Q2**
14 P-B4	**N×B**
15 Q×N	**O-O-O**
16 QR-Q1	**B-B3**
17 P-KB5	

Hereabouts White's play is rather aimless. It would have been better to put a rook on QB1 and to launch some sort of attack on the Q-side.

17 ...	**B-N1**
18 P-N3	**P-KR4?!**
19 P×P	**P-R5**
20 R×P	**RP×P**
21 Q×NP	**QR-N1?**

After 21...P×P or 21...P-Q4, the situation would be quite unclear.

22   P×P!

22 ...	**Q×P**

If 22...R×Q 23 P-B8=Qch R×Q 24 R×Rch K-Q2 25 R-B7ch and 26 R×Q, winning material.

23 R×Q	**R×Q**
24 N-Q5	

The authors, Monroe Newborn (foreground) and David Levy (rear left), discuss a game with Ben Mittman, director of the Vogelbach Computer Center at Northwestern University and coach of the world champion programmers (rear right).

At this point Fenner offered a draw which the program declined.

24	...	B-K1
25	N-N6ch	K-Q1
26	R×NP	B-B3
27	R×Bch	K-B2
28	R-QB8ch!	

Presumably Black had overlooked this move. If 28 R×R??? B×P is mate.

| 28 | ... | R×R |

If 28...K-N2 29 R×B K×R 30 N-Q5, with an easy endgame win.

| 29 | P×R | B×Pch |

| 30 | K-N1 | R-KR1? |

Hoping for a swindle, 30...K×N 31 R×Pch would have been hopeless, objectively, but at least the program would be forced to play an endgame where it was not a piece ahead.

| 31 | N-Q5ch | K-B3 |
| 32 | N-R5ch | Resigns |

If 32...K-B4 33 P-N4 mate or 33...K-Q2 34 N-KB6ch and 35 N×B.

During the remainder of 1977 the program hit the headlines again quite a few times. Its victory in the Minnesota Open qualified it for a place in the state's closed championship the following weekend but there it did not fare so well - its opponents were prepared for it and the program finished in last place with one win, one draw and three losses. A few weeks later it gave a simultaneous exhibition in New York against ten human opponents, including Edward Lasker, Walter Goldwater (President of the Marshall Chess Club) and Burt Hochberg (Editor of *Chess Life and Review*). CHESS 4.5 scored eight wins, one draw and only one loss. In September it competed in the Aronson Open in London, over an open telephone line from Arden Hills, Minnesota where the Cyber computer is located. In this event it achieved a tournament rating of 2000 with a score of $3^1/_2$ out of 6. One of its draws was against the captain of the England junior team who had expressed some contempt for the program before the game but who found himself unable to win a rook ending against it despite having an extra pawn. At the end of the year it gave another exhibition, this time in Paris, against such notables as Monsieur Chandon Moet (of the champagne family) and Roger Vadim, but from the publicity surrounding the event it was clear that the program, not its human opponents, was the celebrity.

The fame of the Northwestern program is quite justifiable. It is already stronger than more than 99% of serious chess players (by serious I mean anyone who finds it worthwhile to join their national federation or subscribe to a chess magazine) and it can accomplish great feats at blitz chess (see chapter 3). What then are its limitations and how likely is it that Slate and Atkin will find some way to surmount them and make a quantum leap forward during the next few years?

Reprinted courtesy of *Minnesota State Chess Association,* The Minnesota Chess Journal, *Vol. 14, No. 2.*

One of the biggest problems still faced by chess programmers is how to develop an evaluation function which performs well in quiet positions. Examples of this failing can be seen in the notes to my games with CHESS 4.5 where the program often thought that it had an advantage when in fact it was quite lost. Another illustration of incorrect evaluation can be seen in the game between CHAOS and CHESS 4.4 (page **32**). On move 22 CHESS 4.4 made a capture which should have given its opponent a positional advantage (with correct play) - obviously CHESS 4.4 thought that after White's best continuation, 23 B-B1 N(Q4) moves 24 B × N P × B, the position was still good for Black.

It does not matter how far you look if you cannot see properly and it does not matter how deeply your program searches if it cannot make an accurate evaluation of the positions at the end of its search. This is why the human is, at the moment, the master of the machine. The human sees relatively little but understands a lot, while the best chess programs see 10,000-50,000 times more but do not understand what they see. I maintain that this blind, brute force approach produces a kind of monkey/typewriter situation in which a program appears to play moderately well whereas it is actually playing very weak chess so many times that its best results resemble the moves of strong players. Some programmers, e.g. Slate and Newborn, my co-author, argue that as the search becomes deeper strategy and tactics merge into one, but in my opinion this view is erroneous.

Let us now look at two further examples.

This position is from the game Perry (White) v CHESS 4.6, played in the Aronson Open Tournament in London, September 1977. CHESS 4.4 (to move) continued:

13	...	N-K4?
14	B-Q5	N-Q6ch
15	K-B1	N(K5) × KBP
16	B × R	N × R

It is not difficult to see that the Black knight on KR8 is trapped. Why did the program follow this continuation? Because when playing 13...N-K4? it would have analyzed the whole of the tactical continuation which was actually played and it would have noticed that 17 K-N1 allows the knight to escape from the corner. It would not, however, have examined the move 17 B-K3 because that is a non-tactical move, i.e. it is not a capture or a check or even a direct threat. The program looks at the "quiescent" position in the above diagram and assesses it as being good for Black who is a pawn up.

Perry naturally played 17 B-K3, trapping the knight in the corner, and eventually he won the game. An average human player with only a moderate conceptual ability can see at a glance, without so much as a 1-ply search, that after 17 B-K3 the capture of the knight on KR1 is inevitable - it can never escape. But how does one explain the concept of "never" to a chess program?

The next position is not taken from a game but is based on a well known idea in the Dragon Variation of the Sicilian Defence.

White is a queen up for a knight and three pawns, an overwhelming material advantage under normal circumstances. Yet Black has a clearly won position because although White's queen is not attacked and may not be attacked (Black's knight can not move without allowing the queen to escape) the queen will never get out of its cage. A brute force program might well see that the queen will not escape during the next 10 or 20 ply, but it will not be able to analyze as far as "never"! Furthermore, if White plays the best moves it will be another 14 ply before Black's win is evident to the program: *1 K-N2 P-K4 2 K-B3 P-R4 3 K-B4 P-R5 4 K-N4 P-K5 5 K×P P-K6 6 K-N3* (say) *P-K7 7 K* moves *P-K8=Q*. If CHESS 4.6 were to reach the diagrammed position at the end of a branch of analysis it would undoubtedly consider the position to be quiescent (which it is) and evaluate it as winning for White (which it is not). It would not see the need to analyze what might happen after another 14 ply. Yet to any average (human) club player the diagrammed position is an obvious win for Black.

If I am correct in assuming that brute force programming will never produce a World Champion, it becomes necessary to question whether or not computer programs will be able to play real chess by other means. If they are constrained to look at trees that are more human in size (50-100 nodes), instead of the monster (1 million - 3 million node) trees examined at present, perhaps the CPU time saved can be used to examine each terminal node with a much better "understanding" (i.e. a more sophisticated evaluation mechanism) than is employed at the moment. This small tree approach has already been shown to produce moderately reasonable results, such as Marsland's WITA (recently renamed AWIT) and Richter's SCHACH MV5.6. Consider, for example, the following game.

White: SCHACH MV5.6
Black: Fischer/Schneider
1st German Computer Tournament
Dortmund 1975
Irregular Opening

1	N-QB3	P-Q4
2	P-Q4	B-N5
3	P-B3	B-B4
4	P-K4	P×P
5	P×P	B-Q2
6	N-B3	

So far White's play has been perfectly logical and he has taken command of the centre.

6	...	N-QB3
7	P-K5	P-K3
8	B-KN5	B-K2
9	Q-Q2	P-KN3
10	B-Q3	P-N3
11	B×B	KN×B
12	0-0-0	

Continuing sensibly, completing his development and preparing for

an attack against Black's K-side.

12	...	0-0
13	Q-R6	

With the terrible threat of 14 N-KN5.

13	...	N-B4
14	B×N	NP×B
15	N-KN5	Q×Nch

Otherwise it's mate.

16	Q×Qch	K-R1
17	P-KN4	

Opening up another line of attack.

17	...	P×P
18	Q×NP	P-B4
19	Q-R4	P-B5
20	N-K4	

Now the other knight joins in the attack.

20	...	P-B6
21	N-N5	R-B2
22	N×Rch	K-N1
23	Q-B6	P-B7
24	N-R6 mate	

White's play is rather crude but it definitely looks as though SCHACH had a plan - to attack the enemy king. Yet SCHACH was playing *without any look-ahead whatsoever!!*

WITA (or AWIT) has competed in a number of computer chess tournaments. Typically, the programs that finish behind it or level with it in these events look at two orders of magnitude times as many positions as WITA when making each move. This, to some extent, confirms the view that it is not only what one looks at that is important but also what one sees.

Having attacked the brute force approach and praised the small tree search we shall now examine some of the problems that will face even those programmers who follow the second path. These problems relate to the assessment of positions that are encountered as terminal nodes on the game tree.

The position on page 60 has already been shown to present evaluation difficulties. Consider now the same position but with Black's pawn removed from K2 and placed on Q2.

This position is a win for *White* because the White king can stop both pawns no matter whose turn it is to move. e.g. *1 K-N2 P-Q4 2 K-N3 P-R4 3 K-R4 P-Q5 4 K-N3*, and now both *4...P-Q6 5 K-B3 P-R5 6 K×P P-R6 7 K-B2 P-R7 8 K-N2* and *4...P-R5ch 5 K×P P-Q6 6 K-N3 P-Q7 7 K-B2*, win for White, because once the pawns have been captured Black must move either his king or his knight, allowing the White queen to become active.

The small difference in position (in comparison with the material situation) between this example and the position in the previous diagram changes a win for Black into a win for White. In order for a program to be able to cope with this delicate a difference it must have an enormous amount of chess knowledge. Here, for example, it would be necessary for a program to know that a lone king cannot stop two unaided passed pawns if they are separated by three empty files but that the king *can* stop the pawns when they are separated by only two files.

Let us next turn to the problem of *zugzwang*. This term describes a situation in which the side whose turn it is to move is at a disadvantage because of and only because of the fact that it is his turn to move. A simple example can be seen in the diagram at the top of page 63.

If it is White to move he is in *zugzwang*. 1 K-K6 is stalemate while any other move allows 1...K×P with an immediate draw. If it is Black to move then he is in *zugzwang* - he must move off K1 and then White plays K-Q7 followed by P-K8 = Q.

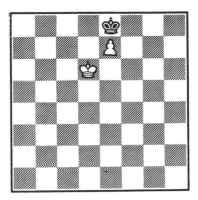

The concept of *zugzwang* is fundamental to a large proportion of endgame theory and many endgames are decided only because of a *zugzwang* possibility. But how is a program to recognize that a position is *zugzwang* when evaluating that position as a terminal node on the game tree? Any static evaluation mechanism must take into account whose turn it is to move, but it is totally alien to the very idea of static evaluation that there can exist positions in which possession of the move constitutes a disadvantage. *Zugzwang* positions, when encountered as terminal nodes, will therefore be assessed wrongly, often leading to disastrous results.

It is not only *zugzwang* positions themselves that can cause problems. Positions that will eventually lead to *zugzwang* can also give rise to incorrect assessments.

White to play draws by *1 K-N2 K-Q1 2 K-B2 K-K2 3 K-Q2 K-B2 4 K-K2 K-N3 5 K-B3 K-R4 6 K-N3*, followed by K-R3-N3-R3 ad infinitum. But with Black to move White loses because the Black king can reach KN5 and

White will then be in *zugzwang*, forced to move away from his defence of the KBP. When encountering the diagrammed position as a terminal node how can a program be expected to realize the *zugzwang* possibility that exists 15-ply further on?

Conclusion

Chess is an extremely complex game in which subtle nuances abound. Brute force methods are clearly inadequate for the task of dealing with subtlety and even the search of small trees, although allowing more time for the evaluation of terminal nodes, does not solve the problem of the inability of programs to conceptualize. Until Artifical Intelligence makes giant strides in the realm of concept formation it will be impossible for chess programs to exhibit the understanding of a Fischer. Until that time they must content themselves with being able to play a particular form of chess very, very well but at the same time admit that they do not play real chess.

With its present level of intelligence and a very fast typewriter the monkey can type innumerable crude sonnets, but without increasing its I.Q. it will never write Hamlet.

With their present level of sophistication, and running on very fast computers, the best chess programs can play innumerable crude games, but without increasing their 'understanding' of chess they will never play with the subtlety of a World Champion.

3 Blitz Play

The term "blitz play" in chess is used to describe a game played at high speed. Instead of moving at an average of from 2 to $3^3/_4$ minutes per move, the players must make all of their moves within a short period of time - usually five minutes. Alternatively, the players are required to move every five or ten seconds.

Blitz chess does not allow the players the luxury of long term planning. Moves are made by instinct, with little or no calculation to back it up. Since strategical planning is denied the players the game is normally highly tactical in nature. Sacrifices are more common than in normal chess because although they are mostly theoretically unsound they are not easy to refute given the time restriction.

Because of their ability to calculate tactical variations with considerable accuracy and to a great depth, the strongest chess programs are very adept blitz players. They will not leave material *en prise* but they will grab any tactical opportunity which presents itself. The only way for a human opponent to outwit a strong program is to avoid all tactics except when they are essential or definitely advantageous. In the game which follows, the human player (an International Grandmaster) outplays the program positionally but then makes the mistake of trying to win by tactical means. As a result he became the first Grandmaster ever to lose to a computer program.

Since programs are not yet linked to robots which can move the pieces for them and punch the button on the chess clock, special rules are used for human v computer blitz play. The human uses a chess clock and makes all his moves in five minutes in the normal way. The program is constrained to move at an average rate of five seconds per move and if it has not given mate or announced mate by move sixty (i.e. when it has consumed five minutes of computing time) then it loses on time.

White: CHESS 4.6
Black: Michael Stean

London, September 1977
Owen's Defence

1	P-K4	P-QN3

Designed to get the program out of its openings book.

2	P-Q4	B-N2
3	N-QB3	P-QB4
4	P×P	

A positional error, leaving Black with more pawns controlling the centre and opening up the QN-file along which Black will eventually be able to counter-attack.

4	...	P×P
5	B-K3	P-Q3
6	B-QN5ch	N-Q2
7	N-B3	P-K3
8	O-O	

White has a big lead in developing but Black's pawns control the centre.

8	...	P-QR3
9	B × Nch	Q × B
10	Q-Q3	N-K2
11	QR-Q1	R-Q1
12	Q-B4	

"Threatening" 13 B × P, since the recapture 13...P × B would leave Black's queen *en prise* to White's rook, but in fact Black can meet 13 B × P with 13...Q-B3, winning a piece.

12	...	N-N3
13	KR-K1	B-K2
14	Q-N3	Q-B3
15	K-R1?!	

A strange move, putting its king on a diagonal dominated by its opponent's queen and bishop. The reason was probably that CHESS 4.6 considered its other pieces to be on their optimal squares and so it decided to move its king as far away from the centre as possible in order that it might be safer.

15	...	O-O
16	B-N5	B-R1

17	B × B	N × B
18	P-QR4	R-N1
19	Q-R2	R-N5
20	P-QN3	

Overprotecting the QRP and the QNP, but shutting the queen even further out of play.

Let us now survey the scene. Black's pawns still dominate the centre, controlling the squares ...Q5, ...Q4, and ...K4, while White's KP attacks only one central square. Black's queen and bishop exert pressure along an important diagonal and his QN5 rook is actively placed. In contrast, White's queen is out of play and he has no active possibilities at his disposal. It is therefore quite reasonable to conclude that Black has a marked positional advantage - in a game between two Grandmasters, with no time shortage, I would expect Black to win every time.

Stean decided that his positional advantage was so overwhelming that the time had come for a tactical assault on White's king along the diagonal. In the ensuing complications he discovers, to his horror, that the program can sometimes calculate better than a Grandmaster.

20 ...   P-B4?!

Attempting to open up the diagonal. 20...P-Q4 was a better way of going about it, and if 21 N-K5 Q-N2 22 N-Q3 R-Q5 23 N × BP R × R 24 R × R Q-B3, followed by 25...P × P.

21 N-KN5   P × P
22 N(B3) × P!

Not 22 N × P(K6) because of 22...R × BP, with a strong attack against the white king.

22 ...   R × P

At first sight this move looks strong, since 23 N × R loses at once to 23...Q × NP mate. But CHESS 4.6 has seen further than its opponent and now plays

23 R × P!

"Bloody iron monster" exclaimed the Grandmaster, who only now realised that his queen is needed to prevent R-Q8 mate. Since it is impossible for the Black queen to defend ...Q1 and remain on the crucial diagonal, Black must lose material.

23 ...   Q × R

The best try.

24 N × Q   R × NP

Now Black is threatening 25...R × Ndis ch, 25...R × BPdis ch (winning the queen) and 25...R-K7dis ch (winning the rook), but CHESS 4.6 had seen this position coming and had everything under control.

25 N(N5)-K4!

Blocking the diagonal. CHESS 4.6 had already "seen" this move when playing its 21st move!

25 ...   R-N5

Apparently winning a piece, since the K4 knight cannot move and cannot be defended again.

26 P-B4!

Cutting the ...QN5 rook off from its attack on the knight.

26 ...   N-B4

So that if 27 N × N P × N, winning the other knight which is pinned against the White king by the bishop.

27 P-R3

"This computer is a genius" Stean.

27 ...   N-N6ch
28 K-R2   R × N
29 Q-KB2!

Yet another tactical blow. Stean had only expected 29 N × R N × N when Black has two minor pieces and a pawn for the queen, but CHESS 4.6 finds a mate threat (30 Q-B7ch K-R1 31 Q-B8mate) which forces an even greater material advantage.

29	...	P-R3
30	N×R	N×N
31	Q-B3	

Winning two pieces for the rook and emerging with queen against rook and pawn.

31	...	R-N1
32	R×N	R-KB1
33	Q-N4	B×R

34	Q×KPch	K-R1
35	Q×B	R-B3
36	Q-K5	R-QN3
37	Q×BP	R×P
38	Q-QB8ch	K-R2
39	Q×P	Resigns

Stean was in no doubt that the program would be able to promote a pawn and force mate by move 60.

David Slate, of CHESS 4.6, records a move.

CHESS 4.6's win against Stean was no fluke. During 1977 it won a number of other games against players holding the title of International Master, including myself, Berliner (former World Correspondence Champion), Day and Vranesic, and it won one game against International Grandmaster Robert Hubner, rated amongst the top dozen players in the world. At the end of 1977 I estimated its ability at blitz chess to be in the range 2300-2400. This, in itself, is a great achievement, which appeared most unlikely a decade ago.

In the remainder of this chapter I shall comment on four more of this program's blitz victories played during 1977. Each of its opponents is an International Master.

White: CHESS 4.6

Black: Hans Berliner

Pittsburgh, March 1977

Bird's Opening

1	P-KB4	P-KN3
2	N-QB3	B-N2
3	P-K4	P-QB4

Transposing into a Sicilian Defence.

4	N-B3	N-QB3
5	B-B4	P-K3
6	O-O	KN-K2
7	P-K5	

Otherwise Black plays 7...P-Q4, with advantage.

7	...	P-Q3
8	N-K4	

The tactics are already beginning. If 8...P-Q4 9 N-Q6ch K-B1 10 B-N5, and Black's king is awkwardly placed.

8	...	P×P
9	P×P	N×P
10	B-N5ch	N(K2)-B3
11	P-Q3	O-O
12	N×N	N×N
13	B-K3	

White has some pressure for the pawn, but objectively speaking this should not be enough.

13	...	P-QR3
14	B-R4	P-QN4
15	B×NP!?	

Complicating the position still fur-

ther, but at the cost of a piece.

15	...	P×B
16	B×P	R-K1
17	P-Q4	N-B3
18	P-B3	P-K4

18...Q-B2 should have led to an easy win, since 19 N-Q6 R-Q1 gives White nothing. I imagine that in this position Black was confident of victory no matter what he played - after all, he is a piece up.

19	N-Q6	P×P

If 19...R-K3 20 Q-B3, attacking QB6 and KB7.

20	Q-B3	

20	...	N-K4??

Admitting defeat. Black had to play 20...B-Q2.

21	Q×R	P-Q6
22	N×R	Q×N
23	P-QR4	P-R4

24	P × P	N-N5
25	R-R7	Q-K4

One last try.

26	Q × Bch	K-R2
27	Q-B7	Q-K7
28	Q × P	Resigns

White: CHESS 4.6
Black: Lawrence Day

Toronto, August 1977
Sicilian Defence

1	P-K4	P-QB4
2	N-KB3	N-QB3
3	B-N5	P-Q3
4	O-O	B-Q2
5	P-B3	N-B3
6	R-K1	P-QR3
7	B-R4	P-QN4
8	B-B2	B-N5
9	P-KR3	B × N
10	Q × B	

White is handling the opening rather well, considering that it is not a tactical system.

10	...	P-KN3
11	P-Q3	B-N2
12	B-B4	

12	...	N-Q2
13	N-Q2	O-O

14 B-QN3

Not a bad move but a negative one, illustrating the program's inability to form a concrete plan.

14	...	R-B1
15	P-QR4	N(B3)-K4
16	Q-K2	Q-N3
17	P × P	P × P
18	B-K3	N-QB3

Black was afraid of 19 P-KB4.

19	N-B3	Q-N2
20	N-N5	N(B3)-K4
21	P-KB4	

21 ... P-B5

Once again the human goes in for tactics, but he has overlooked White's strong reply.

22 R-R7!

Now White begins to take complete command of the situation.

22	...	Q-B3
23	P × N	P × B
24	P-Q4!	P-Q4

The point of White's previous move is that 24...P × P loses to 25 P-Q5 Q-B5 26 Q × Q and 27 R × N, when White has an extra piece.

25	P × P	Q × QP
26	R(1)-R1	P-B3

27	P×P	P×P
28	Q-N4!	

A strong tactical blow, threatening to complete White's control of the seventh rank.

28	...	P-B4
29	Q-B3	Q×Q
30	N×Q	

White does not yet have any advantage in material but its positional plus is of decisive proportions. With a rook on the seventh rank, complete domination of the QR-file and the possibility of attacking Black's weak, doubled QNPs, CHESS 4.6 has a winning position.

A few years ago the best chess programs would not be able to win this position against a strong human opponent. Here, however, CHESS 4.6 exhibits excellent technique in converting its positional advantage into the full point.

30	...	N-B3
31	R(1)-R3	N-Q4
32	B-B2	P-N5!

The best chance, but not good enough.

33 R×P

Not 33 P×P R-B8ch 34 K-R2 R-B7, attacking the bishop, followed by 35...R×QNP, ...R-N8 and ...P-N7, when Black might win.

33	...	P×P
34	R(3)-N7!	B-R3
35	P×P	R×P
36	R×P	R-B8ch
37	K-R2	B-B5ch
38	B-N3	B×Bch
39	K×B	R-KB3
40	N-K5	R-B6ch
41	K-R2	N-B5

CHESS 4.6 now announces mate in four!

42	R(QR7)-KN7ch	K-B1
43	N-Q7ch	K-K1
44	R-N8ch	R-B1
45	R×R mate	

White: CHESS 4.6
Black: Zvonko Vranesic

London, September 1977
Sicilian Defence

1	P-K4	P-QB4
2	N-KB3	P-K3
3	P-Q4	P×P
4	N×P	N-KB3

5	N-QB3	B-N5
6	P-B3	

Best is 6 P-K5, which is known to lead to an advantage for White after a complicated sequence. CHESS 4.6 did not know this variation and was uanble to calculate the consequences of 6 P-K5 with sufficient accuracy. It therefore discovered a "new" move.

6	...	O-O
7	B-KB4	P-QR3
8	P-QR3	B-R4?!

8...B × Nch 9 P × B P-Q3 is more solid.

9	B-Q6	R-K1
10	P-QN4	B-B2
11	N-N3	B × B
12	Q × B	Q-K2

Necessary, in order to reduce White's grip on the dark squares.

13	Q × Q	R × Q
14	P-K5!	

As this move demonstrates, Black's troubles on the dark squares are not yet over, because after

14	...	N-Q4

White can continue 15 N-K4 and

then N-Q6.

15	K-Q2?	

Lack of positional appreciation.

15	...	N × N
16	K × N	N-B3
17	R-K1	P-QN4
18	B-Q3	R-N1
19	K-N2	P-Q4?

Black expects to be able to regain the pawn but as usual the program calculates better than its human opponent.

20	P × P e.p.	R-Q2
21	R-Q1	

The move that Vranesic had overlooked. If now 21...R × P?? 22 B × RPch K × B 23 R × R.

21	...	N-K4
22	N-B5	R-Q1
23	P-KB4	N-N5
24	P-Q7!	

The same motif. If 24...B × P 24 N × B R × N 26 B × RPch K × B 27 R × R.

24	...	B-N2
25	R-Q2	B-Q4
26	N × RP	R-N3
27	N-B5	N-B3
28	P-QR4!	

White temporarily returns one of his extra pawns in order to create three connected passed pawns on the Q-side.

| 28 | ... | P×P |
| 29 | P-B4! | B-R1 |

If 29...R×NPch 30 K-B3, winning a piece.

30	K-B3	P-N3
31	B-B2	P-R6
32	K-N3	B-B3
33	K×P	K-B1
34	B-R4	B×B
35	K×B	K-K2

36	R(1)-Q1	R-QR1ch
37	K-N3	R-Q1
38	P-N5	P-R3
39	K-N4	R(3)-N1
40	P-N3	R-QR1
41	P-N6	R(R)-N1
42	K-N5	P-N4
43	P×P	P×P
44	R-Q6	N-N5
45	N-R6	R-QR1
46	P-N7	R-R2
47	P-N8=Q	R×Qch
48	N×R	R-N2ch
49	R-N6	R×P
50	RxRch	K-B3

It is almost superfluous to comment on the strength of White's position but the sixty move rule (see page 88) offers Black some hope. He must try, at all costs, to avoid walking into a forced mate within the next ten moves.

| 51 | P-B5 | N-K4 |
| 52 | P-B6 | K-N3 |

From a practical point of view Black might have tried 52...N×P and hoped to avoid mate for long enough to win on time.

53	P-B7	N×R
54	N×N	K-B4
55	P-B8=Q	K-N3
56	Q-KN8ch	K-B4
57	Q-R7ch	K-N5
58	N-K5 mate	

"I am very impressed" - Vranesic.

White: CHESS 4.6
Black: Zvonko Vranesic

London, September 1977
Sicilian Defence

1	P-K4	P-QB4
2	N-KB3	P-K3
3	P-Q4	P×P

4	N × P	N-QB3
5	N × N	

CHESS 4.6 always seems to make this capture in the Sicilian Defence even though it is usually bad (of my own game against the program, page 16). Although Black's QRP is isolated, Black has an important pawn majority in the centre and the use of the QN-file.

5	...	NP × N
6	B-K3	N-B3
7	N-B3	P-Q4
8	P-K5	N-Q2
9	P-B4	B-K2
10	B-K2	O-O
11	O-O	P-QR4
12	B-Q3	P-KB4

12...P-QB4 seems more natural.

13	P × P e.p.	N × P
14	Q-B3	R-N1
15	B-Q4	P-B4

16 B-K5   P-B5?

The program did not overlook the capture of the rook, it misassessed the position that arises after Black's 18th move.

17	B × R	Q-N3ch
18	K-R1	Q × B

19	B-K2	Q × NP
20	KR-B1	Q-N3
21	QR-N1	Q-B2
22	Q-N3	B-B4
23	R-K1	B-Q2
24	R-KB1	B-Q3
25	N-N5	B × N
26	R × B	N-K5
27	Q-KR3	R-B3
28	B-N4	Q-Q2?

Overlooking a simple, tactical reply.

29	R × QP	Q-K2
30	R × P	P-R3
31	Q-K3	N-B4
32	B-K2	Q-QB2
33	R-R8ch	K-R2
34	P-N3	P-K4

A final, desparate blow directed against White's K-side.

35	P × P	R × Rch
36	B × R	B × P
37	P-QR4	B-B3
38	B-N2	N-Q2
39	R-R7	Q-Q3
40	Q-K4ch	P-N3
41	Q-Q5	

In this hopeless position Vranesic lost on time. Whether or not he exchanges queens Black will lose his knight.

4 Computer Chess Tournaments

Since 1970 the Association for Computing Machinery (ACM) has organized a chess tournament as part of its annual conference. In 1974 the first World Championship for computer programs took place in Stockholm. Since then computer tournaments have become increasingly popular, with events taking place in Germany, Canada, the Netherlands as well as the annual tournament in the U.S.A. In 1978, the first competition exclusively for microcomputers was held - a suggestion of my own which was implemented thanks to Douglas Penrod, founder/editor of the *Computer Chess Newsletter*. There is now an international society for those interested in computer chess and it looks as though interest in the subject is increasing at an almost exponential rate, which is perhaps not so surprising in view of the advent of home computing as a hobby.

The two principal computer chess tournaments continue to be the annual ACM competition and the World Championship which is held every three years. I have written books on the 1975 and 1976 ACM events; this chapter and Appendix B of this volume are devoted to coverage of the 1977 ACM tournament in Seattle and the Second World Comptuer Championship which was held in Toronto earlier in the same year.

Second World Computer Championship
Toronto, August 7th-9th 1977

No.	Program	Rd 1		Rd 2		Rd 3		Rd 4		Total	Place
1	CHESS 4.6 (USA)	W11	1	B 9	1	W2	1	B 4	1	4	1st
2	DUCHESS (USA)	W3	1	B 14	1	B 1	0	B 9	1	3	2nd =
3	KAISSA (USSR)	B 2	0	W16	1	B 5	1	B 6	1	3	2nd =
4	BELLE (USA)	W6	½	B 12	1	W7	1	W1	0	2½	4th =
5	CHAOS (USA)	W15	1	B 7	½	W3	0	B 12	1	2½	4th =
6	BLACK KNIGHT (USA)	B 4	½	W8	½	B 14	1	W3	0	2	6th =
7	DARK HORSE (Sweden)	B 16	1	W5	½	B 4	0	B 10	½	2	6th =
8	ELSA (W. Germany)	W12	½	B 6	½	W9	0	B 15	1	2	6th =
9	MASTER (England)	B 13	1	W1	0	B 8	1	W2	0	2	6th =
10	WITA (Canada)	B 14	0	B 11	1	W15	½	W7	½	2	6th =
11	BCP (England)	B 1	0	W10	0	B 16	1	W14	½	1½	11th =
12	BLITZ V (USA)	B 8	½	W4	0	B 13	1	W5	0	1½	11th =
13	CHUTE 1.2 (Canada)	W9	0	B 7	½	W12	0	B 16	1	1½	11th =
14	OSTRICH (Canada)	W10	1	W2	0	W6	0	B 11	½	1½	11th =
15	BS 6676 (Netherlands)	B 5	0	W13	½	B 10	½	W8	0	1	15th
16	TELL (Switzerland)	W7	0	B 3	0	W11	0	W13	0	0	16th

The sensation of the tournament was KAISSA's loss to DUCHESS in the first round. KAISSA, the defending World Champion, had been seeded number one, but played very much below the level that I had expected. Full credit must go to DUCHESS which demonstrated that it had made a greater improvement during the preceding year than any other program. The

DUCHESS-KAISSA game is annotated below but for reasons of space I have decided to depart from my usual pattern and am giving the remainder of the games from this event (and all of the games from ACM 77) in Appendix B, without notes.

White: DUCHESS
Black: KAISSA

Centre Counter

1	P-K4	P-Q4

KAISSA's favourite defence.

2	P×P	N-KB3
3	P-Q4	N×P
4	N-KB3	P-KN3
5	B-K2	B-N2
6	P-B4	N-N3
7	N-B3	O-O
8	B-K3	B-N5
9	P-B5	

This move drives Black's knight off ...QN3 so that White's eleventh move attacks the black QNP.

9	...	N-Q4
10	O-O	P-K3
11	Q-N3	P-N3

Now or on the previous move Black should have considered the exchange ...N×B.

12	N×N	P×N
13	B-KN5	Q-Q2
14	P-KR3	B-B4
15	Q-B3	R-K1
16	KR-K1	B-K5
17	N-Q2	Q-B4

Somewhat pointless. While White has been playing fairly methodically, improving its position very slightly move by move, KAISSA has been floundering around without any sort of plan in sight. Black should be aiming to complete its development.

18	B-K3	Q-K3
19	N×B	P×N

If 19...Q×N 20 B-KR6!, followed by B-QN5.

20	P×P	BP×P
21	KR-QB1!	

Keeping the QB-file firmly under control, White makes it clear that the Black knight will not find it easy to reach a comfortable square.

21	...	N-Q2
22	B-N4	Q-Q4
23	Q-B6	N-B3
24	B-K2	QR-Q1
25	Q-R4	R-K2
26	B-QN5	Q-KB4
27	R-B2	N-Q4

At last the knight has reached a sensible looking square but it is too late to do anything about the invasion of the QB-file by White's major pieces.

28	R(1)-QB1	B-B3
29	Q-N3	P-QR4
30	P-N4	Q-K3
31	R-B6	

The invasion of Black's position is complete. For KAISSA there is no satisfactory move.

31	...	P-R5
32	Q×P	R-Q3
33	R×R	Q×R
34	Q-R8ch	

34   ...   R-K1

I had expected KAISSA to play 34...K-N2, which allows White to win a piece by 35 P-N5. When KAISSA played its rook back to K1 I commented to the audience that I thought there must be a bug in the program. How else could one explain away the voluntary loss of the rook? Nobody, not even ex-World Champion Botvinnik, who was sitting in the audience, could suggest why KAISSA had played this move, and its programmers, Messrs Donskoy and Arlazarov, agreed that the answer was a bug.

Later that night however, the programmers reset this position in order to see what their program had been thinking about. The result was astounding: KAISSA had seen the continuation 34...K-N2 35 Q-KB8ch!! K×Q 36 B-KR6ch followed by R-B8ch and a forced mate.

The time is fast approaching when I am going to have to admit that chess programs are smarter than I am.

| 35 | Q×Rch | K-N2 |
| 36 | P-N5 | |

Now 36 Q-KB8ch does not work because after 36...K×Q 37 B-KR6ch the black king can escape to K2, which square was previously occupied by Black's rook.

36	...	B-Q1
37	B-QB4	Q-K2
38	Q×Q	N×Q
39	B-B4	N-B4
40	B-Q5	K-B1
41	R-B8	K-K2
42	R-B4	N-N2
43	B×KP	N-K3
44	B-K3	N-B2
45	P-Q5	N-N4
46	B-B3	K-Q2
47	P-QR4	N-Q3
48	R-B6	N-B4

and KAISSA's programmers resigned for their program.

After KAISSA's loss in this game, the hoped-for clash between KAISSA and CHESS 4.6 did not take place because of the way that the Swiss pairing system operates. The same situation occurred in the first World Computer Championship in Stockholm - CHESS 4.0 lost in an early round and was never paired against KAISSA. The spectators (and the programmers) were naturally anxious to see what would happen when these two giants of the computer chess world met in mortal combat, so the same solution was applied to this situation as had been employed in Stockholm three years earlier. An exhibition game was arranged, after the tournament, between KAISSA and CHESS 4.6. Since CHESS 4.0 had White in their Stockholm encounter (which was drawn) I suggested that KAISSA be given White for the Toronto game, and no-one objected.

White: KAISSA
Black: CHESS 4.6

Toronto 1977
Nimzowitsch's Defence

| 1 | P-K4 | N-QB3 |

An unusual move (in human chess) which can lead to interesting positions after only a few moves.

2	N-KB3	P-K3
3	P-Q4	P-Q4
4	B-Q3	

4 N-B3 or 4 P-K5 would give White more chance of keeping the advantage.

4	...	P × P
5	B × P	B-Q2
6	O-O	N-B3
7	R-K1	N × B
8	R × N	B-K2
9	P-B4	

Black has equalized and should continue with 9...B-B3.

| 9 | ... | P-B4? |

A weak move, leaving a backward pawn on K3 and a weak square on K4.

| 10 | R-K1 | O-O |
| 11 | N-B3 | P-B5 |

Somewhat artificial but quite well motivated. Black's KBP restricts White's bishop and cramps his K-side.

| 12 | Q-Q3 | Q-K1 |
| 13 | P-KN3? | |

Opening up the KB-file which can be used by Black for an attack against the White king. This move also allows Black to exchange off a potentially weak pawn.

13	...	P × P
14	RP × P	Q-R2
15	B-B4	P-KN4!

Striking out in the right direction - towards White's king.

| 16 | P-Q5 | |

The best chance for counterplay.

| 16 | ... | P × P? |

A tactical miscalculation and a strategic error as well. Firstly CHESS 4.6 overlooks the effect of 17 (which KAISSA does not play) and secondly it is far more sensible to proceed with the K-side attack by 16...P × B rather than be diverted to another arena.

17 QN×P??

This leads to a position in which White has slightly the better ending. Instead, 17 R×B would have kept White very much in the game, e.g. 17...Q×R 18 N×QP or 17...N×R 18 N×NP.

17 ...	P×B
18 N×Bch	N×N
19 Q×B	N-N3
20 Q×Qch	R×Q
21 P-KN4	R-Q2

The ending is marginally better for White because Black's K-side pawns are isolated, but in a game between two strong human opponents I would expect the result to be a draw. From now on however, CHESS 4.6 demonstrates that its slightly deeper exhaustive search is extremely useful in certain situations.

22 QR-Q1	QR-Q1
23 R×R	R×R
24 K-N2	K-N2
25 N-N5??	

Already a fatal error. The Black rook must not be allowed onto the seventh rank.

| 25 ... | R-Q7 |
| 26 R-QN1 | R-B7 |

27 P-N3	N-K4
28 R-KR1	R×RP
29 R-R4	

After 29 R×Pch K-N3 30 R-K7 K×N 31 R×Nch K×P, Black is a pawn up with an easy endgame win.

29 ...	N-Q6
30 N-R3	R-N7
31 P-N5	K-N1

32 N×P??

Making Black's task simple. Up to this point I had grave doubts as to whether CHESS 4.6 would be able to force a win against a careful defense but it seems that KAISSA did not know about one of the golden rules of endgame play - when you are a pawn or two down you should exchange pawns but not pieces.

32 ...	R×BPch
33 K-N3	R×N
34 R×R	N×R
35 K×N	K-B2
36 P-N4	K-K3
37 K-K4	P-QR3
38 K-B4	K-Q3
39 K-K4	P-B4

Creating a passed pawn.

40	P × Pch	K × P	43	K-Q3	K-N5
41	K-Q3	P-R4	44	K-B2	K × P
42	K-B3	P-R5			

KAISSA's programmers resigned.

Eighth ACM Computer Championship
Seattle, October 15th-17th 1977

No.	Program	Rd 1		Rd 2		Rd 3		Rd 4		Total	Place
1	CHESS 4.6	W8	1	B 4	1	W3	1	B 2	½	3½	1st=
2	DUCHESS	B 6	1	W5	1	B 7	1	W1	½	3½	1st=
3	CHAOS	W10	1	B 12	1	B 1	0	W6	1	3	3rd
4	XENARBOR	W11	1	W1	0	B 5	1	B 8	½	2½	4th
5	BLACK KNIGHT	W9	1	B 2	0	W4	0	B 11	1	2	5th=
6	BLITZ V	W2	0	B 8	1	W12	1	B 3	0	2	5th=
7	OSTRICH	B 12	0	W9	1	W2	0	B 10	1	2	5th=
8	CHUTE 1.2	B 1	0	W6	0	B 10	1	W4	½	1½	8th
9	BRUTE FORCE	B 5	0	B 7	0	W11	0	W12	1	1	9th=
10	TYRO	B 3	0	B 11	1	W8	0	W7	0	1	9th=
11	WITA	B 4	0	W10	0	B 9	1	W5	0	1	9th−
12	8080 CHESS	W7	1	W3	0	B 6	0	B 9	0	1	9th=

This tournament was notable for the appearance, for the first time in the history of the event, of a chess program running on a microprocessor (8080 Chess). Although the program did not perform well, and its sole point came about from good fortune rather than good play, its participation was a nudge in the ribs for the big programs running on much larger and faster machines. In future years I would hope that the leading programs in each year's microprocessor tournament will be allowed to compete with the 'big guys' in the ACM tournaments. Just as computer chess tournaments have done much to stimulate work in the field, so the competition between small and large machines will probably inspire microprocessor programmers to find new programming strategies that are not limited by small trees and slower machines.

Probably everyone expected that the eighth ACM tournament would be won with a 100% score by CHESS 4.6, just as so many previous events had been won by this program's predecessors. Before the start, and right up to the middle of the last round, this was my opinion. In fact, I rather rashly gave odds of 100 to 1 that if the CHESS 4.6 v DUCHESS game ended in a decisive result then the Northwestern program would be the winner. My co-author risked a dollar, which he retrieved, and I had a few anxious moments in the endgame, when DUCHESS had the better position. For the games of this event the reader is referred to Appendix B.

During the tournament I gave a simultaneous exhibition against all twelve programs. In a similar match in 1975 I had scored ten wins and two draws. This time I again won ten, but drew one and lost one, to CHESS 4.6. The time has come when I can no longer hold off the world's strongest program when giving it only a fraction of my concentration. Ten years ago this possibility would have seemed extremely remote.

5 Microcomputers and Chess

Researchers who first described how computers might be programmed to play chess were talking about machines costing millions of dollars. These machines occupied entire laboratories, ran on vacuum tubes or mechanical relays, required large amounts of electricity, generated vast amounts of heat, and failed at intervals measured in minutes or hours. They executed approximately 10,000 instructions per second, compared with 10,000,000 or more on some big fast machines currently available. They had to be programmed in machine language, a language that must have driven a certain number of programmers in the 1950's into a permanent state of insanity. Memory space was measured in bits rather than in kilowords as it is now, thereby placing severe restrictions on the size of programs. Finding mistakes in programs was a tremendous task. Programmers complained that their programs failed because of hardware problems while the technicians called in to find the mysterious bugs countered that the problems were with the programs. The two were always seen working together and blaming each other for their own woes.

The first chess programs were developed in such an environment, and it is little wonder they didn't play particularly strong chess. The first program, in fact, played on a 6 x 6 board (without Bishops) because of limitations caused by these factors.

In the 1960's, transistors replaced vacuum tubes and relays and the second generation of computers was born. Computer centers sprang up at a large number of universities, research centers, and commercial establishments. They were supported by staffs of dozens of programmers, system analysts, operators and technicians. High level languages such as FORTRAN became available as did editors, assemblers, compilers, and operating systems. Time sharing systems became the rule - a single computer servicing as many as a hundred users with each being oblivious of the other's presence. Charges for computing time typically ran from $5 to $10 per minute.

Smaller computers called minicomputers also started to be produced by several firms. Rather than costing millions of dollars and requiring a large staff to maintain, these systems cost $50,000 - $200,000 and were kept running by small staffs of two or three. They found their way into the laboratories of universities, mainly in engineering and computer science departments, although as time went on and costs dropped, they invaded other departments as well including geography, music, and linguistics. They differed from their larger brothers mainly in (1) their word size: typically 12 to 24 bits (2) memory size: ranging from 4K to 64K words, (3) their ability to support a number of users; they could support only one person at a time, (4) the peripheral equipment they could control: usually much less and slower, and (5) the cost of using them: once acquired there was often no charge for computer time.

Throughout the 1960's and early 1970's great advances were made in computer hardware and software. The third generation computers born in the late 1960's were characterized by the introduction of integrated circuits. These circuits crammed the electronic equivalent of a radio onto a piece of semiconductor material smaller than a penny. Computer systems of all sizes and prices became available from a lower limit of about $5,000 to as much as $20,000,000 and more.

By the middle 1970's, approximately 200 chess programs had been developed. The performances of a number of them are well known, but there are many others which never acquired much of a reputation. Many special endgame and mating programs also were written. Perhaps 500 - 2000 people around the world had taken a shot at programming chess in one way or another. Thousands of others were probably interested in programming chess but were restrained by the unavailability of computing facilities.

Paralleling the interest to program computers to play chess, people have shown an equal interest and desire to play against them. People love to play games and computers are becoming increasingly popular opponents. They never get upset when they lose (perhaps this is a negative consideration - maybe people like to see their opponent fret and fume and squirm!), they never tire and are always ready to start another game when the last one ends, they can play at any desired speed, they can be insulted, ridiculed, and ultimately unplugged! They never rave to their colleagues about victories or seek excuses for defeats. One can discuss strategy in their presence (for now anyway, until the day arrives when they listen!), eat, make noise, and in general, show them none of the courtesies normally given a warmblooded opponent. They serve as tireless teachers, having infinite patience. They become friends and often are talked to as though they are human.

For many years, game playing programs with small computing requirements have flourished on university campuses. STARTRECK, probably the most popular of these, has been a grand success for a number of years. While students of. the 1950's and 1960's found themselves in academic difficulties because of excesses in bridge and other human versus human games, more recently electronic games have caused similar problems. Chess programs have been available on a number of computers but they have been used sparingly because of their large computing requirements. MAC HACK, various versions of COKO, BELLE, OSTRICH, and CHESS 3.0 - 4.6 have been widely distributed and are used after hours (when computing costs are lower) by thousands of chess enthusiasts.

In 1975, as a result of great progress in the miniaturization of transistor circuitry leading to the introduction of large scale integrated (LSI) circuits the microcomputer became commercially available at the retail store level. Computer circuitry that once occupied rooms and cost millions of dollars could now be manufactured for only several dollars and placed on the head of a penny. A revolution was born. Cost fell to the point where it became feasible for someone to have his own computer. For $1000, the cost of a good stereo system, an individual could purchase a computer for his own home, a computer more powerful than any in existence 25 years earlier. In the 1950's and 1960's, it was in vogue for the middle and upper class to spend hundreds of dollars on stereo equipment in order to obtain distortion-free sound at frequencies only their pet cats could appreciate. Starting in the late 1970's, the home computer has assumed in some sense the same role. This movement has only begun, but its prospects for the future are awesome. One never finishes building a computer system. There is always something else to add. First, one can add more memory, then a good floppy disc, then a video display, then a magnetic tape unit, then a new and faster processing unit, and then again more memory and on and on. While there is really only one thing that can be done with a stereo system - i.e., play records - the possible applications for home computers fathom the imagination. Today, almost every home in North America has several hundred dollars worth of stereo equipment; in twenty years they will all have several thousand dollars in computing equipment.

The capabilities of current microcomputers differ from those of minicomputers in essentially the same ways as minicomputers differ from larger computers. The differences are related to the 8-bit word size around which the calculating and control units of almost all microcomputers are designed. This is in contrast to the 12 to 24-bit word sizes used by minicomputers and 32 to 64-bit word sizes used by larger computers. These calculating and control units, called microprocessors, are manufactured by such well known semiconductor giants as Texas Instruments, Motorola, RCA, and Intel. They typically cost in the order of $50. The 8-bit word size has two important effects. First, arithmetic on numbers exceeding ± 128 is awkward! It is necessary to store numbers larger than ± 128 in two memory locations with the least significant bits stored in one location and the most significant bits stored in another. The basic arithmetic operations consequently are more complicated and take longer than on larger machines. Second, most instructions require several memory locations (two or three) because the problem of addressing (or referring to) memory locations requires it. This also causes a loss in speed. In a big machine, it usually requires three instructions to add two positive numbers in locations X and Y and store the results in a third location Z:

Instruction 1: Transfer X to the adder A
Instruction 2: Add Y to A forming X + Y

Instruction 3: Store A at Z.

These three instructions occupy three (consecutive) memory locations say M_1, M_2, and M_3: X, Y and Z occupy three locations also. The addition requires a minimum of six machine cycles:

Cycle 1: Get instruction from M_1,

Cycle 2: Decode and perform instruction, i.e., transfer the number in X to the adder A,

Cycle 3: Get next instruction from M_2,

Cycle 4: Decode and perform instruction, i.e., add Y to A,

Cycle 5: Get next instruction from M_3

Cycle 6: Decode and perform instruction, i.e., store A at Z.

Additional cycles may be necessary in order to decode the instructions if locations X, Y, or Z must be "indirectly addressed", a term whose definition is beyond the scope of this presentation. Typically, seven, rather than six, cycles might be required.

For a microcomputer, instead of three instructions, six instructions are necessary assuming that positive numbers larger than 128 are to be added. The three numbers stored in X, Y, and Z in the previous example would have to be stored in six locations, X_2 X_1, Y_2, Y_1, and Z_2, Z_1. Then the program would:

Instruction 1: Transfer X_1 to the adder A

Instruction 2: Add Y_1 to A forming $X_1 + Y_1$ and possibly a carry C.

Instruction 3: Store A in Z_1.

Instruction 4: Transfer X_2 to the adder A

Instruction 5: Add Y_2 and C to A forming $X_2 + Y_2 + C$.

Instruction 6: Store A in Z_2

These six instructions would most likely occupy eighteen consecutive memory locations and the addition would require about 13 or 14 machine cycles. Thus even if the two machines just described were designed of circuits capable of operating at the same speed, the microcomputer would take more than twice the time of the larger machine to carry out the equivalent operation.

Memory sizes on microcomputers currently range from 2K 8-byte words to 16K 8-byte words. This is about 1/10 the size of minicomputer memories and about 1/100 the size of large computer memories. A limit of 64K arises because two memory locations can store a number from 0 to $2^{16} = 64K$. This small memory size places restrictions on program sizes. The better chess programs, CHESS 4.6, DUCHESS, BELLE, and so on require considerably more memory space than this. OSTRICH 79s*, a special

---

*Available through Computer Game Programs, 1700 Ohio Savings Plaza, 1801 East Ninth St., Cleveland, Ohio 44114.

version of OSTRICH which is commercially available, runs on 16K 16-bit words. SARGON, currently the best of the microcomputer programs however only uses 16K of 8-bit words. Most of the big programs have between 5,000 - 20,000 instructions but in addition they use additional memory space to store information gathered while searching the move tree. In the case of CHESS 4.7, this can be as much as a million words! Other programs use anywhere from about 10K to 200K and more. OSTRICH 79S has about 8K instructions and requires about 8K for storing information about the move tree.

Not only are main memories smaller, secondary memories are also smaller. Secondary memory refers to disc and tape storage. In microcomputers, they are at least an order of magnitude smaller than they are on minicomputers and they also function more slowly. Secondary memory is used during program development and thus developing programs for microcomputers is a slower procedure than on big computers.

Software for microcomputers is getting more sophisticated but presently is way behind that available on larger systems. The only high level programming language widely available for microcomputers is BASIC and this executes in an "interpretive mode". In an interpretive mode, each BASIC instruction is translated into machine language as it is executed, resulting in relatively slow program execution when compared to programs which are completely translated before execution begins. Programs written for larger machines in FORTRAN, PL1, or other high level programming languages are almost always translated before execution.

All of the aforementioned problems will disappear in the next few years. Sixteen-bit microcomputers are already on the market and it won't be long before the microcomputer of tomorrow looks like the minicomputer of today. Software will improve quickly with high level languages such as FORTRAN becoming widely available by 1980. Soon it will be no handicap whatsoever to develop a chess program on microcomputer. In another ten years, there will be microcomputers as powerful as any large computer on the market today! Chess-playing machines the size of cigar boxes will then make mincemeat of the best human players! Beware, David!

The Programs

There are two different types of microcomputer systems used for playing chess. First, there are microcomputers which are designed only to play chess. In my opinion, the most notable of these are CHESS CHALLENGER and BORIS. Two others, COMPU-CHESS and CHESSMATE are also available but they play more weakly. Prices are in the range of $150 to $300 and are falling. The second type are general purpose microcomputers for which home-brewed chess programs have been developed. These machines, of course, can handle the usual variety of non-chess programs as well. The most notable programs in this category are SARGON II and MIKE. There are at least twenty others in existence but they are considerably weaker. Several hundred others are at various stages of development.

CHESS CHALLENGER

CHESS CHALLENGER is manufactured by Fidelity Electronics, a Chicago based firm that advertises itself as the "world's largest manufacturer of self-contained, microprocessor based board games." In addition to CHESS CHALLENGER, they also produce CHECKER CHALLENGER and an electronic backgammon machine. When CHESS CHALLENGER first appeared on the market, it played disasterously. It both accepted and made illegal moves. However, more recent versions play quite respectably and are no longer subject to this criticism. The system is neatly packaged, runs on batteries or plugs into the wall, and weighs about five pounds. Two versions are marketed - CHESS CHALLENGER "3" and CHESS CHALLENGER "10". The "10" version is far superior and I give it credit for playing at about the 1300 USCF level when running in its "tournament mode", one of ten different modes in which it can play. Given a certain position, the computer's response is not always the same; if two or more moves look about as good as one another, the computer picks one randomly. Certain opening lines are programmed. A Fairchild F8 8-bit microprocessor is the brains of the machine. The program requires 4K of ROM (Read Only Memory - memory which can be read but not changed) and ½K of RAM (Random Access Memory - memory which can be read and changed). The program resides in the ROM and uses the RAM to store information found as the search progresses. The program is similar to CHESS 3.0. It carries out forward pruning at all levels in the tree.

CHESS CHALLENGER 10 took on OSTRICH several months ago at McGill and an interesting game ensued. Neither side made a serious tactical error. OSTRICH's positional play however made the difference. With each trade, OSTRICH's position improved slightly. By move 26, OSTRICH had the game wrapped up. OSTRICH earned a provisional Quebec Chess Federation rating of 1508 this summer based on tournament play. QCF ratings are very similar to USCF ratings.

White: OSTRICH
Black: CHESS CHALLENGER

Move times in seconds are denoted after each move. OSTRICH was set to play at a speed of 140 seconds per move; CHESS CHALLENGER 10

played in tournament mode.

1	P-K4(B)	P-QB4(32)
2	N-KB3(B)	P-Q3(30)
3	B-N5ch(B)	B-Q2(77)
4	N-B3(53)	N-KB3(181)
5	Q-K2(60)	N-B3(182)

6 O-O(110)   P-K4(657)

CHESS CHALLENGER 10 takes eleven minutes to find this move. Lights blinking on the console from time to time told us that it had not crashed. This move weakens the queen pawn and causes long term problems for CHESS CHALLENGER 10.

7 P-Q3(14)   N-Q5(199)
8 B × Bch(70)   Q × B(75)
9 Q-Q1(141)   B-K2(153)
10 B-N5(106)   ...

CHESS CHALLENGER 10 has developed nicely to this point - certainly as well as a 1300 level player. With the exception of its weak queen pawn, all its pieces are on good squares. For the next few moves, however, aimless play takes over.

10 ...   P-QR4(640)
11 P-KR3(160)   R-KN1(547)
12 P-R3(146)   P-R3(176)
13 B × N(121)   P × B(152)
14 K-R1(148)   P-R5(275)
15 N-Q5(223)   B-Q1(261)
16 P-B3(231)   N-N6(167)
17 R-R2(125)   R-QB1(392)
18 N-Q2(180)   ...

OSTRICH forces CHESS CHALLENGER 10 to give up its well positioned knight.

18 ...   N × N(174)
19 Q × N(92)   R-N3(174)
20 P-Q4(141)   BP × P(160)
21 P × P(151)   Q-N4(80)
22 R-Q1(342)   Q-B5(238)
23 QR-R1(321)   R-B3(333)
24 N-K3(373)   Q × P(273)
25 Q × Q(233)   P × Q(131)
26 R × P(112)   ...

While no outright mistakes have been made, CHESS CHALLENGER 10 finds itself with poorly placed pawns.

26 ...   P-N4(123)
27 QR-Q1(179)   B-K2(146)
28 N-B5!(277)   R-B7(190)

A move that reflects the horizon problem. R-B7 pushes the loss of a pawn, either the queen's or the knight's, over the search horizon of CHESS CHALLENGER 10.

29 R/4-Q2(151)   R × R(90)
30 R × R(98)   P-R4(107)
31 R-Q5   ...

OSTRICH is more interested in winning the knight's pawn than the queen's pawn. CHESS CHALLENGER 10 doesn't seem to have algorithms that encourage centralizing the king in the end game, a necessary maneuver here.

31 ...   R-N1(161)
32 R × NP(100)   R-N3(126)
33 R-N8ch(191)   B-Q1
34 N × Pch(146)   K-K2(47)
35 N-B5ch(128)   K-Q2(77)
36 R-N4(153)   B-B2(92)
37 R × P(243)   R-N1(110)

38	P-QN3(328)	B-N3(125)	44	N-N7ch(115)	K-K2(73)
39	P-B4(134)	B-B2(215)	45	R-B4(431)	B-Q3(90)
40	P-N3(125)	R-N1(83)	46	N-B5ch(103)	K-K3(246)
41	P-QN4(86)	R-K1(84)	47	R-B6(66)	R-Q1(197)
42	P-N5(63)	R-QN1(93)	48	P-QR4(54)	P-R5(54)
43	R-Q4ch(37)	K-K3(47)	49	P × P(42)	Resigns

BORIS

Named after Bobby Fischer's 1974 opponent in Reykjavik, BORIS is made by Chafitz Inc. of Rockville, Maryland. It has gone through a series of revisions. The current version reflects the influence of David Slate and Larry Atkin who have been discussing their ideas with Chafitz during the last year. Recently, Slate and Atkin have been hired as consultants by Chafitz. BORIS is based on an F8 microprocessor, the same one used by Fidelity in CHESS CHALLENGER 3 and 10. It requires 2½K of ROM and ¼K of RAM, the smallest amount of memory used by any program that plays "respectable" chess. BORIS carries out an iterated full-width search going as deeply as time allows. Because of the small amount of RAM, BORIS is unable to store much information as the search progresses. Moves are generated as needed, a necessary procedure.

BORIS is not quite as strong as CHESS CHALLENGER 10. It is, however, superior in its ability to interact with the user. It is able to recommend moves for its opponent. This is done by storing the continuation figured out for its own last move and then displaying the second move on this sequence when asked. It can change places with its opponent at any time in the middle of a game. Comments such as "I expected that," "illegal move," and "congratulations," add a nice touch. New versions that may be on the market by the time this book appears will have the ability to speak moves. An electronic chess board is also anticipated, according to Dan Newmayer of Chafitz.

MIKE

Although it might be hard for Americans to comprehend, the microcomputer revolution which began in California has spread well beyond the North American continent - even as far as the western countries of Europe - to England for example! It was in London that Mike Johnson, a programmer with the British Post Office, programmed his own Motorola 6800 system to play chess. The 6800 is to the microcomputer world as was the model T Ford to the automobile world. Named after its author, MIKE is written in assembly language and requires 10K to execute. Although the Motorola 6800 is a relatively slow microprocessor (it takes 2 microseconds to add together two 8-bit numbers), MIKE searches trees at a rate of about 200 nodes/sec, a most impressive statistic. This, of course, means that about 36,000 nodes are examined during the course of a three minute move. In September 1978, MIKE won the first European Microcomputer Chess Championship. Participants included BORIS (2nd place) and CHESS CHALLENGER 10 (3rd place). The five round round-robin actually ended in a tie between MIKE and BORIS but MIKE defeated BORIS in a playoff for the $200 first place prize. Three months later, Johnson came to Washington, D.C. and guided MIKE through a most respectable performance in the ACM's Ninth North American Computer Chess Championship finishing with 1 1/2 points out of a possible 4. MIKE drew with SARGON II, BLACK KNIGHT, and BS6676. Its game with SARGON II is presented on pages 84-85.

SARGON II

SARGON II, the current king of the microcomputer chess world was named after an ancient Mesopotamian king of the same name. Its authors, the husband and wife team of Kathe and Dan Spracklen, have invested all their free time since September 1977 developing first, SARGON I, and then its successor SARGON II. Being both programmers and chess players, the Spracklens have been captured by the excitement of watching their protege progress. SARGON II is playing stronger chess than any of its microcomputer contemporaries, a rating of about the 1450-1500 USCF level seems to be the consensus of opinion. SARGON II runs on Z-80 based microcomputers such as the TRS-80 (Radio Shack's computer) and the fast Wavemate Jupitor III which uses a 4.3 megahertz clock. The program occupies 12½K bytes and is growing. It carries out a full-width search at a rate of about 50 nodes/sec. When participating in the ACM's Washington tournament, SARGON carried out three level searches in about two minutes. Checking moves at the last ply caused search to be extended. The program has an exchange evaluator which carried out a careful analysis of exchanges at terminal nodes. The program's strength, to a good measure, can be credited to the performance of this algorithm. A book having about 4000 positions is also included in the program.

SARGON I captured first place at the West Coast Computer Faire's Microcomputer Chess Tournament in March of 1978. In so doing, it polished off five opponents without a loss. Deciding to take on the giants with an improved version called SARGON II, the Spracklens brought their Jupiter Wavemate III to Washington to participate in the ACM's annual tournament. Originally seeded eighth in a field of twelve, SARGON II mildly surprise the competition by finishing with 2 1/2 out of 4 points. This placed it in a three-way tie for third place with CHAOS and BLITZ 6.5. The program's most impressive game was a victory over Tony Marsland's much improved AWIT in the final round. We present here its draw with MIKE one round earlier. In this game, SARGON II shows strength in gaining a two pawn advantage and then weakness in failing to understand how to proceed.

White: MIKE
Black: SARGON II

1	P-K4	P-K4		
2	P-Q4	N-QB3		
3	P-Q5	N-N5		
4	P-QB3	N-R3		
5	P-KB4	N-B4		
6	P×P	...		

Stronger is B-Q3. This prevents 6 ... Q-R5+ while simultaneously developing a bishop. MIKE would much rather bag a pawn.

6	...	Q-R5ch
7	K-Q2	N×Pch
8	K-B2	N-B7
9	Q-K1	...

Again, MIKE is better off with the developing move 9 N-B3.

9	...	B-B4
10	N-B3	Q-R4
11	R-N1	N-K2
12	B-K3	Q-N3ch
13	K-B1	B×Bch
14	Q×B	N-N5
15	Q-Q2	P-Q3
16	B-Q3	Q-R4
17	B-N5ch	B-Q2
18	B×Bch	K×B
19	P×P	P×P
20	P-KR3	N-KB3
21	Q-N5	Q×Q
22	N×Q	KR-KB1
23	P-B4	QR-B1
24	N-Q2	N/7×P

MIKE now is paying for his slow development. It will fall behind by two pawns by move 27.

25	K-N1	N-K6
26	N/5-K4	N×N
27	N×N	R×P
28	N-B3	P-B4
29	P-QR4	P-Q4
30	P-KN3	R-KB3
31	R-K1	P-Q5
32	N-N5	P-QR3
33	N×P	P-B5
34	P×P	R×N
35	R×N	R/3×P
36	P-R5	R-Q8ch
37	K-R2	R-QR5ch
38	R-QR3	R/5×Rch
39	P×R	R-Q7ch
40	K-N3	R-Q6ch
41	K-B4	R×KRP
42	R-Q1ch	K-B3
43	P-R4	...

SARGON II can win easily by advancing the two passed kingside pawns. However, the program gives a lot of credit to attacking moves and not enough relatively to advancing pawns in such a situation. Consequently SARGON II leaves the passed pawns on their original squares while fruitlessly attacking with the rook. SARGON II, only programmed to detect draws by repetition of position when an identical position is repeated on alternative moves, fails to avoid a slightly more complicated drawing sequence, and thus the game ends in a draw in seven more moves. Newer versions of the Spracklen program will handle this position correctly.

43	...	R-R4
44	K-N4	R-R5ch
45	K-N3	R-R6ch
46	K-B4	R-R4
47	K-N4	R-R5ch
48	K-N3	R-R6ch
49	K-B4	R-R4
50	K-N4	R-R5ch
		Drawn by repetition.

How to keep up with events

Two magazines have taken the lead in publishing articles on computer chess and chess on microcomputers. *Personal Computing*, 1050 Commonwealth Avenue, Boston, Mass. 02215, USA, provides the most extensive coverage, about ten pages of news items and invited articles every month. Editor Harry Shershow has expanded coverage with every successive issue. Material is divided between large and small computers. *Byte Magazine*, the most widely distributed magazine dedicated to microcomputers, has published a number of invited articles on computer chess. Their address is BYTE Publications Inc., 70 Main Street, Peterborough, New Hampshire 03458, USA.

6 Computer Chess Miscellany

Programs to solve chess problems

A number of people are interested in problems of the "White to play and mate in two" variety. Although these problems are not really part of chess (since the positions are normally quite artificial) the same techniques that are used in chess programming could easily be employed to solve problems. In fact the Northwestern program has, for some time, announced mate whenever it detected a forced mate within its horizon. A program could be made to find all mates within a certain number of moves simply by performing an exhaustive search to the required depth, and for this reason such a program would be, in my opinion, of little value. (But that is because I dislike both chess problems and exhaustive searches). Some of the microprocessor machines described above already solve such problems.

Programs to do Swiss system pairings

Various programs exist to perform the pairings for Swiss system tournaments. One such program was used at the 1976 Chess Olympiad in Haifa, Israel. It not only paired the teams for each round in accordance with the rules of the Swiss system, it also gave printouts, day by day, on which all the players could see at a glance the scores of every individual in the event.

At a tournament where the rounds are played at the rate of one per day (or even more slowly), such a program presents few problems. If there is a hardware fault or a communication problem the pairings can always be done by hand as a last resort. There is, however, a danger that if such a program were to be used for a large individual tournament of the type that is extremely common in the U.S.A. (many competitors and two or three rounds per day), it might lead to a state of utter chaos. Imagine the situation between rounds, when eight of the nine games have been played in an event and there is a break of only an hour or so before the next round is due to begin. Suddenly the computer goes down, or there is a line fault, or the terminal malfunctions. What does the tournament director do? He must pair the players by hand, so he needs a set of pairing cards on which are written the pairings and results for each player for all the previous rounds. This means that each time the program outputs the pairings for a round it should also print out an updated pairing card for use by the tournament director in cases of emergency. So far I have not heard of a program which will do this, even though it is (in my opinion) an essential failsafe device. I would hate to be a T.D. in a tournament with 500 angry players, eagerly waiting for their pairings, when something went wrong with the program and there was no backup system.

Openings Innovations

Chess is a game in which the frontiers of knowledge are continually being expanded. In every tournament and match played at the master level, some new idea or ideas are seen in the openings. There is no real reason why chess programs should not be able to discover openings innovations in certain types of positions since innovations are often surprising moves and computer programs are prone to make surprising moves rather often.

Some months ago I happened to be analyzing a variation of the French Defence which leads to extremely sharp play - the kind that programs revel in. Eventually I noticed that in a certain position, reached in a master game in 1935, White had a crushing continuation which was overlooked both by the players of the time and by the openings monograph which was devoted entirely to this particular system of the French. O.K., so an International Master finds a new move in the openings; hardly a matter for the headlines. But I felt at the time that the position was so sharp that a good computer program might well find the same continuation. So at the 1977 ACM tournament in Seattle I asked Larry Atkin to try this position on the Northwestern program.

The game Chistiakov-Orlov, Moscow Championship 1935 opened:

1	P-K4	P-K3
2	P-Q4	P-Q4
3	N-QB3	B-N5
4	P-QR3	B × Nch
5	P × B	P × P
6	Q-N4	N-KB3
7	Q × NP	R-N1
8	Q-R6	P-N3
9	B-KN5	R-N3
10	Q-R4	QN-Q2
11	B-N5	P-B3

In this position Chistiakov retreated his bishop with 12 B-QB4. As pointed out in the book *"French Poisoned Pawn"* by Zeuthen and Jarlnaes (Copenhagen 1971), if White captures on QB6 with 12 BxP, Black plays 12...Q-B2 with an excellent game (13 BxR QxBPch and 14...QxR). The innovation in the diagrammed position is 12 BxN! When the position was 'shown' to CHESS 4.6 it found the move 12 BxN in about 90 seconds, thereby improving on existing theory. After the program had printed out this move one of the spectators asked why Black cannot play 12...Q-B2 in reply - after all, White then has two bishops attacked and so must lose one of them. I asked Larry Atkin to make the reply move 12...Q-B2 but he informed me that it was not necessary. The program had predicted 12...Q-B2 as its main variation and had intended to continue 13 B-Q8!! This is probably what Chistiakov had missed. If Black does not capture the bishop on Q1 he is mated on K2 and if he plays 13...QxB then 14 QxQch KxQ 15 BxP R-N1 16 BxP leaves White two pawns up. The alternative to 12...Q-B2 is 12...RxB, but then comes 13 BxP Q-B2 14 P-Q5! (the difference - if White is allowed to capture on KB6 his queen will protect the QB3 pawn), when White will win.

After discovering this innovation CHESS 4.6 wrote a letter to the Readers' Questions column of the openings magazine *Modern Chess Theory*, and was told by Grandmaster Michael Stean that its new move was indeed correct!

Endgames

I described in my earlier volume *Chess and Computers* how I lost a case of whiskey to Dr. Arlazarov when he wrote a routine that would play perfectly in the ending of rook and pawn v rook. Since then a database has been created by Ken Thompson for the ending of queen v rook. This ending is a win, with correct play, for the side with the queen, but it is by no means an easy task for even a strong player to force the win within fifty moves*. Indeed, I well remember a good friend of mine defending just this ending in a World Student Team Championship, only to lose after forty-five of the fifty moves. Ken Thompson's program will always win this ending from the superior side and will always make the optimal defensive move when playing with the rook. Against masters, at speed chess, it rarely loses within fifty moves!

Professor Donald Michie has been developing a technique which he calls advice tables, whereby it is possible to program a computer to play such endgames by giving a set of heuristic rules (i.e. pieces of advice). This does not quite result in optimal play but it does result in sensible play without the

---

*A game is drawn if fifty successive moves are played by each side without a pawn being moved or a capture being made

need for exhaustive search. I wholeheartedly support any attempt to get away from brute force programming in chess and I therefore congratulate Michie for his invention of this technique.

Botvinnik's program PIONEER has been working on endgame studies with some success. I published an article by his colleague Stilman in my book on the 1976 U.S. Computer Chess Championship. When Botvinnik came to Toronto in 1977, he brought with him the tree created by PIONEER to solve the following problem:

The tree which is reproduced below contains only 200 moves and was generated in 3½ hours of computing time.

7 Postscript: 1978 - 80 and BELLE The World Champion

Since the original manuscript for this book was completed, four major computer chess tournaments have been held: three ACM tournaments—Washington in 1978, Detroit in 1979, and Nashville in 1980—and the Third World Computer Chess Championship in Linz, Austria. The story of these events has been the remarkable success of Ken Thompson's and Joe Condon's BELLE. BELLE won the 1978 ACM tournament, became world champion at Linz on September 28, 1980, and won the 1980 ACM tournament one month later. A second place finish in the 1979 ACM tournament marred an otherwise perfect record.

During this period, CHESS 4.9 (the latest version) underwent only minor changes; its playing strength remained essentially fixed at just over a USCF rating of 2000. Meanwhile, Slate proceeded independently of Atkin and Cahlander to develop a FORTRAN-based version of CHESS 4.9 called NUCHESS (Northwestern University CHESS). That program made its debut in Linz finishing with a disappointing two out of four points, though only a half point behind its "brother" who incredibly could only manage 2½ points and a tie for fourth place!

Besides BELLE, a number of other programs made significant progress during the last three years, most notably CHAOS and Claude Jarry's L'EXCENTRIQUE (Jarry began his program in 1976 as a class project while a student in the second author's class). Both CHAOS and L'EXCENTRIQUE were rated at the Expert level for their showings in the world championship. (Eight of the eighteen programs in Linz received performance ratings in excess of 1700.) CHAOS carries out a relatively selective search, while L'EXCENTRIQUE carries out a large search, second only to BELLE's. Jarry's program uses the minimax algorithm (without the alpha-beta algorithm!) for the first few iterations in order to find and save the strongest continuation for each first level move. On deeper iterations, L'EXCENTRIQUE employs the alpha-beta algorithm. Jarry argues that finding the strongest continuation for each first ply move on the initial few iterations results in faster searches on later iterations.

It was BELLE, however, which attracted everyone's attention and admiration. In 1978 and after adding special move generation circuitry to their PDP 11 computer at Bell Telephone Laboratories in Murray Hill, New Jersey, Thompson and Condon found that BELLE was able to search trees a bit larger than those searched by CHESS 4.9. Through a lot of skill and a bit of good fortune, the new Murray Hill masher defeated the world champion in the second round of the 1978 tournament in Washington. The audience was spellbound as the game developed incredible complications. CHAOS fell to BELLE in the third round, and BLITZ 6.5 was mated in only 14 moves in the final round. BELLE and CHESS 4.9 met again at the 1979 ACM tournament. Both programs had undergone only minor changes, and perhaps the good fortune that followed BELLE around in 1978 decided to hover over CHESS 4.9 this time. The latter recaptured the ACM tournament, possibly for the last time. Six of the twelve participants received at least B level performance ratings.

During the following months Thompson and Condon developed a second generation special chess machine which they tied into a PDP 11/23 computer. The new system gave vast speedups in move generation and position evaluation. When Thompson arrived at the 1980 World Championship in Linz (Condon stayed at BTL and spoke with Thompson over an open phone during the game), he said they had souped up BELLE to the point where it searched trees having 30,000,000 nodes per three minute move! Thompson and Condon gave it a few test games prior to the tournament, and they felt it was playing very near Master level strength.

After L'EXCENTRIQUE upset CHESS 4.9 in Round 1, BELLE emerged as the tournament favorite. However, Slate's NUCHESS set BELLE back a notch by drawing with the latter in Round 2. In Round 3, BELLE routinely defeated the upstart L'EXCENTRIQUE; in Round 4, Truscott's DUCHESS quietly succumbed. However, three and a half points gave BELLE only a tie for first place with CHAOS after regularly scheduled play. An extra game was necessary to determine a new champion (a procedure agreed upon by the participants before the tournament began). BELLE won that game in style announcing mate in six on the thirty-fourth move! The new champion will reign at least until 1983 when the Fourth World Championship will be held, possibly in New York.

The event, hosted by the city of Linz, was held on the bank of the Danube River. The city graciously housed the participants in the Turotel, adjacent to the Brucknerhaus where the games were played. Austrian and German television networks gave extensive coverage to the games. Claude Shannon and Fridrik Olafsson (President of FIDE) attended the tournament as special guests, and both were sought out by the press for their opinions on the future of computer chess activities.

For each of the four tournaments, we present the final standings and a listing of all games played between programs which finished with more than two out of four points. We also present the results of a special man/machine versus man match played as a special event at the 1979 ACM tournament. The final game between BELLE and CHESS SENSORY CHALLENGER is annotated and concludes this chapter.

Ninth ACM Computer Chess Championship
Washington D.C., December 3-5, 1978

No.	Program	Rating*	Perf. Rating	1	2	3	4	Total
1	BELLE	1950	2244	8W	2W	3W	4W	4
2	CHESS 4.7	2040	1961	9W	1L	6W	7W	3
3	CHAOS	1775	1797	5W	7W	1L	6D	2½
4	BLITZ 6.5	1670	1724	10W	6D	11W	1L	2½
5	SARGON II	0	1448	3L	12W	8D	11W	2½
6	DUCHESS	1850	1744	11W	4D	2L	3D	2
7	OSTRICH	1450	1454	12W	3L	9W	2L	2
8	MIKE	0	1268	1L	9D	5D	10D	1½
9	BLACK KNIGHT	1174	1183	2L	8D	7L	12W	1½
10	BS '66 '76	0	1133	4L	11L	12W	8D	1½
11	AWIT	1300	1275	6L	10W	4L	5L	1
12	BRUTE FORCE	0	592	7L	5L	10L	9L	0

*Ratings are based on performances in previous computer and human tournament play and were provided by Ken Thompson.

Brief descriptions of the programs

BELLE: Ken Thompson, Joe Condon; PDP 11/70 with home built move generator, Bell Telephone Laboratories, Murray Hill, New Jersey; C language; 400,000–800,000 nodes/move; 100,000 positions in book.

CHESS 4.7: David Slate, Larry Atkin, David Cahlander; CDC CYBER 176, CDC Corporate Headquarters, Arden Hills, Minnesota; assembly language; 500,000 nodes/move; 7,000 positions in book.

CHAOS: Mike Alexander, Fred Swartz, Jack O'Keefe; Amdahl V/6, Amdahl Corporation, Sunnyvale, California; FORTRAN; 25,000 nodes/move; 7,500 positions in book.

BLITZ 6.5: Robert Hyatt; UNIVAC 1100, UNIVAC, Washington D.C.; FORTRAN; 100,000 nodes/move; 3,000 moves in book.

SARGON II: Dan Spracklen, Kathe Spracklen, Wavemate Jupiter (Z-80 based microcomputer), at site; Z-80 assembly language; 9,000 nodes/move; 4,000 positions in book.

DUCHESS: Tom Truscott, Eric Wright, Bruce Jensen; IBM 370/165, TUCC, Research Triangle Park, North Carolina; IBM S/360 assembly language; 50,000–200,000 nodes/move; 3,000 positions in book.

OSTRICH: Monroe Newborn, Ilan Vardi; Data General Nova 3, McGill University, Montreal, Quebec; assembly language; 10,000–15,000 nodes/move; 300 positions in book.

MIKE: Mike Johnson; Motorola M6800, at site; assembly language; 36,000 nodes/move; no book.

BLACK KNIGHT: Fred Prouse, Ken Sogge, Lonny Lebahn; UNIVAC 1100/40, UNIVAC, Washington, D.C.; FORTRAN; 10,000 nodes/move; 96,000 positions in book.

BS '66'76: Barend Swets; IBM 370/168, Datacrown, Ltd., Toronto, Ontario; FORTRAN; 300 nodes/move; 3,000 positions in book.

AWIT: Tony Marsland; Amdahl V/6, University of Alberta, Edmonton, Alberta; Algol W; 250 nodes/move; 10,000 positions in book.

BRUTE FORCE: Louis Kessler; IBM 370/168, University of Manitoba, Winnipeg, Manitoba; FORTRAN H; 400,000 nodes/move; no book.

Note that there were two microcomputers at the tournament site and that for the first time one of them, SARGON II, put on a most respectable performance. There were also three selective search programs, CHAOS, AWIT, and BS '66'76, although CHAOS examines a large number of nodes on each move.

Grandmaster Robert Byrne attended the tournament as a guest of the organizers. His article in the December 11, 1978 edition of *The New York Times* reviews the tournament and the sharp 14 move victory of BELLE over BLITZ 6.5 in the last round. Regarding BELLE's victory over CHESS 4.7 in the second round, Bryne observed that both sides *"waltzed around aimlessly in a would-be positional battle."* He went on to say that *"despite enormous progress in the last year, computers lack positional judgement and often do not know what to do in tranquil situations. However, tactically they are freer from error than the average human player."*

THE GAMES			8	B×N	P×B
			9	O-O	N-B3
Round 1			10	Q-N3	P-B3
White: CHAOS			11	Q×P	P×P
Black: SARGON II			12	Q-B6ch	N-Q2
			13	N×P	R-B1
	Queen's Gambit		14	N-B7ch	R×N
1	P-Q4	P-Q4	15	B×R	Q-B1
2	P-QB4	N-QB3	16	KR-Q1	P-N4
3	N-QB3	P×P	17	R×P	P-K3
4	N-B3	B-N5	18	QR-Q1	B-N2
5	P-Q5	B×N	19	R×N	O-O
6	KP×B	N-K4	20	R-Q8	B×P
7	B-B4	N-Q6ch			

21	R × Q	R × R
22	Q-N7	R × B
23	Q × R	B-N2
24	R-Q8ch	B-B1
25	Q-K7	P-KR4
26	R × Bch	K-N2
27	R × Pch	K-N3
28	Q × KPmate	

Round 2
White: BELLE
Black: CHESS 4.7

Nimzowitsch Defense

1	P-K4	N-QB3
2	P-Q4	P-Q4
3	N-QB3	P-K3
4	N-B3	B-N5
5	P-K5	KN-K2
6	B-Q2	N-B4
7	N-K2	B-K2
8	P-B3	O-O
9	N-B4	P-B3
10	B-Q3	P × P
11	P × P	P-KN4
12	P-KN4	N-N2
13	N-N2	P-N3
14	Q-K2	B-N2
15	R-KN1	P-QR4
16	P-QR4	K-R1
17	P-R3	K-N1
18	R-R1	P-R3
19	P-R4	P-Q5
20	RP × P	N-N5
21	P × RP	N × Bch
22	Q × N	P × P
23	Q-N6	P × Bch
24	N × P	R-B2
25	P × N	R × NP
26	Q × Pch	R-B2
27	Q-R6	R-N2
28	Q-R8ch	K-B2
29	P-K6ch	K × P

30	Q × R	B × N
31	R-R6ch	K-Q2
32	O-O-O	B-Q4
33	N-K4	K-B1
34	R-R8	B × N
35	QR × Qch	B × R
36	Q-K7	K-N2
37	Q × B(K4)ch	K-R2
38	R-N8	R-N1
39	P-N5	B-K2
40	R × R	B × Pch
41	P-B4	B × Pch
42	Q × B	K × R
43	K-Q2	K-N2
44	K-Q3	K-B1
45	P-N4	P × P
46	Q × NP	K-Q2
47	Q-N5ch	K-Q1
48	K-K4	resigns

White: DUCHESS
Black: BLITZ 6.5

Ruy Lopez

1	P-K4	P-K4
2	N-KB3	N-QB3
3	B-N5	P-QR3
4	B-R4	N-B3
5	O-O	B-K2
6	Q-K2	P-QN4
7	B-N3	O-O
8	P-B3	P-Q4
9	P-Q3	P × P
10	P × P	B-N2
11	R-Q1	Q-K1
12	P-QR4	N-QR4
13	B-B2	B-Q3
14	P-QN4	N-QB5
15	N-QR3	N × N
16	R × N	Q-B3
17	N-N5	P-R3
18	N-B3	N × P
19	P × P	Q × NP

20	P-B4	Q-B3
21	P-B5	N×QBP
22	R-B3	P-K5
23	N-Q2	Q-N4
24	Q×Q	P×Q
25	P×N	B-K4
26	R-QN3	P-QB3
27	N×P	R-R7
28	B-N1	QR-R1
29	P-B4	B-N1
30	N-Q6	R-Q1
31	R(N3)-Q3	B-R3
32	B-R2	P-N5
33	R-Q4	B-R2
34	N×P	R×R
35	R×R	B×P
36	N-K5ch	K-R1
37	B-N2	B×Rch
38	B×B	B-N2
39	B-K6	K-R2
40	B-QB5	R-R5
41	N-Q3	K-N3
42	B×P	B-R3
43	P-B5ch	K-R2
44	N-B5	R×B
45	N×B	R-N7
46	N-B5	R-Q7
47	N-Q7	R-Q5
48	N-K5	P-B4
49	N-Q7	R-Q8ch
50	K-B2	R-Q7ch
51	K-B3	R-QB7
52	N-B8ch	K-R1
53	N-N6ch	K-R2
54	N-K5	R-B3ch
55	K-N4	R-B7
56	K-N3	R-K7
57	N-Q7	R-K3ch
58	K-B4	R-K7
59	N-B8ch	K-R1
60	N-N6ch	K-R2
61	B-Q5	R-B7ch

62	K-K5	R-K7ch
63	B-K4	P-B5
64	N-B4	R-K8
65	K-Q4	K-R1
66	B-Q5	R-KR8
67	P-R3	R-KB8
68	P-N3	P-B6
69	K×P	R-KN8
70	P-N4	R-QR8
71	K-Q4	K-R2
72	K-K3	R-R5
73	K-B3	R-R6ch
74	K-N2	R-QB6
75	B-K6	R-R6
76	N-N6	R-QB6
77	N-B8ch	K-R1
78	B-B7	R-B7ch
79	K-N3	R-QB2
80	N-N6ch	K-R2
81	B-Q5	R-B6ch
82	K-R4	R-B8
83	K-R5	R-QN8
84	N-B4	R-N4
85	B-B7	R-N2
86	B-R2	R-N7
87	B-K6	R-N8
88	K-R4	R-QR8
89	N-N6	R-QR1
90	B-N3	R-QN1
91	B-B7	R-QB1
92	B-Q5	R-B4
93	B-R2	R-B1
94	N-B4 drawn	

Round 3
White: CHESS 4.7
Black: DUCHESS

Petroff Defense

1	P-K4	P-K4
2	N-KB3	N-KB3
3	P-Q4	P×P
4	P-K5	N-K5

5	Q×P	P-Q4
6	P×Pe.p.	N×QP
7	B-Q3	N-B3
8	Q-KB4	P-KN3
9	O-O	B-N2
10	B-Q2	Q-B3
11	Q×Q	B×Q
12	N-B3	B-K3
13	N-KN5	B-B5
14	N(N5)-K4	N×N
15	N×N	B×NP
16	B×B	B×R
17	R×B	R-Q1
18	R-K1	O-O
19	B-KR6	P-N3
20	N-B6ch	K-R1
21	B×R	R×B
22	B-N3	N-Q5
23	N-Q7	R-Q1
24	N-K5	R-KB1
25	N×BPch	K-N2
26	N-N5	K-R3
27	N-K6	R-K8
28	K-B1	N×N
29	R×N	R-Q1
30	R-K7	P-B3
31	R×QRP	R-Q8ch
32	K-K2	R-Q1
33	R-QB7	P-B4
34	P-KB4	R-Q5
35	K-B3	P-KN4
36	P-N3	P×P
37	P×P	K-N3
38	R-B6ch	K-B4
39	B-K6ch	K-B3
40	R×NP	K-K2
41	B-B5	R-R5
42	B×P	R-R6ch
43	K-N4	R×P
44	P-B5	K-Q2
45	P-B6	R-R5ch
46	K-N5	R-R8

47	P-B7	R-R1
48	K-B6	P-B5
49	B-B5ch	K-B2
50	R-B6ch	K-N2
51	K-K7	R-R1
52	R×P	R×P
53	P-B8=Q	R-K7ch
54	K-B7	R-K4
55	Q-B8ch	K-N3
56	Q-B7ch	K-R3
57	R-R4ch	K-N4
58	B-Q7 mate	

White: CHAOS
Black: BELLE

Queen's Gambit Accepted

1	P-Q4	P-Q4
2	P-QB4	P×P
3	N-KB3	N-KB3
4	P-K3	P-K3
5	B×P	P-B4
6	Q-K2	P-QR3
7	O-O	P-QN4
8	B-N3	N-B3
9	N-B3	B-K2
10	R-Q1	P-B5
11	B-B2	N-QN5
12	P-K4	N×B
13	Q×N	B-N2
14	B-B4	P-N5
15	P-K5	N-R4
16	N-K2	N×B
17	N×N	P-N4
18	N-R5	B×N
19	P×B	Q-Q4
20	Q-K4	P-B6
21	Q×Q	P×Q
22	R(Q1)-N1	P-B7
23	R-K1	R-QB1
24	R(R1)-B1	R-B5
25	R-K2	R×P
26	N-B6ch	B×N

27	P×Bch	K-Q2
28	R(K2)×P	R-KB1
29	R-B7ch	K-K3
30	R(B1)-B6ch	K-B4
31	R×RP	R-Q6
32	R-N7	R×P
33	R×NP	K-K4
34	R-N4	R-KN1
35	R-N3	P-N5
36	K-N2	R×P(B3)
37	R-R7	P-Q5
38	K-B1	R-KR3
39	R-K7ch	K-B3
40	R-K4	R×P
41	R×QP	P-R4
42	R-B4ch	K-N3
43	R-QB3	R-R8ch
44	K-N2	R-QN8
45	R-N4	R-QR1
46	R-N6ch	K-N2
47	P-R3	R-R2
48	R(B3)-QN3	R-R5
49	R(N3)-N5	P-R5
50	R-N7	R-Q5
51	R-B7	K-N6
52	R(N5)-N7	R(Q5)-Q8
53	R-B8	R-N8ch
54	K-R2	R-R8ch
55	K-N2	R(N8)-N8
		mate

Round 4

White: BLITZ 6.5
Black: BELLE

Four Knights Game

1	P-K4	P-K4
2	N-KB3	N-QB3
3	N-QB3	N-KB3
4	B-N5	N-Q5
5	B-B4	B-B4
6	N×P	Q-K2
7	B×Pch	K-B1

8	N-N6ch	P×N
9	B-B4	N×KP
10	O-O	R×P
11	K×R	Q-R5ch
12	K-N1	N-KN6
13	Q-R5	P×Q
14	P×N	N-B6 mate

White: DUCHESS
Black: CHAOS

Sicilian Defense

1	P-K4	P-QB4
2	P-Q4	P×P
3	P-QB3	N-KB3
4	P-K5	N-Q4
5	Q×P	P-K3
6	B-QB4	P-Q3
7	N-B3	N-B3
8	B-QN5	B-Q2
9	B×N	B×B
10	O-O	P-B3
11	P×P	P×P
12	R-K1	N-B2
13	Q-Q3	Q-Q2
14	N-Q4	R-QN1
15	N×B	P×N
16	Q-Q4	N-Q4
17	P-QB4	N-B2
18	Q×RP	Q-B1
19	P-QN3	P-K4
20	N-QB3	B-K2
21	B-R6	R-N1
22	Q-K3	R-KN3
23	R(R1)-Q1	Q-N5
24	P-N3	P-QB4
25	Q-Q2	P-B4
26	B-K3	P-B5
27	B×QBP	Q-R6
28	N-Q5	N×N
29	Q×N	Q-B1
30	B-R7	R-R1
31	B-N6	P×P

32	BP×P	R×RP	45	Q-K4	B-K2
33	R-KB1	Q-R6	46	R-Q3	R-B8ch
34	Q-B6ch	Q-Q2	47	K-N2	R-QR8
35	Q-K4	Q-B1	48	K-R3	R-KN8
36	R-Q5	Q-R6	49	R-N3	R×Rch
37	B-B2	R-KR3	50	P×R	Q-N1
38	Q-N2	Q-Q2	51	Q×RP	Q×P
39	K-R1	R-B3	52	Q-R5ch	K-Q1
40	R-N5	Q-B1	53	Q×P	Q×BP
41	P-KN4	R-B2	54	Q-KR5	B-B3
42	R-N6	B-R5	55	Q-N6	Q-B8ch
43	R×P	R(B2)×B	56	K-R2	Q-B6
44	R×R	R×R	57	Q-B7	drawn

Tenth ACM Computer Chess Championship
Detroit, October 28–30, 1979

No.	Program	Rating*	Perf. Rating	1	2	3	4	Total
1	CHESS 4.9	2040	2099	8W	9W	3W	2D	3½
2	BELLE	1950	1982	5W	4D	7W	1D	3
3	DUCHESS	1889	1942	10W	7W	1L	4W	3
4	CHAOS	1775	1794	12W	2D	9W	3L	2½
5	L'EXCENTRIQUE	0	1640	2L	12W	8W	6D	2½
6	MYCHESS	0	1552	7L	10W	11W	5D	2½
7	SARGON III	0	1614	6W	3L	2L	9D	1½
8	OSTRICH80	1450	1374	1L	11W	5L	10D	1½
9	BLITZ 6.9	0	1516	11W	1L	4L	7D	1½
10	AWIT	1325	1314	3L	6L	12W	8D	1½
11	BS '66 '76	0	1045	9L	8L	6L	12W	1
12	RUFUS	0	644	4L	5L	10L	11L	0

Brief description of the programs

CHESS 4.9, BELLE, DUCHESS, CHAOS, SARGON III, OSTRICH80, BLITZ 6.9, AWIT and BS '66 '76 had all participated in the 1978 ACM tournament, and they all underwent relatively minor modification. All were playing on the same computer used at ACM 78 or on one having equivalent power. L'EXCENTRIQUE had participated in the 1976 ACM tournament and then rested for a few years while being converted from DEC code to IBM 360 assembly language code. MYCHESS and RUFUS were new programs.

L'EXCENTRIQUE: Claude Jarry; Amdahl V/7, McGill University, Montreal, Quebec; assembly language; 2,000,000 nodes/move; 600 opening lines in book.

MYCHESS: David Kittinger; Cromemco Z-2D, at site; Z-80 assembly language; 9,000 nodes/move; 3,000 positions in book.

RUFUS: Charles Sullivan; Apple II microcomputer; 6502 assembly language; 90,000 nodes/move; 2,000 opening lines in book.

On the day before the regular tournament began, a special one-game match was held featuring for the first time man/machine versus man. Dan McCracken, president of the ACM at that time, felt it would be interesting to see whether a chess program working with a human could produce a combined playing strength greater than either could achieve individually. Mc-Cracken pointed out that in a number of areas man and machine function better as a pair than they do individually.

Ben Mittman and Monroe Newborn put together the match. It was necessary that both man and machine be of roughly equal playing strength, otherwise the stronger one would wind up deciding all the moves. Slate and CHESS 4.9 seemed to be an ideal pair since both were rated at just over 2000. Their opponent had to be someone who, while stronger, was within reach; David Levy seemed to fit the bill. Thus, on Saturday, October 27, 1979, David Slate and CHESS 4.9 sat down as a team to tackle David Levy.

As the game progressed, it became clear that Slate did not have sufficient interaction with his program, and that he was not able to get the information he wanted to assist him in choosing moves. Levy won the game in a relatively straightforward manner, and Slate later regretted having listened to his machine as frequently as he did. If he were to play again, Slate said he would most likely chose more of his own moves. One might attempt to conclude that the match showed (1) for man and machine to work together, considerable planning is necessary to take best advantage of the machine, (2) if the machine (or man) is clearly the stronger, it (he) might as well play alone, and (3) it does not seem that, even under optimal interactive conditions, Slate/CHESS 4.9 could outplay Levy.

THE GAME

White: Slate/CHESS 4.9
Black: Levy

Bird's Opening

1	P-KB4	P-Q4
2	N-KB3	N-KB3
3	P-K3	B-N5
4	P-QN3	QN-Q2
5	B-N2	P-B3
6	B-K2	B×N
7	B×B	Q-B2
8	N-B3	P-K4
9	P×P	N×P
10	Q-K2	B-Q3
11	P-N3	Q-K2
12	O-O-O	O-O
13	B-N2	B-R6
14	K-N1	B×B
15	K×B	P-QN4
16	QR-KB1	N/B3-Q2
17	P-Q4	N-B5ch

18	P×N	Q-N5ch		35	R-R4	R-QB1
19	K-B1	Q×N		36	R-R5	Q-K5
20	P×NP	P×P		37	R×P	Q×BPch
21	B×P	N-N3		38	Q-Q2	Q-K5
22	B-N3	N-B5		39	Q-K1	P-B6
23	B×N	P×B		40	K-B2	P-R4
24	Q-K1	Q-R6ch		41	R-R5	P-R5
25	K-Q2	QR-N1		42	R-R1	P-R6
26	K-K2	R-N7		43	Q-R1	Q-B7ch
27	Q-Q2	R×RP		44	K-B3	R-B3
28	R-QN1	Q-K2		45	Q-QN1	R-B3ch
29	R-R1	Q-K5		46	K-N4	Q-K7ch
30	KR-QB1	R×R		47	K-R4	R-R3ch
31	R×R	Q-N7ch		48	K-N5	Q-R4ch
32	K-Q1	Q-R8ch		49	K-B4	R-KB3ch
33	Q-K1	Q-N2		50	resigns	
34	K-K2	R-N1				

George Koltanowski (left) and Max Euwe discuss who stands better early in the Slate/CHESS 4.9 vs Levy game.

Slate said he selected 10 Q-K2 over the advice of his computer, which recommended castling kingside. He feared Levy would play B-Q3 followed by P-KR4, and N/K4-N5. After 17 P-Q4, Levy had a clear upper hand. The regular four round tournament produced few surprises. CHAOS drew with BELLE in round 2, requiring BELLE, when it met CHESS 4.9 in the final round, to obtain a full point to win the tournament. BELLE was unable to do that; the game was an exciting battle that ended in a draw by agreement with equal material on the board.

John McCarthy, George Koltanowski (former president of the USCF and the world's most famous blindfold chess player), and Max Euwe (former president of FIDE) attended the tournament as guests of the ACM. Koltanowski and Euwe served as commentators for the Slate/CHESS 4.9 vs. Levy match, and their vast repertoire of stories and jokes added flavor to the entire tournament. John McCarthy awarded the trophies at a conference luncheon following the tournament and stressed the importance of viewing the tournament as both a scientific experiment and a competitive event.

THE GAMES

Round 1
White: L'EXCENTRIQUE
Black: BELLE

Ruy Lopez

1	P-K4	P-K4	20	P-QB4	B-B6
2	N-KB3	N-QB3	21	R×Rch	R×R
3	B-N5	P-QR3	22	N-Q4	B-K5
4	B-R4	N-KB3	23	P-B3	P-QB4
5	O-O	N×P	24	P×B	P×N
6	Q-K2	N-B4	25	B-Q2	P-Q6
7	B×N	QP×B	26	K-N2	P-KB3
8	P-Q4	N-K3	27	P×P	B×P
9	P×P	N-Q5	28	R-KB1	P-B3
10	N×N	Q×N	29	P-N5	B-K4
11	P-KR3	B-K2	30	P-B5	P-KN3
12	R-Q1	Q-N3	31	P-R4	B-Q5
13	P-QN3	B-KB4	32	P-N4	R-Q2
14	P-KN4	B-K3	33	R-B3	B-K4
15	P-QR4	O-O	34	R-B1	R-Q1
16	P-R5	Q-N4	35	R-Q1	K-B2
17	N-B3	Q×Q	36	R-KR1	K-K3
18	N×Q	KR-Q1	37	P-R5	B-N2
19	B-K3	B-Q4	38	P-R6	B-R1
			39	R-KB1	K-K2
			40	K-N3	B-Q5
			41	K-R3	B-K4
			42	K-N4	R-Q5
			43	K-B3	K-K3
			44	R-KR1	B-B2

45	R-QR1	B-Q1	14	B-N5	N-R4
46	R-KB1	R-Q2	15	Q-B2	B-R3
47	K-N3	B-B2ch	16	Q-R2	Q-R5
48	K-N2	K-K4	17	P-N4	N-B5
49	R-B4	K-Q5	18	N×N	P×N
50	R-B3	K×P	19	B×P	B×P
51	R-B1	K-Q5	20	B×B	N×B
52	R-K1	R-B2	21	K-N2	N-K4
53	R-K3	B-K4	22	Q-K2	KR-K1
54	R-K1	R-B4	23	KR-K1	N-B5
55	B-K3ch	K-B6	24	Q-R2	N-R4
56	P-N5	P-Q7	25	K-B3	P-B3
57	R-Q1	K-Q6	26	P-Q6ch	K-R1
58	B×P	K-K7	27	Q-Q5	Q-Q2
59	P×RP	K×R	28	Q-B5	QR-Q1
60	P-R7	R-B1	29	Q×Q	R×Q
61	B-N4	B-B5	30	P-K5	P×P
62	B-B3	B×P	31	R×P	R×R
63	B-K5	R-QR1	32	B×R	N-B5
64	K-B3	R×P	33	B-B4	P-QN4
65	B-B7	B×P	34	P-QR4	P-N4
66	Resigns		35	B×P	P×P
			36	R×P	N×P
			37	R-R5	R-B2ch

Round 2
White: BELLE
Black: CHAOS

Nimzowitsch Indian Defense

1	P-Q4	N-KB3	38	B-B4	P-B5
2	P-QB4	P-K3	39	R-QB5	R-B1
3	N-QB3	B-N5	40	R-B6	N-B2
4	P-K3	P-B4	41	K-N3	K-N2
5	B-Q3	O-O	42	R×P	P-QR3
6	P-QR3	B×Nch	43	R-B7	R-QR1
7	P×B	N-B3	44	P-B4	P-QR4
8	N-K2	P-Q3	45	P-B5	P-R5
9	P-K4	P-K4	46	B-K5ch	K-B1
10	P-Q5	N-QR4	47	B-R1	P-R6
11	O-O	P-QN3	48	P-B6	R-R3
12	P-B4	Q-K1	49	B-B6	R-R1
13	P×P	P×P	50	R-N7	P-R7
			51	P-B7	R-B1
			52	R-N8	N-Q3
			53	K-B4	K-K1
			54	R×Rch	N×R
			55	K-N5	K-Q2

56	K-R6	K×P
57	K×P	N-Q3
58	B-K5	K-Q2
59	P-N5	N-B2
60	B-N2	N×Pch
61	K-N6	N-B6
62	K-B5	N×P
63	K-K4	K-B3
64	K-Q4	K-N4
65	K-B3	K-R5
66	K-B2	N-B6
67	B-B6	K-R6
68	B-K7ch	K-R5
69	K-N2	P-R8=Q
70	K×Q	drawn

Round 3
White: CHESS 4.9
Black: DUCHESS

Center Counter Defense

1	P-K4	P-Q4
2	P×P	Q×P
3	N-QB3	Q-Q3
4	P-Q4	B-B4
5	N-KB3	N-QB3
6	N-QN5	Q-Q2
7	B-KB4	R-B1
8	N-K5	N×N
9	P×N	Q-B3
10	Q-B3	Q×Q
11	P×Q	P-QR3
12	N-Q4	B-Q2
13	O-O-O	P-KN3
14	N-N3	R-Q1
15	N-R5	B-B1
16	R×Rch	K×R
17	B-B4	K-K1
18	R-Q1	B-R3
19	B-Q2	B-N2
20	B-B3	P-QB3
21	P-K6	B-R3ch
22	K-N1	P-B3
23	N×NP	B×N
24	B-R5	K-B1
25	R-Q7	B-B5
26	P-KR3	B-K4
27	R×B	P-N4
28	B×P	P-R4
29	P-QR4	R-R3
30	B-B4	P-KB4
31	B-Q2	R-N3
32	P-R5	B-Q5
33	P-R6	B×BP
34	P-R7	B×P
35	R×B	P-N5
36	B-B3	N-B3
37	B-N4	N-N1
38	R-R8ch	K-N2
39	B-B3ch	K-R3
40	B-Q2ch	K-N2
41	BP×P	RP×P
42	P×P	R×NP
43	B-Q3	P-B5
44	B-B3ch	K-R3
45	R-KB8	P-B4
46	B-K5	P-B6
47	R×P	P-B5
48	R-B4	R-N8ch
49	B-B1	K-N4
50	R-B7	K-R3
51	K-R2	R-R8
52	B×P	R-K8
53	B-N7ch	K-N4
54	B-B8	R-K5
55	R-N7ch	K-B3
56	B-Q3	R-QR5ch
57	K-N3	R-R2
58	R×N	K×P
59	B-B4ch	K-K4
60	R-N7	R-N2ch
61	K-B3	resigns

Round 4
White: BELLE
Black: CHESS 4.9

Benoni Defense

1	P-Q4	N-KB3
2	P-QB4	P-QB4
3	P-Q5	P-K3
4	N-QB3	P×P
5	P×P	P-Q3
6	P-K4	P-KN3
7	N-B3	B-N2
8	B-K2	O-O
9	O-O	R-K1
10	N-Q2	N-R3
11	P-B3	N-B2
12	P-QR4	P-N3
13	N-B4	B-QR3
14	B-N5	P-KR3
15	B-R4	P-KN4
16	B-B2	N-R4
17	N-K3	B-QB1
18	Q-B2	N-B5
19	B-B4	B-Q2
20	KR-Q1	Q-B3
21	B-KN3	N-R4
22	B-K1	N-B5
23	K-R1	P-R3
24	B-KN3	P-N4
25	P×P	P×P
26	R×R	R×R
27	B-B1	P-QN5
28	N-K2	P-N6
29	Q-N1	N-R4
30	B-B2	N-B5
31	N-B4	N×N
32	B×N	B-N4
33	B-N3	R-R5
34	Q-B1	B-B1
35	R-Q2	Q-Q1
36	Q-B1	P-R4
37	K-N1	P-R5

38	B-B2	B-N2
39	N-K3	B×B
40	Q×B	R-R8ch
41	R-Q1	R-R7
42	Q-Q3	R×P
43	N-B4	R-B7
44	P-K5	B×P
45	N×B	P×N
46	Q×P	R-K7
47	K-B1	P-B5
48	Q-N7	R-R7
49	B-N6	P-R6
50	Q×N	Q-B3
51	Q-Q8ch	Q×Q
52	B×Q	R×P
53	R-K1	P-B6
54	R×P	P-B7
55	R-K8ch	K-N2
56	B×P	R×B
57	R-QB8	R-N7
58	P-Q6	R×P
59	P-Q7	R-Q7
60	K-N1	R×P
61	R×P	R-Q6
62	R-B2	K-B3
63	K-R2	drawn

White: DUCHESS
Black: CHAOS

Sicilian Defense

1	P-K4	P-QB4
2	N-QB3	N-QB3
3	P-KN3	P-K3
4	N-B3	P-Q4
5	P×P	P×P
6	P-Q4	B-N5
7	B-K2	N-B3
8	B-KN5	B×N
9	B×B	Q-K2ch
10	K-B1	P×P
11	N×P	Q-Q1
12	Q-K2ch	K-Q2

13	Q-N5	R-QN1		55	B-N3ch	K-B4
14	N×Nch	P×N		56	K-K4	K-Q3
15	Q-B5ch	K-B2		57	K-B5	K-Q2
16	B×P	B-K2		58	K-N6	K-K2
17	B×R	Q×B		59	P-B5	B-K4
18	Q×BP	Q-N1		60	B-B2	B-B3
19	Q×Q	R×Q		61	B-K4	B-R1
20	B-K4	R-KR1		62	B-B3	B-K4
21	P-KB4	N-R4		63	B-B6	B-B3
22	K-K2	N-B5		64	B-K8	B-K4
23	KR-QN1	B-B3		65	B-N5	B-R1
24	K-Q3	N-N3		66	B-B4	P-R5
25	R-K1	K-N1		67	B-N8	B-B3
26	QR-N1	N-R5		68	B-Q5	B-K4
27	B-B5	P-KR4		69	K-N5	B-B3ch
28	B-N6	N-B4ch		70	K-B4	K-B1
29	K-B4	N-Q2		71	K-K4	K-K2
30	R-K8ch	R×R		72	B-K6	P-R6
31	B×R	N-N3ch		73	K-Q3	B-R1
32	K-B5	P-R5		74	K-R4	B-B6
33	P×P	K-B1		75	K-B5	K-Q1
34	P-R5	K-Q1		76	K-Q6	K-K1
35	B-N5	K-B2		77	B-N3	B-N7
36	P-R6	P-R3		78	K-K6	B-R1
37	B-Q3	B-R1		79	B-R4ch	K-B1
38	B-B5	N-R4ch		80	B-Q1	K-K1
39	K-N4	P-N4		81	P-B6	K-B1
40	K-R5	K-N2		82	B-N3	K-K1
41	B-K4ch	K-R2		83	B-R4ch	K-B1
42	P-R7	N-N3		84	B-Q1	K-K1
43	P-KR4	N-B5ch		85	B-N3	K-B1
44	K-N4	K-N3		86	B-B4	K-K1
45	P-B3	P-R4ch		87	B-N5ch	K-B1
46	K-N3	QP×P		88	B-R4	P-N6
47	R-Q1	N-Q7ch		89	B×P	K-K1
48	R×N	P×R		90	B-B2	K-B1
49	K-B2	P-N5		91	B-Q3	K-K1
50	P-R5	K-B4		92	B-N5ch	K-B1
51	K×P	B×P		93	B-R6	K-K1
52	P-R6	B-R1		94	B-Q3	K-B1
53	K-K3	K-B5		95	B-K2	K-K1
54	B-B2	K-Q4		96	B-R5ch	K-B1

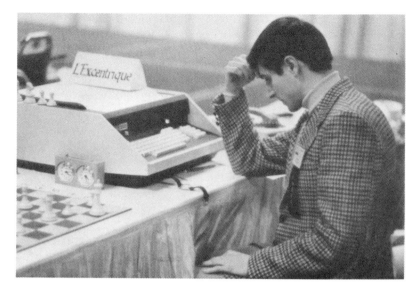

Claude Jarry anxiously waits for L'EXCENTRIQUE to make a move.

97	B-N4	K-K1
98	B-B3	K-B1
99	B-K4	K-K1
100	B-N6ch	K-B1
101	B-B5	K-K1
102	B-K4	K-B1
103	B-N1	K-K1
104	B-B5	K-B1
105	B-B2	K-K1
106	B-R4ch	K-B1
107	B-Q1	K-K1
108	B-K2	K-B1
109	B-B3	K-K1
110	B-B6ch	K-B1
111	B-Q5	resigns

White: MYCHESS
Black: L'EXCENTRIQUE

Petroff Defense

1	P-K4	P-K4
2	N-KB3	N-KB3

3	N×P	P-Q3
4	N-KB3	N×P
5	P-Q4	P-Q4
6	B-Q3	N-QB3
7	O-O	B-K2
8	R-K1	B-KN5
9	B×N	P×B
10	R×P	B×N
11	P×B	O-O
12	P-Q5	Q-Q2
13	Q-K2	Q×P
14	N-B3	Q-Q3
15	B-B4	Q-N3ch
16	K-R1	Q-B4
17	B×P	Q-Q2
18	R-Q1	Q×B
19	N-Q5	Q-R4
20	N×Bch	N×N
21	R×N	Q×P·
22	R×NP	Q-K3
23	Q×Q	P×Q

24	R(Q1)-Q7	R×P
25	R×NPch	K-B1
26	R×KRP	K-K1
27	R(R7)-K7ch	K-Q1
28	K-N2	R-B3
29	R(K7)-Q7ch	K-K1
30	R-K7ch	K-B1
31	R×RP	R-N3ch
32	K-B3	R×R

33	R×R	R-R3
34	R-R8ch	K-K2
35	K-N3	R-N3ch
36	K-B3	R-R3
37	K-N3	R-N3ch
38	K-B3	R-R3
39	K-N3	R-N3
	drawn	

The Third World Computer Chess Championship
Linz, Austria, September 25–29, 1980

No.	Program (Country)	Rating*	Perf. Rating	1	2	3	4	Total
1	BELLE (USA)	2150	2189	8W	6D	4W	3W	3½
2	CHAOS (USA)	1800	2025	17W	4D	6W	7W	3½
3	DUCHESS (USA)	1900	1945	18W	12W	7W	1L	3
4	L'EXCENTRIQUE (CAN)	0	2030	5W	2D	1L	12W	2½
5	CHESS 4.9 (USA)	2050	1903	4L	9D	11W	10W	2½
6	NUCHESS (USA)	0	1759	16W	1D	2L	9D	2
7	KAISSA (USSR)	0	1631	14W	13W	3L	2L	2
8	BCP (UK)	0	1584	1L	10D	14D	15W	2
9	BEBE (USA)	0	1781	10D	5D	12D	6D	2
10	SCHACH 2.3 (FRG)	0	1706	9D	8D	13W	5L	2
11	AWIT (CAN)	1400	1249	13L	17W	5L	18W	2
12	MASTER (UK)	0	1643	15W	3L	9D	4L	1½
13	OSTRICH (CAN)	1450	1431	11W	7L	10L	14D	1½
14	MYCHESS (USA)	0	1380	7L	15D	8D	13D	1½
15	PARWELL (FRG)	0	1256	12L	14D	16W	8L	1½
16	ADVANCE 1.0 (UK)	0	754	6L	18D	15L	17W	1½
17	DARK HORSE (SWE)	0	636	2L	11L	18W	16L	1
18	CSC (USA)	0	505	3L	16D	17L	11L	0

This tournament was remarkable for (1) BELLE's performance, (2) the fact that *all* programs played well (ratings for programs that finished far down the list are way off target), (3) the domination by North American programs (the first five places went to programs from the USA and Canada), (4) the trend toward special hardware (BELLE, BEBE, PARWELL, and ADVANCE 1.0 were all home-brewed devices to a major degree), and (5) the great progress in world wide communications (satellite communication linked computers in the USA, Canada, England, Germany, and Italy (KAISSA ran on an IBM 370 computer in Pisa) to Linz, and there was only an occasional loss of line.)

Brief description of the programs

BELLE: Ken Thompson and Joe Condon; PDP 11/23 with special hardware, Bell Telephone Laboratories, Murray Hill, New Jersey; C language; 30,000,000 nodes/move; 280,000 positions in book.

CHAOS: Fred Swartz, Mike Alexander, Jack O'Keefe, Victor Berman; Amdahl 470, Amdahl Corporation, Sunnyvale, California; FORTRAN; 25,000 nodes/move; 10,000 positions in book.

DUCHESS: Tom Truscott, Bruce Wright, Eric Jensen; IBM 370/165, TUCC, Research Triangle Park, North Carolina; assembly language; 200,000 nodes/move; 3,000 positions in book.

L'EXCENTRIQUE: Claude Jarry; Amdahl V/7, McGill University, Montreal, Quebec; assembly language; 2,000,000–4,000,000 nodes/move; 3,000 positions in book.

CHESS 4.9: Larry Atkin, David Cahlander; CDC CYBER 176, CDC Headquarters, Arden Hills, Minnesota; assembly language; 500,000 nodes/move; 7,000 positions in book.

NUCHESS: David Slate, William Blanchard; CDC 6600, Northwestern University, Evanston, Illinois; FORTRAN; 200,000–500,000 nodes/move; 6,000 positions in book.

KAISSA: Mikhail Donskoy, Vladimir Arlazarov; IBM 370/168, Pisa, Italy; assembly language; 100,000–200,000 nodes/move; book size not available.

BCP: Don Beal, PDP 11/70, Queen Mary College, London; C and assembly language; 100,000 nodes/move; 1,000 lines in book.

BEBE: Tony Scherzer; Special purpose hardware at site; assembly language; 1,000,000 nodes/move; no book.

SCHACH 2.3: Matthias Engelbach; Burroughs 7800, HSBW Newbiberg/Munich; ALGOL; 100,000–200,000 nodes/move; 6,000 positions in book.

AWIT: Tony Marsland; Amdahl 470 V/7, University of Alberta, Edmonton, Alberta; ALGOL W; 250 nodes/move; 10,000 positions in book.

MASTER: John Birmingham, Peter Kent; IBM 3033, U.K. Atomic Energy Authority, Harwell, England; PL1; 50,000–150,000 nodes/move; 700 lines in book.

OSTRICH: Monroe Newborn, Data General Nova 4 at site; assembly language; 20,000 nodes/move; 1,000 lines in book.

MYCHESS: David Kittinger, Cromemco Z-2D at site; Z-80 assembly language; 15,000 nodes/move; 850 moves in book.

PARWELL: Thomas Nitsche, Elmar Henne, Wolfram Wolff; SMS2 (Siemens) with 128 8080s attached; FORTRAN and 8080 assembly language; 50,000 nodes/move; 3,000 moves in book.

ADVANCE 1.0: Mike Johnson, Dave Wilson; 6502 plus special chess hardware; assembly language; 500,000 nodes/move; 5,000 positions in book.

DARK HORSE: Ulf Rathsman, UNIVAC 1100/81, Stockholm, Sweden; FORTRAN; 20,000–30,000 nodes/move; 46 positions in book.

CSC: Dan Spracklen, Kathe Spracklen, Ron Nelson, Frank Duasson, Ed English; Chess Sensory Challenger at site based on 6502 microprocessor; assembly language; 50,000–100,000 nodes/move; 1,000 moves in book.

THE GAMES

Round 1
White: L'EXCENTRIQUE
Black: CHESS 4.9

Petroff Defense

1	P-K4	P-K4
2	N-KB3	N-KB3
3	P-Q4	N×P
4	B-Q3	P-Q4
5	N×P	B-Q3
6	P-QB4	B×N
7	P×B	N-QB3
8	B-B2	N×KP
9	Q×P	Q×Q
10	P×Q	B-B4
11	O-O	P-QB3
12	P-B4	N-N5
13	P-KR3	N(N5)-B3
14	P-KN4	N-Q7
15	R-K1ch	K-B1
16	B-Q1	B×N
17	B×N	B-Q6
18	R-K3	B-B5
19	B-N4ch	K-N1
20	P-Q6	N-Q4
21	R-K4	B-Q6
22	R-Q4	N×B
23	R×N	P-QN3
24	R-Q4	B-N4
25	P-QR4	P-QB4
26	R-Q2	B-B3
27	P-R5	R-Q1
28	P-R6	P-R4
29	P×P	R-R3
30	B-N4	KR×QP
31	R×R	R×R
32	K-B2	R-Q7ch
33	K-K3	R×P
34	R-Q1	R-N6ch
35	K-B2	B-K5
36	R-Q8ch	K-R2
37	R-KB8	P-B3
38	R-B7	R-R6
39	R×RP	P-B4
40	B-K2	R×KRP
41	R-Q7	R-R7ch
42	K-K3	R-R8
43	R-Q8	R-R6ch
44	K-Q2	R-QN6
45	B-B4	R-N5
46	B-B7	R-Q5ch

47	R × R	P × R	26	B-N5	Q-N1
48	P-R7	K-R3	27	B-Q3	Q-K1
49	B-N6	B-N7	28	K-R1	P-QR4
50	K-Q3	P-N4	29	B-N5	Q-Q1
51	B × P	P-N4	30	B-B4	R-QB7
52	B-K4	B-B8ch	31	R-N7	Q-R1
53	K × P	K × P	32	B × Pch	K-R1
54	P-B5	P-KN5	33	B-Q5	Q-K1
55	P-R8 = Q	K-R5	34	R-N1	N × B
56	K-K3	K-R3	35	Q × N	R × BP
57	K-B2	resigns	36	Q-K5	Q-R1ch
			37	P-Q5	R-B1

Round 2
White: NUCHESS
Black: BELLE

King's Gambit Accepted

1	P-KB4	P-K4	38	R-N1	Q-N2
2	P-K4	P × P	39	P-B5	Q-KB2
3	N-KB3	P-Q4	40	R-N1	P-R5
4	P × P	N-KB3	41	R-N8	R × R
5	B-N5ch	P-B3	42	Q × Rch	Q-N1
6	P × P	N × P	43	Q-K5	P-R6
7	P-Q4	B-Q3	44	P-B6	P-R3
8	O-O	O-O	45	P × Pch	Q × P
9	N-B3	B-KN5	46	Q-K8ch	K-R2
10	B-B4	B-N5	47	Q-K4ch	K-R1
11	N-K2	B-Q3	48	Q-K8ch	K-R2
12	N × P	B(N5) × N	49	Q-K4ch	K-R1
13	R × B	B-B4	50	Q-K8ch	drawn

14	P-B3	N-K4
15	B-K2	N × Rch
16	B × N	B-Q3
17	B × P	R-N1
18	Q-B3	R-K1
19	B-B6	R-K8ch
20	K-B2	R × B
21	R × R	R × Pch
22	K-N1	Q-B2
23	P-N3	B × N
24	P × B	R × QRP
25	R-N1	Q-Q3

White: L'EXCENTRIQUE
Black: CHAOS

Alekhine Defense

1	P-K4	N-KB3
2	P-K5	N-Q4
3	P-Q4	P-Q3
4	N-KB3	P × P
5	N × P	P-KN3
6	P-QB4	N-N3
7	P-B5	N(N3)-Q2
8	B-QB4	N × N
9	P × N	Q × Qch
10	K × Q	N-Q2
11	P-K6	P × P
12	B-K3	N-K4

13	B-Q4	B-N2	55	K-R3	B-Q8
14	R-K1	N×B	56	R-B3ch	K-K5
15	B×B	R-KN1	57	K-R2	R×P
16	B-B3	P-N3	58	B-N8	R-R4ch
17	P-QN3	N-R4	59	K-N2	K-B4
18	P-QN4	N-N2	60	K-B1	R-Q4
19	P×P	BP×P	61	R-KN3	B-N5
20	B-K5	K-B2	62	R-K3	P-N4
21	R-K3	N-Q3	63	R-K5ch	R×R
22	P-N4	B-N2	64	drawn	
23	N-Q2	QR-QB1			
24	R-KR3	P-KR4			
25	P-R4	N-B5		**Round 3**	
26	N×N	R×N		**White: BELLE**	
27	K-Q2	R-Q1ch		**Black: L'EXCENTRIQUE**	
28	R-Q3	R×R			
29	K×R	R×KNP		**Caro-Kann Defense**	
30	P-B4	R-N7	1	P-K4	P-QB3
31	P-R4	R-KR7	2	P-Q4	P-Q4
32	R-QB1	P-R3	3	N-QB3	P×P
33	R-B7	B-Q4	4	N×P	N-Q2
34	B-Q6	R×P	5	B-QB4	QN-B3
35	R×Pch	K-N1	6	N-N5	P-K3
36	R-K8ch	K-N2	7	N-K2	P-KR3
37	R-K7ch	K-B3	8	N-KB3	B-Q3
38	R-QR7	R-R6ch	9	O-O	P-QN4
39	K-Q4	R-R6	10	B-Q3	N-K2
40	R×P	P-R5	11	P-QR4	P×P
41	R-R7	K-B4	12	R×P	O-O
42	R-B7ch	K-N5	13	B-K3	N-N5
43	R-KN7	R×P	14	B-KB4	B×B
44	R×Pch	K-B6	15	N×B	Q-Q3
45	R-R6	R-R7	16	N-R5	P-N3
46	R×RP	R-Q7ch	17	N-N3	P-KB4
47	K-B3	R-KN7	18	Q-R1	P-R3
48	P-N5	R-QR7	19	R-K1	N-B3
49	R-R3ch	K-N5	20	B×RP	B×B
50	R-R8	R-R4	21	R×B	R×R
51	K-N4	R-R8	22	Q×R	P-B5
52	R-KN8ch	K-B6	23	N-K4	N×N
53	R-QB8	R-N1ch	24	R×N	P-N4
54	K-R4	B-N6ch	25	P-B4	R-N1
			26	P-B5	Q-Q4

The scene in the game room in Linz.

27	R-K2	P-N5
28	Q-R7	R-K1
29	R-K5	Q-Q1
30	N-K1	N-B4
31	Q-R6	N×P
32	Q-Q3	K-N2
33	Q-K4	R-B1
34	K-R1	R-B4
35	N-Q3	K-B3
36	N×P	P-N6
37	P-B3	P×P
38	R×Pch	N×R
39	Q×Nch	K-N2
40	Q×R	K-N1
41	Q-N6ch	K-R1
42	Q-B7	Q-N4
43	N-N6ch	Q×N
44	Q×Q	P-R4
45	P-B4	P-R5

46	P-B5	P-R6
47	P-B6	P×Pch
48	Q×P	resigns

Round 4
White: DUCHESS
Black: BELLE

Two Knights' Defense

1	P-K4	P-K4
2	N-KB3	N-QB3
3	B-B4	N-KB3
4	P-Q4	P×P
5	O-O	N×P
6	R-K1	P-Q4
7	B×P	Q×B
8	N-B3	Q-QR4
9	N×N	B-K3
10	B-Q2	B-QN5
11	N×P	N×N

12	P-QB3	B-K2
13	PxN	Q-Q4
14	R-QB1	P-QB3
15	B-N5	BxB
16	R-B5	QxRP
17	NxB	O-O-O
18	NxB	PxN
19	Q-Q2	R-Q4
20	R(B5)-B1	R-N4
21	R-K2	R-Q1
22	Q-B3	R-Q3
23	Q-B2	P-KN3
24	R-Q1	R(N4)-Q4
25	R-K4	P-K4
26	R-K3	RxP
27	R(Q1)-K1	R-Q7
28	Q-B5	QxP
29	RxP	Q-N3
30	R-K8ch	R-Q1
31	RxRch	RxR
32	Q-K7	Q-R4
33	R-N1	R-Q2
34	Q-K3	Q-N3
35	Q-K8ch	Q-Q1
36	Q-K6	Q-K2
37	Q-N8ch	R-Q1
38	Q-B4	P-KR4
39	P-B4	R-K1
40	R-R1	Q-K6ch
41	K-B1	P-R3
42	R-Q1	P-KN4
43	P-B5	Q-K4
44	Q-Q3	R-B1
45	Q-Q7ch	K-N1
46	K-N1	Q-B4ch
47	K-R1	QxP
48	Q-Q6ch	K-B1
49	P-R3	P-N5
50	PxP	PxP
51	R-K1	R-Q1
52	Q-R6	Q-B7
	resigns	

Round: Playoff
White: BELLE
Black: CHAOS

Alekhine Defense

1	P-K4	N-KB3
2	P-K5	N-Q4
3	P-Q4	P-Q3
4	N-KB3	PxP
5	NxP	P-KN3
6	P-KN3	B-B4
7	P-QB4	N-N5
8	Q-R4ch	N(N5)-B3
9	P-Q5	B-B7
10	Q-N5	Q-Q3
11	NxN	NxN
12	N-B3	B-N2
13	QxP	O-O
14	QxN	Q-N5
15	K-Q2	B-K5
16	KR-N1	KR-N1
17	B-R3	B-R3ch
18	P-B4	Q-R4
19	R-K1	P-B4
20	Q-K6ch	K-B1
21	P-N3	B-N2
22	B-QN2	B-Q5
23	P-KN4	R-N3
24	Q-Q7	R-Q3
25	Q-R4	Q-N3
26	B-R3	BxNch
27	KxB	R(Q3)-Q1
28	QR-Q1	Q-B7
29	PxP	Q-B7ch
30	K-Q4	PxP
31	Q-B6	Q-B7ch
32	K-K5	K-N1
33	R-N1ch	K-R1
34	BxKP	Q-N7ch
35	R-Q4	Q-N7
36	Q-B6ch	K-N1
37	BxQ	RxPch

| 38 | K-K6 | P-KR3 | 40 | P×R | R-KB1 |
| 39 | Q×RP | R-K4ch | 41 | B-B3 | mate |

Eleventh ACM Computer Chess Championship
Nashville, October 26–28, 1980

			Perf.			Round		
No.	Program	Rating*	Rating	1	2	3	4	Total
1	BELLE	2150	2294	9W	5W	2W	3W	4
2	CHAOS	1800	1952	7W	9W	1L	5W	3
3	CHAMPION SENSORY CHALLENGER (CSC)	0	1807	4D	7W	9L	1W	2½
4	BEBE	0	1762	3D	6W	5W	9L	2½
5	CRAY BLITZ	1850	1791	8W	1L	4W	2L	2
6	MYCHESS	0	1545	1L	4L	8W	10W	2
7	OSTRICH	1450	1372	2L	3L	10W	8D	1½
8	CUBE 2.0	0	1334	5L	10W	6L	7D	1½
9	AWIT	1400	1337	10W	2L	3L	4L	1
10	CLASH	1000	875	9L	8L	7L	5L	0

Seven of the participants from Linz gathered for a second time in less than a month. They were joined by CRAY BLITZ, which sat out the world championship and aimed instead for this event, and two new programs, CUBE 2.0 and CLASH. CHESS 4.9, L'EXCENTRIQUE, and DUCHESS were unable to participate because their authors were unable to attend. Only a blitz chess round robin between the participants and an exciting final round game between BELLE and CSC spared this event from being a rather dull affair. CRAY BLITZ captured this sideshow by winning all nine games. BELLE was second with an 8-1 record. Of note was the fact that five of the ten participants were present and, well, beeping—BELLE, BEBE, CSC, MYCHESS, and CLASH—and that two CRAY computers participated for the first time. They were used by CRAY BLITZ and CUBE 2.0. The CRAY executes 80,000,000 instructions per second!

Brief description of the programs

With the exception of CRAY BLITZ, CUBE 2.0, and CLASH, brief descriptions of the participants can be found in the section describing the Linz tournament.

CLASH: Chris Peters, Texas Instruments TX990 at site; FORTRAN IV; 1,000–2,000 nodes/move; small book.

CRAY BLITZ: Robert Hyatt, Albert Gower; CRAY-1, CRAY Research, Mendota Heights, Minnesota; 500,000–1,000,000 nodes/move; 3,000 positions in book.

CUBE 2.0: Lloyd Lank, James Lank; CRAY-1, United Computing, Kansas City, Missouri, 4,000,000–6,000,000 nodes/move; 2,000 moves in book.

THE GAMES

Round 1
White: CSC
Black: BEBE

Sicilian Defense

1	P-K4	P-QB4
2	N-KB3	P-Q3
3	P-Q4	P×P
4	N×P	N-KB3
5	N-QB3	P-KN3
6	P-B4	QN-Q2
7	B-K2	B-N2
8	O-O	O-O
9	B-K3	P-QR3
10	R-B1	P-K3
11	N-B3	N-N5
12	Q-Q2	N×B
13	Q×N	Q-B2
14	QR-Q1	P-QN4
15	Q-Q2	P-N5
16	N-QR4	R-N1
17	P-QN3	P-Q4
18	P×P	P×P
19	Q×P	Q×P(B5)
20	B-B4	N-N3
21	N×N	Q-K6ch
22	K-R1	Q×N(N3)
23	N-N5	B-N2
24	Q-Q7	B-B1
25	B×BPch	K-R1
26	Q-Q6	B-B4
27	B-B4	Q×Q
28	R×Q	B-B6
29	B×P	B×P
30	R-Q7	R×Rch
31	B×R	B-N2
32	B-B4	P-R3
33	N-B7ch	K-R2

34	N-Q8	B-B4
35	N-K6	B×N
36	B×B	R-QR1
37	R-Q2	R-R6
38	B-B4	R-R2
39	K-N1	P-R4
40	R-K2	B-Q5ch
41	K-B1	K-N2
42	R-K4	B-N7
43	B-Q3	B-B6
44	R-K2	R-KB2ch
45	R-KB2	R-Q2
46	B-N5	R-Q4
47	B-B4	R-R4
48	P-N3	B-Q5
49	R-Q2	B-B6
50	R-K2	P-N4
51	R-KB2	P-R5
52	P-N4	P-R6
53	R-B5	R×Rch
54	P×R	K-B3
	drawn	

Round 3
White: BELLE
Black: CHAOS

Sicilian Defense

1	P-K4	P-QB4
2	P-QB3	N-KB3
3	P-K5	N-Q4
4	P-Q4	P×P
5	P×P	P-Q3
6	N-KB3	N-QB3
7	B-QB4	N-N3
8	B-QN5	P-K3
9	O-O	B-K2
10	P×P	Q×P
11	N-B3	O-O

12	R-K1	B-Q2
13	B-K3	N-Q4
14	B-R4	N×B
15	P×N	KR-B1
16	P-K4	P-QR3
17	B×N	R×B
18	N-K5	R-B2
19	R-K2	B-K1
20	N-B3	QR-B1
21	P-K5	Q-N5
22	P-Q5	Q-B4ch
23	K-R1	P×P
24	N×P	R-Q1
25	R-Q2	R(B2)-Q2
26	P-QN4	Q×N
27	R×Q	R×R
28	Q-K1	B-QR5
29	Q-B3	B-QB3
30	P-QR3	B-KN4
31	Q-B2	B-B5
32	R-K1	R-Q6
33	Q-B4	B-R3
34	P-K6	R×P
35	P×Pch	K-B1
36	Q-B5ch	K×P
37	Q-K7ch	K-N1
38	Q×Rch	resigns

Round 4

What follows is one of the most exciting games in the history of the ACM tournaments. The notes are by David Levy.

White: CSC
Black: BELLE

Ruy Lopez

1	P-K4	P-K4
2	N-KB3	N-QB3
3	B-B5	P-QR3
4	B-R4	N-B3
5	O-O	N×P

The opening variation, which leads to very lively play, has long been a favorite of Victor Korchnoi and was used by him several times during his 1978 world championship match against Karpov.

6	P-Q4	P-QN4
7	B-N3	P-Q4
8	P×P	B-K3
9	P-B3	B-QB4

Up to now both programs have been following well known opening theory, taken directly from their opening books. Now, however, CSC is out of book and at once makes a serious strategic mistake.

10 B-K3?

This allows Black to saddle its opponent with doubled isolated pawns. Normal here is 10 QN-Q2.

10	...	B×B
11	P×B	R-QN1
12	QN-Q2	N-B4

Threatening 13 N-Q6, forking the pawns on K4 and N7, as well as the slower plan of 13 O-O followed by N-Q2, R-K1, N-B1, and the white pawn at K4 would soon be lost.

13	Q-K1	N-Q6
14	Q-N3	O-O
15	QR-N1?	

Perhaps it is a little unfair to give this move a question mark, since the correct continuation requires a deep analysis well beyond the scope of CSC. However, from the pure chess point of view, White should be criticized.

The correct move was 15 B-B2 when Black would almost certainly have played 15 ...N×NP allowing the continuation 16 B×Pch K×B 17 N-N5ch K-N1 18 Q-R4 R-K1 19 Q-R7ch K-B1 20 N×P B×N 21 R×Bch K×R 22 R-KB1ch Q-B3 (22 ... K-K3 23 Q-B5ch K-K2 24 Q-B7 mate) 23 P×Q and White will win.

15	...	Q-K2?
16	B-B2	Q-B4

BELLE has pinned all its hopes on this move when making the previous one but a better plan would have been 15 ...P-R3. Now White cannot capture on Q3 because of 16 ... Q×KP, but there is something better for White.

17	N-N5!	N(B3)×P
18	N×RP	KR-Q1

And not 18 ...K×N 19 Q×N losing the knight on Q6 as well.

19	N-B6ch	K-B1
20	B×N	N×B
21	N-R5	P-N3
22	N-B6	B-B4

This move soon lands Black in trouble. There were numerous alternatives such as 22 ...P-N5.

23	Q-N5	P-N5
24	N-R7ch	K-K1
25	N-B6ch	K-B1

Here and for a few moves, White could force a draw.

26	N-N3	Q-B5
27	N-R7ch	K-K1
28	P×P	R×P
29	N-B6ch	K-B1
30	N-N4	R-Q3
31	N-R6	Q-K5!

A dual purpose move putting pressure on White's KN2 and supporting Black's own K-side.

32 R×B!?

An interesting exchange sacrifice that just fails. But if White vacilates, Black will play 32 ...B-K3 or 32 ...N-K4 followed by 33 N-N5 where Black has the more active game.

32	...	P×R
33	Q-N8ch	K-K2
34	Q×Pch	K-Q1
35	N×P	R-QB3
36	P-KR4	

A typical computer move and not a bad try. In many variations White only just fails to promote this pawn.

36	...	R-B7!
37	Q-B8ch	K-Q2
38	Q-B7ch	K-B1
39	Q-N6	K-N2
40	N-R5ch	K-R1!!

A very profound move. Black gives up a pawn with check in order to cause its opponent to lose a tempo (a move). White then finds its queen on the wrong flank, and in bringing it back to the K-side, White hands over the initiative for just long enough.

41	Q×Pch	K-N1
42	Q-KN6	

Preventing mate on KN2, but now comes the deadly blow.

42	...	N-K4!

Threatening the queen as well as R×KNPch.

42	Q-N8ch	K-R2
44	R-KB1	R(N5)×P
45	K-R1	R×NP

White could well resign here to save further embarrassment.

46	N-B6ch	N × N
47	Q-QR8ch	K × Q
48	P-R4	

Having delayed mate for as long as possible, White finally runs out of checks, but a bug appears in BELLE!

48	...	K-N1
49	P-QR5	K-R1
50	P-R6	K-R2
51	P-R5	K-N3
52	P-R7	R-KN8ch

At last!

| 53 | K × R | Q-N7 mate. |

Appendix A: An Unsolved Problem

It is a well-known empirical law of tree searching that the deeper the search the better the result. As chess programs, for example, search larger and larger trees, their performance improves. Many researchers in this field assume this law to guarantee ultimate success in chess programming, and in other problem domains that depend on heuristic search. I am not quite so convinced that this is the case. In my own opinion it is quite possible that deeper searches of the game tree will result in performances that asymptotically approach some fixed level and there is nothing to prove whether or not this level, in chess, will be at World Championship class.

I have long felt that there ought to be some theoretical method or computational experiment which would determine exactly how the parameters of the tree search affect the performance of the search. If a functional relationship could be found that related the performance of the tree searching system (P_t) to the branching factor (b), the depth of search (d) and the performance of the evaluation function (P_e), it would be possible to determine what increase in depth would be required in order to reach some desired performance level (e.g. World Chess Champion). In this chapter I shall describe an experiment which I think will solve this important problem and I leave it to others to implement my suggestion or to discover a theoretical alternative.

First let us define our problem domain and parameters. We shall assume that in our trees all paths are of depth d and that there are b branches at each non-terminal node. The evaluation function used to score the terminal nodes has performance P_e and the whole tree searching system has performance P_t.

P_e can be defined in various ways. It might be the correlation between the actual order of merit of a group of successor nodes (or moves) and the order of merit as determined by the evaluation function. Another possibility, and the one which I suggest is used for this experiment, is given by the expression

$$P_e = \frac{b + 1 - 2i}{b - 1} \qquad (1)$$

where i is the mean ranking of the move chosen by P_e in the actual order of merit. Note that if i = 1 (for which the evaluation function always chooses the best move), $P_e = 1$. If i = (b + 1)/2, (for which the evaluation function chooses at random), $P_e = 0$. If i = b (for which the worst move is always chosen), $P_e = -1$.

Similarly, P_t is given by

$$P_t = \frac{b + 1 - 2j}{b - 1} \qquad (2)$$

where j is the mean ranking of the move chosen at the root of the tree in the actual order of merit.

Clearly, when i = 1 and P_e = 1, j = 1 and P_t = 1.

Next we must build a model of an evaluation function that conforms to (1). We shall assume that the b terminal node successors of the same parent node have scores S_1, S_2, S_3, ... S_b, which are generated randomly on the range $0 \leqslant S_k \leqslant R$. If we add, to each of these scores S_k, a different random number S_k' generated on the range $-E \leqslant S_k' \leqslant E$, then we have two sets of scores for the same group of nodes: S_1, S_2, ..., S_b and $S_1 + S_1'$, $S_2 + S_2'$, $S_3 + S_3'$ ..., $S_b + S_b'$. If we look for the best score in the second group (let us assume that it is $S_3 + S_3'$) we have, from the subscript 3, the fact that on this particular occasion our evaluation function (normally an inexact model) has picked the third best move as being best. By conducting a large number of experiments of this kind for various values of E it is possible to determine the mean value of i for each value of E. It is then possible to find a relationship between E and i so that we can produce a model of an evaluation function with any desired, positive value of P_e, simply by varying E.

(Note, incidentally, that P_e = 1 when E = 0 and P_e = 0 when E = ∞).

We are now ready to conduct the most important part of the experiment. For each group of b terminal nodes (all sharing a common parent node) generate the random scores S_1, S_2, S_3, ... S_b. Using some value of E (i.e. some value of P_e) generate the modified scores $S_1 + S_1'$, ... etc., which are assigned to a similar group of nodes on a second tree. Perform a normal search of both trees, generating terminal scores in the manner described above. We will then have determined which move, at the root of the tree, would be chosen by the search of the tree with modified terminal scores. By determining where, in the actual order of merit (as found by the search of the unknown tree), this chosen move lies, we have the index j from which we can calculate P_t using (2).

By conducting a large number of experiments for different values of b, d and E, we will be able to derive a relationship expressing P_t as a function of P_e, b and d.

Applications

The most interesting application of this relationship is that it will enable us to estimate the depth of search necessary before (say) CHESS 4.6 can beat Bobby Fischer. I conjecture that for a World Champion, P_t lies somewhere around 0.99 (I estimate j to be around 1.15).

Another useful experiment would be to determine the effect of forward pruning. One could determine the relationship between P_t, P_e, b and d when a certain fraction f of the nodes at each non-terminal level were pruned, using an evaluation function of performance P_{pr} to do the pruning.

Further studies

The experiments described above can first be performed with trees for which the terminal scores are randomly generated. In a game situation however, there is some relation between the scores of the nodes in any successor group - this relationship being the fact that these successor nodes share the same parent. The significance of this fact can be seen from the following tree.

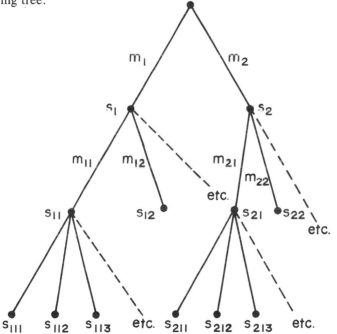

Let us assume that m_1 is a bad move which loses the queen to the reply m_{11} but that m_2 is a respectable move which does not lose material to the best reply m_{21}. Then the scores s_{111}, s_{112}, s_{113}, ... etc., and s_{211}, s_{212}, si_{213}, ... etc., are not random scores but are separated by the fact that in one group the scores will, in general, be much higher than those in the other group because of the enormous difference caused by the loss of the queen. Clearly even though the evaluation function may not choose the best move in either or both of the two groups, the tree search is still likely to prefer m_2 to m_1.

In order to allow for this effect the experiments should be performed on trees that have been grown to simulate game situations. Typically, in chess, there is a small number of moves (normally less than four) which appear either to maintain the status quo or to improve one's position. There is a larger number of moves which are slightly disadvantageous and more moves which are extremely disadvantageous. A graph of the apparent change in score brought about by making the nth best move in a chess position will look something like this.

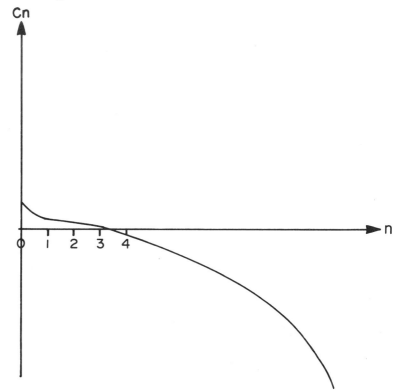

If we choose some function $f(n) = c_n$ which approximates to this curve we can determine the score for the nth best successor of a node (whose own score is s) from the equation

$$s_n = s + f(n + E_n)$$

where E_n is some number randomly generated on the range $-\frac{1}{2} \leqslant E_n \leqslant \frac{1}{2}$.

Now, starting at the root of the tree, we can grow the tree and assign apparent scores for all the nodes down to terminal depth in such a way as to simulate a chess tree. Then the tree can be searched in the manner described above.

If these experiments lead to the conclusion that exhaustive search techniques are not going to produce a World Chess Champion then those programmers who have placed all their faith in the search of enormous trees will try a different approach, possibly with greater success. I shall be very pleased to hear from any reader who performs these experiments and/or discovers a theoretical solution to the problem.

Reprinted, with permission, from Creative Computing, *Vol. 2, No. 1*

Appendix B: Games from 1977 Tournaments

Eighth ACM Tournament

Round 1

White: CHAOS
Black: TYRO

Queen's Gambit Declined

1 P-Q4 P-Q4 2 P-QB4 P-K3 3 N-QB3 N-KB3 4 B-N5 P-KR3 5 B×N P×B 6 P×P P×P 7 N-B3 B-QN5 8 P-KN3 O-O 9 B-N2 B×Nch 10 P×B R-K1 11 Q-Q2 K-N2 12 O-O B-B4 13 Q-N2 P-N3 14 N-R4 Q-Q2 15 N×Bch Q×N 16 P-QB4 P-B3 17 P×P P×P 18 Q-N5 R-Q1 19 P-K4 Q-Q2 20 Q×QP N-B3 21 Q×Q R×Q 22 P-K5 R-QB1 23 B-R3 R(B1)-B2 24 P×Pch K×P 25 B×R R×B 26 QR-B1 N×P 27 K-N2 N-K7 28 KR-Q1 N×R 29 R×R N×P 30 R×RP N-N5 31 K-B3 N-Q4 32 K-K2 P-N4 33 K-Q3 N-K2 34 R-N7 N-N3 35 R×NP N-K4ch 36 K-K4 N-N5 37 P-B3 N×P 38 R-N1 K-K3 39 R-KR1 P-B4ch 40 K-B4 N×P 41 R×Pch K-B2 42 K×N K-N2 43 R-QN6 K-B2 44 K-B4 K-K2 45 K×P K-Q2 46 K-B6 K-B2 47 R-K6 K-Q2 48 P-N4 K-B2 49 P-N5 K-Q2 50 P-N6 K-B2 51 P-N7 K-Q2 52 P-N8=Q K-B2 53 Q-B7ch K-Q1 R-K8mate.

White: BLACK KNIGHT
Black: BRUTE FORCE

Centre Counter

1 P-K4 P-Q4 2 P×P Q×P 3 N-QB3 Q-K3ch 4 KN-K2 B-Q2 5 P-Q4

N-QR3 6 B-N5 P-R3 7 B-K3 Q-QN3 8 Q-N1 P-N4 9 P-KR4 P×P 10 P-Q5
Q-N5 11 B-Q4 P-K4 12 P×Pe.p P-KB3 13 P-R3 Q-K2 14 P×Bch K-Q1 15
Q-R2 P-QB4 16 O-O-O P×B 17 N×P N-B4 18 B-B4 Q-N2 19 K-K4 Q×NP
20 N×N Q-N4ch 21 R-Q2 Q×Rch 22 K×Q B×N 23 N-K6ch K×P 24
N×Bch K-B2 25 B-Q5 N-K2 26 B×P QR-Q1ch 27 K-B3 R-QN1 28 Q-K6
N-N1 29 Q-B6ch K-Q1 30 Q-Q7mate.

White: XENARBOR
Black: WITA
King's Indian Defence
1 P-Q4 N-KB3 2 P-QB4 P-KN3 3 N-QB3 B-N2 4 P-K4 P-K3 5 N-KB3 P-Q3
6 P-KN3 N-QB3 7 B-N2 P-KR3 8 O-O O-O 9 P-Q5 P×P 10 BP×P N-N1 11 B-
K3 R-K1 12 Q-B2 Q-K2 13 KR-Q1 N×KP 14 N×N Q×N 15 Q×P B×P
16 QR-N1 N-R3 17 Q×QP B-N2 18 N-Q4 B-K4 19 B×Q B×Q 20 B-N2 B-
B1 21 KR-QB1 B-QB4 22 P-QR4 P-B3 23 P-R5 R-N1 24 R×B N×R 25 N-
B6 B-B4 26 R-N5 P-R3 37 R-N6 P×N 28 P×P R×R 29 P×R R-K4 30 P-
B7 P-KR4 31 P-R4 P-R4 32 B-KB1 P-R5 33 B-Q4 P-R6 34 B×R P×B 35 B-
B4ch K-B1 36 K-R2 K-K2 37 P-R3 B-B1 38 P-R4 P×P 39 P×P N-Q2 40 B-
N3 B-N2 41 B-R2 K-B3 42 B-N3 K-N2 43 P-B5 P×P 44 B-Q5 B-B1 45 P-N7
P-R7 46 P×B=Q N-B3 47 B×P P-B5 48 Q-B5 P-B6 49 Q-KN5ch Resigns.

White: 8080 CHESS
Black: OSTRICH
Centre Game
1 P-K4 P-K4 2 P-Q4 N-KB3 3 P×P N×P 4 N-KB3 B-B4 5 N-Q4 N-QB3 6
N×N B×Pch 7 K-K2 QP×N 8 Q×Qch K×Q 9 B-B4 B-Q5 10 P-B3 B-
N5ch 11 K-Q3 N-B7ch 12 K×B N×R 13 B-B4 B-K3 14 B-Q3 K-B1 15 N-
Q2 R-Q1ch 16 K-K3 N-B7 17 B×P N-N5ch 18 K-K2 R-R1 19 B-K4 N×RP
20 P-QN4 R-R5 21 P-N3 R-R4 22 P-R4 B-Q4 23 B-Q3 N-N5 24 P-B4 B-N7
25 R-KN1 B-R6 26 N-B3 P-R4 27 P×P R×P 28 N-Q4 N×P 29 B×N
KR×Bch 30 K-B3 P-QB4 31 N-K2 R×P 32 N-B4 B-K3 33 R-QB1 P-KN4
34 N-K2 R-R7 35 R-B3 B-B4 36 N-B1 R-Q7 37 B-K2 R-K5 38 B-Q3 Black
lost on time. Black's next move, 38... P-N5 mate, could not be printed
because of a program bug. The analysis part of the program was aware of
the mate, but crashed in the process of trying to print the move. Contest
rules forbid any program changes, so time ran out for Monty Newborn, the
author of OSTRICH. The irony of the situation is that Monty was co-author
of this very rule!

White: CHESS 4.6
Black: CHUTE

Ruy Lopez

1 P-K4 P-K4 2 N-KB3 N-QB3 3 B-N5 KN-K2 4 P-Q4 P×P 5 N×P N×N 6
Q×N P-QR3 7 B-K2 N-B3 8 Q-B4 B-Q3 9 B-K3 O-O 10 N-B3 P-
QN4 11 Q-Q5 B-N2 12 O-O Q-K1 13 P-QR3 Q-K3 14 P-B4 QR-K1 15 Q×Q
BP×Q 16 QR-Q1 P-K4 17 P-B5 N-K2 18 P-QN3 R-B3 19 P-QN4 R-R1 20
B-N5 R-B2 21 B-R5 P-N3 22 B×N B×B 23 P×P R×Rch 24 K×R R-
KB1ch 25 K-K1 B-R5ch 26 P-N3 B×NPch 27 P×B P×P 28 B×P R-B6 29
R-Q3 R×R 30 P×R K-N2 31 B-B5 P-Q3 32 N-Q5 P-B3 33 N-N6 K-R1 34
N-B8 P-Q4 35 N-Q6 B-R1 36 P×P P×P 37 B-B8 P-K5 38 B×P B-B3 39
B×P B×B 40 N×B P×P 41 P-R4 K-N2 42 P-R5 K-R3 43 P-R6 K-R4 44 P-
R7 P-Q7ch 45 K×P K-N5 46 P-R8=Q K×P 47 N-R3 P-Q5 48 P-N5 K-B7
49 P-N6 K-N6 50 Q-K4 K-B7 51 P-N7 K-N8 52 P-N8=Q K-B7 53 Q-K1ch
K-N7 54 Q(N8)-KN3mate.

White: BLITZ
Black: DUCHESS

Ruy Lopez

1 P-K4 P-K4 2 N-KB3 N-QB3 3 B-N5 P-QR3 4 B×N QP×B 5 P-Q4 P×P 6
Q×P Q×Q 7 N×Q B-Q2 8 B-K3 O-O-O 9 N-QB3 B-Q3 10 O-O-O N-B3 11
R-Q3 N-N5 12 P-KN3 N×B R×N B-QB4 14 R-Q3 B-KN5 15 P-B3 B-R4 16
N(B3)-K2 B×N 17 N×B P-QB4 18 N-B5 R×R 19 P×R B×P 20 R-B1
B-K7 21 N-K7ch K-Q1 22 R×P B×P 23 N-Q5 B×P 24 N×P R-N1 25 N-
K6ch K-K1 26 R×KNP R×R 27 N×Rch K-K2 28 N-R5 K-Q3 29 N-B4 P-
B5 30 K-Q2 B-N8 31 P-QR3 P-N4 32 P-KN4 K-K4 33 N-K2 B-Q6 34 P-KR4
B×N 35 K×B K-B5 36 P-N5 K-N5 37 K-K3 K×P 38 K-B4 P-QR4 39 K-B5
P-N5 40 P×P P×P 41 P-N6 P×Pch 42 K-K4 P-N4 43 K-Q4 P-N5 44 K×P
P-KN6 45 K×P K-N4 46 K-R5 P-N7 47 P-N4 P-N8=Q 48 P-N5 Q-R2ch 49
K-N4 K-B4 50 K-B4 K-K4 51 K-N4 Adjudicated a win for Black.

Round 2

White: 8080 CHESS
Black: CHAOS

Sicilian Defence

1 P-K4 P-QB4 2 P-Q4 P×P 3 Q×P N-QB3 4 Q-Q5 N-B3 5 Q-Q3 P-K4 6 N-
KB3 B-B4 7 B-N5 Q-N3 8 B×N B×Pch 9 K-Q2 Q×P 10 B×NP R-KN1 11
Q-B3 Q×Qch 12 K×Q R×B 13 N-Q2 P-Q3 14 N-B4 B-QB4 15 P-KR4 B-
K3 16 N-N2 R-N5 White lost on time.

White: WITA
Black: TYRO

Queen's Gambit Declined

1 P-Q4 P-Q4 2 P-QB4 P-K3 3 P-K4 P×KP 4 N-QB3 B-N5 5 P-QR3 B×Nch 6 P×B N-KB3 7 R-N1 O-O 8 B-K2 P-QN3 9 B-B4 P-B3 10 N-R3 Q-K2 11 Q-R4 KN-Q2 12 O-O B-R3 13 B×N N×B 14 KR-Q1 P-KB4 15 K-R1 P-K4 16 P×P Q×KP 17 Q-N3 K-R1 18 N-N5 Q-B3 19 N-R3 R-Q1 20 R×Rch Q×R 21 N-B4 Q-R5 22 P-N3 Q-B3 23 R-Q1 B-B1 24 N-R5 Q-K2 25 P-R3 P-N3 26 P-B5 P×N 37 P×P P×P 28 P-KB4 P-N4 29 B×RP B-K3 30 Q-N4 Q×Q 31 BP×Q B-Q4 32 P-N4 P×P 33 K-R2 P×P 34 P-B5 R×P 35 B-N4 R-R7ch 36 K×P N-Q2 37 B-R5 N-B3 38 K-R4 R-R7ch 39 K-N5 N×B 40 P-B6 K-N1 41 R-KN1 K-B2 42 R-QR1 N×P 43 K-B5 R-KB7ch 44 K-N5 P-R4 45 K-R6 R-KN7 46 R-R7ch K-K3 47 R-R1 P-K6 48 R-R6 K-B4 49 R-R2 R-N3mate.

White: CHUTE
Black: BLITZ

Petroff Defence

1 P-K4 P-K4 2 N-KB3 N-KB3 3 N×P P-Q3 4 N-KB3 N×P 5 Q-K2 Q-K2 6 P-Q3 N-KB3 7 B-N5 QN-Q2 8 Q×Qch B×Q 9 B-K2 O-O 10 O-O P-KR3 11 B-Q2 N-N3 12 B-R5 B-K3 13 N-B3 KR-K1 14 B×N RP×B 15 N-Q4 B-Q4 16 N×B N×N 17 B-B3 P-QB3 18 B×N P×B 19 N-B5 QR-B1 20 QR-K1 B-B1 21 R×R R×R 22 P-Q4 R-K7 23 N-K3 R-Q7 24 N×P R×BP 25 R-N1 R-Q7 26 N×P R×QP 27 N-Q7 R-Q7 28 K-B1 P-Q4 39 K-K1 R-B7 30 N×B K×N 31 R-Q1 R×NP 32 P-QR4 R-R7 33 R×P R×RP 34 R-Q8ch K-K2 35 R-Q3 P-QN4 36 R-K3ch K-Q3 37 R-Q3ch K-B3 38 R-B3ch K-N3 39 R-B1 R-K5ch 40 K-Q2 P-N5 41 P-B3 R-K4 42 R-B4 R-QN4 43 P-N3 P-N6 44 R-B8 K-N2 45 R-B8 P-N7 46 R×Pch K-N3 47 R×P P-N8=Q 48 R-Q7 Q-R7ch 49 K-Q3 Q×P White resigns.

White: DUCHESS
Black: BLACK KNIGHT

Sicilian Defence

1 P-K4 P-QB4 2 P-Q4 P×P 3 P-QB3 P×P 4 N×P N-QB3 5 N-B3 P-Q3 6 B-QB4 P-K3 7 O-O N-B3 8 Q-K2 B-K2 9 R-Q1 P-K4 10 B-K3 N-KN5 11 B-Q2 B-R5 12 B-K1 B-K2 13 B-Q2 B-K3 14 B×B P×B 15 N-KN5 B×N 16 Q×N B×B 17 Q×NP R-KB1 18 Q×NP Q-N3 19 Q×Rch K-K2 20 Q×Rch K×Q 21 R×B Q-B2 22 R(R1)-Q1 N-Q5 23 P-B4 Q-KN2 24 R-Q3 P-KR4 25 K-R1 P-R3 26 P×P P×P 37 R-KB1ch K-K1 38 R-N3 Q-K2 29 R-N8ch K-Q2 30 R-QR8 K-B3 31 R×Pch K-N2 32 R-R4 K-B3 33 R-R5 Q-N5 34 R×P Q×P 35 R-QB5ch K-Q3 36 P-K5ch K-K2 37 R-QN1 Q-KB7 38 R-B7ch K-Q1 39 R-KR7 N-B3 40 R-R8ch K-B2 41 N-N5ch K-Q2 42 R-R7ch K-Q1 43 N-Q6 Q-B1 44 K-N1 P-R5 45 R(N1)-N7 N-K2 46 R-N8ch K-B2 47 R×Q P-R6 48 R×Nch K-B3 49 P×P K-Q4 50 N-B7 K-Q5 51 R×P K-Q4

52 R-Q6ch K-K5 53 R-B8 K-B6 54 R-B4 K-K7 55 R-K4ch K-B6 56 N-N5mate.

White: OSTRICH
Black: BRUTE FORCE
                        Centre Counter Defence
1 P-K4 P-Q4 2 P×P Q×P 3 N-QB3 Q-K4ch 4 KN-K2 P-QR4 5 P-Q4 Q-KB4 6 B-K3 P-KN4 7 N-N3 Q-N3 8 B-Q3 P-KB4 9 O-O N-KB3 10 N-N5 K-Q1 11 P-Q5 P-N5 12 B-Q4 P-K3 13 P×P B-N5 14 B×P K-K2 15 B×Q P×B 16 B×Nch K×B 17 Q-Q4ch K-K2 18 Q-N7ch K×P 19 N×Pch K-Q3 20 N×R R-K1 21 Q-QB7ch K-K3 22 KR-K1ch B×R 23 R×Bch K-B3 24 R×R B-Q2 25 Q-K5ch K-B2 26 Q-K7mate.

White: XENARBOR
Black: CHESS 4.6
                        Benoni Defence
1 P-Q4 N-KB3 2 P-QB4 P-B4 3 P-Q5 P-K3 4 N-KB3 P×P 5 P×P P-Q3 6 P-K3 B-B4 7 N-B3 QN-Q2 8 P-KN3 N-K4 9 N×N P×N 10 Q-N3 Q-N3 11 Q×Q P×Q 12 B-N2 B-Q6 13 P-K4 B-Q3 14 B-K3 O-O 15 O-O-O B-B5 16 P-N3 B-R3 17 N-R4 B-N4 18 N×NP R-R3 19 P-QR4 B-K7 20 R-Q2 R×N 21 R×B R×P 22 R-B2 R-B1 23 B-R3 R-R1 24 R-B4 P-QN4 25 R-B2 R×P 26 B-N2 P-B5 27 P-R4 P-B6 28 R-K2 N×KP 29 B×N R×B 30 R-QR2 R-R6 31 R×R B×Rch 32 K-B2 B-N5 33 R-R1 P-B4 34 R-R8ch K-B2 35 R-QN8 P-B5 36 K-Q3 P×B 37 P×P R-QB5 38 R×P P-B7 39 K×R B-K2 40 P-K4 P-B8=Qch 41 K-Q3 Q-B8ch 42 K-K3 Q×R 43 P-N4 B×P 44 K-Q2 Q-B5 45 P-Q6 Q×P 46 P-N5 B×Pch 47 K-B3 P-R4 48 K-N3 P-R5 49 K-R2 Q-QN5 50 K-R1 B-B8 51 K-R2 Q-N7mate.

                        Round 3
White: CHESS 4.6
Black: CHAOS
                        Sicilian Defence
1 P-K4 P-QB4 2 N-KB3 N-QB3 3 B-N5 N-B3 4 P-K5 N-Q4 5 O-O P-K3 6 B×N QP×B 7 P-Q3 B-K2 8 N-R3 O-O 9 B-Q2 B-Q2 10 Q-K2 Q-N3 11 N-B4 Q-Q1 12 N-Q6 Q-N3 13 P-B4 Q×P 15 P×N BP×P 15 KR-N1 Q-R6 16 R×P Q-R5 17 R-QB1 QR-N1 18 R-B7 R-N7 19 R(B7)×BP KR-N1 20 Q-K3 Q×P 21 R-B7 B×N 22 R×B B-R6 23 Q-B4 P-B4 24 P×Pe.p. B-B1 25 P×P B-K2 26 R×B P-KR3 27 Q-B7ch K-R2 28 P-N8=Qmate.

White: TYRO
Black: CHUTE

Queen's Gambit Declined

1 P-Q4 P-Q4 2 P-QB4 P-K3 3 P-KN3 P×P 4 N-KB3 N-QB3 5 P-QR3 N-B3 6 N-B3 P-QR3 7 P-K4 P-QN4 8 B-B4 N-KR4 9 B-R3 N×B 10 P×N Q-B3 11 Q-Q2 Q-R3 12 N-N5 N-Q1 13 P-Q5 B-K2 14 B-N4 P-KB4 15 KP×P P×BP 16 B-B3 B-N2 17 O-O Q-QN3 18 QR-K1 P-R3 19 Q-K3 Q-KB3 20 N-K6 R-QB1 21 N×N K×N 22 B-R5 P-N4 23 K-R1 P×P 24 Q×P B-Q3 25 Q-B3 R-KN1 26 R-KN1 R×Rch 27 R×R Q-K4 28 Q-N2 K-Q2 29 R-Q1 B-B4 30 R-Q2 Q-K8ch 31 Q-N1 Q×R 32 Q-N7ch B-K2 33 Q-K5 Q×BP 34 Q-K6ch K-Q1 35 Q×KRP Q-B8mate.

White: BLACK KNIGHT
Black: XENARBOR

Sicilian Defence

1 P-K4 P-QB4 2 N-KB3 N-QB3 3 N-B3 P-Q3 4 P-Q4 P×P 5 N×P N×N 6 Q×N N-B3 7 P-K5 P×P 7 Q×KP P-QR3 9 B-K2 Q-Q3 10 Q×Q P×Q 11 B-KN5 B-K3 12 B×N P×B 13 B-B3 O-O-O 14 O-O-O B-R3ch 15 K-N1 B-N2 16 R-Q3 P-B4 17 KR-Q1 B-K4 18 B-Q5 B×B 19 N×B B×RP 20 R-KR3 B-K4 21 P-KB4 P-KR4 22 P×B P×P 23 R-KB3 P-B5 24 P-KN3 P×P 25 R×NP P-R5 26 R-N7 P-B4 27 N-N6ch K-N1 28 R(Q1)-Q7 R×R 29 N×Rch K-R2 30 N×P R-K1 31 N-B6ch K-R1 32 N-K7 P-B5 33 R-N8 R×R 34 P-R4 R-N8ch 35 K-B2 P-B6 36 N-Q8 K-N1 37 N-N6 P-B7 38 N-Q7ch K-R2 39 N-K5 P-B8=Q 40 K-B3 P-R6 41 P-B5 P-R7 42 P-R4 P-R8=Q 43 P-N4 Q-R8ch 44 K-Q3 Q×N 45 P-R5 Q(R8)-K5ch 46 K-Q2 Q(K4)-Q5mate.

White: BLITZ V
Black: 8080 CHESS

King Pawn Opening

1 P-K4 P-K4 2 N-KB3 P-Q4 3 N×P P×P 4 B-B4 N-KR3 5 O-O N-B3 6 N×N P×N 7 Q-K2 B-KB4 8 P-Q3 B-B4 9 B×N P×B 10 Q-R5 Q-B3 11 P×P Q×P 12 Q×BPch K-Q1 13 Q×B B×Pch 14 Q×B Q×R 15 Q-R4ch K-Q2 16 R-Q1ch K-K1 17 Q-R5 ch Resigns.

White: OSTRICH
Black: DUCHESS

Petroff Defence

1 P-K4 P-K4 2 N-KB3 N-KB3 3 B-B4 N×P 4 Q-K2 P-Q4 5 N×P B-K3 6 O-O B-Q3 7 N-KB3 O-O 8 P-Q3 P×B 9 P×N N-B3 10 N-N5 N-Q5 11 Q-R5 P-KR3 12 N×B P×N 13 Q-Q1 P-B4 14 P-QB3 N-B3 15 N-R3 Q-N1 16 P-R4 N-K4 17 B-K3 B-K2 18 P-B4 N-Q6 19 N×P N×BP 20 P-KN3 N-N3 21 Q-N4 K-R2 22 P-R5 N-K4 23 R×R N×Q 24 R×Q R×R 25 B-B4 R-Q1 26 N-K5 N×N 27 B×N B-B3 28 B×B P×B 29 R-KB1 K-N2 30 K-N2 K-B2 31 K-B3 R-Q6ch 32 K-N4 R-Q7 33 R-QN1 R-KB7 34 P-R4 K-K2 35 P-N4 P-B5

36 R-K1 R-B7 37 R-K3 P-N3 38 P-R5 P×P 39 P×P K-Q3 40 K-B4 R-QR7
41 R-B3 R×P 42 K-K3 K-K4 43 R-B2 R-R8 44 R-B2 R-K8ch 45 K-Q2
R×P 46 R-B1 R-N5 47 R-K1ch K-Q4 White resigns.

White: BRUTE FORCE
Black: WITA

Queen Pawn Opening

1 P-Q4 N-KB3 2 N-QB3 N-B3 3 P-Q5 N×P 4 Q×N P-Q3 5 P-QR3 P-K3 6
Q-Q2 B-K2 7 P-QN4 B-B3 8 P-N5 N-K4 9 P-B4 N-N5 10 N-B3 P-B3 11
P×P P×P 12 P-R3 B-R5ch 13 K-Q1 N-B7ch 14 K-K1 N×Rch 15 P-N3
N×P 16 Q-Q3 Q-B3 17 N×B Q×N/R5 18 Q-B3 P-Q4 19 Q-N4 Q×Q 20
P×Q N×B 21 K×N P-QR3 22 B-K3 P-K4 23 P×P B×P 24 P-R4 P-KR4
25 P-R5 P-R5 26 R-R4 B-K3 27 B-B2 P-R6 28 P-K3 P-R7 29 B-N3
P-R8=Qch 30 K-K2 Q-QB8 31 K-Q3 R-QN1 32 P-K4 R-N7 33 R-R3 R×P
34 N-R2 Q-Q7mate.

Round 4

White: WITA
Black: BLACK KNIGHT

Sicilian Defence

1 P-K4 P-QB4 2 N-KB3 N-QB3 3 P-Q4 P×P 4 N×P N-B3 5 N-QB3 P-Q3 6
P-KR3 P-QR3 7 P-KN4 N×N 8 Q×N P-K4 9 Q-Q3 B-K3 10 B-N2 B-K2 11
B-K3 R-QB1 12 Q-Q2 P-KR4 13 P-N5 N-Q2 14 N-Q5 B×N 15 P×B R-B5
16 Q-K2 P-N4 17 P-N3 R-KR5 18 P-KB4 O-O 19 O-O P×P 20 B-B2 P-B6 21
Q×BP B×P 22 B×R B×B 23 Q×RP B-B3 24 QR-K1 B-B6 25 P-R3 Q-
N3ch 26 K-R2 N-B3 27 Q-Q1 B×R 28 R×B R-B1 29 R-K2 R-B6 30 Q-Q2
Q-R4 31 R-K3 R×NP 32 Q×Q R×R 33 P-QR4 R-K7 34 Q×RP R×P 35
Q-R8ch K-R2 36 P×P R-N7 37 Q-B6 N-K5 38 Q-K8 N-N4 39 Q-K7 K-R3
40 P-N6 P-B4 41 Q-K3 K-N3 42 P-R4 N-K5 43 K-N1 R-N8ch 44 Q-K1
R×Qch 45 K-R2 R-QN8 46 B-B1 R×B 47 P-N7 R-QN8 48 P-N8=Q R×Q
49 K-N1 N-B6 50 P-R5ch K×P 51 K-R2 P-N4 52 K-N3 P-N5 53 K-N2 P-B5
54 K-B2 R-N8 55 K-N2 N-K5 56 K-R2 K-R5 57 K-N2 P-B6ch 58 K-R2 P-
N6mate.

White: DUCHESS
Black: CHESS 4.6

Sicilian Defence

1 P-K4 P-QB4 2 P-Q4 P×P 3 P-QB3 P×P 4 N×P N-QB3 5 N-B3 P-Q3 6 B-QB4 P-K3 7 O-O N-B3 8 Q-K2 B-K2 9 R-Q1 P-K4 10 B-K3 N-KN5 11 B-Q2 N-K5 12 N×N P×N 13 N-N5 Q-N3 14 B-B4 N-K4 15 N×P(Q4) N×B 16 Q×N B-N5 17 Q-R4ch B-Q2 18 Q-N3 O-O 19 Q×Q P×Q 20 P-QR3 KR-B1 21 QR-B1 R×R 22 R×R R-R5 23 B-K3 B-Q1 24 P-B3 R-R4 25 R-Q1 B-KB3 26 R-Q2 R-QB4 27 N-K2 R-B3 28 P-QR4 B-K3 29 N-Q4 R-B8ch 30 K-B2 B-Q2 31 N-N5 B×N 32 P×B R-QN8 33 B×P R×P 34 R×R B×R 35 K-K3 K-B1 36 B-Q4 B×Bch 37 K×B K-K1 38 K-Q5 K-Q2 39 P-N6 P-N3 40 P-B4 K-K2 41 P-R3 P-B3 42 P-R4 K-Q2 43 P-N4 P-R3 44 P-R5 P×P 46 P×P K-K2 46 K-Q4 K-K3 47 K-B4 K-K2 48 P-B5 K-Q1 49 K-N4 K-Q2 50 K-N5 K-K1 51 K-R4 K-K2 52 K-N4 K-Q1 53 K-B4 K-K1 54 K-Q4 K-Q2 55 K-Q5 K-K2 56 K-Q4 K-K1 57 K-B4 K-B2 Adjudicated drawn.

White: BRUTE FORCE
Black: 8080 CHESS

Queen Pawn Opening

1 P-Q4 P-Q4 2 N-QB3 N-QB3 3 B-B4 N-B3 4 N-N5 P-K4 5 B×P B-N5ch 6 P-QB3 N×B 7 P×N B×Pch 8 N×B N-K5 9 N×N P×N 10 Q-R4ch B-Q2 11 Q×KP P-QN4 12 P-KN4 O-O 13 B-N2 P-QB3 14 P-KR4 P-QR4 15 O O O R-R3 16 Q-Q4 P-KB4 17 Q×B Q×Q 18 R×Q P×P 19 R-Q6 R×P 20 B×P R-B4 21 B-Q5ch K-B1 22 R×R R×P 23 P-K4 P-R5 24 R-QN6 P-N4 25 P×P K-N2 26 R-N7ch K-N3 27 R(R1)×P K×P 28 R×P K-B5 29 R-QR5 P-R6 30 R-KB7ch K-K6 31 R×Pch K-Q5 32 R-KN7 K-B4 33 R×P K-Q3 34 R-R6ch K-B4 35 N-B3 R-K2 36 R-QB6ch K-N5 37 P-K5ch K-N4 38 N-Q4ch K-R4 39 N-N3ch Resigns.

White: CHUTE
Black: XENARBOR

Sicilian Defence

1 P-K4 P-QB4 2 P-QB4 N-QB3 3 N-KB3 P-K4 4 N-B3 N-B3 5 B-K2 P-Q3 6 O-O P-KN3 7 P-Q3 B-N2 8 B-N5 N-Q5 9 N×N BP×N 10 N-Q5 P-KR3 11 N×Nch B×N 12 B×B Q×B 13 Q-R4ch B-Q2 14 Q-R5 P-N3 15 Q-Q5 R-QN1 16 QR-B1 P-QR4 17 P-QN3 P-R4 18 B-B3 P-KR5 19 P-R4 P-R6 20 KR-K1 R-QB1 21 Q-N7 Q-Q1 22 Q-R7 B-B3 23 P×P R-R1 24 Q×R Q×Q 25 B-N4 P-KN4 26 R-B2 Q-Q1 27 R(B2)-K2 Q-K2 28 P-B3 Q-B3 29 K-N2 Q-B5 30 B-B5 O-O 31 B-N4 P-B3 32 B-K6ch K-R1 33 B-B5 R-KN1 34 B-N4 R-K1 35 B-R5 R-KN1 36 B-N4 R-N2 37 B-B8 R-KR2 38 B-B5 R-R5 39 B-N4 R-R2 40 B-B5 R-R3 41 B-N4 R-R5 42 B-B5 R-R4 43 B-N4 R-R3 44 B-K6 R-R2 45 B-B5 R-KN2 46 B-N4 Drawn by repetition of moves.

White: CHAOS
Black: BLITZ

Queen's Gambit Declined

1 P-Q4 P-Q4 2 P-QB4 P-K3 3 N-QB3 N-KB3 4 B-N5 B-K2 5 P-K3 O-O 6 N-B3 P-KR3 7 B-R4 N-K5 8 B×B Q×B 9 P×P N×N 10 P×N P×P 11 Q-N3 R-Q1 12 B-Q3 N-B3 13 O-O R-Q3 14 KR-B1 P-QN3 15 P-B4 P×P 16 Q×BP B-N5 17 N-Q2 QR-Q1 18 B-K4 B-Q2 19 QR-N1 P-QR4 20 B-Q5 N-N5 21 B×Pch Q×B 22 Q×P B-K3 23 P-QR3 Q×Q 24 R×Q N-Q4 25 R(B7)-B1 R-QB1 26 R×Rch B×R 27 R-QB1 B-N2 28 P-N3 P-QN4 29 N-N3 P-R5 30 N-B5 B-B3 31 P-K4 N-N3 32 P-Q5 B-K1 33 N-N7 R-Q2 34 N-B5 R-QB2 35 R-B3 B-N3 36 P-B4 N-B5 37 N-R6 R-K2 38 P-K5 B-K5 39 P-Q6 R-KB2 40 N-B7 B-B3 41 P-K6 R-B1 42 P-K7 R-B1 43 R-Q3 B-Q2 44 N-R6 K-B2 45 K-B2 K-K1 46 N-B7ch R×N 47 P×R K×P 48 K-B3 B-B4 49 R-Q5 B-N5ch 50 K×B N-Q3 51 R×N Resigns.

White: TYRO
Black: OSTRICH

Queen's Gambit Accepted

1 P-Q4 P-Q4 2 P-QB4 P×P 3 P-K4 N-QB3 4 P-Q5 N-K4 5 P-B4 B-N5 6 N-KB3 B×N 7 P×B N-Q6ch 8 B×N P×B 9 Q×P P-QB3 10 K-K2 Q-Q2 11 P×P Q×Qch 12 K×Q O-O-Och 13 K-K2 P×P 14 R-Q1 R-Q3 15 B-K3 R-R3 16 B×P R×Pch 17 B-B2 P-R4 18 P-N3 R-R3 19 P-R4 R-B3 20 K-K3 R-R6 21 P-N4 P-K4 22 P×P R(B3)×Pch 23 K-K2 B×P 24 B-N6 N-K2 25 R-Q4 R-K6ch 26 K-B2 B-K8ch 27 K-B1 R(R6)-B6ch 28 K-N1 R-K7 29 R-Q8ch K-N2 30 B-Q4 R×P 31 R-Q7ch K-B1 32 R×N R-N5ch 33 K-R2 R×B 34 K-N2 R-B7ch 35 K-N3 R-Q6ch 36 K-R4 R-B4mate.

Second World Computer Championship

Note that the round one game between DUCHESS and KAISSA is found on page 69.

Round 1

White: CHESS 4.6
Black: BCP

Scotch Gambit

1 P-K4 P-K4 2 N-KB3 N-QB3 3 P-Q4 P×P 4 P-B3 Q-K2 5 P×P Q×Pch 6 B-K2 P-Q4 7 N-B3 B-QN5 8 O-O B×N 9 B-Q3 Q-K2 10 P×B N-B3 11 Q-N3 N-K5 12 R-K1 Q-K3 13 N-N5 Q-Q2 14 P-B3 P-B4 15 P×N BP×P 16 B×P P×B 17 R×Pch N-K2 18 Q-B7ch K-Q1 19 Q×P Q-K1 20 N-B7ch K-Q2 21 N×R K-Q3 22 R×N Q×R 23 B-R3ch K-B3 24 Q×Q P-KR4 25 Q-B5ch K-Q2 26 R-K1 P-R3 27 Q-Q5mate.

White: CHUTE
Black: MASTER
Pirc Defence
1 P-K4 P-Q3 2 N-QB3 P-KN3 3 B-B4 B-K3 4 B×B P×B 5 N-B3 N-QB3 6
Q-K2 B-N2 7 O-O Q-Q2 8 P-QR3 O-O-O 9 P-QN3 P-Q4 10 P×P P×P 11 R-
R2 P-Q5 12 N-Q1 P-Q6 13 P×P Q-Q4 14 B-N2 P-K4 15 R-K1 Q×NP 16 N-
B3 N-Q5 17 Q-K4 N×Nch 18 Q×N N-R3 19 Q-K3 R-Q5 20 B-R1 N-N5 21
Q-R3 K-N1 22 R-K4 P-KR4 23 Q-N3 Q-K3 24 P-R3 N-R3 25 P-B4 N-B4 26
Q-B3 N-Q3 27 R×R P×R 28 N-Q5 P-B3 29 N-N4 Q-K8ch 30 Q-B1 R-K1
31 Q×Q R×Qch 32 K-B2 R-R8 33 P-QR4 K-B2 34 N-B2 P-B4 35 N-K1 N-
B4 36 R-B2 K-Q3 37 R-N2 P-N3 38 R-N1 P-R5 39 R-B1 N-N6 40 K-B3 R-
B8ch 41 K-N4 N-K7 42 R-N1 B-B3 43 P-N3 P×P 44 P-R4 P-N7 46 B×P
Adjudicated a win for Black.

White: CHAOS
Black: BS 66/76
Albin Counter Gambit
1 P-Q4 P-Q4 2 P-QB4 P-K4 3 QP×P P-Q5 4 N-KB3 N-QB3 5 QN-Q2 B-K3
6 P-KN3 P-KR4 7 B-N2 P-Q6 8 O-O R-N1 9 P×P Q×P 10 Q-N3 Q-Q1 11 N-
K4 N-Q5 12 N×N Q×N 13 B-K3 R-Q1 14 B×Q R×B 15 Q×P B×P 16
KR-Q1 B-Q6 17 Q-N8ch K-Q2 18 Q×B P-QB4 19 R×B K-B2 20
Q×QBPch K-N1 21 Q-KB8ch K-B2 22 R×R N-K2 23 Q×Nch K-N3 24 Q-
N4ch Black lost on time.

White: BELLE
Black: BLACK KNIGHT
Sicilian Defence
1 P-K4 P-QB4 2 N-KB3 N-QB3 3 P-Q4 P×P 4 N×P N-B3 5 N-QB3 P-Q3 6
B-QN5 B-Q2 7 O-O N×N 8 Q×N B×B 9 N×B P-K4 10 Q-R4 N-Q2 11 R-
Q1 P-QR3 12 N×Pch B×N 13 R×B Q-B2 14 R-Q3 P-QN4 15 Q-N3 O-O 16
B-N5 N-B4 17 Q-QB3 R-R2 18 B-Q8 R×B 19 Q×N R×R 20 Q×Q R×Q
21 P×R R×P 22 P-QN3 P-QR4 23 P-B3 P-B3 24 P-QR4 P-N5 25 P-B4 R-
B6 26 P×P P×P 27 R-N1 R-Q3 28 K-B2 P-N4 29 R-N2 P-R4 30 K-K2 R-
QB6 31 R-N1 R-B7ch 32 K-B1 R-Q7 33 R-B1 R-N7 34 R-B8ch K-N2 35 R-
B7ch K-B3 36 R-B6ch K-B2 37 R-B5 R-N8ch 38 K-B2 Adjudicated drawn.

White: OSTRICH
Black: WITA
Sicilian Defence
1 P-K4 P-QB4 2 N-KB3 P-Q3 3 B-B4 N-KB3 4 N-QB3 P-K3 5 O-O B-K2 6 P-
Q3 B-Q2 7 B-K3 N-B3 8 B-QN5 O-O 9 N-N5 P-KR3 10 B×N B×B 11 N-R3
K-R1 12 Q-B3 N-Q2 12 KR-N1 Q-R4 14 Q-N4 B-B3 15 B-Q2 B-Q5 16 Q-

R4 Q-Q1 17 Q×Q QR×Q 18 N-K2 P-B4 19 N×B P×N 20 N-B4 QR-K1 21 N-K2 P-K4 22 P×P R×P 23 P-KB4 N-B4 24 B-N4 P-KN3 25 P×P R(B4)×P 26 N×P B-Q4 27 P-B4 N×P 28 B×P R-K5 29 N-N5 B×P 30 N×P R-R1 31 P-QN3 B-R3 32 P-QN4 R×N 33 P-N5 P-N3 34 P×B R×P 35 B-B7 N-N5 36 P-QR3 N-B7 37 R-R2 R-K8ch 38 R×R N×R 39 K-B2 N-Q6ch 40 K-B3 N-N5 41 R-N2 N-Q4 42 B-Q6 P-QN4 43 B-B5 R-KB3 ch 44 K-K4 N-B2 45 R-KB2 N-K1 46 R×R N×Rch 47 K-Q3 K-N2 48 B-Q4 K-B2 49 B×N K×B 50 K-Q4 K-K2 51 K-B5 K-Q1 52 K×P K-B2 53 P-QR4 P-N4 54 P-R5 K-N1 55 K-N6 K-B1 56 P-R6 K-N1 57 P-N4 K-R1 58 P-R7 P-R4 59 P×P P-N5 60 P-R6 P-N6 61 P-R7 Resigns.

White: ELSA
Black: BLITZ V
Queen's Gambit Declined
1 P-Q4 P-Q4 2 P-QB4 P-K3 3 N-QB3 N-KB3 4 B-N5 K-K2 5 N-B3 O-O 6 Q-N3 P×P 7 Q×BP QN-Q2 8 O-O-O N-N3 9 Q-Q3 B-Q2 10 N-K5 R-B1 11 Q-B3 N(B3)-Q4 12 B×B Q×B 13 N×B Q×N 14 P-K4 N×N 15 Q×N Q-R5 16 P-QR3 KR-Q1 17 Q-B5 R-Q3 18 B-N5 Q-R4 19 P-B4 P-QR3 20 B-K8 Q×Qch 21 P×Q R×Rch 22 R×R R×B 23 P×N P×P 24 P-QN4 P-R3 25 K-N2 R-K2 26 R-Q6 P-QN4 27 P-N4 R-B2 28 K-N3 K-B1 29 P-K5 R-B5 30 R-Q8ch K-K2 31 R-QN8 R-B2 32 P-KR4 P-KN3 33 P-N5 P-KR4 34 R-QR8 K-Q2 35 R-QN8 K-B3 36 R-Q8 R-Q2 37 R×R K×R 38 K-B3 K-B3 39 K-Q4 P-N3 40 K-K4 P-R4 41 K-Q4 P-R5 42 K-K4 K-Q2 43 K-Q4 K-K2 44 K-K4 K-B1 45 K-Q4 K-K1 Adjudicated drawn.

White: TELL
Black: DARK HORSE
Alekhine Defence
1 P-K4 N-KB3 2 N-QB3 N-B3 3 P-Q4 P-Q3 4 B-QN5 B-Q2 5 B-N5 P-K4 6 B×KN Q×B 7 N-Q5 Q-Q1 8 N-KB3 P×P 9 N×QP B-K2 10 B×N B×B 11 N×QB P×N 12 N-N4 Q-Q2 13 Q-Q4 B-B3 14 Q-K3 B×P 15 R-QN1 B-B3 16 N-QR6 O-O 17 R-N7 KR-B1 18 R×RP Q-N5 19 O-O R×R 20 Q×R Q×KP 21 Q-N7 R-B1 22 Q×P(B7) B-K4 23 R-Q1 Q-K7 24 R-N1 Q×N 25 R-N8 P-N3 26 R×Rch K×R 27 P-N3 Q-B5 28 Q-Q8ch K-N2 29 P-B4 B-Q5ch 30 K-N2 Q×BPch 31 K-B3 Q-B7ch 32 K-N4 Q×KRP 33 Q-R5 P-KB4ch 34 Q×P P×Qch 35 K×P Q×NP 36 K-K4 P-B4 37 P-R4 Q-N7ch 38 K-Q3 Q-B6ch 39 K-B4 Q×P 40 P-R5 Q-KB8ch 41 Q-Q5 B-K4 42 P-R6 Q-B6ch 43 K-B4 Q-K7ch 44 K-Q5 Q×P 45 K-K4 Q-K7ch 46 K-Q5 Q-B6ch 47 K-B4 B-Q5 48 K-N5 Q-N2ch 49 K-B4 P-R3 50 K-Q3 Q-QN7 52 K-B4 B-K4 52 K-Q5 Adjudicated a win for Black.

Round 2

White: KAISSA
Black: TELL

Ruy Lopez

1 P-K4 P-K4 2 N-KB3 N-QB3 3 B-N5 N-B3 4 O-O N×P 5 P-Q4 N×QP 6 N×N P×N 7 Q×P N-B4 8 R-K1ch N-K3 9 N-B3 P-QB4 10 Q-K5 P-KR4 11 N-Q5 B-K2 12 B-N5 Q-R4 13 B×B P-R3 14 Q×NP R-R3 15 Q-N8ch N-B1 16 Q×Nmate.

White: MASTER
Black: CHESS 4.6

Reti Opening

1 N-KB3 P-Q4 2 P-B4 P×P 3 N-R3 P-K3 4 Q-R4ch B-Q2 5 Q×BP N-QB3 6 P-K3 N-B3 7 B-Q3 P-QR3 8 N-B2 P-QN4 9 Q-B4 B-Q3 10 Q-N5 O-O 11 O-O P-K4 12 Q-R4 Q-K2 13 B-K4 N×B 14 Q×N K-R1 15 P-KN4 N-R4 16 P-N5 B-B3 17 Q-KN4 B×N 18 Q×B Q×Pch 19 Q-N2 Q×Qch 20 K×Q P-K5 21 P-R3 P×Pch 22 R×P P-KB4 23 P-N3 N-B3 24 B-N2 N K4 25 B×N B×B 26 R(R1)-KB1 P-N3 27 P-KR3 P-B4 28 P-Q4 P×P 29 P×P B-Q3 30 N-K3 R(B1)-K1 31 R(B1)-B2 R(R1)-Q1 32 R-Q2 B-N5 33 R-Q3 B-B1 34 P-Q5 R-K4 35 P-QR4 P×P 36 P×P B-B4 37 P-Q6 B×P 38 N-R4 R-K3 39 N×B R(K3)×N 40 R×R R×R 41 R-QB3 R-Q5 White resigns.

White: DARK HORSE
Black: CHAOS

Three Knights

1 N-QB3 P-K4 2 N-B3 N-QB3 3 P-K4 B-N5 4 N-Q5 N-B3 5 N×B N×N 6 P-B3 N-B3 7 Q-K2 O-O 8 P-Q4 P-Q3 9 P-QN3 B-N5 10 P-Q5 N-K2 11 P-N3 P-B3 12 P×P P×P 13 B-N5 Q-R4 14 Q-K3 N(B3)-Q4 15 P×N N×P 16 Q-Q2 B×N 17 P-QN4 Q-R6 18 R-KN1 Q×BP 19 Q×Q N×Q 20 B-K7 KR-K1 21 B×P N-K5 22 B-B5 N×B 23 P×N QR-Q1 24 B-K2 B×B 25 K×B R-Q4 26 QR-QB1 R(K1)-Q1 27 KR-Q1 R×R 28 R×R R-K1 29 R-Q6 R-QB1 30 K-B3 P-QR4 31 K-K4 P-B3 32 K-B3 P-R5 33 R-Q7 R-R1 34 R-Q6 R-R3 35 K-N2 P-R3 36 P R4 K B2 37 P-R5 K-N1 38 P-B3 K-B1 39 R-Q8ch K-K2 40 R-Q6 K-B1 41 R-Q8ch K-K2 42 R-Q6 K-K1 43 P-R3 K-K2 44 K-B2 K-B1 45 R-Q8ch K-K2 46 R-Q6 K-B1 47 R-Q8ch K-B2 48 R-Q7ch K-N1 49 R-Q8ch K-R2 50 R-QB8 P-N4 51 P×Pe.p.ch K×P 52 R-KN8ch K-B2 53 R-QB8 K-K3 54 R-K8ch K-B2 55 R-QB8 K-N3 56 R-KN8ch K-R4 57 P-N4ch K-R5 58 R-N6 P-R4 59 P×P K×P 60 R×P K-N4 61 R-K6 K-B4 62 R-R6 K-N4 63 R-Q6 K-B5 64 R-N6 K-B4 65 R-N4 R-R4 66 R-QB4 K-K3 67 K-K2 K-Q4 68 R-K4 R×P 69 R×RP R-B6 70 R-R7 P-B4 Adjudicated drawn.

White: BLACK KNIGHT
Black: ELSA

Ruy Lopez

1 P-K4 P-K4 2 N-NB3 N-QB3 3 B-N5 P-Q3 4 P-Q4 P×P 5 Q×P B-Q2 6
B×N B×B 7 N-B3 Q-B3 8 B-K3 B-K2 9 N-Q5 Q×Q 10 N×Q B×N 11
P×B O-O-O 12 N-N5 P-QR3 13 N-R7ch K-N1 14 O-O-O N-B3 15 P-KB3 KR-
K1 16 KR-K1 B-B1 17 R-Q2 R×B 18 R×R K×N 19 R-Q1 R-Q2 20 P-QB4
P-QN4 21 P×P P×P 22 R-N3 K-R3 23 R-R3ch K-N3 24 R-N3 P-N3 25 P-
QR4 B-R3ch 26 K-N1 K-R4 37 R×Pch K×P 28 R-N7 R-K2 29 R-Q3 R-
K8ch 30 K-R2 R-K6 31 R-Q4ch K-R4 32 R×P B-N4 33 P-R4 N-K1 34 R×P
B-B3 35 R-K4 R×R 36 P×R B×RP 37 R×P Adjudicated a draw.

White: DUCHESS
Black: OSTRICH

Petroff Defence

1 P-K4 P-K4 2 N-KB3 N-KB3 3 P-Q4 B-K2 4 P×P N×P 5 B-Q3 P-Q4 6
P×Pe.p. N×QP 7 O-O O-O 8 R-K1 B-N5 9 P-B3 K-R1 10 B-KB4 N-B3 11
QN-Q2 P-KN4 12 B-K3 N-B4 13 Q-K2 B×N 14 N×B N×B 15 Q×N P-N5
16 B-B5 R-KN1 17 N-K5 N×N 18 Q×Nch B-B3 19 Q-B4 B-N4 20 Q-K4 B-
Q7 21 QR-Q1 Q-N4 22 R-K2 B-B5 23 R-Q7 QR-K1 24 Q×R R×Q 25
R×Rch K-N2 26 B-K6 P-QR4 27 R×KBPch K-R3 28 R(K8)-K7 Q-N3 29
B-B5 Q-N1 30 B-K4 Q-Q1 31 R-K6ch K-N4 32 R-B5ch K-R5 33 R-KR6ch
Resigns.

White: BLITZ V
Black: BELLE

Ruy Lopez

1 P-K4 P-K4 2 N-KB3 N-QB3 3 B-N5 N-B3 4 O-O N×P 5 R-K1 N-Q3 6
N×P B-K2 7 B×N QP×B 8 N-QB3 O-O 9 Q-R5 R-K1 10 P-Q4 B-K3 11 B-
B4 N-N4 12 N×N P×N 13 N-B3 Q-Q2 14 R-K3 P-R4 15 P-KR3 P-R5 16 B-
K5 Q-B3 17 P-B3 P-R3 18 P-R3 QR-Q1 19 N-Q2 B-N4 20 R-K2 P-KN3 21
Q-B3 Q×Q 22 N×Q B-QB5 23 R(K2)-K1 P-QB3 24 N×B P×N 25 B-B6
R-QB1 26 B×P R-R1 27 R-K7 R×R 28 B×R R-K1 29 R-K1 B-N6 30 R-
K5 B-R7 31 P-KB4 B-K3 32 B-B6 R-KB1 33 P-R4 B-N5 34 R-K7 B-B1 35 P-
KN3 K-R2 36 K-N2 K-N1 37 K-B3 P-N3 38 K-K4 B-B4ch 39 K-K3 R-B1 40
KB3 R-N1 41 R-K5 B-B7 42 P-Q5 P×P 43 R×P P-N5 44 RP×P R-K1 45
R-Q6 B-K5ch 46 K-K3 P-QN4 47 R-Q4 B-B3ch 48 B-K5 B-N7 49 K-B2 B-
B3 50 K-K2 B-N7 51 K-K3 P-B3 52 R-Q6 P×B 53 R×Pch K-B2 54 P-B5 B-
R6 55 P-N4 R-KN1 56 R×R K×R 57 K-B3 P-K5 ch 58 K-B4 P-K6 59 K×P
B×P 60 K-K4 K-N2 61 K-B4 B-K7 62 K-N5 B-Q8 63 P-B6 ch K-R2 64 P-B4
P×P 65 P-N5 P-B6 66 P×P P-R6 67 P-B7 K-N2 68 P-B8=Qch K×Q White
resigns.

White: BCP
Black: WITA

Sicilian Defence

1 P-K4 P-QB4 2 N-QB3 P-Q3 3 P-Q4 N-KB3 4 B-K3 P-K3 5 N-B3 B-K2 6
P-K5 QP×P 7 B-QN5ch B-Q2 8 P×KP N-N5 9 O-O N-QB3 10 B×N B×B
11 Q×Qch R×Q 12 B-B4 O-O 13 P-KR3 B×N 14 P×B N-R3 15 B×N
P×B 16 N-K4 P-B4 17 P×Pe.p. B×P 18 N×P R-Q7 19 N×KP R-K1 20 N-
B5 R×QBP 21 N×P R-B2 22 N-Q6 R-KB1 23 QR-N1 B-K4 24 KR-Q1 R-
KN2ch 25 K-B1 R×P 26 N-B4 B-B3 27 R-Q6 B-R5 28 K-K2 R×BPch 39
K-K3 R-B7 30 K-Q4 R-QB2 31 R-N1ch K-B2 32 N-K3 R-Q7ch 33 K-K4
R×R 34 N-B5 R-B5ch 35 K-K5 R-K1ch 36 K-Q5 R-QN5 37 R-N7ch K-B3
38 R-N4 R×R 39 P×R R-K4ch 40 K-B4 R×N 41 P×R P-KR4 42 P-R4
K×P 43 P-R5 P-KR3 44 P-R6 B-B3 45 P-N4 P-R5 46 P-N5 P-R6 47 P-N6 P-
R7 48 P×P P-R8=Q 49 K-N3 P-R4 50 K-R4 Q-B3ch 51 K-R3 Q-R1 52 K-
N4 B-Q5 53 K-B4 K-K5 54 K-N5 P-R5 55 K-B4 P-R6 56 K-N3 P-R7 57 K-
B4 Q-Q4ch 58 K-N4 P-R8=Q 59 K-R3 Q-R8ch 60 K-N4 Q(R8)-R4mate.

White: BS 66/76
Black: CHUTE

Blackmar Gambit

1 P-Q4 P-Q4 2 P-K4 P×P 3 N-QB3 N-KB3 4 P-B3 P×P 5 Q×P Q×P 6 B-
K3 Q-QN5 7 0-0-0 B-N5 8 N-N5 N-R3 9 Q×P B×R 10 N-Q6ch Q×N 11 B-
QN5ch P-B3 12 B×Pch N-Q2 13 Q×Rch QN-N1 14 B-QN5 P-QR3 15
B×Nch K×B 16 Q-N7ch K-K3 18 Q-K4ch K-Q2 18 B-B4 P-K4 19 B×P Q-
R3ch 30 K×B B-Q3 21 N-B3 R-QB1 22 Q-N7ch B-B2 23 Q-Q5ch K-K1 24
B×B R×B 25 R-K1ch R-K2 26 R×Rch K×R 27 Q-K5ch Q-K3 28 Q×N
Q-Q4ch 29 K-B1 Q×P 30 Q-N7ch K-B3 31 Q-B6ch Q-K3 32 Q-B3ch K-N3
33 N-R4ch K-R4 34 Q-B3ch K×N 35 Q-B4ch K-R4 36 P-N4ch Q×P 37
Q×Pch K-R3 38 Q-B1 Q-N4ch 39 K-N1 Q-QR4 40 Q-R3 ch Q-R4 41 Q-
K6ch Q-N3 42 Q-K3ch Q-N4 43 Q-K6ch Q-B3 44 Q-R3ch K-N3 45 Q-N4ch
K-B2 46 Q-QB4ch K-N3 47 Q-K4ch K-R3 48 P-N4 Q-B8ch 49 K-R2 Q-B2ch
50 K-R3 Q-B3 51 Q-K3ch K-N3 52 Q-Q3ch K-R3 53 Q-R3ch K-N3 54 K-N3
Q-B2ch 55 K-R3 Q-QB5 56 Q-KN3ch K-B2 57 Q-KB3ch K-N3 58 Q-KN3ch
K-B2 Draw agreed.

Round 3

White: CHAOS
Black: KAISSA

King's Indian Defence

1 P-Q4 N-KB3 2 P-QB4 P-B4 3 P-Q5 P-Q3 4 N-QB3 P-KN3 5 P-K4 B-N2 6
B-K2 O-O 7 B-N5 P-KR3 8 B-K3 Q-N3 9 Q-Q2 N-N5 10 B×N B×B 11 P-B3

B-Q2 12 B×RP B×B 13 Q×B Q×P 14 R-N1 Q×Nch 15 Q-Q2 Q×Qch 16 K×Q B-B1 17 N-K2 K-N2 18 P-KR4 R-R1 19 N-B4 N-Q2 20 P-R5 P-KN4 21 N-Q3 R-QN1 22 P-B4 N-B3 23 P-K5 N-K5ch 24 K-K3 N-N6 25 R-R2 P×Pch 26 K×P N×Pch 27 K-B3 B-B4 28 R-Q1 B×N 29 R×B P×P 30 R-KR3 N-B3 31 R-KN3ch K-B1 32 R-K3 P-N4 33 R×P P×P 34 R-B5 P-B6 35 P-Q6 P×P 36 K-K3 R-K1ch 37 K-Q3 P-B5ch 38 K×P(B4) R-B1ch 39 K-N3 P-B7 40 R×N P-B8=Q 41 R(N3)-KB3 R-QN1ch 42 K-R4 Q-QB5ch 43 K-R5 Q-N4 mate.

White: CHESS 4.6
Black: DUCHESS
Petroff Defence
1 P-K4 P-K4 2 N-KB3 N-KB3 3 P-Q4 P×P 4 P-K5 N-K5 5 Q×P P-Q4 6 P×Pe.p N×QP 7 B-Q3 N-B3 8 Q-KB4 P-KN3 9 O-O B-N2 10 B-Q2 Q-B3 11 Q×Q B×Q 12 N-B3 O-O 13 N-Q5 B×P 14 QR-N1 B-N2 15 N×P R-N1 16 B-KB4 R-Q1 17 N-QN5 B-B1 18 B-N5 R-Q2 19 KR-K1 P-N3 20 N-B3 P-B4 21 N-Q5 K-R1 22 B-KB4 B-QN2 23 N-N5 R-B1 24 N-B6 R(Q2)-QB2 25 N-K6 R-B2 26 N×B R(B2)×N(B1) 27 N×P K×N 28 B×N R(B1)-Q1 29 B-KB4 R-Q5 30 B-KN5 R-KN5 31 P-KB4 N-QR4 32 R-K7ch K-N1 33 P-N3 K-B1 34 R(N1)-K1 B-B6 35 B-KR6ch K-N1 36 R(K1)-K3 B-K5 37 B×B P×B 38 P-KR3 R×KBP 39 B×R R×P 40 R(K3)×P R-QN7 41 R-K8ch K-B2 42 R(K4)-K7ch K-B3 43 B-K5ch K-N4 44 B×R N-B5 45 B-B1ch K-B3 46 R-K6ch K-N2 47 B-N5 N-Q3 48 R×N K-B2 49 R-K7ch K-N1 50 R-Q8mate.

White: ELSA
Black: MASTER
Pirc Defence
1 P-K4 P-Q3 2 P-Q4 N-KB3 3 N-QB3 P-KN3 4 N-B3 BN2 5 B-K2 O-O 6 O-O P-N3 7 B-KN5 B-N2 8 P-K5 N-K5 9 N×N B×N 10 B-Q3 B-N2 11 Q-K2 P×P 12 P×P P-KB3 13 B-QB4ch K-R1 14 QR-Q1 Q-B1 15 B-R4 Q-N5 16 P-KR3 Q-R4 17 P-KN4 Q-R3 18 R-Q3 P×P 19 B×P Q×P 20 B×R Q×Pch 21 K-R1 Q×B 22 B×Bch K×B 34 Q×Pch K-R3 24 Q-K3ch K-N2 25 Q-K7ch Q-B2 26 Q-K5ch Q-B3 27 Q×Pch Q-B2 28 Q-K5ch Q-B3 29 Q×Qch K×Q 30 R(B1)-Q1 P-KR4 31 P-B4 P-KN4 32 P-R4 P-N5 33 R-Q6ch K-K2 34 K-N1 B×N 35 R(Q1)-Q2 P-R5 36 P-R5 N-B3 37 P×P P×P 38 R-Q7ch K-B1 39 R-Q1 B×R 40 R×B N-K4 41 P-N3 N-B6ch 42 K-N2 K-K2 43 R-QN1 R-R7 44 R-QB1 R-N7 45 R-B3 K-B3 46 R-B1 R×NP 47 P-B5 P×P 48 R×P R-N8 49 R-B5ch K-K3 50 R×N P×Rch 51 K×P R-N8 52 K-K4 P-R6 53 P-B4 R-KB8 54 K-Q4 P-R7 55 K-Q3 P-R8=Q 56 P-B5ch K×P 57 K-Q4 R-B8 58 K-Q3 Q-K8 59 K-Q4 Q-K5mate.

White: OSTRICH
Black: BLACK KNIGHT

Sicilian Defence

1 P-K4 P-QB4 2 N-KB3 N-QB3 3 B-B4 N-B3 4 N-B3 N×P 5 B×Pch K×B
6 N×N P-Q4 7 N×P P-K4 8 N-N3 B-KB4 9 O-O B-K2 10 P-Q3 P-Q5 11 R-
K1 Q-B2 12 Q-K2 B-Q3 13 B-Q2 Q-N3 14 P-B3 KR-K1 15 P×P P×P
White resigns. OSTRICH's computer broke down—(blew a fuse).

White: CHUTE
Black: BLITZ V

Petroff Defence

1 P-K4 P-K4 2 N-KB3 N-KB3 3 N×P P-Q3 4 N-KB3 N×P 5 Q-K2 Q-K2 6
P-Q3 N-KB3 7 Q×Qch B×Q 8 N-R3 B-N5 9 P-R3 B×N 10 P×B O-O 11 N-
N5 N-R3 12 B-K3 P-B3 13 N×RP N-B4 14 B×N P×B 15 N×P P×N 16 P-
QR4 QR-K1 17 O-O-O B-Q3 18 P-N3 R-K4 19 K-N1 R(B1)-K1 20 K-N2 P-R3
21 R-KN1 R-K8 22 R×R R×R 23 P-B3 B-R7 24 R-R1 B-K4 25 K-B2 N-Q4
26 P-QB4 N-N5ch 27 K-Q2 R-N8 28 K-K3 R×P 29 K-K4 B-Q5 30 R-R2 R-
R6 31 R-N2 R-R8 32 B-K2 R-K8 33 P-B4 R×Bch 34 K-B3 R-Q7 35 P-R5
N×P 36 R-N3 R×Pch 37 K-K4 N-N7 38 R-N3 N×P 39 R-N8ch K-R2 40 P-
R6 R×Pch 41 K×R B-K4ch 42 K-B5 B×R 43 K-K4 N-Q3ch 44 K-K3 P-B4
45 P-R4 P-N4 46 P×P P×P 47 K-K2 P-N5 48 K-K3 P-QB5 49 K-Q4 P-N6
50 K-K3 P-B6 51 K-Q3 P-N7 52 P-R7 B×P 53 K×P P-N8−Q 54 K-N3 Q
N8ch 55 K-R4 Q-N7 56 K-R5 Q-R6mate.

White: TELL
Black: BCP

Two Knights Defence

1 P-K4 P-K4 2 N-KB3 3 N-QB3 B-B4 N-B3 4 N-B3 B-K2 5 O-O O-O 6 B-Q5
P-Q3 7 B×N P×B 8 P-Q4 B-N5 9 P×P B×N 10 Q×B P×P 11 R-Q1 B-
Q3 12 B-K3 P-QR4 13 B-B5 Q-N1 14 B×B P×B 15 QR-N1 P-R5 16 P-
QN4 R-B1 17 Q-B5 R-Q1 18 P-N5 P×P 19 R×NP Q-B1 20 Q×Q KR×Q
21 R-Q3 R-R3 22 R-N4 P-R6 23 R-N7 P-R3 24 P-B3 R(R3)-B3 25 N-Q5
N×N 26 P×N R-R3 27 R-Q2 R-R5 28 P-N4 P-K5 29 P×P R×KP 30 P-R3
R-K8ch 31 K-N2 R-QR8 32 R-B2 R×RP 33 R(N7)×P R(R7)×P 34
R(B7)-B3 R×Rch 35 R×R P-N4 36 R-B6 P-R7 37 R-N6ch K-B2 38 R-
N7ch K×R 39 P-R4 P×P 40 K-R3 P-R8=Q 41 K-N2 Q-Q5 42 K-R3
Q×QP 43 K-R2 R-B7ch 44 K-R3 Q-R8mate.

White: WITA
Black: BS 66/76

Albin Counter Gambit

1 P-Q4 P-Q4 2 P-QB4 P-K4 3 QP×P P-Q5 4 P-K4 P-KB4 5 B-Q3 N-QB3 6

N-KB3 B-N5ch 7 K-K2 P×P 8 B×P B-N5 9 Q-R4 P-Q6ch 10 K-B1 Q-Q2 11 B×N Q×B 12 Q×B B×N 13 P×B Q×KBP 14 R-N1 P-Q7 15 B×PQ-Q8ch 16 B-K1 Q-Q6ch 17 K-N2 Q-N3ch 18 K-R1 Q-K5ch 19 R-N2 P-QR4 20 Q-B3 Q-B4 21 R×P O-O-O 22 Q×P Q-K5ch 23 P-B3 Q×KBPch 24 K-N1 Q-K6ch 25 K-R1 Q-K5ch 26 K-N1 Q-K6ch 27 K-R1 Q-K5ch 28 K-N1 Q-K6ch Draw by repetition.

White: BELLE
Black: DARK HORSE

Alekhine Defence

1 P-K4 N-KB3 2 P-K5 N-Q4 3 P-Q4 P-K3 4 B-Q3 N-QB3 5 N-KB3 B-K2 6 O-O O-O 7 P-B3 P-Q3 8 R-K1 P×P 9 P×P P-QN3 10 Q-B2 P-N3 11 B-KR6 N(Q4)-N5 12 P×N N×NP 13 Q-N3 N×B 14 B×R B×B 15 R-Q1 B-QR3 16 N-K1 N×N 17 R×Q R×R 18 Q-R4 P-QN4 19 Q×B N-B7 20 N-B3 N×R 21 Q×NP R-Q7 22 Q-B1 N-B7 23 Q-B1 B-R3 24 N-K4 R-Q4 25 N-B6ch K-N2 26 Q×N R×P 27 N-K8ch K-B1 28 Q-B3 R-Q4 29 Q-R8ch K-K2 30 P-KN3 P-QB3 31 N-B6 R-Q8ch 32 K-N2 B-N4 33 N×P B-R3 34 Q-QN8 B-N2 35 Q×Pch R-Q2 36 Q-B5ch R-Q3 37 Q-KN5ch K-Q2 38 N-B6ch B×N 39 Q×B K-K1 40 P-QR4 R-Q4 41 Q-QB3 P-QB4 42 P-R5 R-B4 43 P-R6 P-B3 44 P-R7 R-Q4 45 P-R8=Qch K-K2 46 Q-N7ch R-Q2 47 Q×QBPch K-K1 48 Q(N7)-B8ch R-Q1 49 Q×Pmate.

Round 4

White: MASTER
Black: DUCHESS

Reti Opening

1 N-KB3 N-KB3 2 P-B4 P-Q4 3 P×P N×P 4 P-KN3 P-QB3 5 B-N2 P-K3 6 O-O B-K2 7 P-Q4 O-O 8 P-K4 N-B3 9 N-B3 P-QN3 10 N-K5 B-R3 11 R-K1 Q-B1 12 B-K3 QN-Q2 13 N×N Q×N 14 P-K5 N-Q4 15 Q-R4 B-QN4 16 N×B P×N 17 Q-QN3 KR-Q1 18 B-Q2 QR-B1 19 QR-B1 P-QR4 20 R×R R×R 21 R-QB1 R×Rch 22 B×R P-R5 23 Q-Q1 N-N5 24 B-K3 N×P 25 P-Q5 P×P 26 Q×QP Q×Q 27 B×Q N-N5 28 B-K4 B-B4 29 K-N2 B×B 30 P×B P-R3 31 K-B3 K-B1 32 P-R4 K-K2 33 P-R5 K-K3 34 K-B4 N-Q4ch 35 B×Nch K×B 36 P-KN4 P-N5 37 K-B5 P-R6 38 P-K4ch K-B4 39 P×P P×P 40 P-K6 P×Pch 41 K-K5 P-R7 42 K×P P-R8=Q 43 P-N5 P×P 44 P-K5 Q-Q5 45 K-B5 Q-KB5ch 46 K-K6 P-N5 47 K-K7 P-N6 White resigns.

White: BS 66/76
Black: ELSA

King's Indian Defence

1 P-Q4 N-KB3 2 P-QB4 P-KN3 3 N-KB3 B-N2 4 N-B3 O-O 5 B-B4 N-R4 6 P-

K3 N×B 7 P×N P-QB4 8 P×P B×Nch 9 P×B Q-B2 10 Q-Q4 N-R3 11 P-B6 QP×P 12 P-KR3 R-Q1 13 Q-K3 Q-Q3 14 Q-K5 B-B4 15 P-N4 B-K3 16 P-N5 N-B4 17 R-QN1 Q-Q6 18 B×Q N×Bch 19 K-K2 N×Q 20 N×N P-B3 21 N×NP B×BPch 22 K-K3 P×N 23 P×P P×P 24 R×P R-Q6ch 25 K-K2 R-K1ch 26 R-K7 R×Rch 27 K-B1 R-N6mate.

White: BCP
Black: OSTRICH
Bishop's Opening
1 P-K4 P-K4 2 B-B4 N-KB3 3 P-Q4 P-Q3 4 N-KB3 B-N5 5 P×P B×N 6 P×B P×P 7 B×Pch K-K2 8 Q×Qch K×Q 9 O-O QN-Q2 10 B-N5 P-KR3 11 B×Nch N×B 12 N-B3 B-N5 13 N-Q5 N×N 14 B×N P-B3 15 B-K6 K-K1 16 P-QR3 B-K2 17 KR-Q1 R-Q1 18 R×Rch B×R 19 R-Q1 R-B1 20 K-N2 B-N3 21 B-B5 R-B3 22 B-B8 R-B2 23 B-B5 K-B1 24 R-Q7 R×R 25 B×R B-Q5 26 P-B3 B-B4 27 P-N4 B-Q3 28 P-QB4 P-B4 29 P-N5 K-K2 30 B-B5 K-B3 31 P-KR4 P-KN3 32 B-Q7 P-KR4 33 P-R4 P-N4 34 P×Pch K×P 35 P-R5 P-R5 36 P-N6 P×P 37 P×P B-K2 38 B-K6 B-Q1 39 B-Q5 K-B5 40 B×P P-R6ch 41 K×P K×P 42 B Q5 B×P 43 K R2 K×P 44 K-R3 K-B6 45 K-R2 B-Q1 46 K R3 B-N4 47 K-R2 B-B5ch 48 K-R3 B-N6 49 B-B6 B-K8 50 B-Q5 Draw agreed.

White: BLITZ V
Black: CHAOS
Sicilian Defence
1 P-K4 P-QB4 2 N-KB3 N-QB3 3 P-Q4 P×P 4 N×P N-B3 5 N-QB3 P-K3 6 B-K2 B-N5 7 O-O B×N 8 P×B N×P 9 N×N QP×N 10 Q×Qch K×Q 11 B-Q3 N-B4 12 B-K3 N×B 13 KR-Q1 P-K4 14 P×N K-B2 15 QR-N1 B-B4 16 R-N3 P-QN3 17 R-Q2 P-B3 18 P-KR3 QR-Q1 19 P-Q4 K-B1 20 P×P R×R 21 B×R P×P 22 B-N5 P-KR3 23 B-R4 P-QN4 24 P-R3 P-QR4 25 P-B3 K-Q2 26 K-R2 K-K3 27 R-N2 R-KB1 28 R-K2 B-Q6 29 R-Q2 B-B8 30 K-N1 B-B5 31 B-Q8 P-R5 32 B-B7 K-B4 33 P-N4ch K-N4 34 B×P R×P 35 R-Q6 B-Q4 36 K-R2 K-R5 37 B×P R×RPch 38 K-N1 P-R4 39 B-K5 K×P 40 B-Q4 R-N6ch 41 K-B2 P-R5 42 R-N6h K-B5 43 R-R6 R-N7ch 44 K-B1 K-N6 45 R-N6ch K-R6 46 R-Q6 B-B5ch 47 K-K1 R-K7ch 48 K-Q1 R-K3 49 R-Q7 K-R7 50 K-Q2 R-K7ch 51 K-Q1 P-R6 52 R-Q6 R-K3 53 R-Q7 B-N6ch 54 K-Q2 K-R8 55 B-K3 B-B7 56 K×B R×B 57 R-Q6 K-N7 58 R×P P-R7 59 R-KN6ch R-N6 60 R-KR6 P-R8=Q 61 R×Q K×R 62 K-Q2 K-N8 63 K-B2 R-N5 64 K-Q2 K-B8 65 K-Q1 R-QB5 66 K-Q2 K-B7 67 K-Q3 K-K8 68 K-B2 K-K7 69 K-N2 K-Q7 70 K-N1 K×P 71 K-B1 R-B3 72 K-Q1 R-K373 K-B1 R-K8mate.

White: TELL
Black: CHUTE

Sicilian Defence

1 P-K4 P-QB4 2 B-B4 P-Q3 3 Q-R5 P-K3 4 B-N5ch N-Q2 5 N-QB3 KN-B3 6 Q-R4 P-QR3 7 B-K2 P-Q4 8 P×P P×P 9 N-B3 P-QN4 10 N×QP N×N 11 Q-K4ch B-K2 12 Q×N N-N3 13 Q-B6ch B-Q2 14 Q-K4 O-O 15 O-O P-B4 16 Q-K5 R-B3 17 B-Q3 B-Q3 18 Q-B3 N-Q4 19 Q-N3 P-QB5 20 B×QBP P×B 21 Q×P B-K3 22 N-N5 R-R3 23 P-KR4 N-K6 24 N×B B-R7ch 25 K-R1 N×Q 26 N×Q R×P 27 N-K6 B-B5ch 28 K-N1 B-R7ch 29 K-R1 B-K4ch 30 K-N1 R-K1 31 N-B5 B-R7ch 32 K-R1 B-Q3ch 33 K-N1 B×N 34 P-Q3 N-K4 35 B-N5 R-KN5 36 B-B1 N-B6ch 37 K-R1 R-KR5 mate.

White: BELLE
Black: CHESS 4.6

French Defence

1 P-K4 N-QB3 2 N-KB3 P-K3 3 P-Q4 P-Q4 4 N-B3 B-N5 5 P-K5 KN-K2 6 P-QR3 B×Nch 7 P×B N-R4 8 B-QN5ch B-Q2 9 B-Q3 R-QB1 10 N-N5 P-KR3 11 N-B3 P-QB4 12 P×P R×P 13 B-K3 R×P 14 B×QRP N-B5 15 O-O R×RP 16 R×R N×R 17 B-QB5 Q-R4 18 B-Q6 N-B5 19 Q-R1 N-B3 20 Q×Q N(B3)×Q 21 R-R1 B-B1 22 P-B3 N-B3 23 R-R4 N×B 24 P×N K-Q2 25 R-KN4 P-KN4 26 B-B2 K×P 27 R-QR4 P-N4 28 R-R1 P-QN5 29 P×P N×P 30 B-N1 B-Q2 31 K-R1 P-B4 32 N-Q4 R-QB1 33 N-K2 B-N4 34 N-N1 R-B8 35 R-R5 R×B 36 P-B3 B-B8 37 P-R4 R-N7 38 P×P B×Pch 39 K-R2 P×P 40 R-R4 B×Pch 41 K-N3 B-R4 42 K-R3 P-B5 43 R-R8 B-N3 44 K-N4 R-N7ch 45 K-R3 R×N 46 K-R2 R-N5 47 R-Q8ch K-K4 48 R-KN8 B-K5 49 R-N7 B-B6 50 R-KR7 N-Q6 51 R-R3 R-N7ch 52 K-R1 N-B7mate.

White: WITA
Black: DARK HORSE

English Opening

1 P-QB4 N-QB3 2 P-KN3 P-K4 3 B-N2 Q-B3 4 N-QB3 B-B4 5 N-B3 P-Q3 6 P-Q3 Q-Q1 7 B-K3 B×B 8 P×B N-B3 9 O-O B-K3 10 N-KN5 K-Q2 11 Q-R4 P-QR4 12 Q-N5 R-QN1 13 N-R4 P-KN3 14 P-QR3 R-K1 15 QR-B1 P-R3 16 N×B P×N 17 N-B3 Q-K2 18 P-R3 P-N4 19 P-N3 P-N5 20 P-Q4 P×RP 21 B×P Q-N2 22 K-R1 Q×P 23 R-B3 Q-N3 24 R-KN1 Q-B7 25 R×N Q×N 26 P-Q5 Q×KP 27 P×Nch K-Q1 28 B-N4 Q-N4 29 R-B2 P-N3 30 B-R3 Q-K6 31 R-B3 Q×KP 32 R-B6 Q-K5ch 33 K-R2 Q-B7ch 34 R-N2 Q-K5 35 R×KP Q-B5ch 36 K-R1 Q-KB8ch 37 K-R2 R×R 38 R-N8ch K-K2 39 B×R Q-B7ch 40 K-R3 Q-B6ch 41 K-R2 Q-R4ch 42 K-N3 R×Rch 43 B×R Q-N4ch 44 K-B2 Q×B 45 P-N4 P×P 46 P(R3)×P Q-KB1ch 47 K-N2 K-Q1 48 Q-Q5 P-R4 49 P-N5 P-R5 50 K-R3 Q-R3 51 Q-N8ch K-K2 52 Q-N8 Q-K6ch Draw agreed.

White: BLACK KNIGHT
Black: KAISSA

Centre Counter Defence

1 P-K4 P-Q4 2 P×P N-KB3 3 P-Q4 N×P 4 P-QB4 N-N3 5 N-KB3 P-N3 6 N-B3 B-N2 7 P-KR3 O-O 8 B-K3 N-B3 9 Q-Q2 P-K4 10 P-Q5 N-K2 11 P-KN4 P-KB4 12 O-O-O P-K5 13 N-R2 B-Q2 14 B-K2 B-R5 15 N×B N×N 16 B-Q4 B×B 17 Q×B Q-Q3 18 R-Q2 P-B4 19 Q-K3 QR-K1 20 Q-N5 P×P 21 P×P R×P 22 B-Q1 R×R 23 B×N R×N 24 R×R Q×R 25 B×R Q-N8ch 26 K-B2 Q-N7ch 27 Q-Q2 Q×P 28 Q-B2 N-B4 29 Q×P Q-N7ch 30 K-N3 Q-N6ch 31 K-R4 P-QR3 32 Q-QB8 N-Q3 33 Q-K6ch K-B1 34 B-Q7 Q-B5 35 P-B5 P-K6ch 36 K-R3 N-B5ch 37 K-N3 N-R4ch 38 K-R3 N-B5ch 39 K-N3 N-K4 40 Q-K8ch K-N2 41 Q-K7ch K-R3 42 Q-K6 Q-B5ch 43 K-R3 Q×BPch 44 K-N3 Q-B5ch 45 K-R3 Q-Q6ch 46 P-N3 N-B5ch 47 K-N4 P-K7 48 K-B5 N-Q3 49 K-N6 N-K5 50 K×P N-B4ch 51 K-N6 N×Q 52 P×N P-K8=Q 53 K-N7 Q-R4 54 P-N4 Q(Q6)-Q4ch 55 B-B6 Q(R4)×NPch 56 K-B7 Q(Q4)-Q3ch 57 K-B8 Q(N5)-N1mate.

Bibliography

Chess and Computers (1976), Levy, D., (Computer Science Press, Rockville, Maryland) contains an extensive bibliography of English and Russian language publications on our subject. Since the time of publication of that work many new publications have appeared and we list a number of them below. We have separated them into three categories - books, papers of general interest and technical articles.

Books

Advances in Computer Chess (1977), Clark, M. (Ed.), University of Edinburgh Press.

Chess Skill in Man and Machine (1977), Frey, P.W. (Ed.), Springer-Verlag, New York.

The World Computer Chess Championship (1976), Hayes, J. and Levy, D., University of Edinburgh Press.

1975 U.S. Computer Chess Championship (1976), Levy, D., Computer Science Press, Rockville, Maryland.

1976 U.S. Computer Chess Championship (1977), Levy, D., Computer Science Press, Rockville, Maryland.

General Interest

Benko, P. (1978). "The "Amateur" World Champion: An interview with Max Euwe," *Chess Life and Review* 33, 410-413.

Berliner, H. (1976). "Outstanding performances by CHESS 4.5 against human competition," *SIGART Newsletter*, No. 60, 12-13.

Berliner, H. (1977). "Two games from the Minnesota Open," *SIGART Newsletter*, No. 62, 9-10.

Berliner, H. (1977). "CHESS 4.5 vs. Levy," *SIGART Newsletter* No. 62, 11.

Berliner, H. (1978). "A chronology of computer chess and its literature," *Artificial Intelligence* 10, 201-214.

Byrne, R. (1978). "Fischer vs. the computer," *The New York Times*. July 30, 30.

Cahlander, D. (1977). "The computer is a fish, or is it?" *SIGART Newsletter, No. 62, 8-9.*

Douglas, J.R. (1978). "GM Walter Browne vs. CHESS 4.6" *Chess Life and Review* 33, 363-364.

"First microcomputer chest tournament," (1978). *Chess Life and Review* 33, 311.

Goldwater, W. (1977). "My game and animadversions," *Chess Life and Review* 32, 323-314.

Kaplan, J. (1977). "Let's go, big beige machine!" *Sports Illustrated,* August 22,42.

Lasker, Edward. (1977). "But will it fly?" *Chess Life and Review* 32, 314.

Levy, D. (1977a). "Invasion from cyberland," *Chess Life and Review* 32, 312-313.

Marsland, T.A. (1976). "1976 Canadian computer-chess workshop," *SI-GART Newsletter, No. 60, 22.*

Marsland, T.A. (1977). "A comprehensive list of computer chess literature," Tech. Report TR77-4, Dept. of Comput. Sci., Univ. of Alberta.

Michie, D. (1977). "David Levy challenge game, 1 April 1977," *SIGART Newsletter*, No. 62, 10-11.

Morrison, M.E. (1976). "4th Annual Paul Masson American Class Championship," *Chess Life and Review* 31, 553.

Newborn, M.M. (1978). "Computer chess: recent progress and future expectations," *Proc. Jerusalem Conf. on Inf. Tech.*

Richter, H. (1976). "The first German computer chess championship at Dortmund," *SIGART Newsletter*, No. 56, 2.

Soule, S. and Marsland, T.A. (1975). "Canadian computer chess tournament," *SIGART Newsletter*, No. 54, 12-13.

Technical Articles

Adelson-Velskiy, G.M., Arlazarov, V.L., and Donskoy, M.V. (1975). "Some methods of controlling the tree search in chess programs," *Artificial Intelligence* 6, 361-371.

Akl, S. and Newborn, M.M. (1977). "The principal continuation and the killer heuristic," *Proc. 1977 Annual Conf. of the Asoc. Comput. Mach.* 466-473.

Arlazarov, V.L. and Futer, A.V. (1978). "Computer analysis of a Rook end-game," *Machine Intelligence* 9 (J.E. Hayes, D. Michie, and L.I. Milulich, eds.) University of Edinburgh Press (in press).

Baudet, G.M. (1978). "On the branching factor of the alpha-beta pruning algorithm," *Artificial Intelligence* 9, 177-199.

Berliner, H. (1975). "A new subfield of computer chess," *SIGART Newsletter*, No. 53, 20-21.

Griffith, A.K. (1976). "Empirical exploration of the performance of the alpha-beta tree search heuristic," *IEEE Trans. on Computers*, 6-10.

Knuth, D.E., and Moore, R.N. (1975). "An analysis of alpha-beta pruning," *Artificial Intelligence* 6, 293-326.

Michalski, R. and Negri, P. (1975). "An experiment on inductive learning in chess endgames: the King-Pawn case," *NATO Adv. Study Inst. on Machine Repres. of Knowledge*, Santa Cruz.

Michie, D. (1976). "An advice taking system for computer chess," *Computer Bulletin*, December 12-14.

Michie, D., and Bratko, I., (1978). "Advice tables representations of chess end-game knowledge," *Proc. AISB Summer Conference*, Hamburg.

Newborn, M.M. (1977). "The efficiency of the alpha-beta search on trees with branch-dependent terminal node scores," *Artificial Intelligence* 8, 137-153.

Slate, D. and Mittman, B. (1978). "CHESS 4.6 - Where do we go from here?" *Proc. Jerusalem on Information Tech.* 84-88.

CHESS NOTES

CHESS NOTES

CHESS NOTES

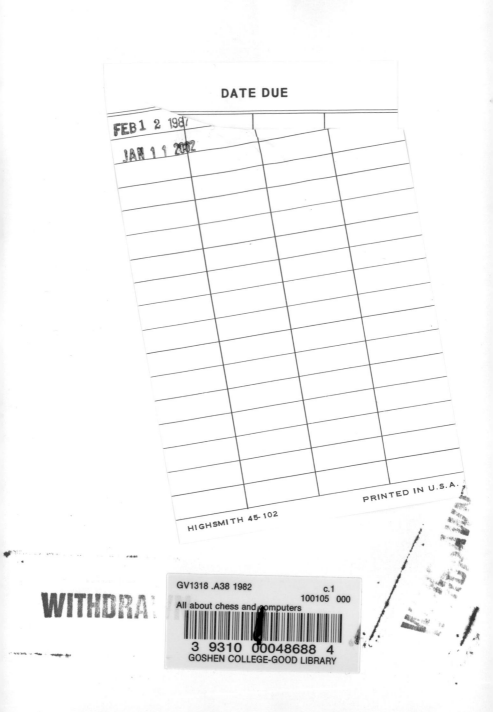

DATE DUE

FEB 1 2 1987

JAN 1 1 2002